By Sword and Plow

JENNIFER E. SESSIONS

By SWORD
AND PLOW

France *and the* Conquest
of Algeria

CORNELL UNIVERSITY PRESS   ITHACA AND LONDON

Cornell University Press gratefully acknowledges financial support from the University of Iowa Office of the Vice President for Research and the University of Iowa Department of History, which aided in the publication of this book.

First published 2011 by Cornell University Press
First printing, Cornell Paperbacks, 2014
Printed in the United States of America

Library of Congress Cataloging-in-Publication Data

Sessions, Jennifer E. (Jennifer Elson), 1974–
   By sword and plow : France and the conquest of Algeria / Jennifer E. Sessions.
     p. cm.
   Includes bibliographical references and index.
   ISBN 978-0-8014-4975-8 (cloth : alk. paper)
   ISBN 978-0-8014-5652-7 (pbk. : alk. paper)
   1. Algeria—History—French Expedition, 1830.   2. France—History—July
Revolution, 1830.   3. Algeria—History—1830–1962.   I. Title.
   DT294.S44 2011
   965'.03—dc22   2011017247

Cloth printing   10 9 8 7 6 5 4 3 2 1
Paperback printing   10 9 8 7 6 5 4 3 2 1

For my parents

Contents

Illustrations

Acknowledgments

I N RESEARCHING AND writing this book, I have incurred debts that my thanks here can only begin to repay. Initial research for this project was supported by grants and fellowships from the Ford Foundation, the French Ministry of Foreign Affairs, the Société des professeurs français et francophones d'Amérique, and the University of Pennsylvania. The National Endowment for the Humanities, the Getty Research Institute, and, at the University of Iowa, International Programs, the Stanley Foundation-UI Support Organization, and the Office of the Vice President for Research enabled me to complete my research in France and the United States. A Kluge Fellowship at the Library of Congress and support from the University of Iowa gave me time to write. I am grateful for the generous assistance of the many librarians, archivists, and curators who made my research possible. Jean-Marie Lincolas at the Service historique de la Défense, Valérie Bajou at the Musée de Versailles, and Frédéric Maguet at the Musée national des arts et traditions populaires (now Musée des civilisations de l'Europe et de la Méditerranée), as well as the interlibrary loan staff at Van Pelt Library at the University of Pennsylvania and the University of Iowa Libraries, deserve particular thanks for their patience with my requests for obscure works. Discovering the riches of French departmental and municipal archives was one of the great joys of this project, as was the kindness of their archivists, who went out of their way to help me locate documents and to make photocopies when I could not visit in person.

My thinking about French colonialism has benefited from the conversation, encouragement, and thoughtful criticism of many people. At the University of Pennsylvania, where this book began, I had the great good fortune to work with Lynn Hunt and Lynn Hollen Lees, and my first thanks must go to them. As a historian, I have learned immeasurably from their teaching and scholarship, and their intellectual influences will be evident in the pages that follow. But each has also been an inspiring model of what it is to be a mentor, a colleague, and a friend. I hope that I can pass on to my own students even part of what I learned from seminars and discussions with them and other Penn faculty. Lee Cassanelli supported my interest in African history, and Susan Sidlauskas encouraged me to consider the visual aspects of colonial culture. Jonathan Steinberg and Marion Kant opened their home, their intellectual enthusiasm, and their friendship to me. My fellows in seminars and discussions both formal and informal made Penn a warm and exciting place to study history.

Many colleagues and friends have read and discussed the various iterations of this book over the years, and I am grateful for their questions, criticisms, and suggestions. Naomi Andrews, Julia Clancy-Smith, Lauren Clay, and Becky Pulju read all or part of the manuscript and offered valuable feedback. FayeLin Bartram, Sarita Patnaik, John Sessions, David Uhrig, and Noelle Yasso provided invaluable research assistance compiling data on French colonial emigration. I would like to thank the two anonymous readers at Cornell University Press, as well as my editor, John Ackerman, for his interest in this book, and Susan Specter for her help in bringing it to fruition.

My colleagues in the History Department at the University of Iowa have been unfailingly generous with their time, ideas, and support. In particular, Lisa Heineman and Johanna Schoen read and commented on chapters. Paula Michaels, Kevin Mumford, Jacki Rand, and Glenn Penny have shared long discussions of colonialism and its cultures. Many other colleagues and friends have enlivened my research, writing, and life. I owe particular thanks to Sung Choi, Brenda Longfellow, Kathy Nasstrom, Jennifer Olmsted, Tracy Osborn, Amanda Owen, Ben Read, Shira Robinson, Rebecca Scales, Rebecca Hartkopf Schloss, Andrea Smith, CJ Voci, and Chuck Walton. Allyson Delnore has discussed all aspects of this project over the years and shared with me her friendship and her knowledge of French imperialism. She read the entire manuscript at a critical point, and this book is much improved for her thoughtful, detailed comments. Jae-Jae Spoon has been a comrade and general co-conspirator in all things French throughout my time in Iowa City. Amy Freund has been unstinting with her warmth, humor, and wisdom. Sophie Bryan, Deborah Hearey, and Sarah Reber have given me support, hospitality, and dear friendships. The Dupuis and de Lussys made me at home in France, and I am grateful for their welcome.

My deepest thanks go to my family, whose love has sustained me through the long years spent writing this book. My sister and her family keep me laughing and put things in perspective. My grandparents offered moral and financial support at many stages of this project. But it is to my parents, who took me to France and taught me to love it, that I owe the greatest debt. My mother's love, advice, and unflagging faith in me keep me going in everything that I do. My father is one of the best historians I know, and his enthusiasm inspired me to follow in his footsteps. He has been a researcher, reader, editor, and sounding board every step of the way, and words cannot convey the depth of my gratitude for his help. For this and so much else, I dedicate this book to them.

Abbreviations

AC	Archives Condé, Chantilly
AD	Archives départementales
AL	Archives du Louvre, Paris
AM	Archives municipales
AN	Archives nationales, Paris
AP	*Archives parlementaires*, ser. 2
APP	Archives de la Préfecture de Police, Paris
BNEst	Bibliothèque nationale de France, Département des Estampes et de la photographie
CAOM	Centre des archives d'outre-mer, Aix-en-Provence
CRANL	*Compte-rendu des séances de l'Assemblée nationale législative*
PVD	*Procès-verbaux des séances de la Chambre des députés*
RAGA	*Recueil des actes du gouvernement de l'Algérie*
SHD	Service historique de la Défense, Vincennes
TEFA	*Tableau de la situation des établissements français dans l'Algérie*

Introduction

The Cultural Origins of French Algeria

WHEN THE FRENCH invaded the Ottoman regency of Algiers in the summer of 1830, they took the first step in a process of conquest and colonization that dominated France's modern imperial history and that has shaped French political culture to this day. Establishing a permanent colony was far from the minds of French planners at the time of the invasion, whose primary aim was to rally support for a tottering regime at home. "The expedition of Algiers was," historians agree, "not connected with the colonial policy of the Restoration Bourbon monarchy," but "a makeshift expedient for internal political consumption, carried out by a government in difficulty seeking the prestige of a military victory."[1] In this, it failed, and King Charles X was overthrown just weeks after Algiers fell. But Charles's successor, his cousin Louis-Philippe d'Orléans, did not withdraw from North Africa after taking power. Instead, the new monarch expanded the temporary military occupation into a permanent settler colony. By the time Louis-Philippe's July Monarchy was overthrown in its turn in February 1848, the French presence in Algeria had swelled to almost one hundred thousand troops and over one hundred thousand European colonists.

From these foundations, Algeria was built over the next century into the jewel of the French empire and its only colony of large-scale European settlement. Throughout the colonial era, the settler presence gave Algeria stronger political,

---

1. Charles-Robert Ageron, *Modern Algeria: A History from 1830 to the Present*, trans. and ed. Michael Brett (Trenton, 1991), 5.

social, and cultural ties to France than those enjoyed by any other colony. It was here that the imperial ideology of "assimilation" came closest to full realization, at least for the growing European population. Indigenous Muslims remained subject to military rule and a separate body of "native" law, but the colonists pressed with relative success for the "constantly more intimate union" with the metropole toward which assimilationist doctrine aspired. In 1848, the Second Republic (1848–52) granted citizenship to the inhabitants of Guadeloupe, Martinique, Guiana, Réunion, Saint-Louis, and Gorée, including the right to elect deputies to the French parliament. But only Algeria came to be "considered a simple prolongation of the soil of the mother country," divided in 1848 into three departments whose European citizens benefited both from political representation in Paris and from administrative structures that were, at least in theory, the same as those of metropolitan France.[2]

These peculiar ties to France and the drastic inequities they entailed between the settlers and the precolonial inhabitants help to explain why decolonization, achieved through the Algerian War of 1954–62, was such a long, traumatic process. But equally pressing is the matter of the colony's origins: What was the impetus for the French conquest of Algeria? How and why did settler colonialism and assimilation become the defining features of the French presence there? In the answers to these questions can be found the imperatives that led France a century later to cling to Algeria with such tenacity and with such traumatic consequences for all parties to this most intimate of colonial relationships.

The basic proposition of this book is that the roots of French Algeria lay in contests over political legitimacy sparked by the Atlantic revolutions of the eighteenth century. The French and Haitian revolutions shattered the foundations of political and social authority throughout the French imperium, leaving the Old Regime's defining structures of political and social privilege in ruins. From the rubble of absolute monarchy, the regimes of the nineteenth century had to reconstitute and, in the process, reconceive the forms and legitimizing principles of sovereignty, citizenship, and political power. The Bourbon Restoration (1815–30) and the Orleanist July Monarchy (1830–48) both sought to reconcile the revolutionary principles of popular sovereignty and participation with prerevolutionary ideals of kingship and royal authority. And to legitimize these experiments with constitutional monarchy, both turned to aggressive warfare and overseas expansion.

---

2. Arthur Girault, *Principes de colonisation et de législation coloniale* (Paris, 1895), quoted in Martin Deming Lewis, "One Hundred Million Frenchmen: The 'Assimilation' Theory in French Colonial Policy," *Comparative Studies in Society and History* 4, no. 2 (1962): 132. New Caledonia saw concerted settlement efforts in the late nineteenth century but had only 18,000 European colonists by 1931.

At the same time, the successful slave revolt that began in Saint-Domingue in 1791 dramatically demonstrated the precariousness of the Old Regime's colonial order and fed French criticism of a political economy predicated on forced labor, whether overseas or at home. In the postrevolutionary period, fears of colonial violence triggered by the Haitian Revolution and the rise of an international abolitionist movement converged with anxieties about the domestic consequences of industrialization and urbanization, leading political thinkers and social reformers alike to seek alternatives to colonial slavery and domestic proletarianization. A new model of colonial settlement, grounded in both a profoundly backward-looking rural agrarianism and a distinctly modern conception of autonomous male citizenship, offered such an alternative, just as the Algerian conquest opened a seemingly ideal field on which to implement it. Although the crisis of colonial legitimacy that resulted from the Haitian Revolution differed in important ways from the crisis of political legitimacy engendered by the French Revolution, together they pushed forward the processes of military conquest and settlement colonization that made Algeria not just a French colony, but ultimately part of France itself.

Algeria between Empires

Nineteenth-century colonialists had a keen sense that they were reinventing empire as a political and social category, and in doing so, they worked from assumptions and lessons derived from two precedents: the "first" French colonial empire in the Atlantic world and the continental Empire of Napoleon Bonaparte.[3] These imperial legacies manifested themselves in quite different ways, but they weighed equally on colonial ideology and practice in the mid-nineteenth century. The Algerian conquest thus stood at a critical crossroads both between the "first" and "second" French empires, and between continental and overseas empire.

To approach Algerian colonization from this perspective links histories that are usually considered separately and blurs the traditional conceptual and chronological boundaries of French colonial history. The distinction between first and second colonial empires is not, of course, entirely arbitrary. The administrative, social, and ideological transformations of the revolutionary decades did not end at the "natural" frontiers so dear to the men of 1789, and they created important differences between the colonialisms of the early modern and modern periods. But taking the Revolution as a strict line of demarcation for research and interpretation masks both the progressive development of these differences and significant

3. For clarity, I will capitalize references to both Napoleonic Empires and refer to the overseas colonial empire in lower case. "Imperial/imperial" is treated the same way.

continuities across the revolutionary divide. Looking carefully at the postrevolutionary decades highlights the extent to which imperial expansion transcended the regime changes of France's tumultuous nineteenth century. Not only was the French Republic "never not an imperial nation-state,"[4] but the French nation-state in *all* of its political guises was never not also an empire. Preoccupation in recent scholarship with the paradoxes of republican imperialism has illuminated profound cleavages within the republican tradition, but it has also overshadowed the ways in which French political culture has been intertwined with empire throughout the modern period. The shifting winds that buffeted kings, republics, and Empires between 1789 and 1914 altered the principles and meanings but never the fact of colonial expansion.

In the traditional periodization, the first French empire encompasses the territories acquired in the seventeenth and eighteenth centuries: Quebec, Louisiana, Saint-Pierre and Miquelon in North America; Martinique, Guadeloupe, and Saint-Domingue, as well as a handful of smaller islands and Guiana in the Caribbean; the West African trading posts of Saint-Louis and Gorée; the Île Bourbon, Île de France (Mauritius), and sporadic settlements on Madagascar in the Indian Ocean; and a handful of factories in India. Despite their geographical, economic, and cultural diversity, these territories were united by a mercantilist policy that bound, however imperfectly, Canadian fur traders, Atlantic cod fishermen, Antillais planters, and West African and Indian merchants into a self-sustaining, monopoly system designed to enrich the French crown. The defining features of this empire, as both contemporaries and subsequent historians have insisted, were slavery and the commercial regime of the *exclusif*.

The geopolitical rivalries and revolutionary upheavals of the eighteenth century took a heavy toll on the first empire. Defeated in the Seven Years' War (1756–63), France ceded Louisiana to Spain and New France to Great Britain, in exchange for the return of the islands of Guadeloupe, Martinique and Sainte-Lucie. In 1757, the British adventurer Robert Clive overcame the nawab of Bengal and his French allies at the Battle of Plassey, effectively ending French pretensions in the Indian subcontinent. The Revolutionary and Napoleonic wars, and the colonial revolutions they sparked, further eroded what remained of French imperial power, even as they generated new ideological and political motivations for expansion.

Armed with a new, universalist conception of their own political and cultural superiority, the Jacobin revolutionaries and Napoleon Bonaparte set out to remake the world in the French image. After renouncing aggressive war as an act

4. Gary Wilder, *The French Imperial Nation-State: Negritude and Colonial Humanism between the Two World Wars* (Chicago, 2005), 3.

of despotism and pledging that the French nation would "undertake no war in-tended to make conquests," the revolutionaries abandoned their pacific commit-ments in favor of a "crusade for universal liberty."[5] In November 1792, the Edict of Fraternity pledged France to liberate the peoples of monarchical Europe and to bestow upon them, by force if necessary, the gifts of republican liberty and equal-ity. Imperial expansion remained a cornerstone of revolutionary ideology as the Republic's fortunes ebbed and flowed over the ensuing years. When Napoleon Bonaparte seized power and declared himself the "savior of the Revolution" in 1799, he also assumed the torch of universalist republican imperialism. From the Egyptian expedition of 1798–99 to the disastrous invasion of Russia in 1812, "the [revolutionary] attack on privilege, seigneurialism and the power of the Church was carried . . . in the wake of Bonaparte's all-conquering regiments" by an army of administrators and savants dedicated to the institution of Enlightened "prog-ress" and French "civilization" in the "backward" regions of Europe and the Middle East. Elsewhere, Napoleon fought to capture the overseas dominions of states now under French suzerainty and to reconquer the lost French colonies in the Atlantic world.[6]

The expansionist ambitions of both Republic and Empire ultimately came to naught. Napoleon's ill-fated foray into Egypt, often seen as the first experiment in modern imperialism, ended in ignominious defeat, and his vast continental empire was dismembered in the wake of Waterloo. In the Antilles, which were a battleground throughout the Revolutionary and Napoleonic wars, islands traded hands with dizzying speed in the conflicts that pitted Europe's imperial powers against one another from 1792 to 1815. At the same time, slaves and people of color throughout the region seized the opportunity to stake their own claims to liberty and equality, with dramatic results for both the landscape of French em-pire and the basic tenets of French political culture. *Gens de couleur* pushed suc-cessfully for the rights of republican citizenship; and slaves revolted, compelling the National Assembly to abolish colonial slavery and extend them citizenship rights in 1794. Napoleon forcibly restored slavery in Martinique and Guadeloupe

5. Decree of 22 May 1790, quoted in Jacques Godechot, *La grande nation: L'expansion révolutionnaire de la France dans le monde de 1789 à 1799*, 2nd ed. (Paris, 1983), 66; also Title VI of the Constitution of 1791, in *Les constitutions de la France depuis 1789*, ed. Jacques Godechot (Paris, 1970), 65. Jacques-Pierre Brissot, speech of 30 December 1792, quoted in Michael Rapport, "Robespierre and the Universal Rights of Man, 1791–1794," *French History* 10, no. 3 (1996): 313. All translations mine unless otherwise noted.
6. Martyn Lyons, *Napoleon Bonaparte and the Legacy of the French Revolution* (New York, 1994), 229. See also Stuart Woolf, *Napoleon's Integration of Europe* (London, 1991); Michael Broers, *The Napoleonic Empire in Italy, 1796–1814: Cultural Imperialism in a European Context?* (London, 2005); W. M. Sloane, "Napoleon's Plans for a Colonial System," *American Historical Review* 4, no. 3 (1899): 439–55; Juan Cole, *Napoleon's Egypt: Invading the Middle East* (New York, 2007).

in 1802, but the "Pearl of the Antilles," Saint-Domingue, was lost for good in the bloody revolution that created the independent Republic of Haiti in 1804.[7] Despite their mixed outcomes, the slave uprisings of the 1790s, especially the Haitian Revolution, decisively challenged the legitimacy of forced labor as the basis for the political economy of empire.

The fall of Napoleon was accompanied by military defeat, territorial loss, and occupation that made 1815 a symbol of national humiliation for many Frenchmen. The Treaty of Paris stripped away many of France's few remaining colonial territories, leaving behind little more than the "debris" of the Old Regime empire. After Napoleon's return during the Hundred Days, the Allies stationed an occupying army across eastern France to guarantee the payment of massive war reparations. Yet the collapse of the Napoleonic Empire also contained the seeds of renewed expansion, as its successors, the Bourbon Restoration, July Monarchy, and Second Republic, all set out to prove, albeit for different reasons, that "Waterloo took nothing from us."[8]

The French invasion and conquest of Algeria must be seen, in this regard, as a legacy of the revolutionary and Napoleonic decades. Napoleon's Egyptian expedition has been seen as the genesis of the "civilizing mission" championed by nineteenth-century French imperialists, and this precedent loomed large in the minds of the planners and observers of the Algerian conquest.[9] Indeed the phrase *mission civilisatrice* first entered the French lexicon around 1840 to describe colonization efforts in Algeria.[10] But Napoleon played other, even more critical roles in shaping the Algerian conquest. Throughout the July Monarchy, Imperial veterans led the French army and military administration in North Africa, while Napoleonic ideals defined the Algerian conquest in the French collective imagi-

---

7. On revolution in the Caribbean, see, among others, C. L. R. James, *Black Jacobins: Toussaint L'Ouverture and the San Domingo Revolution*, 2nd ed. (New York, 1989); David Gaspar and David Geggus, eds., *A Turbulent Time: The French Revolution and the Greater Caribbean* (Bloomington, 1997); Laurent Dubois, *A Colony of Citizens: Revolution and Slave Emancipation in the French Caribbean, 1787–1804* (Chapel Hill, 2004).

8. Th[éodore] Wains-des-Fontaines, "Mazagran: Fragment d'un poème couronné par l'Association-Lionnaise, le 18 juin 1840," *Affiches, annonces judiciaires, avis divers du Mans, et du département de la Sarthe*, 28 August 1840. Manuscript copy, dated 28 March 1840, in CAOM 1E 87.

9. Alice Conklin, *A Mission to Civilize: The Republican Idea of Empire in France and West Africa, 1895–1930* (Stanford, 1997), 17–19; Patricia Lorcin, *Imperial Identities: Stereotyping, Prejudice and Race in Colonial Algeria* (1995; London, 1999), 102–7; Patricia Lorcin, "Rome and France in North Africa: Recovering Algeria's Latin Past," *French Historical Studies* 25, no. 2 (2002): 297–99.

10. The first occurrence is S. Dutot, *De l'expatriation, considérée sous ses rapports économiques, politiques et moraux . . .* (Paris, 1840), 321. See also J.-J.-O. Pellion, "Alger.—Algérie," in *Dictionnaire politique: Encyclopédie du langage et de la science politiques*, ed. Louis-Antoine Garnier-Pagès (Paris, 1842), 48.

nation. Both royal propaganda and popular culture framed the new colonial enterprise in a Bonapartist idiom that cast Algeria's conquerors and colonists as a reincarnation of their Imperial forebears.[11]

If the Algerian conquest had roots in the imperial crises of the Old Regime and Revolution, it was also the critical point of transition from the early modern Atlantic empire to the "New Imperialism" of the late nineteenth and early twentieth centuries. The African empire of the Third Republic (1870–1940) was built on foundations laid in Algeria in the postrevolutionary decades. As the power of the Ottoman Empire waned and European imperial rivalries intensified after 1850, France's Maghrebi outpost became a strategic stronghold in the struggle with Britain for geopolitical primacy in the Mediterranean and the jumping-off point for expansion into Sub-Saharan Africa. Long before 1830, not just French, but a cosmopolitan assortment of Enlightened Europeans had suggested that conquering Ottoman Algiers would bring control over valuable trans-Saharan trade routes and, eventually, commercial and political dominion over the whole continent. After the invasion, imperial policymakers became fixated on linking Algeria to the French possessions in West Africa, and this counterpart to British ambitions for "Cape-to-Cairo" domination helped to drive French participation in the Scramble for Africa later in the century.[12] The Algerian conquest further shaped French imperial practices as a training ground for three generations of colonial administrators, and a blueprint for strategies of rule ranging from military conquest to relations with Islamic authorities elsewhere in North and West Africa.[13]

Algeria remained the heart of the "second" French empire, however. In the commercial arena, it alone accounted for between one-third and one-half of French empire trade and, by the 1930s, had become France's primary external trading partner, much as the self-governing white dominions and a former settler colony, the United States, dominated British trade.[14] The protectorates established

---

11. The term "Bonapartism," indicating the political values associated with Napoleon, must be distinguished from "Imperialism," which describes the political movement that sought to restore the Empire.

12. Ann Thomson, *Barbary and Enlightenment: European Attitudes towards the Maghreb in the 18th Century* (Leiden, 1987), 134, 145; Ann Thomson, "Arguments for the Conquest of Algiers in the Late Eighteenth and Early Nineteenth Centuries," *Maghreb Review* 14, no. 1–2 (1989): 114; C. W. Newbury and A. S. Kanya-Forstner, "French Policy and the Origins of the Scramble for West Africa," *Journal of African History* 10, no. 2 (1969): 254–55.

13. Donal Cruise O'Brien, "Towards an 'Islamic Policy' in French West Africa, 1854–1914," *Journal of African History* 8, no. 2 (1967): 306–7; Antony Thrall Sullivan, *Thomas-Robert Bugeaud: France and Algeria, 1784–1849: Politics, Power, and the Good Society* (Hamden, 1983), 165–70; Christopher Harrison, *France and Islam in West Africa, 1860–1960* (Cambridge, 1988), esp. chap. 2.

14. A. W. Flux, "The Flag and Trade: A Summary Review of the Trade of the Chief Colonial Empires," *Journal of the Royal Statistical Society* 62, no. 3 (1899): 498, 521; C. M. Andrew and A. S. Kanya-Forstner, "French Business and the French Colonialists," *Historical Journal* 19, no. 4 (1976): 987.

in Tunisia (1881) and Morocco (1912) were motivated by the desire to protect Algeria's borders from Italian and British incursions, as well as by the desire to maintain the balance of power in the Mediterranean.[15] Algeria's economic and geopolitical primacy mirrored its importance to imperialist ideologues like Paul Leroy-Beaulieu and Anatole Prévost-Paradol, who saw in the colony France's "supreme chance" for salvation in the face of growing international competition.[16] Just as protecting India was a key driver for British expansion in Africa and Asia, Algeria became the lynchpin of French imperial thought in the age of empire.

By the end of the nineteenth century, it was axiomatic that Algeria occupied an exceptional place in the French empire and that its unique status as a settler colony was the wellspring of its economic and geopolitical strength. Looking ahead to the centenary of the Algiers expedition, Leroy-Beaulieu predicted in 1874 that by 1930 three or four million European colonists would secure a North African base from which France would dominate all of northwest Africa.[17] When that centennial arrived—the first and last the *colons* (settlers) would celebrate—the colony's promoters boasted that this prophecy had been fulfilled. Thanks to its heroic settlers, Algeria had become a "monument of civilization and colonial power that has never been surpassed nor equaled."[18] But, at the same time, its European population made it unlike any other part of the empire. "Never forget that Algeria is not a colony," one journalist reminded metropolitan readers; "Algeria is a magnificent French province that was added to the others just as, over the course of centuries, the Île-de-France, Normandy, Champagne, etc. were."[19]

Leroy-Beaulieu and centennial boosters alike vastly overestimated both the prosperity of the Algerian "miracle" and the benefits of French civilization to the colony's inhabitants. From half a million at the turn of the century, the European population had grown to 880,000 by 1930, enough to undermine the structures of indigenous Algerian society but a far cry from the predicted millions. The settlers enjoyed high standards of living compared with the metropole and enormous privilege relative to the colony's 5.6 million Muslims, but they were also beginning to think of themselves as a people as distinct from the metropolitan French as from indigenous Arabs, Berbers, and Jews. The emergence of a separate *algéri-*

---

15. Henri Brunschwig, *French Colonialism, 1871–1914: Myths and Realities,* trans. William Glanville Brown (1960; repr., New York, 1964), 53–54, 118–19.
16. Anatole Prévost-Paradol, *La France nouvelle,* 2nd ed. (Paris, 1868), 415.
17. Paul Leroy-Beaulieu, *De la colonisation chez les peuples modernes,* 2nd ed. (Paris, 1882), 389–91.
18. Octave Depont, *L'Algérie du centenaire* (1928), quoted in Daniel Lefeuvre, *Chère Algérie: La France et sa colonie, 1930–1962* (Paris, 2005), 26.
19. P. Mille, quoted in Charles-Robert Ageron, *Histoire de l'Algérie contemporaine,* vol. 2, *De l'insurrection de 1871 au déclenchement de la guerre de libération (1954)* (Paris, 1979), 406.

aniste identity after World War I was accompanied by calls for autonomy and even independence from France. The French did little to satisfy these demands, and even less to ameliorate the deteriorating social and economic conditions of the Muslim majority. Already devastated by earlier territorial expropriations, the indigenous population was further squeezed in the interwar years by continuing fragmentation of their remaining lands. At the time of the centennial, half were living at or below subsistence level, and Algerian and metropolitan French cities swelled with *fellahs* (peasants) fleeing famine and unemployment. Paeans to France's benevolent influence were belied by the first stirrings of the nationalist agitation that would erupt into open revolt after World War II.[20]

While avoiding any mention of nascent settler and indigenous nationalisms, centenary celebrations reflected and reinforced the now well-established assumptions about Algeria's exceptional status as a French land. This belief that the Algerian colony was fundamentally different from other overseas territories and had a correspondingly unique relationship to France can be traced to the conquest decades. It was postrevolutionary imperialists, working from the conviction that "a new system of colonization is necessary" if empire was to remain "one of [France's] greatest claims to glory in the eyes of posterity,"[21] that laid down the ideological and policy foundations for the transformation of Algeria into what was variously described as *l'Algérie française, la France africaine,* or *la nouvelle France.*

Politics, Culture, and Colonialism

My concerns in this book are both historical and theoretical, and stem from two sets of questions about European empires that are too often isolated from each other. On the one hand, I seek to explain the policy choices that led France back onto the colonial stage between 1830 and 1848. On the other, I aim to understand how contemporary culture shaped the processes of military conquest and settler colonization that made Algeria French. Together, these questions allow us to understand why the founding of France's most important modern colony took place when and how it did.

This double approach, I believe, will help to bridge an important explanatory gap between older histories of the motives for imperial expansion and more

20. See, among others, David Prochaska, *Making Algeria French: Colonialism in Bône, 1870–1920* (Cambridge, 1990), chap. 7; Lorcin, *Imperial Identities,* chap. 9; Jonathan Gosnell, *The Politics of Frenchness in Colonial Algeria, 1930–1954* (Rochester, 2002), chap. 6; Ageron, *De l'insurrection;* Neil MacMaster, *Colonial Migrants and Racism: Algerians in France, 1900–1962* (Houndsmills, UK, 1997), chap. 1.
21. Jean-Gustave Courcelle-Seneuil, "Colonie," in Garnier-Pagès, *Dictionnaire politique,* 235.

recent inquiries into the cultural "norms and forms" of Western colonialism that have generally moved away from questions of causality.[22] Debate about the origins of European empires long focused on the relative weight of economic and geopolitical factors in imperial expansion, especially during the New Imperialism.[23] In the French case, historians found that the colonies offered little, if any net economic benefit and that empire impeded rather than promoted the development of capitalism. Especially in comparison with Great Britain, where empire was perceived to proceed "for good economic reasons,"[24] the economics of colonialism in France appeared highly irrational, as evidenced by the fact that decolonization met with little opposition from business circles and caused no crisis of French capitalism.[25] Since economic interpretations could not account for either expansion in the nineteenth century or France's dogged attachment to its colonial possessions in the twentieth, historians turned to political explanations. Scholars of parliamentary politics discerned the disproportionate influence of a "colonial lobby" or *parti colonial* made up of colonial representatives, merchants, and ideologues, while others found that "the real cause of French colonial expansion was the spread of nationalist fervor" after the Franco-Prussian War (1870–71).[26] Whether they saw it sparked at the elite or the popular level, however, historians could generally agree that "the French colonialist movement represents the highest stage, not of French capitalism, but of French nationalism."[27]

Studies of the colonialist movement have taught us a great deal about how influential politicians, such as Jules Ferry, and pressure groups like the regional committees of the *parti colonial* and the Union Coloniale Française sought to overcome what they saw as popular ignorance of the colonies. They have had little to say, however, about the responses of ordinary French people to these

---

22. The phrase is Paul Rabinow's: *French Modern: The Norms and Forms of the Social Environment* (Cambridge, Mass., 1989; Chicago, 1995).
23. For key contributions to the "origins debate," see Harrison Wright, ed., *The 'New Imperialism': Analysis of Late-Nineteenth Century Expansion*, 2nd ed. (Lexington, Mass., 1976).
24. Ronald Robinson, introduction to Brunschwig, *French Colonialism*, vii.
25. Jacques Marseille, *Empire colonial et capitalisme français: Histoire d'un divorce* (Paris, 1984); Lefeuvre, *Chère Algérie*.
26. Brunschwig, *French Colonialism*, 182. See also Charles-Robert Ageron, *France coloniale ou parti colonial?* (Paris, 1978); Stuart Persell, *The French Colonial Lobby, 1889–1938* (Stanford, 1983); and articles by Christopher Andrew and A. S. Kanya-Forstner: "The French 'Colonial Party': Its Composition, Aims and Influence, 1885–1914," *Historical Journal* 14, no. 1 (March 1971): 99–128; "The French Colonial Party and French Colonial War Aims, 1914–1918," *Historical Journal* 17, no. 1 (March 1974): 79–106; "The Groupe Colonial in the French Chamber of Deputies, 1892–1932," *Historical Journal* 17, no. 4 (December 1974): 837–66.
27. Christopher Andrew, "The French Colonialist Movement during the Third Republic: The Unofficial Mind of Imperialism," *Transactions of the Royal Historical Society*, 5th ser., 26 (1976): 148.

efforts. More recent scholarship has begun to investigate the popular image of empire developed in cultural fields including, among others, travel literature, advertising, and film. Inspired by the approaches to colonial studies pioneered by Edward Said, these works have begun to expand our knowledge of the ways that empire was embedded in daily life and shaped conceptions of self and nation in modern France. The shift towards the cultural history of empire has also prompted new questions about the categories that structured colonial rule, leading to new understandings of the ways that cultural forms shaped the ideology and practices of French empire overseas.[28]

Too often, however, work that sees culture as constitutive of imperial identities and ideologies fails to address the questions of causality that are vital to understanding the historical origins of empire. Said's claim that "the enterprise of empire depends upon the *idea* of *having an empire*" and that this idea was forged in the cultural arena has stimulated scholarly interest in the relationship between culture and imperialism.[29] But to say, in the words of William Blake, that "the foundation of Empire is Art and Science" and that "Empire follows Art and not vice versa"[30] is not to make a historical argument about the timing or form of a particular instance of colonial domination. Conceptions of colonial culture grounded in the theories of Antonio Gramsci and Michel Foucault make it difficult to differentiate imperialism from any other assertion of discursive power and thus to grasp the particularities of specific colonial histories. Like the "new cultural history" with which they share many methodological and theoretical assumptions, discursive approaches to the study of colonial culture have tended to privilege "the demystification and deconstruction of power" at the expense of causal explanation.[31]

A brief discussion of three key terms used in this book—"representation," "image," and "culture"—will help to outline a more concrete understanding of colonial culture that, while retaining the insights of colonial studies, reclaims the explanatory force required to answer historical questions about empire's origins.

---

28. On this shift, see Alice Conklin and Julia Clancy-Smith, introduction to *French Historical Studies* 27, no. 3 (2004): 497–505; Frederick Cooper, "The Rise, Fall, and Rise of Colonial Studies, 1951–2001," in *Colonialism in Question: Theory, Knowledge, History* (Berkeley, 2005), 33–55; Sophie Dulucq, ed., dossier "L'écriture de l'histoire de la colonisation en France depuis 1960," *Afrique et Histoire* 2, no. 6 (2006): 235–76.

29. *Culture and Imperialism* (New York, 1993), 11–12. See also Edward Said, *Orientalism* (New York, 1979).

30. Quoted in Said, *Culture and Imperialism,* 13.

31. Victoria Bonnell and Lynn Hunt, introduction to *Beyond the Cultural Turn: New Directions in the Study of Society and Culture,* ed. Victoria Bonnell and Lynn Hunt (Berkeley, 1999), 10–11. See also William Sewell, *Logics of History: Social Theory and Social Transformation* (Chicago, 2005), esp. 49, 139–40, 162–68, chap. 6.

I use "representation" in both its physical and abstract senses, as "a material image or figure, a reproduction in some material or tangible form," such as an engraving or painting, and as "an image, likeness, or reproduction in some manner *of* a thing" (for example, the Armée d'Afrique served as an idealized representation of French manhood).[32] "Image" similarly serves to describe both a physical object that bears a mimetic representation and a mental "image," or conception in the mind, which can be real or fictitious, figurative or not.[33] "Culture," the most polyvalent of these terms, has several distinct understandings in historical and cultural criticism that together shed particularly revealing light on the historical role of colonial culture.[34]

In its first meaning, "culture" connotes a shared set of beliefs and practices thought to define discrete social groups. Like the related terms "civilization," "race," and "nation," this usage was intimately involved in the elaboration of the racial and ethnic categories on which European imperial rule rested.[35] Especially before the rise of scientific racism, culture served as the primary criterion for demarcating "civilized" colonizers from the "savage" colonized. In Algeria, ethnographic observation of local cultural differences led French military officers, administrators, anthropologists, and pseudo-intellectuals to develop racialized distinctions—between Arabs and Kabyles and later between natives and settlers—that structured colonial law and society.[36]

The deconstruction of hierarchies of difference is also of central concern to literary conceptions of culture as "an institutional sphere devoted to the making of meaning."[37] This is the sense adopted by Said, who uses "culture" to indicate "all those practices, like the arts of description, communication, and representation, that have relative autonomy from the economic, social, and political realms and that often exist in aesthetic forms, one of whose principal aims is pleasure." Literary and artistic representations, in this analysis, played an essential role in

32. *Oxford English Dictionary*, 2nd ed., s.v. "Representation."
33. On the meaning of "image," see W.J.T. Mitchell, *Iconology: Image, Text, Ideology* (Chicago, 1987), esp. chap. 1, "What Is an Image?"
34. See William Sewell, "The Concept(s) of Culture," in *Logics*, 152–74.
35. Raymond Williams, "Culture," in *Keywords: A Vocabulary of Culture and Society*, rev. ed. (New York, 1983), 89–90. See among others, Talal Asad, ed., *Anthropology and the Colonial Encounter* (New York, 1973); George Stocking, *Victorian Anthropology* (New York, 1987); Nicholas Thomas, *Colonialism's Culture: Anthropology, Travel and Government* (Princeton, 1994); Emmanuelle Sibeud, *Une science impériale pour l'Afrique? La construction des savoirs africanistes en France, 1878–1930* (Paris, 2002).
36. Lorcin, *Imperial Identities*; Paul Silverstein, *Algeria in France: Transpolitics, Race, and Nation* (Bloomington, 2004), chap. 2.
37. Sewell, "Concept(s)," 158. See also Raymond Williams, "Culture is Ordinary," in *The Raymond Williams Reader*, ed. John Higgins (London, 2001), 10–24; Williams, "Culture," 90–92.

forging distinctions between colonizing Self and colonized Other that "nurtured the sentiment, rationale, and above all the imagination of empire." Orientalism, in particular, has been held responsible for naturalizing views of the Islamic Maghreb as a mysterious land of exotic sexual, religious, and political mores diametrically opposed to those of Christian Europe. Such Orientalist oppositions posit the East as a passive subject of Western agency and thus "support, elaborate, and consolidate the practice of empire" in the region.[38]

In basing much of my study on the art, literature, and drama of nineteenth-century France, I employ "culture" in this second sense both as a documentary source and as an object of inquiry. Rather than focus on the canonical works that have interested art historians and literary critics, however, I have cast a wider net that includes "lesser" genres, commercial media, and official rituals like those studied by John MacKenzie and others in British imperial studies.[39] By broadening our definition of colonial culture in this way, we discover a world of colonial consciousness quite different from the exoticism enshrined in "high" art and literature. In cheap prints, vaudeville plays, popular songs, illustrated magazines, Academic painting, and public festivals, patriotic military imagery and picturesque landscapes predominate over sensual harem women or sublime desert scenes.[40] The extent and diversity of these representations belie a near consensus that few in France paid much attention to the colonies before 1870.[41] This is not to say that popular and official culture conveyed accurate knowledge of Algeria

38. Said, *Culture and Imperialism*, xii, 12, 14. On visual Orientalism, see, for example, Linda Nochlin, "The Imaginary Orient," in *The Politics of Vision: Essays on Nineteenth-Century Art and Society* (New York, 1989), 33–59; Roger Benjamin, *Orientalism: Delacroix to Klee* (Sydney, 1997); Benjamin, *Orientalist Aesthetics: Art, Colonialism, and French North Africa, 1880–1930* (Berkeley, 2003).
39. John MacKenzie, *Propaganda and Empire: The Manipulation of British Public Opinion, 1880–1960* (Manchester, 1984); John MacKenzie, ed., *Imperialism and Popular Culture* (Manchester, 1986).
40. Art historians have recently begun to challenge the assumption that leading French artists ignored empire. See Darcy Grimaldo Grigsby, *Extremities: Painting Empire in Post-Revolutionary France* (New Haven, 2002); Peter Benson Miller, "By the Sword and the Plow: Théodore Chassériau's Cour des Comptes Murals and Algeria," *Art Bulletin* 86, no. 4 (2004): 690–718; Jennifer Olmsted, "Reinventing the Protagonist: Eugène Delacroix's Representations of Arab Men" (Ph.D. diss., Northwestern University, 2005); John Zarobell, *Empire of Landscape: Space and Ideology in French Colonial Algeria* (University Park, 2010).
41. Raoul Girardet, *L'idée coloniale en France de 1871 à 1962* (Paris, 1972), 23–24, 109–44; William Schneider, *An Empire for the Masses: The French Popular Image of Africa, 1870–1900* (Westport, Conn., 1982); Thomas August, *The Selling of the Empire: British and French Imperialist Propaganda, 1890–1940* (Westport, Conn., 1985); Dominique Lejeune, *Les sociétés de géographie en France et l'expansion coloniale au XIXe siècle* (Paris, 1993); Tony Chafer and Amanda Sackur, introduction to *Promoting the Colonial Idea: Propaganda and Visions of Empire in France*, ed. Tony Chafer and Amanda Sackur (London, 2002), 1–9.

or the French colonial enterprise. Often, Algeria served as a backdrop for narratives that had as much to do with domestic political and social concerns as with the colony itself. As we shall see, the cultural politics of colonialism were always also metropolitan politics. But recognizing this fact points the way towards a more historical understanding of the broad range of Algerian imagery available to mid-century audiences.

Discursive analyses of colonial culture presume a causal relationship in which the specific relations of cause and effect are ambiguous. On the one hand, they presume that culture is prior to empire, that "colonial rule was justified in advance by Orientalism" and other cultural forms.[42] On the other hand, colonial culture is understood to be constituted by representations of an empire that already exists. This circular chronology of cultural and military-political processes challenges the temporal logic of history, even as it overdetermines the outcome of imperial domination and leaves little room for the agency of historical actors or the contingency of historical events.[43] Culture is assigned a diffuse but totalizing power that loses much of its explanatory force when we try to connect cultural representations with specific policies of conquest or exploitation. Orientalist artists, for example, did not limit themselves to territories that were or would come under European rule.[44] Other cultural agents of empire, such as anthropologists or missionaries, similarly ignored the temporal and geographical boundaries of imperial states. It is only when such actors and the representations they produced are situated in specific places, times, and relationships of power that we can begin to discern their actual historical effects.

Such a situated reading of the production, dissemination, and reception of images of empire is facilitated by anthropological understandings of culture as a system of symbolic meaning and as a social practice. Defined as an autonomous system of signification with an internal logic that can be decoded by the careful observer, culture articulates the expected behaviors and actions that guide people through the social world, much as a map provides an exteriorized representation of the rules for navigating the physical world.[45] This Geertzian conception of culture, which has been so profitably mobilized by historians of French politics, provides a powerful tool for deciphering the meanings assigned to images of Algeria. Specifically, it was political culture, "the set of discourses or symbolic practices by which . . . individuals and groups in any society articulate, negotiate, imple-

---

42. Said, *Orientalism*, 39; also *Culture and Orientalism*, 11, 53.
43. On temporality in historical thinking, see Sewell, *Logics*, 6–11.
44. John MacKenzie, *Orientalism: History, Theory and the Arts* (Manchester, 1995), 54.
45. Sewell, "Concept(s)," 160–61; Pierre Bourdieu, *Outline of a Theory of Practice*, trans. Richard Nice (Cambridge, 1977), 2.

ment and enforce the competing claims they make on one another and upon the whole,"[46] that provided the map by which nineteenth-century Frenchmen made sense of the colonial conquest unfolding on their public squares, stages, canvases, and print stalls.

A Geertzian approach has the advantage of extracting representations of Algeria from the binary relation of colonizer and colonized and resituating them within the broader symbolic logics by which their producers and consumers operated. It has the disadvantage, however, of being largely synchronic and thus more descriptive than explanatory.[47] Colonialism risks emerging from such an analysis as an "order" or "situation" to be exposed, rather than a process to be explained. Conceptions of culture as practice, characterized by the work of Pierre Bourdieu and Michel de Certeau, reanimate cultural symbols by reinserting them into the temporal realm of the social. Meaning in this view consists not in static "symbolic facts, finished products, to be *deciphered* by reference to a code (which may be called culture)" (like the map), but in the dynamic performance of such a code's provisions.[48] In the conflicts generated by the cultural practices of specific historical actors in particular social and political contexts we can begin to see the causes of historical change. Recent histories of French Algeria have enlisted such a dynamic, historicized approach to great effect. Historically grounded accounts of the colonial state, in particular, have shown the importance of military and administrative encounters with Algerians in shaping French policies and the complex relations of power between colonizer and colonized, as well as the contradictions that such encounters produced within imperialist ideologies such as "assimilation" and the "civilizing mission."[49] Histories of the internal logics of the colonial state, however, have relatively little to say about either aesthetic, especially visual, cultural forms or the processes by which French imperial rule and the structures of settler colonialism came into being in the first place.

To answer these historical questions, I combine conceptions of culture as representation, culture as system, and culture as practice to attend not only to the symbolic content of French representations of Algeria and the social and political

---

46. Keith Michael Baker, *Inventing the French Revolution: Essays on French Political Culture in the Eighteenth Century* (Cambridge, 1990), 4.

47. On historians' use of Geertz, see Sewell, "History, Synchrony, and Culture: Reflections on the Work of Clifford Geertz," in *Logics*, 175–96.

48. Bourdieu, *Outline*, 4–9, quote 23.

49. E.g. Lorcin, *Imperial Identities*; Julia Clancy-Smith, *Rebel and Saint: Muslim Notables, Populist Protest, Colonial Encounters (Algeria and Tunisia, 1800–1904)* (Berkeley, 1997); Benjamin Brower, *A Desert Named Peace: The Violence of France's Empire in the Algerian Sahara, 1844–1902* (New York, 2009); Osama Abi-Mershed, *Apostles of Modernity: Saint-Simonians and the Civilizing Mission in Algeria* (Stanford, 2010).

meanings assigned to particular representational modes, but also to the ways that both content and meaning participated in postrevolutionary debates about the nature of empire, sovereignty, and citizenship. Imagery and ritual will be read as a discourse presenting Algeria in specific ways, but also as an object of social practice, part of a field of multiple discourses in constant dialogue with one another. Representations of war and landscape, for example, must be considered in light of contemporary conventions for representing male citizenship and territorial space. Their full causal force, however, emerges only when they are considered in relationship both to each other and to the broader political and cultural contexts that produced them.

Michel de Certeau's formulations about the reciprocity between reader and text offer a useful means of understanding the cultural politics of empire in postrevolutionary France and the causal role of culture in the French conquest of Algeria. For de Certeau, representations, like texts, serve as "a cultural weapon" in the hands of social elites who seek to legitimize particular interpretations of historical events by controlling their production. At the same time, readers maintain the power to misinterpret and subvert authorized interpretations in their private reading practice. They may "insinuate" themselves into the "cracks in a cultural orthodoxy" and therein find ways to exercise their inventiveness.[50] A look at the vibrant cultural economy of mid–nineteenth-century France suggests that orthodoxy was plagued not with microscopic cracks, however, but with gaping faults in which readers' and viewers' values, demands, and alternative sources of knowledge challenged the ability of political or intellectual authorities to impose their vision of Algerian affairs. The market for imagery (and ideas) about Algeria was shaped by the political and cultural tastes of its consumers and by the existence of multiple, often contradictory discourses about the nascent colony. The conditions under which images of Algeria were created and circulated—their "social life"[51]—is thus one of the central concerns of this book. Combining symbolic analysis of official and popular representations with historical analysis of their dissemination and reception uncovers a contestatory politics masked by more monolithic, abstract conceptions of colonial culture. Despite significant tensions between them, these varied representations converged to push forward the processes of conquest, colonization, and assimilation that came to define French Algeria in the years after 1830.

50. Michel de Certeau, *The Practice of Everyday Life*, trans. Steven Rendall (Berkeley, 1984), 171–73, quote 172.
51. Arjun Appadurai, ed., *The Social Life of Things: Commodities in Cultural Perspective* (Cambridge, 1986), esp. introduction, 3–63.

PART I

By the Sword

1

A Tale of Two Despots

The Invasion of Algeria and the Revolution of 1830

ALMOST ANY ACCOUNT of the French conquest of Algeria begins with the July Revolution of 1830. According to historians of both French politics and North African colonialism, the invasion of the then–Ottoman regency was a by-product of the Bourbon Restoration's final collapse. Faced with widespread popular opposition and a strong liberal majority in the elected Chamber of Deputies, King Charles X and his ultraroyalist prime minister, Jules de Polignac, engineered the expedition against Algiers in a last, desperate bid for public and electoral support. To no avail. Barely three weeks after the fall of Algiers on 5 July 1830, a revolutionary coalition of liberal deputies, journalists, artisans, and workers took to the streets of Paris. When the smoke cleared at the end of the "Three Glorious Days" of 27, 28, and 29 July, Charles had abdicated, and his cousin, Louis-Philippe d'Orléans, had assumed the throne as "King of the French."

This turn of events, which so quickly transformed the conqueror into the conquered, delighted the monarchy's many opponents. Satirists unleashed a gleeful torrent of caricatures like *The Royal Evacuation*, by the Parisian lithographer Langlumé (fig. 1).[1] Printed less than a week after the revolution, *The Royal Evacuation* made crude fun of the brief interval separating the fall of Algiers from the fall of Paris. The cartoon depicts Charles X straining to swallow a generically "Oriental" building, identified by the caption as the city of Algiers, while

---

1. I have translated the titles of all illustrations into English.

his backside extrudes a Parisian-style edifice that falls to join the silhouette of Notre Dame cathedral on the ground behind him. The caption, in which Charles exclaims, "How funny! I swallow Algiers and I give up Paris," mocks the king's political naïveté in expecting to rally popular support with military victory in North Africa.

Much of the humor of Langlumé's cartoon derived from its scatological play on the timing of the two capitals' respective falls. But it also carried a more serious message about the links between the Algiers expedition and the July Revolution, which became one of the most popular themes in revolutionary political satire in 1830.[2] By linking the two events through the body of the king, Langlumé gave visual expression to the entanglement of the Algerian invasion in the politics of monarchy in postrevolutionary France. Invoking Rabelais' gluttonous Gargantua, the print satirized Charles X's unmeasured appetite for power and its fatal consequences for the legitimacy of royal authority. More subtly, the identifying features of the two cities reference the confrontation between sacred and secular authority that defined the political culture of the late Restoration. The minarets of the Algiers skyline and the towers of Notre Dame stand in silent contrast to the tricolor flags and civic architecture of the unidentified Parisian building. Coarse as it is, *The Royal Evacuation* encapsulates the ways that the invasion of the Ottoman regency, justified by Charles X and the Polignac ministry as a righteous attack on religious fanaticism and despotic rule, articulated the competing political ideals at stake in the Revolution of 1830.

The popularity of such satires reflects the fact that there was more to the relationship between the July Revolution and the Algiers expedition than a simple campaign stratagem. The monarchy did, as we will see, intend the expedition to divert public attention from domestic travails, including a worsening economic recession, a wave of mysterious fires in Normandy, and the growing unpopularity of the Polignac government. In this respect, the *Journal des débats* newspaper was correct to describe the invasion as the work of "ministers without a majority in the Chambers or the electoral colleges who simplemindedly think they can escape their fate with smoke and noise!"[3] But the specific forms of that smoke and noise had a deeper political significance, as well. Closer investigation of the ways that the government and its opponents represented the expedition shows not only why it failed to salvage the monarchy, but how it actually served to further undermine

2. Langlumé himself published seven other caricatures on the theme. I have identified over fifty similar images in collections De Vinck, Hennin, and Qb1 Histoire de France; George McKee, ed., *The Image of France, 1795–1880,* http://www.lib.uchicago.edu/efts/ARTFL/projects/mckee; AM Lyon Fi; Jean-Pierre Séguin and Julie-Emilie Adès, *Les canards illustrés du 19e siècle: Fascination du fait divers* (Paris, 1982).
3. *Journal des débats,* 17 May 1830.

FIGURE 1. *The Royal Evacuation*, lith. Langlumé (Paris), 1830. Bibliothèque nationale de France, Département des Estampes et de la photographie.

the legitimacy of the Bourbon regime. Charles X and his supporters publicly portrayed the invasion as an expression of their ultraroyalist conception of Christian kingship, but simultaneously justified it by invoking the values of secular liberalism. Royalists claimed to act in the name of liberty and reason against political despotism and religious fanaticism, even as they celebrated the expedition as an act of divinely inspired royal power. Caricatures like *The Royal Evacuation* encapsulated this contradiction and, in this regard, embody both the roots of the Algerian conquest in the conflicted political culture of the Bourbon Restoration and the role of the expedition in precipitating the crisis of legitimacy that brought it down.

The Political Origins of the Algiers Expedition

Accomplished in just three days, the July Revolution of 1830 lacked the bloody drama and radical outcomes of the other nineteenth-century French revolutions. The men of 1830 did not proclaim a republic and institute universal (male) suffrage. Instead, they installed Charles's cousin, Louis-Philippe, as "King of the French" under a constitutional Charter little different from the one it replaced. Property qualifications for the suffrage were extended only minimally, and voting remained the privilege of a small group of wealthy notables. The Revolution of 1830 thus constituted less a struggle between republicanism and monarchy than a crisis of legitimacy within the system of constitutional monarchy instituted after the fall of Napoleon. Because of its apparent moderation, 1830 remains the least-studied of all the French revolutions.[4] Yet it was this crisis that provided both the immediate trigger and the symbolic framework for the invasion of Algiers. Viewed from an imperial perspective, the July Revolution stands as one of the most significant events in modern French history.

The political culture of the Bourbon Restoration was characterized from the outset by "a continuous public and participatory negotiation over the nature of legitimate authority."[5] Conservative ultraroyalists saw the return of the Bourbons in 1814 as an opportunity to revive the sacred kingship of the Old Regime. Liberals, by contrast, interpreted the restored monarchy as a constitutional re-

---

4. This despite periodic calls for renewed attention to the events of 1830. See David Pinkney, "A New Look at the French Revolution of 1830," *Review of Politics* 23, no. 4 (1961): 490–506; John Merriman, introduction to *1830 in France*, ed. John Merriman (New York, 1975), 1–16; Pamela Pilbeam, *The 1830 Revolution in France* (New York, 1991), 1; Jeremy Popkin, *Press, Revolution, and Social Identities in France, 1830–1835* (University Park, 2002), 4–5.
5. Sheryl Kroen, *Politics and Theater: The Crisis of Legitimacy in Restoration France, 1815–1830* (Berkeley, 2000), 110. My interpretation of Restoration political culture owes a great debt to Kroen, although she does not address colonial questions. See also Maurice Agulhon, *Marianne au combat: L'imagerie et la symbolique républicaines de 1789 à 1880* (Paris, 1979); Pierre Rosanvallon, *La*

gime based on the secular principles of popular sovereignty, the rule of law, and parliamentary governance. These contradictions were embodied in the constitutional Charter of 1814. Issued in the name of "Louis, by the grace of God, King of France and Navarre," as a gift rather than an obligation to his subjects, the Charter vested sovereignty in a sacred, inviolable royal person and reestablished Catholicism as the state religion. Yet it also maintained certain revolutionary rights and institutions, including equality before the law, freedom of expression and of religion, and a Chamber of Deputies elected by some ninety thousand of the kingdom's wealthiest taxpayers.[6] Ultraroyalists read the regime's founding document as reconstituting the absolute monarchy of the Old Regime, while liberals construed it as a contract between monarch and nation that subjected the king to the will of the people. The restored Bourbon kings were thus caught between two incompatible views of sovereignty and royal legitimacy.

Contradictions between sacred and secular royal authority pervaded the ceremonial and parliamentary politics of the Restoration, especially after the accession of Charles X in 1824.[7] Under Louis XVIII (r. 1814–24), a policy of *oubli*, or compulsory forgetting, aimed to simply ignore divisive revolutionary memories. His devout brother, however, sought to reinstate the symbolic foundations of the Old Regime monarchy. Royal rituals, from Charles X's elaborate coronation in May 1825 to the papal jubilee of 1826, proclaimed the king's divine authority and identified the regime with the Church in both elite and popular political discourse. Restoration liberals, on the other hand, were united by a resolute anticlericalism and what they saw as the political principles of 1789: popular sovereignty, patriotism, and the rule of law.[8] A loose coalition of moderate constitutionalists, republicans, and Bonapartists, they saw efforts to "resacralize" the monarchy as a plot led by counterrevolutionary priests to resurrect the clerical, aristocratic, and royal privileges of the Old Regime. Seditious placards, songs, caricatures, defaced

---

monarchie impossible: Les Chartes de 1814 et 1830 (Paris, 1994); David Skuy, *Assassination, Politics and Miracles: France and the Royalist Reaction of 1820* (Montreal, 2003); Jean-Yves Mollier, Martine Reid, and Jean-Claude Yon, eds., *Repenser la restauration* (Paris, 2005).

6. "Charte constitutionnelle du 4 juin 1814," in *Les constitutions de la France depuis 1789*, ed. Jacques Godechot (Paris, 1970), 217–24. On the Charter, see ibid., 209–16; Rosanvallon, *La monarchie impossible*, 93–104.

7. On Restoration ceremonial practices, see Kroen, *Politics and Theater*; Françoise Waquet, *Les fêtes royales sous la Restauration, ou l'Ancien Régime retrouvé* (Geneva, 1981); Rémi Dalisson, *Les trois couleurs, Marianne et l'Empereur: Fêtes libérales et politiques symboliques en France, 1815–1870* (Paris, 2004), chap. 1; Martin Wrede, "Le portrait du roi restauré, ou la fabrication de Louis XVIII," *Revue d'histoire moderne et contemporaine* 53, no. 2 (2006): 112–38.

8. Robert S. Alexander, *Bonapartism and the Revolutionary Tradition in France: The Fédérés of 1815* (Cambridge, 1991), chap. 11; Sudhir Hazareesingh, "Memory and Political Imagination: The Legend of Napoleon Revisited," *French History* 18, no. 4 (2004): 463–83; Sudhir Hazareesingh, *The Legend of Napoleon* (London, 2004), 129–36.

coins, even baked goods portrayed Charles as a Jesuit or a bishop, and spread rumors of a clerical conspiracy through French society.[9]

A series of laws indemnifying aristocrats for property confiscated during the Revolution, reauthorizing female religious communities, and making sacrilege a capital offense aggravated electors' disquiet about the reactionary turn of the "Jesuit-king," and liberals gained a majority in the Chamber of Deputies from 1827, escalating the struggle between conceptions of monarchy into a full-blown constitutional crisis. The appointment in August 1829 of the extreme ultra Polignac government brought matters to a head over the question of ministerial responsibility.[10] Polignac's views were diametrically opposed to those of the liberal majority, and his nomination seemed to confirm liberals' fears of a plot to "return [our country] to the yoke of ultramontane fanaticism and absolute power."[11] Liberal deputies, writers, and caricaturists responded with a deafening chorus of outrage about the new ministry and began to predict a royalist coup d'état against the Charter. Ultras, who believed the appointment of ministers was an unfettered royal prerogative, saw in the storm of protest the seeds of revolution. They called on the king to invoke Article 14 of the Charter, suspending the Chambers and asserting dictatorial powers in the name of "state security."[12]

At the opening of the 1830 parliamentary session, Charles X concluded his annual address with a ringing assertion of the sacred nature of royal power and, in a thinly veiled reference to Article 14, of his duty "to maintain the public peace" in case of "criminal maneuvers" against the government.[13] Liberals responded with a statement, signed by 221 deputies and presented to the king on 18 March, that the Polignac ministry posed a direct threat to the Charter and to public liberty.[14] The next day, the king prorogued the session, raising expectations that the

9. Kroen, *Politics and Theater*, 190–96, 216–27; Barbara Day-Hickman, *Napoleonic Art: Nationalism and the Spirit of Rebellion in France (1815–1848)* (Newark, Del., 1999), 26–35; Robert Goldstein, *Censorship of Political Caricature in Nineteenth-Century France* (Kent, Ohio, 1989), 113–17.

10. On the parliamentary crisis of the late 1820s, see Guillaume de Bertier de Sauvigny, *Au soir de la monarchie: Histoire de la Restauration*, 3rd ed. (Paris, 1955), 423–35, 444–58; Vincent Beach, "The Fall of Charles X: A Case Study of Revolution," *University of Colorado Studies Series in History* 2 (November 1961): 21–60; Pamela Pilbeam, "The Growth of Liberalism and the Crisis of the Bourbon Restoration, 1827–1830," *Historical Journal* 25, no. 2 (1982): 351–66; Rosanvallon, *La monarchie impossible*, 93–104.

11. *La Tribune des départements*, 9 August 1829, quoted in Charles Ledré, *La presse à l'assaut de la monarchie* (Paris, 1960), 89–90.

12. *1787–1831, Souvenirs du comte de Montbel, ministre de Charles X*, ed. Guy de Montbel (Paris, 1913), 227–30; Baptiste Capefigue, *Histoire de la Restauration et des causes qui ont amené la chute de la branche aînée des Bourbons, par un homme d'État*, 2nd ed., vol. 10 (Paris, 1833), 293.

13. "Procès-verbal de la séance royale d'ouverture de la session de 1830," 2 March 1830, *AP* 61:543–44.

14. Adresse au roi, 18 March 1830, *Moniteur universel*, 19 March 1830.

Chamber would be dissolved at an opportune moment. That moment came on 17 May, as an invasion force of thirty-seven thousand prepared to sail from Toulon to Algiers. By the time the fleet left port on 25 May, campaigning was well underway for elections now set for late June and early July.

Officially, the French expedition against Algiers was a punitive one. The Algerian merchant house of Bacri had supplied grain to the French army during the Directory, payment for which had never been entirely settled.[15] In April of 1827, during a discussion of the Algerians' demands for reimbursement, Hussein, the dey (governor) of Ottoman Algiers, struck the French consul with a fly swatter. The French responded to this "outrage" by declaring war and instituting a naval blockade of the regency.[16] Two years later, a French parley ship was fired upon in Algiers harbor after the commander of the blockade squadron met with the dey to propose an armistice. Polignac, then minister of foreign affairs, rejected Hussein's apologies and, instead, proposed an invasion of the regency. Charles X approved this plan in October 1829, just two months after Polignac's installation as president of the Council of Ministers. Initially, Polignac suggested collaborating with Russia to subsidize an attack by Egyptian troops. But this so-called *grand projet* collapsed and, on 31 January 1830, the Council voted to take direct action. Charles mobilized the army and navy, appointed the minister of war, General de Bourmont, to command the expedition, and ordered him to prepare for a rapid departure of the amphibious invasion force.[17]

Some historians have seen the "fly-swatter affair" as a fig leaf for seizing the dey's treasury in order to refill the crown's depleted coffers without raising taxes at home.[18] French planners did see potential financial advantages in an invasion, but both revenge and financial gain paled beside domestic political concerns in the decision to go to war, whose true objectives were "the glory that will be reflected onto the KING [and] the force that such an expedition will give to his government."[19] Charles-André Julien's detailed analysis of parliamentary and

15. That Bacri and his associate, Busnach, were Jewish gave an anti-Semitic tenor to public debate on the blockade. E.g. Auguste Barthélémy and Joseph Méry, *La Bacriade, ou la guerre d'Alger: Poëme héroï-comique en cinq chants* (Paris, 1827).
16. An agreement signed in 1819 collapsed when France refused to recognize the dey as a Bacri creditor. A full account of the convoluted *affaire des Bacri* can be found in Charles-André Julien, *Histoire de l'Algérie contemporaine*, vol. 1, *La conquête et les débuts de la colonisation (1827–1871)* (Paris, 1964), 21–29.
17. Ibid., 38, 43.
18. Marcel Emérit, *Une cause de l'expédition d'Alger, le trésor de la Casbah* (Paris, 1955); Amar Hamdan, *La vérité sur l'expédition d'Alger* (Paris, 1985), esp. 84–85, 115–20, 349–61; Pierre Péan, *Main basse sur Alger: Enquête sur un pillage, juillet 1830* (Paris, 2004).
19. SHD 1H 1, ministre de la Guerre (Clermont-Tonnerre), "Rapport au Roi sur Alger," 14 October 1827.

press debates shows how the "Algiers question" had become entangled in the constitutional struggle between crown and parliament in the 1820s.[20] The ministries of the period defended the treaty settling the Bacri claims and then the blockade and invasion as matters of royal prerogative. The opposition challenged the government at every turn on the grounds that the deputies' right of financial oversight empowered them to intervene in all matters involving the public treasury, including diplomacy and war.

On both sides, attitudes towards Algiers itself were subordinated to the ongoing political conflict. Restoration liberals had traditionally espoused a bellicose militarism, celebrating the army and the glories of the republican and Imperial past in ostentatious contrast to the European peace ushered in with the return of the Bourbons.[21] But when the government instituted the blockade of Algiers in 1827, liberal deputies and journalists protested, declaring it an overreaction to a minor infraction of consular etiquette. A year later, they reversed course to criticize the blockade as inadequate punishment for the dey's insult, while the government defended it as a prudently limited measure. The parties exchanged positions once again after the appointment of the Polignac ministry, and the expedition— the only significant action taken by the new government—became a central locus of the unfolding constitutional crisis. When Charles X announced the expedition as a point of national honor, the opposition denounced it as militarily risky, diplomatically dangerous, and, above all, unconstitutional because the government had failed to seek the Chambers' approval for war-related expenses. "Unjust in its origin, imprudent in its haste, fruitless in its results, and . . . *reprehensible and criminal* in its execution," Alexandre de Laborde proclaimed on behalf of the deputies, the expedition "compromises our [the Chamber's] most cherished rights."[22] According to liberals, such disregard amounted to no less than the suppression of representative government and a decisive step "onto the uncertain road of arbitrary rule."[23] Ultras in turn charged the opposition with "spreading calumnies whose fruits they hope will benefit revolution against the monarchy."[24]

20. "La question d'Alger devant les Chambres sous la Restauration," *Revue africaine* 311 (1922): 270–305; "La question d'Alger devant les Chambres sous la Restauration," pt. 2, *Revue africaine,* 312–13 (1922): 425–58; *L'opposition et la guerre d'Alger à la veille de la conquête* (Oran, 1921); *La question d'Alger devant l'opinion de 1827 à 1830* (Oran, 1922); "L'avenir d'Alger et l'opposition des libéraux et des économistes en 1830," *Bulletin de la Société de Géographie et d'Archéologie d'Oran* 42 (1922): 23–54; Julien, *La conquête,* chap. 1.
21. Raoul Girardet, *La société militaire de 1815 à nos jours* (Paris, 1998), 20–24.
22. Alexandre de Laborde, *Au Roi et aux Chambres: Sur les véritables causes de la rupture avec Alger et sur l'expédition qui se prépare* (Paris, 1830), ii, 109 (emphasis in original).
23. *Le Courrier français,* 3 May 1830, quoted in Julien, *L'opposition et la guerre,* 4.
24. *Gazette de France,* in *Moniteur universel,* 16 March 1830.

As the expedition provoked further wrangling over the limits of royal power, it was also drawn into the intensifying struggle for control of the Chamber of Deputies. The very notion of an attack on Algiers was a response to liberal electoral gains in the late 1820s. The initial proposal for an invasion, presented to Charles X shortly after the blockade began in 1827, cited political utility as its first advantage. "It could be useful to Your Majesty to have a pretext for organizing an army," War Minister Clermont-Tonnerre wrote, "to remind France . . . that military glory survived the Revolution and that the legitimate Monarchy not only guarantees the country against foreign invasion, but that it can also can carry our standards into distant countries." Any expedition should therefore be timed to coincide with parliamentary elections, it being "desirable that those events that give new strength to governments and present a salutary object to the spirit of peoples should coincide with times of political ferment." To go before the nation with "the keys to Algiers in hand," the minister concluded, would benefit the monarchy at the ballot box.[25] Political concerns remained uppermost in the final decision to go to war, which the new war minister, General de Bourmont, endorsed in December of 1829: "An expedition against Algiers would capture the national imagination (*esprit*); it would give new vigor to the army, stoke the hopes of trade, and reunite all opinions by uniting all interests."[26]

Following this logic, the Polignac government set the electoral calendar in the spring of 1830 to coincide with the anticipated stages of the expedition. The dissolution of the Chamber and the date of new elections were announced as soon as the fleet was ready to sail, so that the electoral colleges would meet just after the expected victory. The army's landing in North Africa in mid-June provided the occasion to strike against leading liberal candidates, notably the revolutionary hero, General Lamarque, who was forced into retirement just before the first round of voting on 23 June. When Hussein Dey capitulated on 5 July, the monarchy and its defenders greeted the news as an opportunity to sway electors in twenty departments where electoral college meetings had been delayed until mid-

---

25. SHD 1H 1, "Rapport au Roi sur Alger," 14 October 1827. The Council of Ministers rejected the proposal, but Polignac exhumed the project on coming to power in 1829. While contemplating the dissolution of the Chamber during the winter and spring of 1829–30, the Council devoted its remaining attention to preparations for the expedition. See Alfred de Nettement, *Histoire de la conquête d'Alger écrite sur des documents inédits et authentiques* (Paris, 1856), 123–217; Alfred de Nettement, *Histoire de la Restauration*, 8 vols. (Paris, 1860–1872), 7:589–93, 8:383–87; Ferdinand de Bertier, *Souvenirs d'un ultraroyaliste (1815–1832)*, ed. Guillaume de Bertier de Sauvigny (Paris, 1993), 338–39; Jules de Polignac, *Considérations politiques sur l'époque actuelle, adressées à l'auteur anonyme de l'ouvrage intitulé* Histoire de la Restauration par un homme d'État (Brussels and Leipzig, 1832), 90–91 n. 1; *Journal d'un ministre: Œuvre posthume du Cte de Guernon-Ranville . . .*, ed. Julien Travers (Caen, 1874), 1–35.
26. SHD 1H 1, Bourmont, "Rapport au Roi," December 1829.

July. On learning of the victory on the ninth, Charles X immediately forwarded the news to Polignac in "hope that it [would] be useful" in royalist candidates' final appeals to voters.[27] Within hours the king had also issued orders for a celebratory *Te Deum* that was, as we will see, intended to consolidate the effects of the victory on public and electoral opinion.

For all the violent parliamentary rhetoric surrounding the expedition, public events and celebrations like the *Te Deum* were equally, if not more, important in anchoring the invasion in the revolutionary politics of 1830. Organized by military, civic, and religious authorities across France to cheer the mobilization of the expeditionary force, to solicit divine benediction for the king's army, and to celebrate Hussein Dey's defeat, such festivities represented the expedition to a wider public that included not only wealthy electors, but also ordinary people of all classes. Here, more than anywhere else in the months before the July Revolution, the symbolic, electoral, and imperial politics of legitimacy converged and tied the expedition inextricably to the Bourbon monarchy. As Chateaubriand wrote, "the ships that carried liberty over the seas to Numidia carried legitimacy; the fleet under the white flag was the monarchy itself sailing forth."[28] His remark applies equally well to celebrations of the expedition at home, in which nothing less than the fate of the Bourbon regime was perceived to be at stake.

With the election process moving forward, festivities honoring the Armée d'Afrique conflated the defense of Christian monarchy abroad with the defense of the Bourbon regime at home. Designed to rally the nation to the monarchy and reinforce its legitimizing principles, the public spectacles orchestrated around the expedition sought to demonstrate the power of sacred kingship to protect civilization from barbarism, Christianity from Islam, and freedom from tyranny. In choosing this symbolic framework, however, the monarchy opened the expedition to an alternative interpretation as part of a revolutionary confrontation between liberty and despotism. At a time when "Liberty!" and "War against tyrants and despots!" served as rallying cries for the government's critics,[29] declaring war on despotism in the name of liberty was a dangerous venture.

---

27. Guernon-Ranville, *Journal*, 67–68; David Pinkney, *The French Revolution of 1830* (Princeton, 1972), 24–27; Vincent Beach, "The Polignac Ministry: A Re-evaluation," *University of Colorado Studies: Series in History* 3 (January 1964): 120–21, quote 127; *Mémoires du chancelier Pasquier: Histoire de mon temps*, pt. 2, *La Restauration*, vol. 6, *1824–1830*, 2nd ed., ed. duc d'Audiffret-Pasquier (Paris, 1895), 232; Jean Vidalenc, *Le département de l'Eure sous la monarchie constitutionnelle, 1814–1848* (Paris, 1952), 270. French elections in 1830 involved two rounds of voting in colleges at the arrondissement and then departmental levels.
28. François-René de Chateaubriand, *Mémoires d'outre-tombe*, in *Œuvres complètes de F.-R. de Chateaubriand* (1861–1865; repr., Paris, 1997), pt. 1, bk. 31, chap. 6.
29. Placards found in Saint-Céré (Lot), 29 May and 5 June 1825, quoted in Kroen, *Politics and Theater*, 169.

Of Monarchs and Despots: Staging
the Algiers Expedition

In media ranging from newspapers to guidebooks, poems, placards, and public ceremonies, the monarchy and its ultraroyalist supporters presented the Algiers expedition to the French public as a confrontation between Oriental despotism, embodied by Hussein Dey, and Christian monarchy, identified with Charles himself. This opposition drew on a venerable tradition in French political culture, where the two terms had served as mutually constitutive models of legitimate and illegitimate rule since the seventeenth century.[30] The concept of Oriental despotism reflected European assumptions that systems of government "in which a single person directs everything by his own will and caprice"[31] were most common among Asian and African peoples. By the end of the seventeenth century, the term had come to stand for a form of "barbaric," arbitrary rule antithetical to the political and material well-being of "civilized" peoples. In the French conception of Christian monarchy, by contrast, the king was charged by God to rule his people with justice and paternal love, rather than violence and fear. Unlike the Oriental despot, he governed according to the laws of the land and in the interest of his subjects, the Catholic Church, and social order. According to one eighteenth-century royal official, it was "this government, for which God has shown us the model in paternal authority, [that was] the most favorable to the liberty of each of the individuals who make up the society."[32]

Oriental despotism and Christian monarchy were particularly closely linked in France, where aristocrats, Huguenots, and *parlementaires* had begun in the seventeenth century to invoke the Ottoman sultan and the mythical Assyrian tyrant Sardanapalus to denounce Louis XIV's divine-right absolutism as arbitrary, oppressive, and "contrary to reason, humanity, [and] the spirit of Christianity itself."[33] Popularized by Montesquieu and the *philosophes* in the eighteenth century, Oriental despotism became a common metaphor for absolute forms of

30. In the large literature on French uses of "Oriental despotism," see, among others, Franco Venturi, "Oriental Despotism," *Journal of the History of Ideas* 24, no. 1 (1963): 133–42; Melvin Richter, "Despotism," in *Dictionary of the History of Ideas: Studies of Selected Pivotal Ideas*, ed. Philip P. Wiener, vol. 2 (New York, 1973), http://xtf.lib.virginia.edu/xtf/view?docId=DicHist/ uvaGenText/tei/DicHist2.xml; Roger Boesche, "Fearing Monarchs and Merchants: Montesquieu's Two Theories of Despotism," *Western Political Quarterly* 43, no. 4 (1990): 741–61; Jeffrey Merrick, *The Desacralization of the French Monarchy in the Eighteenth Century* (Baton Rouge, 1990); Thomas Kaiser, "The Evil Empire? The Debate on Turkish Despotism in Eighteenth-Century French Political Culture," *Journal of Modern History* 72, no. 1 (2000): 6–34.
31. Montesquieu, *L'esprit des lois* (1748), quoted in Boesche, "Fearing Monarchs," 743.
32. Pierre-Louis-Claude Gin, *Les vrais principes du gouvernement français . . .* (Geneva, 1780), quoted in Merrick, *Desacralization*, 13.
33. Richter, "Despotism," 9.

government and rulers perceived to put themselves above the rule of law. Its presumed illegitimacy made its elimination a central tenet of French imperialist doctrine from the time of the Revolution, when the supposedly despotic character of governments was invoked to justify French invasions in Europe, Egypt, and elsewhere.[34] This dual function made Oriental despotism a mighty but double-edged weapon in the hands of French kings.

The Greek War of Independence (1821–29) from the Ottoman Empire brought Oriental despotism back to the forefront of French political culture and set the symbolic stage for the invasion of Algiers.[35] French artists and writers initially championed military intervention in Greece as a modern-day crusade to free the liberty-loving, Greek Christians from their despotic Muslim rulers, and to defend French imperial interests against Anglo-Russian ambitions in the Near East. With the accession of Charles X in 1824, however, support for the Greeks became deeply politicized as the association of religious fanaticism with political tyranny in views of the Greek War converged with liberal fears of a clerical plot to seize political power in France. French philhellenes began to interpret the conflict as one between religious fanaticism and secular reason, as much as between Islam and Christianity. Where they had referred to defenders of Ottoman rule as "Turks," they now applied the term to "fanatical champion[s] of all legitimist power," including the French king.[36] The language of Oriental despotism was thus alive and well when the Algiers question burst onto the public stage.

In 1830, the Bourbons and their supporters seized the double-edged sword of Oriental despotism with both hands. They turned to the revitalized stereotype to portray Hussein Dey as the quintessential Oriental despot and Charles X as a Christian monarch with a divine mission to liberate Algiers and Europe from Algerine oppression. The king and royalist officials nationwide emphasized this contrast to vindicate simultaneously the invasion of Algiers and the ultra vision of Christian kingship. By delegitimizing the rule of the Ottoman governor in Algiers, ultraroyalists hoped to legitimize that of the Bourbon king in Paris.

---

34. Jacques Godechot, *La grande nation: L'expansion révolutionnaire de la France dans le monde de 1789 à 1799*, 2nd ed. (Paris, 1983), esp. chap. 3; Alice Conklin, *A Mission to Civilize: The Republican Idea of Empire in France and West Africa, 1895–1930* (Stanford, 1997), 16–18.

35. Nettement, *Histoire de la Restauration*, 7:568. On the Greek War, see Aristide Dimopoulos, *L'opinion publique française et la révolution grecque, 1821–1827* (Nancy, 1962); Nina Athanassoglou-Kallmyer, *French Images of the Greek War of Independence, 1821–1830* (New Haven, 1989); Elizabeth Fraser, *Delacroix, Art and Patrimony in Post-Revolutionary France* (Cambridge, 2004), chap. 2–3; Gillian Weiss, *Captives and Corsairs: France and Slavery in the Early Modern Mediterranean* (Stanford, 2011), chap. 8; Darcy Grimaldo Grigsby, *Extremities: Painting Empire in Post-Revolutionary France* (New Haven, 2002), chap. 5–6.

36. Quote in Grigsby, *Extremities*, 242, 357n12.

The royalist portrait of Hussein as Oriental despot drew on long-standing stereotypes of the Barbary states in general and Algiers in particular as "the 'scum' of the Turkish empire."[37] Over the course of the seventeenth and eighteenth centuries, scholars, travelers, and diplomats had developed an image of the deys of Algiers as despots rivaled only by the Turkish sultan himself in insolently flouting European standards of civilized government. A "Moral and Political Poem" penned by a Montpellier publicist in 1830 summed up the view of Hussein that had come to predominate in France by the time of the invasion:

> Never does one see a brigand more daring,
> A barbarian more hideous, a tyrant more shameless,
> The disgrace of Europe and of humanity.[38]

This vision of Hussein Dey had three defining characteristics, which were largely echoed in unofficial texts and images circulating at the time: disdain for the rule of law, both at home and abroad; fanatical Islamic faith; and protection of the Barbary pirates. The first of these, the dey's disregard for international law, provided the official *casus belli*. In diplomatic and public statements, ministerial officials cited a litany of illegal attacks by the dey on French commercial and diplomatic interests. A lengthy article printed in the *Moniteur* in late April 1830 enumerated his many crimes: "violation of the principles of the law of nations; infraction of treaties and conventions; arbitrary exactions; insolent demands opposed to the laws of the kingdom and contrary to the rights of French subjects; pillage of our ships; violation of the home of our diplomatic agents; public insult to our consul; attack against the French parley flag."[39]

According to royalist newspapers and other publications sponsored by the Polignac government, Hussein's scorn for international law was a natural extension of his despotic rule at home. A handbook produced by the Ministry of War for distribution to the Armée d'Afrique and later sold to the public exemplifies this official view of the regency government. Compiled largely from eighteenth-century travel accounts, the *Aperçu historique, statistique & topographique sur*

---

37. Ann Thomson, "Arguments for the Conquest of Algiers in the Late Eighteenth and Early Nineteenth Centuries," *Maghreb Review* 14, no. 1–2 (1989): 108–18, quote 109. See also Ann Thomson, *Barbary and Enlightenment: European Attitudes towards the Maghreb in the 18th Century* (Leiden, 1987); Denise Brahimi, *Opinions et regards des Européens sur le Maghreb aux XVIIème et XVIIIème siècles* (Algiers, 1978); Patricia Lorcin, "Historiographies of Algiers: Critical Reflections," in *The Walls of Algiers: Narratives of the City Through Text and Image*, ed. Zeynep Çelik, Julia Clancy-Smith, and Frances Terpak (Los Angeles, 2009), 227–32.
38. A. Poujol, *Guerre d'Alger: Essai de Poëme politique et morale en deux chants . . .* (Montpellier, 1830), 1.
39. *Moniteur universel*, 20 April 1830.

l'etat d'Alger synthesized contemporary stereotypes of Ottoman Algiers as "the scourge of the civilized world" and its governor as "the most despotic and implicitly obeyed monarch on earth."[40] Readers of the *Aperçu* found an account of deylical rule as an endless cycle of intrigue and terror. The dey was elected by the regency's Turkish militia, but "it is rare that the elevation of a dey takes place without a massacre among the electors who want their own favorite to triumph." Since any militiaman could aspire to the position, the handbook's anonymous authors reported, ambitious officers plotted constantly to murder and replace the ruling dey. Once in office, the governor "is the absolute master of the country; he rewards and punishes at will, . . . and accounts to no one for his conduct." With power unfettered by law or standards of civilized behavior, the dey and his lieutenants systematically diverted public revenues into their own pockets, while holding the Algerian population in fear, poverty, and ignorance.[41]

The second feature in the French portrait of Hussein was Islam, which European writers of the eighteenth and early nineteenth centuries held to be a key source of Oriental despotism. The Muslim faith was presumed by many Westerners to be inherently zealotic. If one thing was certain about its adherents, wrote a French cavalry officer in 1828, "it is that they are fanatics."[42] Islamic fanaticism was, in turn, supposed to encourage not only backwardness and ignorance, but also a tendency to impose and to submit to despotic government.[43] "The dey is a Muslim," the *Moniteur* claimed, and as such, "recognizes no other law than force, active and present force."[44] His subjects, however miserable their condition, were said to be accustomed by Koranic strictures to unquestioning obedience to their oppressor's will.

Religion was most important, however, in explaining the dey's support for Barbary piracy, the third and most distinctive feature of Algerian despotism. Since the seventeenth century, Algiers had been identified in the French imagination with the corsairs who sailed from Maghrebi ports to attack Mediterranean shipping, demanding tribute from European states for the safe passage of their vessels and seizing European captives for ransom or sale into slavery. The corsair economy was nearly moribund by 1830, when barely one hundred captives re-

40. William Shaler, *Sketches of Algiers, Political, Historical, and Civil . . .* (Boston, 1826), 15, 18. On the *Aperçu*, see SHD 1H 4, "Dépenses relatives à l'*Aperçu historique, statistique et topographique sur l'État d'Alger,*" 27 July 1830; SHD 3M 181, doss. "Distribution de l'ouvrage sur Alger." The volume met with "a fashionable success," selling out two editions in days. *Journal des débats,* 11 July 1830.

41. *Aperçu historique, statistique et topographique sur l'État d'Alger, à l'usage de l'armée expéditionnaire d'Afrique . . . ,* 2nd ed. (Paris, 1830), 149–50, 157, 160.

42. Le Chevalier Chatelain, *Mémoire sur les moyens à employer pour punir Alger, et détruire la piraterie des puissances barbaresques . . .* (Paris, 1828), v.

43. Thomson, *Barbary and Enlightenment,* 21, 144–45.

44. *Moniteur universel,* 20 April 1830.

mained in Algerine prisons, but there remained broad consensus in France that the regency of Algiers was "the greatest association formed for brigandage that has ever existed on earth."[45] Barbary piracy was not considered a solely earthly crime, however. It was also seen as a form of religious warfare driven by Muslims' purportedly fanatical hatred of Christians, which explained the corsairs' targeting of European ships and their attempts to force Christian captives to apostatize.[46]

These enduring assumptions underpinned French portrayals of Hussein Dey as the captain of the North African pirates. This role quickly eclipsed his legal violations in official speeches and royalist publications, which subsumed France's specific grievances with the regency into a "triple plague" inflicted upon the Christian powers: "the enslavement of their subjects, the tributes that the dey demands from them, and the piracy that eliminates all security from the Mediterranean coast and constantly threatens ships that navigate that sea."[47] The irony of such characterizations is evident, given the systematic subjugation, taxation, and looting that would accompany the French conquest of Algeria, but in 1830, images of Barbary piracy resonated with centuries-old popular fears of "white slavery." Since the 1600s, processions of freed captives, captivity narratives, and engravings had filled the French imagination with the sufferings of Europeans, especially women, enslaved or held captive in North Africa.[48] The Greek War revived interest in the theme in the 1820s, which saw a flood of new and reproduced memoirs, travel accounts, operas, plays, novels, paintings, and prints.[49]

Pamphlets, songs, and verse devoted to the Algiers expedition summoned up these associations for French audiences across the social and political spectrum. Although the circulation of these texts is difficult to determine from the available sources, their themes are strikingly consistent, indicating a wide resonance among contemporary consumers. A royalist ode dedicated to the dauphin offered a typical denunciation of the "audacious pirate" Hussein and his followers, "who disdain / The laws of Gods and man" in committing "so many crimes / Of which

45. Jean-Charles-Léonard Simonde de Sismondi, *De l'expédition contre Alger*, extr. *de* La Revue Encyclopédique, *mai 1830* (Paris, 1830), 5.
46. Gillian Weiss, "From Barbary to France: Processions of Redemption and Early Modern Cultural Identity," in *La liberazione dei 'captivi' tra Christianità e Islam: Oltre la crociata e il gihad, tolleranza e servizi umanitario,* ed. Giulio Cipollone (Rome, 2000), 799.
47. *Moniteur universel,* 20 April 1830. See also Polignac to duc de Laval and French ambassadors, 12 March 1830, in Nettement, *La conquête,* 266–68.
48. These sources are brilliantly analyzed in Weiss, "From Barbary to France," 789–805.
49. Angela Pao, *The Orient of the Boulevards: Exoticism, Empire, and Nineteenth-Century French Theater* (Philadelphia, 1998); Hervé Lacombe and Peter Glidden, "The Writing of Exoticism in the Libretti of the Opéra-Comique, 1825–1862," *Cambridge Opera Journal* 11, no. 2 (1999): 135–58; Athanassoglou-Kallmyer, *French Images*; Grigsby, *Extremities*, chap. 6; Fraser, *Delacroix,* chap. 2.

Christians were the victims."[50] "We must fight now," read another commemorative poem,

> To bring to bay a barbarian corsair,
> The implacable enemy of the Christian Universe,
> And the horror and dread of the European world.[51]

Many such works were produced by avowed legitimists or by writers seeking the favor of royalist patrons, but terms like "barbarian," "pagan," "corsair," "slavery," and "pillage," along with a corresponding emphasis on the victimization of Christians, appeared in works with a wide variety of political perspectives. In inexpensive popular media, the war with Algiers was framed almost exclusively in terms of corsairing and white slavery. For instance, a cheap songbook peddled in the Jura region in the summer of 1830 included lyrics celebrating "our Christian soldiers" gone "to destroy this retreat / Of pagans and corsairs."[52] The text accompanying a Parisian engraving of the French army's landing could have come directly from the Polignac ministry's offices: "For centuries the African barbarians carried on an awful traffic in Europeans, whom they seized, dragging them into slavery, selling them, or drawing a ransom for their liberation, pillaging trading ships and demanding a humiliating tribute from sovereigns to protect [their ships] from piracy. It was up to France to avenge outraged humanity, to purge the seas, and to destroy the power of these pirates."[53]

In the two decades before the French invasion, both the United States and Great Britain had taken military action against Algiers to protect their shipping from the corsairs, but the French used Barbary piracy to claim a much broader moral authority for their armies. Shifting the emphasis from the fly-swatter affair to the despotic character of the dey's rule made deposing Hussein a necessary and just war aim, and authorized a claim that the French were acting not only on their own behalf but also on behalf of the people of Algiers and all of Christendom. If, as the *Moniteur* informed its readers in late March 1830, "it is a religious duty [for the Muslim dey] to violate the sworn faith of [Christian] infidels,"[54] it must also be the divine mission of France's Most Christian King to protect the Christian faithful. Charles X claimed this sacred duty in his addresses to the Chambers of 1828 and 1830. Speaking not only as the French king, but as a latter-day cru-

50. Monbrion, *Ode sur l'expédition d'Alger, dédiée à Son Altesse Royale Monsieur le Dauphin, Grand-Amiral de France* (Paris, 1830), 6–7.
51. Poujol, *Guerre*, 2.
52. Morel, *Chanson nouvelle sur la guerre nouvelle d'Lager* [sic] (Lons-le-Saunier, [1830]), 1–2.
53. BNEst Qb1 1830, *Débarquement des Français* (Paris, 1830).
54. "Expédition d'Alger," *Moniteur universel*, 26 March 1830.

sader and defender of the faith, he announced the expedition in March 1830 as a measure that would, "in satisfying the honor of France, turn with the aid of the Almighty to the benefit of Christianity."[55]

This announcement set the tone for portrayals of Charles X as Christian monarch that served as the counterpart to depictions of Hussein Dey as Oriental despot. Although it suffused royalist odes, songs, and pamphlets, this image gained widest exposure in public ceremonies held across France in the spring and summer of 1830 to celebrate the expedition. These festivities had clear political aims, in particular to ensure the loyalty of the army and the mass of the French population. The army's enduring Bonapartist affinities had strained its relations with a dynasty restored by Napoleon's defeat, but ultras now hoped to win it over to their cause.[56] Units from all nineteen of the country's military divisions were included in the expeditionary army, and its thirty-seven thousand men were fêted in towns and villages along the route to the expedition's staging grounds in the Midi.[57] Le peuple had shown a similarly troubling attachment to the Revolution and the Empire since 1815, and the Polignac government feared a popular uprising in the spring of 1830. But the ministry also believed that martial glory and royal majesty could seduce the people, along with wavering electors, into acting as a bulwark against liberal elites. Festival organizers thus sought to impress upon all French citizens the principles of Christian monarchy and the ultraroyalist vision of the socio-political order. Organized locally but carried out on a national scale, the spectacles surrounding the Algiers expedition constituted a kind of serial "fête of sovereignty," which worked "to affirm the legitimacy of power through the reiteration of the arguments that constituted it."[58]

The first celebrations were initiated by local military, civic, and religious authorities to honor army units designated to take part in the expedition. By turns solemn and joyful, these military festivals varied tremendously from place to place. In Strasbourg, the local clergy and regimental chaplain arranged "an august and touching ceremony" at the cathedral followed by a banquet at the chaplain's home for the local artillery companies assigned to the Armée d'Afrique.[59] It was military authorities, however, that organized a public review and parade of troops

55. "Procès-verbal de la séance royale d'ouverture de la session de 1830," 2 March 1830, AP 61:543.
56. Bertier, Souvenirs, 349; Memoirs of the Comtesse de Boigne, 1820–1830, ed. Charles Nicoullaud, vol. 3 (New York, 1908), 236.
57. Nettement, La conquête, 240; SHD 1H 1, "État indicatif, par division militaire, du nombre d'hommes à diriger sur chacun des corps désignés pour faire partie de l'expédition," [25 February 1830].
58. Alain Corbin, "La fête de souveraineté," in Les usages politiques des fêtes aux XIXe–XXe siècles, ed. Alain Corbin, Noëlle Gérôme, and Danielle Tartakowsky (Paris, 1994), 25.
59. Moniteur universel, 26 March 1830.

departing from Bordeaux.[60] In some cases, spectators also participated in the proceedings, as in Montpellier, where a crowd of residents escorted two engineering companies out of town to the sound of the regimental band playing military tunes.[61] Across the Midi, where the expeditionary force was billeted while waiting to embark at Toulon, everyday life took on a festive air. Locals embraced the soldiers "as friends and as brothers," whose "arrival in the villages was a holiday and [whose] departure a day of mourning."[62]

Royalist accounts of these ceremonies interpreted enthusiasm for the Armée d'Afrique as evidence of the army's identification with the monarchy and of the people's attachment to the king. Legitimist authors highlighted soldiers' zeal for the expedition and the enthusiasm of spectators at send-off ceremonies. Government newspapers recounted striking cases of martial ardor, while royalist poems, songs, and speeches lauded the fervor of young heroes said to "burn" for revenge against the dey and to "rejoice" at the prospect of action.[63] In the throngs that turned out to applaud the soldiers, royalists saw a citizenry united around the throne and a calming of the unrest stirring the country. So Lyon's legitimist organ, the *Gazette de Lyon*, implied in reporting that "all the enemies of the *patrie* seemed to have disappeared" in the cheering at a review of the troops.[64] General de Bourmont's trip to join his command was described by *La Quotidienne* as "one long series of military and popular fêtes," at which crowds "express[ed] in an unequivocal manner the sentiments of recognition [they] felt for the prince who had ordered this eminently French war and for the general to whom its success was confided."[65]

Patriotic themes combined with royal pageantry in festivities organized for Charles's eldest son, the duc d'Angoulême, who traveled to Toulon in early May to review the expeditionary force. A placard posted throughout the department of the Rhône explained that although the dauphin "could not this time lead the arms and share the perils" of the expedition, he nonetheless wished to show the soldiers his moral support and to verify the army's logistical preparations "with the prudence of a chief and the solicitude of a father."[66] To carry this message to as many of his father's subjects as possible, Angoulême followed an itinerary that

60. *Journal de Toulouse*, 31 March 1830.
61. Ibid., 26 March 1830.
62. Fallot de Broignard, quoted in Pierre Guiral, *Marseille et l'Algérie, 1830–1841* (Aix-en-Provence, 1957), 45–46.
63. P. Ledoux, *Le départ pour Alger: Couplets à l'occasion de l'Expédition d'Afrique* (Paris, 1830), 1–2.
64. *Gazette de Lyon*, 24 April, in *Moniteur universel*, 30 April 1830.
65. *La Quotidienne*, 26 April, in *Moniteur universel*, 3 May 1830.
66. AN F7 6760, "Le conseiller d'état, préfet, aux habitants du dépt. du Rhône," 9 May 1830.

wound through fifteen departments, where local authorities mobilized the rituals of the royal entry to celebrate his passage.[67] Smaller communes made do with
tolling church bells and receptions by whatever notables could be mustered. In
the small Beaujolais textile town of Tarare, for example, the prince was greeted
by the adjunct mayor, two *curés*, and an under-inspector of customs.[68] The entry
staged in Vienne on 29 April was characteristic of larger cities with correspondingly greater means. A deputation of government officials and functionaries met
the royal guest at the city limits and escorted him through the streets to the town
hall. Garlands, bunting, and arches made of greenery festooned the parade route,
and private homes were decorated with the white flags and *fleurs de lys* of the
Bourbons. Inhabitants lined the streets and quays, shouting "vive le Dauphin!"
and "vive le Roi!"[69] Authorities in Lyon organized the most elaborate entry of
all, a two-day affair deemed by the *Moniteur* to be one of the most brilliant fêtes
of the period, which included a military and civilian escort into the city, artillery
salvoes on the place Louis-le-Grand, the illumination of public and private buildings, a fireworks display, a banquet at the prefecture, and a public review of the
local garrison.[70]

Angoulême's voyage culminated with a review of the full expeditionary force
assembled at Toulon. On 4 May, thousands gathered on the quays and bluffs
overlooking the harbor for the "glittering, magnificent spectacle," while scores of
private craft followed the dauphin's tour of the fleet.[71] The hundred warships were
hung with colorful banners resembling "enormous garlands of flowers, offered in
homage to the white flag" of the Bourbons, according to one witness, and each
ship's crew fired a broadside salute as the prince passed.[72] The day ended with a
simulation of the planned amphibious landing on a nearby beach, where several
elite companies debarked with great dispatch in specially designed flat-bottomed

67. AN F7 6760, "Itinéraire de Monsieur le Dauphin. 1° de Paris à Toulon" and "Itinéraire de
Monsieur le Dauphin. 2° de Toulon à Paris," n.d. Angoulême ordered that no formal receptions
be organized, but authorities in the fifteen departments along his route ignored his instructions.
Decree of maire de Marseille, 17 April 1830, *Moniteur universel*, 25 April 1830; proclamation of
maire de Lyon, 23 April 1830, *Moniteur universel*, 29 April 1830. Parisian officials were concerned
primarily with security, and the minister of the interior did little beyond arranging police surveillance and a gendarmerie escort for the dauphin. AN F7 6760, ministre de l'Intérieur to préfets of
Loiret, Nièvre, Allier, Loire, Rhône, Isère, Drôme, Vaucluse, Bouches-du-Rhône, and Var, 15 April
1830.
68. *Moniteur universel*, 3 May 1830.
69. Ibid., 7 May 1830.
70. Ibid., 4 May 1830.
71. Auguste Théodore Hilaire Barchou de Penhoën, *Mémoires d'un officier d'état major* (1835; repr.
Geneva, 1977), 88–92, quote 90.
72. Jean-Toussaint Merle, *Anecdotes historiques pour servir à l'histoire de la conquête d'Alger en 1830*
(Paris, 1831), 23.

boats. This performance "enchanted those who witnessed it," while demonstrating to spectators and newspaper readers the government's careful planning for the safety and success of the troops.[73]

Regardless of their scale, royal visits and speeches by local officials situated celebrations of the Algiers expedition firmly within the Bourbon monarchy's efforts to restore the symbolic order of the Old Regime. Voyages by the members of the royal family were among the exceptional festivals that marked political life in Restoration France and, like royal entries of the early modern period, brought the people into direct relation with the holders of royal power.[74] They also provided the occasion for local notables to express their adherence to the principles of legitimacy on which royal power rested. To the extent that they mentioned the impending invasion, prefects, mayors, and other officials repeated ministerial condemnations of Hussein Dey. The central themes in their speeches and proclamations, however, were devotion to the royal family, loyalty to the ultra-royalist vision of kingship, and hope that victory in Algiers would stabilize the monarchy.

Speakers asserted the continuity of royal power across the revolutionary divide by placing the dauphin and his father in the dynastic lineage of French kings and proclaiming their own uninterrupted allegiance to the royal family. They compared the duc d'Angoulême and Charles X to earlier exemplars of heroic French kingship: Louis IX, sainted for his role in the Crusades; Louis XIV, the absolute monarch who had bombarded Algiers repeatedly between 1663 and 1688; and Henri IV, the beloved "good king" whose image the Bourbons worked desperately to recapture throughout the Restoration.[75] Thus, a transparency projected during festivities in Lyon described the dauphin as a "hero of the race [of Louis XIV]," while a report from Moulins claimed that Angoulême's passage recalled for local inhabitants Henri IV's entry into their city in 1595.[76] The president of the Cour royal in Grenoble summed up such dynastic claims by declaring that the expedition would "unite . . . the great names of Saint Louis, Louis XIV and Charles X."[77]

---

73. Barchou de Penhoën, *Mémoires*, 91.
74. On the royal entry, see Ralph Giesey, "The King Imagined," in *The French Revolution and the Creation of Modern Political Culture*, vol. 1, *The Ancien Regime*, ed. Keith Michael Baker (New York, 1987), 41–59; Michèle Fogel, *Les cérémonies de l'information dans la France du XVIe au milieu du XVIIIe siècle* (Paris, 1989).
75. Anne Wagner, "Outrages: Sculpture and Kingship after 1789," in *The Culture of Consumption*, ed. Ann Bermingham and John Brewer (London and New York, 1995), 294–318; Yann Lignereux, "Dans les pas d'Henri IV: La Restauration à Paris, Lyon et Amiens, 1814–1827," in *Imaginaire et représentations des entrées royales au XIXe siècle: Une sémiologie du pouvoir politique*, ed. Corine and Éric Perrin-Saminadayar (Saint-Étienne, 2006), 19–40.
76. *Moniteur universel*, 4 and 7 May 1830.
77. Ibid., 16 May 1830.

At the same time, festival organizers declared their own and their constituents' unshakeable loyalty to the king and the royal family. Officials in the Midi invoked the region's counterrevolutionary tradition as evidence that they and the local population had remained faithful to the crown throughout the Revolution and Empire. In Avignon, the prefect cited the well-known "fidelity" of the Vaucluse to "the white banner," while the mayor of Marseille called on the city's inhabitants to show the dauphin that their fealty had never wavered in the years of revolutionary strife.[78]

Provincial authorities and notables also used the dauphin's visit to voice their support for the crown in the present political crisis. They emphasized the benevolence of Bourbon rule, the wisdom of Charles X's political judgment, and, above all, the ascendancy and sacred character of royal authority under the Charter of 1814. The return of Bourbon rule had brought peace and prosperity to a nation exhausted by decades of revolutionary and Imperial warfare, according to speakers who blithely ignored the incongruity of such statements in celebrations of an impending war. The prefect of the Vaucluse, for example, explained that the Algiers expedition demonstrated "the wisdom of our King for the most precious interest of his people, for the happiness and repose of families, for the security of our future." This evidence of the king's solicitude for his subjects should, he concluded, give them faith in all royal decisions, including "the development of the [political] institutions for which the Charter laid the principles and which must be monarchical in their essence."[79] The mayor of Marseille appealed even more directly to ultraroyalist conceptions of Christian monarchy by welcoming the dauphin's visit and the Algerian expedition as proof of "this truth, that to legitimacy alone . . . did the Supreme Arbiter of kings and peoples attach the power, the glory, and the prosperity of nations."[80]

Civic celebrations of the Armée d'Afrique were reinforced by the Catholic Church, which operated as "the right hand of the State" in public festivals and in the dissemination of royal propaganda during the Restoration, especially in the provinces.[81] While some officials suspected that civic festivities were attended primarily by committed royalists,[82] the clergy could reach a larger pool of potential supporters among the majority of French citizens who regularly attended

---

78. Speech by préfet du Vaucluse, 30 April 1830, *Moniteur universel*, 7 May 1830; proclamation of maire de Marseille, 17 April 1830, *Moniteur universel*, 25 April 1830.
79. Speech by préfet du Vaucluse, 30 April 1830, *Moniteur universel*, 7 May 1830.
80. Proclamation by maire de Marseille, 1 May 1830, *Moniteur universel*.
81. Dalisson, *Les trois couleurs*, 25; Bettina Frederking, "'Il ne faut pas être le roi de deux peuples': Strategies of National Reconciliation in Restoration France," *French History* 22, no. 4 (2008): 468.
82. *Mémoires du baron d'Haussez, dernier ministre de la marine sous la Restauration*, ed. duchesse d'Almazan, 3 vols. (Paris, 1896–97), 2:194.

mass in the early nineteenth century, particularly in rural areas. State authorities acted primarily on their own initiative, but the king himself ordered the bishops and archbishops of France to organize public prayers for divine protection of the Armée d'Afrique and for victory over the dey.[83] The bishops responded by issuing *mandements* (pastoral instructions) that explained the expedition's purpose and specified prayers and liturgy to be included in all masses until the war ended. Read from the pulpit, posted in public places, and circulated in printed form, the episcopal instructions reveal the ways that the monarchy's clerical collaborators presented the Algerian expedition to the whole range of French society, from the wealthiest electors to the humblest peasants.

Not surprisingly, it was the bishops who most clearly articulated the religious dimensions of the struggle between Oriental despotism and Christian monarchy. Prelates described Algiers as "a lair of pirates and of anti-Christian barbarism," populated by "stupid and degraded peoples, stultified by despotism and vice,"[84] and ruled by "a government that had put itself beyond the law, [whose] extermination, humanely speaking, would be a benefit for society."[85] Conversely, they described the soldiers of the expeditionary army as the "sons" of Saint Louis, "new crusaders" endowed with "the heroism of Christian virtue" and designated by God to bring the blessings of Christianity to the "unfortunate inhabitants" of Algiers. This view of the expedition as religious warfare was reflected in the liturgical selections added to masses throughout the month of June, which appealed to the crusader Saint Louis and recalled earlier Christian kings' struggles against the infidel.[86]

Clerical representations of the expedition as a religious crusade also carried an important political message, linking the "sacred" expedition against Islamic despotism with the legitimacy of sacred kingship in France. Charles X's "pure" motives for war, according to the prelates, reflected his virtues as a Christian monarch and the goodness of his rule over the French people. The bishop of Gap (Hautes-Alpes), François-Antoine Arbaud, argued with particular force on this point. A nonjuring priest who had emigrated during the Revolution, now a member of the Jesuit-linked society, La Congrégation, and a supporter of the Missions

83. Charles X to archbishops and bishops, 17 May 1830, in *Moniteur universel*, 26 May 1830.

84. [Charles-Auguste-Marie-Joseph Forbin-Janson], *Mandement de Monseigneur l'Évêque de Nancy et de Toul qui ordonne des prières publiques pour le succès de l'expédition d'Alger, et pour attirer les bénédictions de Dieu sur l'élection générale des députés du Royaume* (Nancy, 1830), 6–7.

85. [Louis Belmas], *Prières ordonnés par Mgr. l'Évêque de Cambrai pour le succès de l'expédition d'Alger* (Roubaix, 1830).

86. Forbin-Janson, *Mandement*, 8–9. See also [François-Antoine] Arbaud, "Mandemen qui ordonne des prières publiques pour le succès de la guerre d'Afrique," 30 May 1830, in *Recueil des circulaires, mandemens, etc. de Mgr. Arbaud, évêque de Gap . . .* , ed. abbé Aucel (Gap, 1838), 299–300.

de France devoted to the re-Christianization of France, Arbaud was aligned with
the most extreme wing of Restoration ultraroyalism.[87] Although unusually vitu-
perative in tone, Arbaud's *mandement* spelled out a link between the eradication
of Algerian despotism and the legitimacy of Christian kingship that ran through
most pastoral instructions.

The core of his text dealt with the sacred justice of the expedition and the
"piety of our monarch" in going to war against Islamic "ignorance" and "supersti-
tion." Unlike the bloodthirsty Napoleon Bonaparte, Charles X was "a king miserly
with the blood and fortune of his people, always anxious to preserve for them the
inestimable benefits of peace." He understood that true honor and glory lay not
in the pursuit of earthly trophies but in defending "the interests of order and of
justice" against anarchy and sacrilege. He had therefore sent his army to fight the
heresy that "a fanatic claiming the title of prophet had forced a multitude of peoples to adopt at sword point almost twelve centuries ago" and the "oppressive laws
and tyrannical vigilance" that kept the word of God from the Algerian population. French victory, the bishop proclaimed, would bring divine grace to the "unfortunate" North Africans and pave the way for a peaceful conquest by Catholic
missionaries. The priests of the diocese, therefore, were to devote all their energy
to obtaining celestial assistance for an army led by "motives of such an elevated
order." Arbaud then turned to the upcoming elections. Addressing both ordinary
citizens and the small group of wealthy electors, he claimed that the Algerian campaign was critical to the defense of order and justice at home, as well:

> The circumstances in which we find ourselves give exceptional importance
> to the expedition's success. Throughout the kingdom, a struggle is about
> to begin between the true friends of the monarchy and those whom . . . se-
> ditious doctrines, disappointed ambition, bruised self-interest, ridiculous
> warnings, or other such reasons have made its enemies. Victories in Africa
> will reawaken in the hearts of the French people their natural love for the
> King and increase the influence of his faithful subjects over choices that, if
> fixed on wise men, will exercise such a useful [influence] on public affairs.[88]

Other bishops sang a similar refrain linking military victory in North Africa to
political victory in France. Charles X publicly denied that prayers for the expedition had any political motivation, but the government had enlisted the Church as

---

87. Aucel, *Recueil*, lxiv–lxxxi; Geoffroy de Grandmaison, *La Congrégation (1801–1830)* (Paris, 1889), 178.
88. Arbaud, "Mandemen," 297–99.

an electoral agent, and the clergy were campaigning "openly" and "systematically" for royalist candidates.[89] Whether on unwritten orders from Paris or at their own initiative, prelates portrayed the Algiers expedition as an extension of this electoral mission. The ultramontane comte de Forbin-Janson, bishop of Nancy and founder of the Missions de France and the Société de la propagation de la foi, appealed to the citizens, charitable associations, and religious communities of Lorraine to pray and do other good works "so as to obtain particular blessings either in favor of the new elections or for the happy and prompt success of the Algiers war."[90] In a special mass for the Algiers expedition, Bishop Pons of Moulins bid his flock "not to become disunited over the sterile, never-ending question of royal prerogative and popular sovereignty." To oppose the two principles was false, he argued, since the people should "join their sovereignty to that of the king."[91]

Not all prelates engaged in such overt politicking, but many did. Even a relative liberal like Bishop Louis Belmas of Cambrai, an ardent Bonapartist and opponent of ultramontane organizations like the Congrégation, called for the preservation of "the peace of the Church and the tranquility of the State."[92] A number of dioceses abandoned all pretense of distinguishing between military and political events, and simply issued a single *mandement* prescribing simultaneous prayers for the Armée d'Afrique and for the elections. A "Paternoster for the use of electors," which appeared on the walls of Paris in late June, took the conflation of the king's divine, political, and military power to its most extreme end. Supposedly authored by the Paris police prefect, this adaptation of the Lord's Prayer not only equated the Algerian enemy with heretical "revolutionaries" at home, but also hailed Charles X as God himself.

> Our Father who art in Saint-Cloud, hallowed be thy name. Let happy and free France add the name liberator to that of CHARLES. Your wisdom and your strength shall finally free us from factions and from demagogic tyranny, just as you freed Greece from Mahmoud's barbarian yoke and from

89. Pilbeam, *1830 Revolution*, 33–34; Frederking, "Il ne faut pas être," 468.
90. Forbin-Janson, *Mandement*, 10.
91. *Mandement de Monseigneur l'évêque de Moulins, qui prescrit des prières publiques pour le succès de nos armes en Afrique, et pour l'élection générale des députés du royaume*, 10 June 1830 (Moulins, 1830), 5. Rumor had Charles X dictating these words in a private audience with Pons on 19 May. Henry Faure, *Histoire de Moulins (Xe siècle–1830)*, vol. 1 (Moulins, 1900), 614.
92. *Prières pour le succès de l'Expédition d'Alger, ordonnés par Mgr. l'Évêque de Cambrai* (Roubaix, 1830), 4. See also [Jean-François-Marie Le Pappe de Trevern], *Mandement de Monseigneur l'évêque de Strasbourg, qui ordonne des prières publiques pour demander le succès de l'expédition contre Alger* (Strasbourg, 1830). On Belmas, see Grandmaison, *La Congrégation*, 247 n. 2; A. Rispal, "Belmas (Louis)," in *Nouvelle biographie générale depuis les temps les plus reculés jusqu'à nos jours*, ed. Dr. Hoefer, vol. 5 (Paris, 1855), 291–92.

the liberalism that hoped to conduct its republican experiments there. In Algiers, your brave and faithful army, which likes Turks no more than it likes men of the pen, shall punish the insolent ally of Paris's factional journals, and Africa shall be freed from her oppressors as Europe is from her carbonari and her *incendiaries*.[93]

When Hussein Dey was finally defeated, ultraroyalists greeted the news as a sign that their prayers had been answered. Contrary winds had slowed the expeditionary fleet during its crossing of the Mediterranean, but once it reached North Africa, the Armée d'Afrique moved rapidly. The French landed at Sidi Ferruch on 14 June and, despite faulty maps, bad weather, and a significant numerical disadvantage, steadily pushed the dey's forces back over the fifteen miles towards the capital (fig. 2).[94] By 19 June, they had captured a key Algerian position at Staouëli, and the Fort de l'Empereur, Algiers's last line of meaningful defense, was destroyed on 4 July. The next morning, Hussein capitulated, and the French took possession of the city. The capitulation treaty called for the surrender of the Casbah and its forts in return for guarantees of the security of the population and the safe passage of the dey and his Turkish militia into exile in Naples.[95] The French casualties of 409 dead and 2,061 wounded were lighter than many had feared, although another 700 would die of disease by the end of August. Algerian losses were significantly heavier, although no specific figures are available.[96]

News of the capitulation reached Paris on 9 July, and the government took immediate steps to publicize the victory. Within hours, a copy of Admiral Duperré's telegraph dispatch was posted at the stock exchange, and the cannon at the Invalides fired to notify the capital of the good news. Reports were prepared for the press and messages were sent to the provinces, where prefects and mayors quickly spread word that Algiers had surrendered, that the king's flag flew over the dey's palace, and that all the sailors from two ships wrecked during the landing had been saved.[97] Within hours, Charles X had also issued orders that a *Te Deum* mass of praise and thanksgiving be sung in all French churches on the

93. "Oraison dominicale à l'usage des électeurs," *Le Globe*, 22 June 1830. The phrase "republican experiments" refers to the Greek War.
94. For a detailed account of the military operations see Gabriel Esquer, *Les commencements d'un empire: La prise d'Alger (1830)* (Paris, 1929); Nettement, *La conquête*, 335–447.
95. Capitulation treaty, 5 July 1830, in Nettement, *La conquête*, 428. After brief sojourns in Paris, Naples, and Leghorn, Hussein settled in Alexandria, where he died in 1838.
96. Julien, *La conquête*, 56. Tens of thousands fled Algiers after the destruction of Fort de l'Empereur, likely preventing major civilian casualties. Jacques Frémeaux, *La France et l'Algérie en guerre, 1830–1870, 1954–1962* (Paris, 2002), 260.
97. Boigne, *Memoirs*, 3:251; SHD 1H 4, Haussez to Sauvo, editor-in-chief of *Le Moniteur universel*, 10 July 1830.

FIGURE 2. *Accurate View of the City and Port of Algiers*, Deckherr frères (Montbéliard), 1830. Bibliothèque nationale de France, Département des Estampes et de la photographie.

following two Sundays.[98] The civic and clerical officials who had orchestrated the mobilization ceremonies were now called upon to celebrate the fall of Algiers.

By 9 July, political developments at home had raised the stakes of the expedition dramatically. The newspapers that reported the fall of Algiers also carried news of electoral disaster for Polignac and the ultraroyalists. The first electoral college meetings had taken place on 23 June and 3 July, and government candidates had been handed a crushing defeat. The government had postponed voting in some twenty left-leaning departments until 13 and 19 July, and held out some hope that the Algerian victory might sway a few undecided electors there. But even an unlikely ultra landslide in these departments could not salvage the situation; the early returns had virtually guaranteed an overwhelming liberal majority in the new Chamber of Deputies. Faced with this catastrophe, the Polignac government did not wait for results from the remaining electoral colleges. On 6 July, the Council of Ministers decided to invoke Article 14 of the Charter giving the king the power to rule by decree and determined the steps to be taken when Charles assumed emergency powers. In light of this decision, public celebrations

98. Beach, "The Polignac Ministry," 127 n. 174; marquis de Dreux-Bréze, 9 July 1830, in *Moniteur universel*, 10 July 1830.

of the fall of Algiers aimed less to sway the remaining elections than to pave the way for a royal coup d'état.

Celebrated in Paris on 11 July and repeated in churches throughout France over the following week, the *Te Deum* was intended to engage the entire population in collective praise for the king and to demonstrate popular support for the monarchy as a warning to liberal politicians and others who might resist the king's seizure of power. In these ceremonies, the monarchy's defenders interpreted the victory over Hussein Dey as evidence of divine sanction for the ultra cause and a promise of divine retribution for its opponents. In ordering the *Te Deum*, Archbishop Quélen of Paris exulted, "Heaven has heard our prayers, the Lord has granted our wishes, God has blessed our arms; ALGIERS is taken!!! . . . Thus shall be treated, everywhere and always, the enemies of our lord King; thus shall be confounded all those who dare to rise up against him."[99] Quélen repeated the sentiment in person at Notre Dame, where he welcomed Charles X with a speech expressing his hope that the victory in Algiers would soon be followed by similar "miracles" at home.[100] In Nancy, Forbin-Janson called so violently for divine punishment of the king's enemies, whom he described as the enemies of God, that he was accused by a group of local notables of trying to provoke civil war in the city.[101] Other clerics adopted less aggressive language, but still equated the government's domestic opponents with its military opponent in North Africa.

Prefects and mayors throughout France organized public festivals to complement the *Te Deum* ceremonies and to cement their political benefits. Officials construed the shared enjoyment of popular entertainments, including military parades, public banquets, concerts, balls, games, and pyrotechnic displays, as an act of devotion to the monarchy, and they enjoined participants to acknowledge this fact. Proclamations and printed programs reminded French men and women that coming together for the *Te Deum* and the pleasures of fireworks, dancing, and greasy-pole races constituted "a just tribute of admiration and thanks to the

---

99. *Mandement de Monseigneur l'archevêque de Paris, qui ordonne que le Te Deum solonnel sera chanté dans toutes les Églises de son Diocèse, en actions de grâces de la PRISE D'ALGER*, 10 July 1830 ([Paris, 1830]), 2. This incendiary phrase was not included in the text of the mandement printed in the *Moniteur universel* (11 July 1830).

100. *Journal des débats*, 13 July 1830. The *Moniteur* also excised this reference, but opposition papers did print it.

101. Andrew Lewis, "A Turbulent Priest: The Forbin-Janson Affair (1824–1839)," *French History* 19, no.3 (2005): 329, 337. The critical passage asked the faithful to pray for victory "no longer over the external enemies who bow before our flags, but in the very heart of the *patrie*, over all those lost or guilty hearts who cannot remain enemies of our King without also being the enemies of God, the enemies of the glory and the happiness of France!" *Mandement de Monseigneur l'évêque de Nancy et de Toul qui ordonne qu'un Te Deum solonnel sera chanté dans toutes les églises de son Diocèse, en actions de grâces de la PRISE D'ALGER* ([Nancy, 1830]), 3.

Monarch who protected our Commerce and who watches with such care over the fate of France."[102] "Charles X has triumphed, as he will always triumph, over his enemies," declared the program for the victory festival in Carcassonne. "Let us, in our turn, triumph over our divisions, and, as Frenchmen like the vanquishers of Algiers, let us share in a single thought, a single sentiment: the glory of our arms, the love of our King."[103]

Charles, according to his advisers, was convinced that victory celebrations had had the desired unifying effect.[104] Despite royalists' early electoral defeats, departmental authorities bolstered the government's confidence with reports of "excesses of joy," "universal delight," and "the greatest enthusiasm" from the populace at Algiers's capitulation.[105] "I cannot express," the mayor of one small Lorraine town reported, "the joy that manifested itself and the good effect that this news spontaneously produced on all classes. I could not finish my reading [of the victory announcement] without interruption because of the unanimous cries of *Vive le Roi.* I am told that it was the same at all the other proclamations."[106] In the capital, police reported that it had been years since they had seen "such great demonstrations of happiness" as on the day of the *Te Deum,* when "the King was saluted by the loud acclamations of the love of his people" during the procession to Notre Dame.[107]

Such reports buoyed the government's faith in the expedition's political effects. As the subprefect of Belfort put it, the fall of Algiers appeared to have "dissipated as if by enchantment the deplorable cloud . . . left by the recent electoral struggle."[108] The ultra newspaper *Le Drapeau blanc* crowed that "Bourmont has vanquished with one blow the Turkish militia of Algiers and the Bedouins of France."[109] With renewed self-assurance, the government began to look forward to more elaborate commemorations of its triumph. Charles X approved a proposal to erect a monument to the expeditionary force in Toulon and commissioned court painter François Gérard to immortalize the event on canvas.[110] Plans

---

102. AD Eure 1M 346, maire d'Evreux, "Prise d'Alger. Proclamation," 11 July 1830. On festive participation, see Claude Ruggieri, *Précis historique sur les fêtes, les spectacles et les réjouissances publiques* (Paris, 1830), esp. 109, 167.
103. AD Aude 4E 69/168, maire de Carcassonne, "Programme des dispositions arrêtées à l'occasion de la prise d'Alger," 15 July 1830.
104. Bertier, *Souvenirs,* 349; Pasquier, *Mémoires,* 236, 240–41.
105. SHD 1H 4, maréchal de camp Gavotz (Marseille) to Bourmont, 9 July 1830; "Rapport analytique de l'État major de la 1re Division militaire," 9–10 July 1830; "Rapport analytique de l'État major" (Lille), 10 July 1830.
106. AD Meurthe-et-Moselle 1M 659, maire de Pont-à-Mousson to préfet de la Meurthe, 10 July 1830.
107. AN F7 3884, Bulletin de Paris, 12 July 1830.
108. AD Haut-Rhin 1M 81, sous-préfet de Belfort to préfet du Haut-Rhin, 11 July 1830.
109. *Le Drapeau blanc,* quoted in Faure, *Moulins,* 616.
110. Haussez, "Rapport au Roi," *Moniteur universel,* 23 July 1830; *Journal des débats,* 12 July 1830.

were set in motion for a national victory festival, perhaps on the order of the three-day celebration that marked the 1823 victory in Spain, to take place later in July.[111] This triumphal confidence was misplaced, however. Not only did the government suffer another crushing defeat in the second round of voting on 13 and 19 July, but barely two weeks after the *Te Deum*, the insurrection that ultra-royalists had feared broke out. By the end of July, it was liberals' turn to proclaim a "double victory" of liberty over "the Barbarians . . . in Paris and in Algiers."[112]

The Conquest of Liberty

It is difficult to gauge popular responses to the monarchy's staging of the Algiers expedition. Contemporary observers offer contradictory accounts of public attitudes. Provincial authorities were ordered to pay particular attention to *esprit public* in the spring and summer of 1830, but their reports are unevenly preserved. Nevertheless, in the surviving archival record and a wealth of printed material from this period, there emerges an alternate interpretation of the invasion that embraced imperial expansion in Algiers, even as it rejected ultraroyalists' celebrations of it. The portrait of Hussein Dey as Oriental despot accorded with liberal understandings of liberty, reason, and the rule of law as the foundations of legitimate authority. But liberals also saw signs of that same despotism in depictions of Charles X as a Christian monarch claiming absolute, sacred authority. In opposition newspapers, pamphlets, songs, poems, and caricatures, the French king, surrounded by his "priestly," "Jesuitical" ministers replaced Hussein Dey as the despotic ruler.

Print media played a critical role in the political culture of the July Revolution.[113] Newspapers and caricatures were seen by postrevolutionary elites as the most dangerous weapons available to the monarchy's opponents, and historians have long recognized their importance as a field of political contestation at this time. While the restored monarchy struggled to assert its legitimacy, constitutionalist, republican, and Bonapartist publishers, journalists, and graphic artists worked equally hard to undermine those efforts. Dynamic overlaps in form and audience made the opposition media a powerful counterweight to the public festivals through which Charles X and his supporters sought to legitimize their vision of Christian monarchy.

111. Rémi Dalisson, "Les 'Journées d'Afrique et des Colonies' pendant la Grande Guerre: Un exemple d'instrumentalisation de l'image africaine (1914–1917)," *Revue TRAMES* 9 (June 2001): 77.
112. D. Laisné, *La Double victoire, ou les Barbares vaincus à Paris et à Alger: Hommage au Roi des Français, S.M. Louis-Philippe Ier* (Versailles, 1830).
113. On the political role of the press and caricatures, see Ledré, *La presse*; Popkin, *Press, Revolution*, 1–16, 29–30; Goldstein, *Censorship*, chap. 1; David Kerr, *Caricature and French Political Culture, 1830–1848: Charles Philipon and the Illustrated Press* (Oxford, 2000).

Beginning with the announcement of the expedition and continuing through the mobilization and victory festivities, these opposition media called into question the motives behind the invasion, and accused the government of seeking "to make of a victory over Algiers a victory over our liberties and to transform [our] glory into a means of corruption or violence" against the French people, the electorate, and the Charter.[114] The true purpose of the expedition, according to liberals, was to salvage the reputation of the Polignac ministry and to lay the groundwork for an ultraroyalist coup d'état. Royalist spectacles were a meant to distract public attention from this counterrevolutionary agenda, to "dazzle" electors into supporting ultraroyalist candidates, and to rouse popular support for the suspension of the Charter.

Suspicion of the monarchy's "ulterior motive of despotism"[115] arose from the moment that Charles X announced the invasion plans in March of 1830. Opposition journalists and caricaturists claimed that the war was intended only to reward ministerial cronies with military contracts and battlefield honors. Particularly vicious were personal attacks on the expedition's commander, Bourmont, who was considered a traitor by many for abandoning Napoleon on the eve of the Battle of Waterloo. The common charge in 1830 held that the Algiers expedition was an excuse "to give the marshal's baton with some decency to the renegade of Waterloo," an effort to "hide an indelible stain [of dishonor] under the embroidery and insignia of a marshal of France," "a sort of baptism of honor" for a cowardly turncoat.[116] One of the few political caricatures on the expedition to escape the censors' vigilance, entitled *Grands projets*, depicts Bourmont striding off to Algiers accompanied by a bulldog and a parrot that symbolize the general's reputed affinity for the English and the royalist media's mindless repetition of the government's message (fig. 3). The caption, "This time there will be no retreat," references both Bourmont's reputed cowardice in 1815 and the Polignac ministry's refusal to bow to the liberal majority in 1830. Other cartoons tagged him with the epithet "Cossack," in reference to the Russian occupation of eastern France that followed Napoleon's defeat.[117]

114. *Journal des débats*, 17 May 1830.
115. "France: L'Expédition d'Alger," *Le Globe*, 26 March 1830.
116. *Mémorial de l'Yonne* and *L'Impartiel* (Besançon), quoted in Ledré, *La presse*, 114, 231n74; "But de l'expédition d'Alger.—Avantages que la France doit en attendre," *Le Constitutionnel*, 6 July 1830; *Le Globe*, 14 March 1830. Several newspapers were prosecuted for disparaging the general's reputation, and the pension of poet and columnist Delphine Gay was revoked after she published a poem denigrating Bourmont's honor. See *Moniteur universel*, 6 May 1830 and 19 May 1830; *Journal de Toulouse*, 26 July 1830.
117. BNEst Qb1 1830, *Cosaque donnant une leçon de pigeon volé aux enfants du dey d'Alger* (Paris, [3 April 1830]); Astoin, *Le Cosaque du Tanaïs volant au pillage d'Alger*, lith. Renou [17 July 1830].

GRANDS PROJETS.

(Attitude calme et imposante)

Pour cette fois, il n'y a plus à reculer

FIGURE 3. Charles Traviés, *Grands projets*, in *La Silhouette*, 13 March 1830. Courtesy Library of Congress, Rare Books and Special Collections Division.

Journalists and caricaturists also satirized preparations for the Armée d'Afrique, thereby undermining the government's claim that the expedition was a matter of the gravest national concern. Comic depictions of unorthodox equipment, including blue-tinted sunglasses, collapsible wooden guardhouses, a pack of dogs to test drinking water, and painted wood and cardboard soldiers to simulate ambushes, trivialized logistical preparations, while drawing attention to the government's desire to guarantee victory within the time frame dictated by the political calendar.[118] Most popular with printmakers and, presumably, their customers, however, were caricatures of French soldiers' sexual conquests in the dey's harem and the misadventures of artists, writers, and other curiosity-seekers who accompanied the expedition. Images of French conscripts' amorous "victories and conquests" over the women of Algiers (fig. 4) and of naïve amateurs' bumbling explorations of the Algerian landscape constituted, as others have argued, a kind of symbolic taking of possession that paralleled the military conquest.[119] But they also ridiculed the monarchy's war effort, making farce of the weighty symbolism of Christian kingship and reinforcing liberal allegations that the expedition was a purely political exercise, a *Military Promenade*, according to one caricature, in which Charles X took French soldiers and electors for a ride, literally and figuratively (fig. 5).

By contrast, there was little humor in liberal criticism of government efforts to publicize and celebrate the expedition. In civic and religious festivities celebrating the Armée d'Afrique, liberals saw both instruments and symptoms of the regime's despotic character. Army bulletins, episcopal *mandements,* and the *Te Deum* festivities all drew their ire. Within days of the expedition's announcement, critics began to decry the publicity surrounding the Armée d'Afrique as a cover for the ministry's illegal maneuvering against the Chamber of Deputies and the Charter. Were this diversionary tactic to succeed, the liberation of Algiers would come at the expense of liberty at home. Emboldened by military success, Polignac and his "absolutist faction" would unveil their "despotic secrets."[120] They would use public rejoicing over the victory as the occasion to dismiss liberal deputies, silence opposition journalists, orchestrate massive electoral fraud, or simply suspend the Charter entirely.

Among liberal critics' first targets were bulletins from the Armée d'Afrique, which were printed and reprinted in metropolitan newspapers, news broadsheets, and placards. Prior to the fleet's departure, they published sarcastic reports that the army's equipment included a lithographic press so as "to send readymade bulletins to France."[121] After the landing at Sidi Ferruch, the main opposition newspapers compared official bulletins with dispatches from their own correspondents and indicted the government for exaggerating the importance of minor engagements, withholding unfavorable news, and falsifying French casu-

118. Julien, "L'opposition," 22; prints in BNEst Qb1 1830.
119. Todd Porterfield, *The Allure of Empire: Art in the Service of French Imperialism, 1798–1836* (Princeton, 1998), 138–40; Gérard de Puymège, *Chauvin, le soldat-laboureur: Contribution à l'étude des nationalismes* (Paris, 1993), 45–49; W. J. T. Mitchell, "Imperial Landscape," in *Landscape and Power,* ed. W. J. T. Mitchell (Chicago, 1994), 19–27.
120. "France: Situation du Ministère," *Le Globe,* 23 March 1830.
121. *Journal des débats,* 4 May 1830.

FIGURE 4. J. J. Grandville, "Oh! the arabesque!" lith. Langlumé (Paris), August 1830. Bibliothèque nationale de France, Département des Estampes et de la photographie.

FIGURE 5. *The Military Promenade*, in *La Silhouette*, August 1830. Courtesy Library of Congress, Rare Books and Special Collections Division.

alty figures. Journalists attributed this misinformation to political strategizing, and alleged that the government was timing the release of good news to coincide with electoral events while repressing bad news to avoid negative publicity.[122] Inflated or delayed reports were an insult to the valor of French soldiers and to the nation, liberals claimed, while the refusal to report casualties accurately left military families in agonizing suspense about the fate of their loved ones. *Le Globe* attacked the "charlatanism" and "glaring deceptions" of a ministry that sought to threaten dissident voters rather than to honor the French fleet, army, and nation as they deserved.[123] "Such despotic manners might be acceptable under a despotic government; such disdain for the families to which the army belongs, such lack of concern for the men killed in combat could be forgiven when the entire nation was devoted to the fighting. But to allow such an infamous tactic under the regime of liberty and transparency in which we live, this cannot be tolerated."[124]

If liberals considered royalist manipulation of the press incompatible with the rule of law and representative government, proponents of secular monarchy found another sign of Bourbon despotism in the abuse of episcopal *mandements* and public prayers. Politicized *mandements* were roundly condemned as counterrevolutionary in both content and form. Even as they were mocked for their overblown rhetoric, bishops came under fire for threatening electors, sowing discord among citizens, and stepping illegally into the realm of politics. As one liberal journalist pointed out, this "descen[t] from the admirable role of priests to the unworthy role of election courtiers" was expressly forbidden by both civil law and the Concordat between the French state and the Catholic Church.[125] Moreover, journalists found it inexcusable that many *mandements* accused them of unpatriotically desiring the defeat of the French army and treasonously corresponding with the enemy.[126]

The *Te Deum* and other victory celebrations marked the high point of liberal condemnations of the Algiers expedition. After predicting that the ministry would use the *Te Deum* to move against its opponents, they seized on the event as evidence of the government's true, reactionary nature. To a certain degree, criticism of the victory celebrations simply continued earlier attacks on the political motives behind the expedition. Eugène Forest, a regular contributor to the influential left-leaning satirical journals *La Silhouette* and *La Caricature*, highlighted

122. E.g. *Le Constitutionnel*, 3 July 1830.
123. "D'une proclamation royale adressée aux électeurs," *Le Globe*, 1 May 1830.
124. "Expédition d'Alger," *Le Globe*, 28 June 1830.
125. "Les mandements électoraux: Monseigneur l'évêque de Montpellier.—L'archevêque d'Avignon.—L'évêque de Dijon," *Le Globe*, 19 June 1830.
126. *Journal des débats*, 22 June 1830; " France: Dernières dépêches d'Afrique," *Le Globe*, 24 June and 26 July 1830.

the monarchy's political uses of the expedition in a lithograph inspired by official rejoicing at a victory that had proved its critics wrong (fig. 6). Published on 17 July, Forest's image depicts a confrontation between a caricaturist and a soldier at the door of a print shop, where the soldier gleefully presents the artist, presumably the author of satires against the expedition, with a broadsheet bearing news of the fall of Algiers. "We showed you, you nay-saying scribbler!" he cries, as two cheering comrades tear up the offending engravings. A closely related image, printed by Langlumé on the same day with the same caption, shows two soldiers expressing their displeasure at the window display of the famous Martinet print shop, in which can be seen copies of caricatures on the expedition, including *Grands projets* and *The Military Promenade*, and prints of the "victories and conquests" type discussed above.[127] These new satires highlighted the regime's fear of caricature, as well as the triumphalist tone of royal celebrations.

In the victory festivities, opposition journalists saw not genuine patriotism, but cynical political manipulation and intimidation. A proclamation by the prefect of the Nièvre, for example, offered proof that the war had been undertaken "with Bible in hand," at the expense of equality before the law, transparent governance, equal taxation, religious, civil and literary freedom, and a host of other liberal achievements, including the abolition of the inquisitorial Holy Office and of the slave trade.[128] Especially revealing are journalistic objections to Archbishop Quélen's incendiary speech at the *Te Deum* in Paris. Widely reprinted, often without commentary, alongside the king's polite response, Quélen's language was seen as evidence of the monarchy's collusion with the counterrevolutionary priesthood. Opponents of the government discerned threats even in the acclamations that greeted Charles X during the procession to Notre Dame, claiming that the ministry had paid hundreds of workers to march through the capital waving a white Bourbon flag and shouting royalist slogans in order to create the proper "festive air" for the *Te Deum* and to demonstrate to liberals the extent of popular support for the monarchy.[129] This incident so struck contemporaries that it was revived a month later in a caricature suggesting that the cheering workers had not been paid, but coerced by the Paris prefect of police (fig. 7). Despite the *Moniteur*'s best efforts to refute such accusations, suspicions persisted that official celebrations of the expedition were intended "to rouse the working classes against the electors."[130] Commenting on the *Te Deum*, *Le Constitutionnel* asked

127. BNEst Qb1 1830, *Enfoncé, artiste de malheur*, lith. Langlumé.
128. "D'une proclamation de Mr. Séguier, préfet de la Nièvre, à l'occasion de la prise d'Alger," *Le Figaro*, 22 July 1830; "Proclamation du préfet de la Nièvre, à l'occasion de la prise d'Alger," *Le Globe*, 24 July 1830.
129. "Singulière démonstration," *Le Constitutionnel*, 13 July 1830.
130. Ibid.

FIGURE 6. Eugène Forest, *Algiers Is Taken.* "We showed you, you nay-saying scribbler!" Lith. Mendouze (Paris), July 1830. Bibliothèque nationale de France, Département des Estampes et de la photographie.

rhetorically if the monarchy believed that "French warriors had gone to destroy the dominion of a ferocious African despotism only . . . to return to establish an exactly similar one in their own *patrie.*"[131]

Although opposition newspapers had their own political motives for questioning public enthusiasm for celebrations of the expedition, there is reason to believe that official accounts of unanimous popular joy were exaggerated and that journalists' suspicions of festivities like the *Te Deum* were quite broadly shared. According to participants' memoirs and accounts printed in opposition newspapers, audiences at many official spectacles manifested either indifference or outright hostility towards the king's representatives. Observers in Lyon, Marseille, and Toulon, for example, reported that Bourmont was met with sullen passivity and that the few shouts of "Vive Bourmont!" were not taken up by the

131. "Le Salut de la France," *Le Constitutionnel*, 12 July 1830.

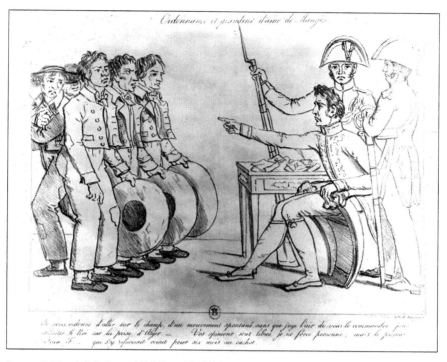

FIGURE 7. *Mangin's Order and Nobility of Soul*, lith. Langlumé (Paris), September 1830. Bibliothèque nationale de France, Département des Estampes et de la photographie.

crowds, which remained "mute."[132] Bourmont seems to have elicited particular resentment, but silent protests extended to the dauphin and the king, as well. In Toulon, where some ten thousand people attended the dauphin's review of the expeditionary fleet on 4 May, residents stood largely quiet during the prince's entry into the city. At the *Te Deum* in Paris, both Haussez and Pasquier commented on the contrast between Parisians' initial rejoicing at the news of the victory and the restless quiet of the crowds that greeted the king along the route to Notre Dame. "The march was silent and sad," Pasquier noted; "a vague anxiety seemed to weigh on the population and to hold back the cries of joy that ought to have welcomed a victory. The King was saluted with only a few, obviously prepared acclamations."[133] Not surprisingly given the heavy police presence at these events, silence appears to have been the most common form of protest against

132. *Journal du commerce de Lyon*, in *Le Globe*, 28 April 1830; quote, "Expédition d'Alger," *Le Globe*, 4 May 1830.
133. Haussez, *Mémoires*, 2:195–96, 2:218; Pasquier, *Mémoires*, 239.

the monarchy's legitimizing rituals. Yet there are a few traces of more active dissent, too. A *Globe* correspondent claimed that those who cheered Bourmont in Marseille were rebuked by other spectators, while government informants in Toulon reported malicious statements circulating in the crowd during Angoulême's tour of the expeditionary fleet.[134] Scattered and fragmentary though they are, such reports suggest that French audiences were well aware of the political significance of the festivities they attended and, at least sometimes, resisted official efforts to use them to promote the ultraroyalist conception of Christian monarchy.

To reject the monarchy's equation of victory in Algiers with the triumph of Christian kingship was not, however, to reject the legitimacy of the expedition itself. As they condemned the Polignac government's attempts to co-opt the army's glory, liberals also sought to reclaim the Armée d'Afrique as a representative of the nation rather than of the monarchy. Opposition journalists insisted with increasing frequency through the spring and summer of 1830 that they could simultaneously revile the government's political uses of the expedition and hope for the army's success. An article that appeared in *Le Constitutionnel* just after the *Te Deum* was typical in declaring it "necessary to distinguish" between the soldiers, "whose intrepid courage has procured us this glorious conquest," and the ministers who had sent them to fight. The army, which had "borne the risks of a stormy sea, the furors of the Bedouin Arab, the fatigue of marches, the threats of the climate," and "taken Algiers at the risk of its life," deserved the nation's praise. The government, however, deserved no share in the glory. Victory celebrations attributing the victory to the Bourbon monarchy, the Polignac government, and its ultraroyalist supporters were, the newspaper argued, the deceptive work of "despots, bad ministers, enemies of common sense, all those who want to oppress or deceive men": "Let the Polignac ministry cease veiling its unpopularity with the mantle of our brave men! Let them cease to insult the army by equating themselves with that ever-valiant force, . . . which would condemn its own valor if, for a single moment, it suspected that [that valor] could be used by men who seek to plunge France back into absolute power." The article concluded with a ringing call for the nation, the electors, and the Chamber of Deputies to reward the victorious army with the "spectacle of oppression vanquished, the King undeceived, and constitutional liberty reconquered."[135]

Le Constitutionnel's rallying cry encapsulates the liberal interpretation of the Algiers expedition, which provided both new arguments against the legitimacy

---

134. "Expédition d'Alger," *Le Globe*, 4 May 1830; AN F7 6760, directeur du Bureau de personnel for ministre de l'Intérieur, confidential to sous-préfet de Toulon, 22 May 1830.
135. "Il faut distinguer," *Le Constitutionnel*, 15 July 1830.

of the Restoration and a basis from which the conquest of Algiers could be reappropriated in the name of liberal values. Rather than reading the fall of Algiers as a sign of Charles X's sacred power, this view portrayed the defeat of Oriental despotism as a prelude to the defeat of fanatical despotism everywhere, including France. Grounded in the principles of secular and popular sovereignty, this alternate interpretation framed the expedition as a victory for constitutional liberty.

The columns of the opposition press beautifully illustrate the coexistence of these seemingly contradictory imperatives. The same newspapers that attacked the expedition as a ministerial plot also covered the mobilization and combat operations in great detail. More often than not, they reprinted official bulletins from the Armée d'Afrique alongside polemical pieces denouncing the government's despotic manipulations of the invasion. Even the most radical opposition journals carried articles about the regency, as well as advertisements for maps, atlases, and engraved landscapes designed to help the reading public follow events in North Africa. "Whatever we might think of the motives and appropriateness of such an enterprise," *Le Globe* declared in introducing a series of articles on the geography, history, economy, and climate of Algiers, "there is no one who does not wish to understand [its] chances for success and the advantages that we may gain from it."[136] Proclaiming their interest in and support for the Armée d'Afrique, liberals sought to reclaim the expedition from its ultraroyalist leaders and to align themselves with the soldiers fighting in North Africa. They and the army both represented the sovereign people and, as such, were locked in a common struggle on behalf of liberty against despotism.

At the heart of the liberal interpretation of the expedition lay a series of oppositions derived from the basic division in Restoration political culture between the liberal understanding of secular, popular sovereignty and the ultraroyalist vision of Christian kingship. Liberals' claims to the Algiers expedition were built upon contrasts between not only liberty and despotism, but also army and ministry, patriotism and partisanship, nation and monarchy. The victory, they argued, belonged not to the king and his ministers but to the army and the nation, to true French patriots devoted to the cause of liberty rather than to partisans in the service of the Bourbon despot.

> In vain [the ministry] tried to make the fall of Algiers a party victory and to confiscate this public triumph for the benefit of a coterie. But France will not be fooled. . . . Where the enemies of her liberties claim to see an expedition conducted in the interests of their cause, she [France] saw a national expedition; by associating herself with it through her wishes, she

---

136. "Alger," *Le Globe*, 13 April 1830.

purified it of the reproach of partisanship and of political calculation. She made it patriotic by taking an interest in it and appropriated success for herself by hoping for it.[137]

In newspapers, poems, songs, and pamphlets, opposition authors attributed the victory to the people and defined both nation and patriotism in terms of what they saw as the universal values of liberalism. "The cannon that resounded in Paris will resound throughout Europe with the consent of all peoples; it proclaims the victory of civilization," wrote the *Journal des débats*. "Civilization," for the *Débats*, did include the destruction of Islamic piracy and white slavery touted by proponents of Christian monarchy but was defined primarily by "patriotism, humanity, and reason" and the desire to "rescue the liberty of all peoples and punish tyranny."[138]

The political implications of such a view were clear. If French soldiers were fighting for liberty on the other side of the Mediterranean, it was the duty of French electors to fight for that same liberty at home. In the weeks before the first round of elections in late June, opposition journals called upon voters to demonstrate their solidarity with the Armée d'Afrique by supporting constitutionalist candidates. The army's exploits, they declared, should strengthen, rather than sap the resolve of liberal electors. True patriots would not be distracted by the government's spectacles; liberals' love of France would allow them to track the dangers run by soldiers in Algiers and those run by electors at home, and to believe that both would triumph in the end. "The same sentiment that leads to the nomination of constitutional deputies makes us applaud the triumph of our soldiers," *Le Constitutionnel* informed the Polignac ministry on the day of the *Te Deum*: "*Let the glorious news ring out in the electoral colleges*, as you put it; you will not change a single one of the names that comes out of the urn to deliver the coup de grâce against you." The singing of the *Te Deum* for Algiers, the satirical *Figaro* predicted, would be followed by a *De profundis* for the ministry.[139]

The announcement of Algiers's fall so close on the heels of the government's electoral defeat seemed to confirm these predictions. An anonymous liberal sympathizer wrote just after learning of the victory that "the soldiers and the citizens of the same nation [have] fulfilled their duties, the former by delivering the world from a people of pirates, the latter by freeing their *patrie* from the plague of ministers."[140] Meanwhile, opposition journalists and publicists demanded that the newly elected Chamber of Deputies prosecute the Polignac ministry for its failure to seek parlia-

137. *Journal des débats*, 10 June 1830.
138. *Le Globe*, 12 July 1830; *Journal des débats*, 10 July 1830.
139. "Bigarrures," *Le Figaro*, 13 July 1830.
140. *À l'Armée d'Afrique! Une Victoire, ou la prise d'Alger* (Paris, 1830), 8.

mentary consent for the war in Algiers: "We will not permit M. de Bourmont to act despotically in a constitutional monarchy. . . . While thanking God for the victory, we will still demand an accounting for the illegality of the war."[141]

Liberals' victory in the first round of electoral college meetings lent their interpretation of the military victory an even more radical cast, and arguments for the invasion of Algiers and the ouster of Hussein Dey began to assume a distinctly revolutionary tone in the last two weeks of July. If the army fought in Algiers by "the right of civilization over barbarism, of humanity over ferocity, of order over piracy, of good over evil," then so should the people of France. And the right by which "force contributes to the general progress of humanity, by which war serves justice, by which victory civilizes the world . . . is the same right that . . . legitimizes revolutions."[142] It was this equation between the army's struggle against Oriental despotism in North Africa and liberals' struggle against Christian kingship at home that made the fall of Algiers such a central theme in the political culture of the revolution that finally erupted on 27 July.

The government's decision to invoke Article 14 of the Charter giving the king emergency powers was made public on 26 July with the publication of the infamous Four Ordinances, which put the final spark to the tinderbox of discontent that had been smoldering since the appointment of the Polignac ministry. Signed by Charles X on 25 July and printed in a special issue of the *Moniteur* the next day, the ordinances rescinded freedom of the press, dissolved the Chamber of Deputies, and revised the electoral law to disqualify three-quarters of eligible voters, presumed to be liberal sympathizers. Deeming these measures unconstitutional, opposition journalists, deputies, and workers immediately began to organize. Crowds gathered in the streets, and violent clashes broke out with government forces on the twenty-seventh. By the time the fighting ended on 29 July, a combination of popular violence, maneuvering by opposition journalists and deputies, and strategic machinations on the part of Charles X's cousin, the duc d'Orléans, had driven the Bourbons from power. Rather than fight the crowd marching on the royal palace of Rambouillet, Charles X and the royal family fled with a small retinue to Cherbourg, whence they sailed for exile in England in mid-August. In the meantime, the Chamber of Deputies had declared the throne vacant and invited the duc d'Orléans to become "King of the French." The duke's acceptance and its "acclamation" by an overwhelming majority of deputies on 7 August gave France a new king, Louis-Philippe I, and inaugurated a new experiment in constitutional monarchy. Charles X's plan

141. *Journal des débats*, 10 July 1830.
142. "Alger: Question politique," *Le Globe*, 15 July 1830.

to save ultraroyalism with a victory over Hussein Dey had failed. The Bourbon Restoration was over.[143]

Historians have attributed liberal attacks on the Algiers expedition to the Polignac ministry's unpopularity, concluding that the invasion was tainted by its association with the hated government.[144] Charles X and his ministers would have agreed, as they equated liberal hostility to the expedition with rejection of royal authority. The government's justification for the Four Ordinances centered on the "unprecedented violence" of press attacks on the Algiers expedition, which they described as "the most grave" of liberal journalists' many offenses against king and country. The text claimed that liberal writers, "insensible to national honor" and "indifferent to the great interests of humanity," would have been happy to leave the French flag "blackened by a barbarian's insults" and Europe "subjected to a cruel slavery and shameful tributes." Worst of all, they had informed the enemy about the equipment, size, and strategy of the expeditionary force, while seeking to undermine the troops' morale and to incite mutiny with gloomy predictions of defeat and personal attacks on Bourmont. These acts, the government concluded, were treasonous and constituted the final betrayal by a group dedicated to dissolving the social bonds, religious faith, and political loyalty that held France together.[145]

Some of the government's focus on liberal coverage of the Algiers expedition was purely polemical, but it also reflects the very real symbolic weight the monarchy had invested in the expedition over the preceding months. The elaborate celebrations organized around the Armée d'Afrique and its victory had transformed the invasion into a symbol of Bourbon rule, but in doing so made it a lightning rod for protest against the regime. Just as ultraroyalists had conflated the Algerians with their domestic enemies, liberals now conflated Charles X with Hussein Dey. Popular anticlericalism and Oriental despotism converged, collapsing the overthrow of the "Oriental" despot of Algiers and the "Christian" despot of Paris into the same process of revolutionary liberation.

The folding of the Algiers expedition into domestic politics became most evident in the aftermath of the July Days, when the Restoration's heavy-handed censorship regime was lifted. As journalists, pamphleteers, and caricaturists unleashed their pent-up hostility towards the fallen regime, they made the

143. The best account of the July Days remains Pinkney, *French Revolution*.
144. E.g. Julien, "Les Chambres," pt. 2, 456; Achille de Vaulabelle, *Histoire des deux Restaurations jusqu'à l'avènement de Louis-Philippe (de janvier 1813 à octobre 1830)*, 5th ed., vol. 8 (Paris, 1860), 118.
145. "Rapport au Roi," 25 July 1830, in *Moniteur universel*, 26 July 1830.

Restoration's ties to the Algerian expedition one of their most popular themes.[146] Like most of the satires that flooded from artists' and writers' pens in these heady weeks, those referencing the Algerian expedition focused on the revolution's victims, especially Charles X and, to a lesser extent, the royal family, Bourmont, and the other members of the Polignac ministry. Satirists' favorite motif, however, was the pairing of Charles X with Hussein Dey, which inspired not only dozens of caricatures, but also comic dialogues and a scene in a popular vaudeville play.[147]

The first of these images, dated 30 July and deposited with the authorities on 7 August, set the tone for the genre, in which the two fallen rulers meet under unexpected circumstances (fig. 8). Here, Hussein encounters the erstwhile French king on the road and exclaims, "And you are also dispossessed!" Charles responds, "Alas, my brother, *mea culpa, mea maxima culpa.*" Charles's bishop's miter invokes the prerevolutionary rumors about the "Jesuit-" or "bishop-king," while his sash, emblazoned "English," reflects allegations that the Algiers expedition had been subject to the approval of Whitehall. The rifle he carries refers to the hunting expedition the king took on the first day of the July Revolution. Later variations on the theme depict Charles and Hussein in similar guises sharing their new, involuntary leisure. They smoke, drink, and play board or card games together, above captions that play on the consonance between the French prefix *dé-* (de-/dis-), and the Algerian ruler's title, "dey," to describe the two rulers as, among other things, deposed, dethroned, decamped, disloyal, dissipated, and debauched.[148]

As in *The Royal Evacuation*, the outpouring of glee that put Charles X and Hussein Dey (sometimes literally) in the same boat focused on the "dey-posed" rulers as representatives of the despotism over which liberty had triumphed, rather than the legitimacy of invasion itself. In several satirical dialogues between Charles X and Hussein Dey, authors made the French king acknowledge the similarities between his own despotic reign and that of his Algerian counterpart.

146. According to *La Caricature*, some four hundred political caricatures on the fall of Charles X were printed in the months following the revolution. Goldstein, *Censorship*, 121. At least fifty of these referenced Algiers. See note 2 above.

147. E.g. Bolognini, *Scènes entre M. de Polignac, Charles X et le Dey d'Alger (les premiers jours d'août 1830)* (Paris, 1830); "Fantaisies: Théâtre de la Porte Saint-Martin, La Caricature, croquis, pochades en un acte," *La Caricature*, 15 September 1831; Théodore Muret, *L'Histoire par le théâtre, 1789–1851,* vol. 3, *Le gouvernement de 1830; La Seconde République* (Paris, 1865), 157.

148. The range of *dé-/*dey jokes can be seen in the caption for an English copy of Victor Ratier's *Les Décampés* (14 August 1830), which reads "En bien cousin ton coup d'état—Eh bien beau-dey ton coup d'éventail / Te voilà dey-frisé, dey-masqué, dey-monté, dey-chu, dey-baté, dey confit. / Et toi dey-baptisé, dey-croté, dey-laissé, dey-coiffé, dey-ferré, dey-tenu. / Ce que c'est que d'être dey-loyal, dey-mesuré, et dey-bauché. / Nous voilà dey-finis, dey-boutés, dey-livrés, dey-bridés, et peut-être bientôt dey-colés." See "Les Deys-Traqués," in *The Royal Menagerie: A Collection of the Best Caricatures Which Have Appeared in Paris Since the Late Revolution.* (Paris and London, 1831), plate 21.

FIGURE 8. "And you too are dispossessed?" Lith. E. Ardet (Paris),
August 1830. Bibliothèque nationale de France, Département
des Estampes et de la photographie.

In one, for instance, Charles laments to the dey that it was not as easy as he had
expected "to be an absolute master, a despot like you" in France. In the end, he
concludes, "one doesn't govern France like Algiers," since "a free nation" has
rights and "people and kings have a just equilibrium."[149] As revolutionary move-

149. Bolognini, *Scènes*, 9–10. For similar examples, many of which cite caricatures, see *Dialogue
entre Charles X et le dey d'Alger* (Paris, 1830); *Charles X et le Dey* (Rouen, 1830); *Polignac et ses confrères jugés par le Dey d'Alger: Grande dispute entre un jésuite et le Dey* (Paris, 1830); *Lettre du Dey
d'Alger au Comte de Bourmont, général en chef de l'expédition d'Alger. Par M. Charles C.* (Paris, 1830);
Raoul Mendès da Costa, *Le Dey d'Alger chez Monsieur Polignac: Scène dramatique* (Paris, 1830).

FIGURE 9. *Royal Menagerie*, lith. Langlumé (Paris), August 1830. Bibliothèque nationale de France, Département des Estampes et de la photographie.

ments blossomed elsewhere in Europe in the fall of 1830, sympathetic French printmakers and buyers expanded their "menagerie" of overthrown despots to include William I of the Netherlands, from whom Belgium won independence, and Charles II, duke of Brunswick, who was actually forced from power, both thanks to popular pressure in the months after the revolution in France (fig. 9). A satirical poem published in Lyon put the political lesson of the summer of 1830 under the pen of Hussein Dey himself, in a fictional letter to his fallen conqueror. And that lesson was simple: "The people of our day strike down tyrants."[150]

The parallels between the French army's mission in Algiers and that of the revolutionaries in Paris were given telling expression in popular prints that placed heroic scenes from the July Days side by side with the fall of Algiers. Images like the cheap, colorful woodcut shown in fig. 10 suggest that neither printmakers nor their customers saw anything inconsistent in celebrating simultaneously the departure of the Armée d'Afrique, the fall of Algiers, and the iconic events of the revolution, in this case Parisian revolutionaries' capture of the Pont d'Arcole

150. *Hussein-Dey, Ex-Dey d'Alger, à Charles X, ex-Roi de France* (Lyon, 1830).

FIGURE 10. *Heroic Deed of Young d'Arcole on the Day of 28 July 1830, Departure of French Troops for Algiers,* and *Attack on the Fort de l'Empereur near Algiers, 4 July 1830,* impr. de Blocquel (Lille), 1830. Réunion des Musées Nationaux/Art Resource, NY.

on 28 July.[151] The July Revolution was thus integrated into a process of liberation that had begun with the invasion of Algiers and, at least some Frenchmen hoped, would not end until despotism had been destroyed the world over. The impulse to spread revolution beyond French borders was less important (and less widely shared), however, than the desire to reclaim the Algiers expedition from the fallen monarchy and to replace, as many prints did, the white flag of the Bourbons with "the noble colors of the nation," the tricolor flag restored by the new July Monarchy as the banner of the Armée d'Afrique (fig. 11).

---

151. On the pont d'Arcole as a "heroic anecdote," see Michael Marrinan, *Painting Politics for Louis-Philippe: Art and Legitimacy in Orleanist France, 1830–1848* (New Haven, 1988), 34–35, figs. 23–27.

FIGURE 11. *Fall of Algiers*, impr. Cereghetti (Paris), October 1830. Bibliothèque nationale de France, Département des Estampes et de la photographie.

In redefining the invasion as a victory for liberty and the nation, the revolutionaries of 1830 also laid the ideological groundwork for the subsequent conquest and colonization of the former Ottoman regency. They contrasted the Bourbons' "wasteful" political aims for the expedition with a vision of productive, agricultural exploitation. From leading opposition deputies to satirical journals, critics of the Restoration argued that the injury caused by its despotic scheming could be healed by the creation of a French colony in Algiers. As *Le Figaro* argued, France could, "out of patriotism," "act nationally by founding a colony" where the Bourbons had sought only to destroy French liberty.[152] "Let them not say that the success of our African army pains patriots," the *Tribune des départements* concurred. "Already our soldiers' enthusiasm makes them [patriots] look forward to the foundation of a French colony on the African coast; they dream of a *Côtes-d'Afrique* department and pore over maps of Algiers showing the monuments, streets, and squares that will house the brave men who must

152. "Des suites de la prise d'Alger," *Le Figaro*, 10 July 1830.

ensure for France *the most beautiful of colonies.*"[153] The expedition was thus recast in terms that bound the conquest to the sovereign nation championed by the
liberal revolutionaries of 1830. Because of the strength of these bonds, the July
Monarchy did not renounce the occupation of Algiers and withdraw the Armée
d'Afrique. Instead, Louis-Philippe embraced the conquest, expanding it to all of
the former Ottoman regency and laying the foundations for France's most important modern colony.

153. *La Tribune des départements,* 11 July 1830, quoted in Charles-Robert Ageron, *France coloniale
ou parti colonial?* (Paris, 1978), 16.

2

Empire of Merit

The July Monarchy and the Algerian War

O N 18 MARCH 1842, King Louis-Philippe d'Orléans met Horace Vernet, one of the best-known and most popular painters of his day, at Versailles. Over the previous decade, the new monarch had transformed the renowned royal palace into a historical museum filled with thousands of paintings and statues representing the great events and great men of the French past. In 1837, Louis-Philippe had commissioned Vernet to add a new gallery to the Musée historique de Versailles, an elaborate room devoted to the military achievements of his own reign and, especially, to his sons' campaigns in Algeria, where three of the princes had served since the mid-1830s (fig. 12). The gallery, of which a huge triptych depicting the 1837 siege of the Algerian city of Constantine was the centerpiece, had taken Vernet four years to complete and cost his royal patron nearly three hundred thousand francs. Upon seeing the final result, Louis-Philippe declared himself thrilled with "the great merit of [Vernet's] paintings and with the felicitous and fine ensemble of the whole" and named the artist a commander of the Legion of Honor to mark his achievement. The gallery opened to the public the following day, and it soon became one of the museum's most popular attractions, which it remained well into the twentieth century.[1]

---

1. Frédéric Nepveu, architecte du Roi, reported to the directeur des Bâtiments de la Couronne on each of the king's 398 visits to Versailles. I identify these reports by the number and date of the visit. On Vernet's presentation of the Constantine Gallery, see AC Ms 1351, no. 238, 18 March 1842; *Moniteur universel*, 22 March 1842.

SALLE DE CONSTANTINE.

FIGURE 12. Charles Gavard, engr. J. Huguenet, *Constantine Gallery*, in Charles Gavard, *Supplément aux Galeries Historiques de Versailles* (Paris, 1848). Bibliothèque nationale de France, Département des Estampes et de la photographie.

The opening of the Constantine Gallery was a revealing moment in the history of the July Monarchy. On coming to power in 1830, Louis-Philippe had rejected the Bourbon model of Christian monarchy, but he did not, as anticolonial deputies demanded, renounce the "grievous bequest" of Algiers.[2] Algerian notables argued that their country deserved a place alongside France, Belgium, and the other European states "liberated" from despotism in 1830, but their claims were summarily dismissed, as well.[3] Instead, after several years of hesitation, Louis-Philippe joined the larger, louder chorus that declared the capture of Algiers the Restoration's only worthwhile legacy and called for the expansion of French power in North Africa. "Absolutism dreamed up this conquest as a means of oppressing liberty," declared the new minister of war, Field Marshal Soult. "Victorious liberty will keep it as a trophy captured from absolutism."[4] For the remainder of his eighteen-year reign, Louis-Philippe put the full symbolic weight of the monarchy behind the conquest, sending each of his five sons to fight in Algeria and celebrating their campaigns with all the means available to the royal family, including public speeches, festivals, the press, and the visual arts. Vernet's Constantine Gallery inaugurated the most spectacular of these celebrations, a suite of three rooms at the Versailles museum that were dedicated to the Algerian conquest and the Orléans princes' role in the war.

The siege of Constantine, where Louis-Philippe's second son, the duc de Nemours, commanded the assault troops, was a strategic turning point in the French push into the Maghrebi interior, as well as the high point of Nemours's military career. Vernet's commemoration of the siege and its royal commander, along with two more "African" galleries added to the Musée historique in the 1840s, perfectly captures Algeria's central place in Orleanist efforts to legitimize the July Monarchy. It figured the conquest as the new regime's most important contribution to French history and staked the future of the Orléans dynasty on the Algerian campaigns of Louis-Philippe's sons. At the same time, it sheds new light on the French pursuit of empire in North Africa. Some contemporary

---

2. Duvergier de Hauranne, speech to the Chamber of Deputies, 9 July 1836, *AP* 105:145.
3. Charles-André Julien, *Histoire de l'Algérie contemporaine*, vol. 1, *La conquête et les débuts de la colonisation (1827–1871)* (Paris, 1964), 73–75; Jennifer Pitts, "Liberalism and Imperialism in a Nineteenth-Century Mirror," *Modern Intellectual History* 6, no. 2 (2009): 287–313; Hamdan Khodja, *Aperçu historique et statistique sur la Régence d'Alger, intitulé en Arabe le Miroir* (Paris, 1833); Hamdan Khodja testimony, 23 January 1834, in *Procès-verbaux et rapports de la Commission d'Afrique instituée par ordonnance du Roi du 12 décembre 1833* (Paris, 1834), 56–57.
4. CAOM F80 1671, "Rapport soumis au Roi par le Président du Conseil, Ministre Secrétaire d'État de la Guerre sur les mesures à prendre pour assurer l'avenir de l'occupation et de l'administration de l'ancienne Régence d'Alger," July 1834.

observers were convinced that the July Monarchy supported the conquest of Algeria less from conviction than out of obedience to public opinion, "the opinion of the street" to one disapproving author and "the imperious will of France" to a more enthusiastic early historian.[5] What we might call a "will to empire" did exist in postrevolutionary France, but it was hardly spontaneous. The symbolic embrace of the Algerian conquest by the Orléans regime was an effort to generate such a will to empire, albeit one whose primary objective was the legitimation not of empire but of the monarchy itself.

Like Charles X's justifications for invading Algiers, pinning the legitimacy of the new July Monarchy to the Algerian war was risky. By associating themselves with the triumphs and sacrifices of the Armée d'Afrique, the Orléans men sought to demonstrate a new model of constitutional kingship in which the personal merits of a "chosen" ruler could reconcile the competing notions of sovereignty that had erupted into revolution in 1830. Doing so in such spectacular fashion, however, highlighted the ambiguities of their novel claims to power. In this chapter, I will discuss Algeria's place in the official culture of the Orléans monarchy, before turning in the next chapter to the popular culture of the period, which offered French audiences a very different understanding of the war and helped to create a will to empire founded on very different understandings of sovereignty and citizenship. There were critical tensions between royal and popular representations of the Algerian conquest, which undermined the monarchy's self-legitimizing efforts, but together they forged symbolic links between the conquest and the nation that became a seemingly irrefutable justification for French colonization in North Africa.

Merit, Militarism, and Monarchy in Orleanist France

Louis-Philippe's political uses of the Algerian conquest bore marked similarities to those of Charles X. The "Three Glorious Days" of 1830 altered its terms, but the crisis of legitimacy that brought down the Bourbon Restoration continued unabated into the new July Monarchy. Like his cousin, Louis-Philippe sought to defuse this crisis by making war in North Africa. Where the Bourbons faced the challenge of reestablishing royal power in the wake of the French Revolution, however, Louis-Philippe had the even more peculiar task of "founding a new dynasty on the rubble of a revolution which had chased one king from the throne

---

5. Paul-Dieudonné Fabar, *L'Algérie et l'opinion* (Paris, 1847), 25; Amédée Gabourd, *Histoire contemporaine comprenant les principaux événements qui se sont accomplis depuis la Révolution de 1830 jusqu'à nos jours . . .*, vol. 2 (Paris, 1864), 2:455.

and demanded an end to the legitimist principle of divine right."[6] It was his efforts to resolve this dilemma that drove the new royal family's personal and political investment in the Algerian conquest.

The paradoxes of revolutionary monarchy pervaded the Orleanist regime. Steeped in the lessons of recent French history, the kingmakers of 1830 tried to steer a middle course that would guarantee the liberal principles of popular sovereignty, individual liberty, and the rule of law while avoiding the extremes of either absolute royal power, identified with the Bourbons, or popular democracy, which they associated with the "anarchy" of 1793 and the Terror. Louis-Philippe himself described the new monarchy as a "*juste milieu* between the abuse of liberty and the abuse of royal authority."[7] In 1830, he declared his accession to the throne to be "the expression of the general will" and swore to uphold the revised constitutional Charter as "King of the French" rather than "King of France."[8] But he also maintained many royal prerogatives, including a full-scale court and royal household, elaborate residences and entertainments, dynastic marriages for his children, and substantial annual appropriations for royal expenses (the Civil List), as well as hereditary transmission of the throne itself.[9] This attempt to balance the protection of liberty and public order, and to combine popular with royal sovereignty, was reflected in the Charter's revisions.[10] The elements most closely associated with Bourbon ultraroyalism—sacred monarchy, the established Church, Article 14, and the hereditary peerage—were suppressed, and sovereignty was attributed to "the French people." Rather than extending political rights to all citizens, however, the authors of the new constitution made them contingent on "capacity," or merit.[11] Eligibility to vote and to stand for public

---

6. Michael Marrinan, *Painting Politics for Louis-Philippe: Art and Ideology in Orleanist France* (New Haven, 1988), 1. See also Alain Corbin, "L'impossible présence du roi: Fêtes politiques et mises en scène du pouvoir sous la Monarchie de Juillet," in *Les usages politiques des fêtes aux XIXe–XXe siècles*, ed. Alain Corbin, Noëlle Gérôme, and Danielle Tartakowsky (Paris, 1994), 77–116; Jo Burr Margadant, "Gender, Vice, and the Political Imaginary in Postrevolutionary France: Reinterpreting the Failure of the July Monarchy, 1830–1848," *American Historical Review* 104, no. 5 (1999): 1461–96; Jean-Claude Caron, "Louis-Philippe face à l'opinion publique, ou l'impossible réconciliation des Français, 1830–1835," *French Historical Studies* 30, no. 4 (2007): 597–621.

7. Response to a delegation from Cosne, 30 August 1830, quoted in Caron, "Louis-Philippe," 607.

8. Declaration to the Chambers, 9 August 1830, quoted in Pierre Rosanvallon, *La monarchie impossible: Les Chartes de 1814 et 1830* (Paris, 1994), 127.

9. Anne Martin-Fugier, *La vie quotidienne de Louis-Philippe et de sa famille, 1830–1848* (Paris, 1992), chaps. 3 and 5; Margadant, "Gender, Vice," 1476–77; H. A. C. Collingham with Robert S. Alexander, *The July Monarchy: A Political History of France, 1830–1848* (London, 1988), chap. 8.

10. Rosanvallon, *La monarchie*, 105–21; David Pinkney, *The French Revolution of 1830* (Princeton, 1972), 183–92.

11. Douglas Johnson, *Guizot: Aspects of French History, 1787–1874* (London and Toronto, 1963), chap. 2; Vincent Starzinger, *Middlingness: Juste Milieu Political Theory in France and England, 1815–1848* (Charlottesville, 1965), 20–27, 55–62; Pierre Rosanvallon, *Le moment Guizot* (Paris, 1985), 95–104, 121–32.

office was restricted to those men whose economic or professional status, as indexed by the tax rolls, was believed to reflect superior reason or significant "interests" in the well-being of French society. Lower age and income thresholds, and the inclusion of commercial wealth and certain professions, doubled the size of the Restoration-era electorate, and earned the new regime the epithet, "the bourgeois monarchy." But the property qualifications set in 1831 still enfranchised less than 1 percent of the population, "removing power from the very rich to share it amongst the wealthy."[12]

The architects of the *juste milieu* hoped to reconcile the partisans of monarchy and republic, but they ultimately satisfied neither. The redistribution of power remained too limited for republicans, who wanted universal suffrage and, as the satirical daily *Le Charivari* noted, saw the very word "royal" as an anachronism in the age of liberty.[13] Conservative Bourbon loyalists believed that the reforms of 1830 went too far in dismantling royal power and aristocratic privilege. Even liberals were split on the proper balance between monarchism and parliamentary institutions. For those in the so-called *parti de résistance*, it was enough to enforce the liberal interpretation of the Charter of 1814. To the leftist *parti de mouvement*, the July Days had promised more thoroughgoing democratic change that the new regime failed to deliver.

Most problematic for all parties was the nascent Orléans dynasty itself. The throne, as Pierre Rosanvallon and Jo Burr Margadant point out, was the only form of political power still transmitted by birth after 1830, and as such it presented an inherent contradiction to liberal and republican principles of individualism and popular sovereignty.[14] Supporters of the senior branch of the royal family saw Louis-Philippe as a usurper, whose throne rightfully belonged to Louis XVIII's grandson, the duc de Bordeaux. Legitimists were further enraged by the fact that the new king was the son of the regicide *conventionnel* Philippe-Égalité, who had voted in 1792 for the execution of Louis XVI. Bonapartists, for their part, saw Napoleon's son, the duc de Reichstadt, as the legitimate ruler of France. After his death in 1832, they transferred their loyalties to the Emperor's nephew, Louis-Napoleon Bonaparte. These challengers put immediate and constant pressure on the legitimacy of the new dynasty. Republic secret societies led a series of uprisings and assassination attempts against the royal family, while both legitimist and Bonapartist pretenders staged attempted coups in the 1830s. Such attacks posed

12. Eligibility for the vote was set at 200 francs in annual taxes and for holding office at 500 francs. The electorate ranged from 167,000 to 241,000 during the July Monarchy, including a few women (mostly widows) who could vote by proxy, while fewer than 10,000 were eligible for office. Collingham, *July Monarchy*, 71.

13. "Le mot Royal est aujourd'hui un anachronisme," *Le Charivari*, 11 February 1833.

14. Margadant, "Gender, Vice," 1467; Rosanvallon, *La monarchie*, 165, 169–75.

a very real, physical threat to the Orléans family, which developed a deep sense of insecurity and an acute sense of the contradictions inherent in its novel mix of monarchical and liberal principles.

Louis-Philippe sought to resolve the founding paradoxes of his "popular throne" by appealing to the concept of capacity and presenting himself as a "citizen-king" whose authority derived from his personal merits and past services to the nation, rather than from his royal blood.[15] Orleanist public festivals and iconography combined the traditional forms of royal ceremonial with a symbolic vocabulary of popular sovereignty, individual merit, and militaristic nationalism drawn from the republican and Bonapartist traditions. The army played a central role in these self-representations from the beginning of the July Monarchy, as Louis-Philippe sought to exploit the popular Bonapartism that suffused post-revolutionary French society and to paint himself as a "soldier of the Nation," who had risked his life to defend the *patrie* from its enemies. The new king's military biography thus became a key element of Orleanist representation, which recalled his service during the Revolution and his affiliation with the National Guard under the Restoration as proof of his patriotic qualities.

As the duc d'Orléans, Louis-Philippe had fought with the armies of the Republic in 1792, most notably at the battles of Valmy and Jemappes, where revolutionary France won its first victories against the invading European Allies. These battles gained symbolic currency as early as the July Days, when Orleanists promoted his candidacy for the throne by proclaiming him "a prince devoted to the cause of the revolution," who had "carried the tricolor flag under fire."[16] Valmy and Jemappes subsequently became one of the July Monarchy's founding myths, celebrated in royal speeches, festivals, and art (including a Gallery of 1792 at Versailles) as evidence of the new king's solidarity with the French people and his devotion to the cause of liberty. The revolutionary origins of Louis-Philippe's throne were also cast in militaristic terms by frequent references to his affiliation with the National Guard, the bourgeois militia that was instrumental in the overthrow of Charles X. Guardsmen featured prominently in public festivals following the July Revolution, and Louis-Philippe's first official portraits depicted him in his National Guard uniform.[17]

15. On meritocracy and Orleanist representation, see Margadant, "Gender, Vice."
16. Placard posted in Paris, 30 July 1830, in Pinkney, *French Revolution*, 150.
17. Caron, "Louis-Philippe," 607; Rémi Dalisson, *Les trois couleurs, Marianne et l'Empereur: Fêtes libérales et politiques symboliques en France, 1815–1870* (Paris, 2004), 115; Mathilde Larrère, "Ainsi paradait le roi des barricades: Les grandes revues royales de la garde nationale, à Paris, sous la Monarchie de Juillet," *Mouvement Social* 179 (1997): 13; Thomas Gaehtgens, *Versailles, de la résidence royale au Musée Historique* (Paris, 1984), 278; Marrinan, *Painting Politics*, 3–19, 77–78, 114, 255–56 n. 233; Philip Mansel, "Monarchy, Uniform and the Rise of the Frac, 1760–1830," *Past and Present* 96 (August 1982): 121–24.

Louis-Philippe's biographical claims to power were bolstered and given a sharper martial edge by an ambitious program of monument building, which sought to appeal to widespread affection for the memory of Napoleon Bonaparte. The new king replaced the statue of Napoleon at the top of the Colonne de Vendôme, completed the Emperor's unfinished Arc de Triomphe, and repatriated Napoleon's ashes from Saint Helena to Paris, where they were installed with great pomp in a splendid tomb at the Hôtel des Invalides. When the Musée historique de Versailles was established, its very first gallery was dedicated to Napoleon's iconic victories. These projects were intended, as Prime Minister Casimir Périer explained in 1831, to show the new king's respect for the popular cult of Napoleon that had been repressed by the Bourbons: "By honoring a great reputation, by reerecting the monument which hallows a memory from which France derives great glory, the King forges . . . one more link between the country and the throne."[18]

The militaristic tenor of Orleanist symbolism stood in stark contrast with Louis-Philippe's deep attachment to peace as a matter of policy. In this regard, the new king shared the views of many postrevolutionary liberals, who identified war with the political extremes of the revolutionary and Napoleonic eras, and considered violence incompatible with a modern civilization defined by the spread of reason, trade, and the rule of law.[19] Louis-Philippe himself considered the "pacific work" of preventing future European conflicts to be "the glory of my reign,"[20] and he adopted a foreign policy of "peace at all costs" based on an alliance with Great Britain and nonintervention in the affairs of other European states. The post-Napoleonic Concert of Europe restrained continental rivalries, and France refused to intervene in revolutionary uprisings in Poland, Italy, and Spain in the early 1830s. Egyptian viceroy Muhammad 'Ali's struggle for independence from the Ottoman Empire nearly broke the Franco-British alliance in 1840, but Louis-Philippe backed down from open confrontation and the war scare passed peacefully.[21]

---

18. Quoted in Marrinan, *Painting Politics*, 159. On the July Monarchy's monument building, see Maurice Agulhon, *Marianne au combat: L'imagerie et la symbolique républicaines de 1789 à 1880* (Paris, 1979), 59–67; Isabelle Rouge-Ducos, *L'Arc de triomphe de l'Étoile, panthéon de la France guerrière: Art et histoire* (Dijon, 2008); Jean Tulard, "Le Retour des cendres," in *Les lieux de mémoire*, ed. Pierre Nora, bk. 2, *La Nation*, vol. 3 (Paris, 1986), 81–110; Michael Paul Driskel, *As Befits a Legend: Building a Tomb for Napoleon, 1840–1861* (Kent, Ohio, 1993).
19. See esp. Benjamin Constant, *De l'esprit de la conquête et de l'usurpation* (1814; repr., Geneva, 1980); Lucien Febvre, "Civilisation: Évolution d'un mot et d'un groupe d'idées," in *Civilisation, le mot et l'idée* (1930; repr., Quebec City, n.d.), http://dx.doi.org/doi:10.1522/cla.fel.civ; Alice Conklin, *A Mission to Civilize: The Republican Idea of Empire in France and West Africa, 1895–1930* (Stanford, 1997), chap. 1.
20. Letter to Metternich (1834), quoted in Collingham, *July Monarchy*, 197.
21. On Louis-Philippe's foreign policy, see Collingham, *July Monarchy*, chaps. 15, 17, and 23.

The king, already fifty-seven years old in 1830, was especially concerned that this pacifist policy should survive him, and he worried that his heir, the duc d'Orléans, was overly enamored of "the bellomania of Louis XIV [and] Napoleon." "In our Century, War and revolutionary Upheaval are inseparable and ignominious," he cautioned the young crown prince: Privileging "the glory of arms and the dangerous *éclat* of victories" over "the pacific needs" of commerce would aid the regime's enemies.[22] Yet Louis-Philippe had himself inculcated in his sons a strong sense of obligation to prove themselves in accordance with the meritocratic spirit of their age and the belief that a career in the French armies was the best means to do so.[23] Instructions drawn up for the education of his eldest son specified that he be taught that his birth and privileged status were the result of pure accident and "that He alone by his actions can prove that he is worthy of them." "Because he must govern one day," Louis-Philippe wrote, the boy must cultivate compassion for "human misfortunes and miseries," as well as physical strength, patriotism, and a courage "founded on reason, duty, and honor."[24] These teachings were reinforced by daily life in the Orléans household during the Restoration, when Bonapartist intellectuals and former Imperial officers frequented the future king's salon and enthralled the young princes with tales of their campaigns under the Republic and the Empire.[25]

On reaching adolescence, each of Louis-Philippe's five sons received a commission in the French armed forces: the two eldest, the duc d'Orléans and the duc de Nemours, and the two youngest, the duc d'Aumale and the duc de Montpensier, in the army; the third, the prince de Joinville, in the navy. Military service had long been the professional vocation of royal men,[26] but with Louis-Philippe's accession to the throne, this tradition gained new political urgency. The new king could say that he had been called to the throne on the basis of his past services to the nation, but his sons held their status purely by birth. As a result, they were subjected to what Jo Burr Margadant describes as a "never-ending need to prove their claim to represent the nation, not as men with royal blood but rather as outstanding men of honor, exemplars of their sex both as family men and in service to the public." Military service was the essential, if not only means by which they could answer this demand. As Margadant observes, "to distinguish

---

22. AN 300 AP III 172, Louis-Philippe to duc d'Orléans, 31 August 1837.
23. Martin-Fugier, *La vie quotidienne*, 193–95, 227–35; Arnaud Teyssier, *Les enfants de Louis-Philippe et la France* (Paris, 2006), 52–62.
24. AN 300 AP III 51, Louis-Philippe, "Instruction pour l'éducation de mon fils François, prince de Joinville," [October 1825]. The contents of this document suggest that the added title is incorrect and that it was written for the duc d'Orléans around 1817.
25. *Vieux souvenirs de Mgr. le Prince de Joinville 1818–1848*, ed. Daniel Meyer (Paris, 1986), 34.
26. Margadant, "Gender, Vice," 1484; Margin-Fugier, *La vie quotidienne*, 228.

their privileged titles in a meritocratic age, honor required a distinguished military record, one recognized as such by other officers, their own troops, and the general public."[27]

In the context of their father's conservative foreign policy, the insistence on military service as a prerequisite for legitimacy posed a nearly insurmountable problem for the princes. They were fully cognizant of this fact, especially the duc d'Orléans, who was agonizingly aware of the need to cultivate a public image that would legitimize his eventual assumption of the throne. "In time of peace, we have so few means of making ourselves known without appearing to throw ourselves at people's heads," he lamented to his brother Nemours; "we must not neglect one, however small it might appear."[28] This awkward position was exacerbated by the regime's use of the army to quell domestic political unrest. Orléans's regiment was sent to restore order after a revolt of radical Lyonnais silk workers in December 1831, and both Orléans and Nemours joined the National Guard in the brutal repression of a major republican uprising in Paris in 1834.[29]

The contradictions between Louis-Philippe's militaristic rhetoric and his pacifist policy provided the regime's many opponents with one of their most powerful weapons. The leftist *parti de mouvement*, in particular, adopted a strident, patriotic militarism as a mark of its oppositional stance and seized every chance to attack the king's "cowardice."[30] But legitimists also drew damning comparisons between the new king's diplomatic caution and the past triumphs of the Bourbon monarchs. The intimate relationship between war and masculinity gave a distinctly gendered cast to such attacks, the most trenchant of which came from caricaturists, whose ceaseless hostility was seen by both contemporary observers and the government as the greatest danger facing the July Monarchy.[31] The words of Bonapartist lithographer Nicolas Charlet exemplify the ways that political satirists sexualized their disgust with Louis-Philippe's conciliatory stance: "My heart

27. Margadant, "Gender, Vice," 1467, 1484.
28. AN 300 AP III 102, Orléans to Nemours, 9 July 1834.
29. The princes did not take part in the "Massacre of the rue Transnonain" that became a potent symbol of state violence, but 1834 still turned many on the left against them. On the use of the army in keeping domestic order, see Jean Delmas, "Armée, Garde nationale et maintien de l'ordre," in *Histoire militaire de la France*, vol. 2, *De 1715 à 1871*, ed. Jean Delmas (Paris, 1992), 538–43.
30. Philippe Darriulat, *Les patriotes: La gauche républicaine et la nation, 1830–1870* (Paris, 2001), esp. pt. 2, chap. 1.
31. See, among others, James Cuno, "Charles Philipon and La Maison Aubert: The Business, Politics, and Public of Caricature in Paris, 1820–1840" (Ph.D. diss., Harvard University, 1985); essays in Raimbond Rütten, Ruth Jung, and Gerhard Schneider, eds., *La caricature entre République et censure. L'imagerie satirique en France de 1830 à 1880: Un discours de résistance?* (Lyon, 1996); Robert Goldstein, *Censorship of Political Caricature in Nineteenth-Century France* (Kent, Ohio, 1989).

is crushed by our foreign policy. Our cockerel plays the hen and does not defend its cock. It has no balls (*sexe*) anymore: it is a herd of vile speculators . . . a people of unscrupulous stockbrokers."[32] *La Caricature* gave harsh visual expression to this sentiment in an 1832 lithograph depicting Louis-Philippe as a naïve farmer "plucking his cock[erel]" to plume the hat of an Englishman ensconced at his hearth, while a Russian, an Austrian, and a Prussian "take liberties with his wife, *France*oise" behind his back (fig. 13). As the journal's editor explained, this domestic melodrama was an allegory for Orléans rule. Despite the bust of Napoleon on his mantle, the farmer-king ignores the foreigners' insults to his wife, France, and the map hanging beside the Napoleonic icon shows the nation reduced to its smallest possible dimensions under the peasant-monarch. The objects scattered about the cottage belie his ostensible devotion to domestic liberty, including scissors used to cut the people down to size, a canner for clamping down on civil servants' autonomy, a salt cellar to hold the taxes imposed on the poor, and a clothesline on which to hang censored newspapers alongside the royal socks.[33]

The impotence of Louis-Philippe's bellicose rhetoric became a favorite subject of opposition satirists. His frequent allusions to his time in uniform, for example, became a leitmotif in anti-Orléans caricature, most pointedly in a highly successful 1831 image of the king as a parrot mindlessly repeating "Valmy! Jemappes!" in answer to all questions (fig. 14). Critics also took note of the pressure that the combination of militaristic language and diplomatic caution placed on his sons. The princes did take part in the few French campaigns of the early 1830s, such as limited interventions in Belgium in 1831 and 1832, and their activities were exhaustively reported in the official and Orleanist press. One contemporary recalled that "the feats of arms of Louis-Philippe's five sons replaced the society column in the papers, and even those hostile to the [government] followed their expeditions with interest."[34] These were minor operations, however, and easily dismissed by critics as "military promenades," which added little to the princes' military prestige. An 1834 print by the republican Honoré Daumier reflects the clarity with which the monarchy's opponents grasped the princes' predicament (fig. 15). Daumier shows the duc d'Orléans standing before a pair of paintings of the battles of Valmy and Jemappes, commissioned by his father from Horace Vernet during the Restoration and well known to French viewers after being displayed

32. Quoted in Gérard de Puymège, *Chauvin, le soldat-laboureur: Contribution à l'étude des nationalismes* (Paris, 1993), 60.

33. *La Caricature*, 4 October 1832.

34. Marie Le Harivel de Gonneville, comtesse de Mirabeau, preface to *Le Prince de Talleyrand et la maison d'Orléans. Lettres du Roi Louis-Philippe, de Madame Adélaïde et du Prince de Talleyrand*, ed. comtesse de Mirabeau (Paris, 1890), 24.

FIGURE 13. After J.-J. Grandville, "While he plucks his cock[erel], the Russian, the Austrian, and the Prussian take liberties with his wife, *France*oise," in *La Caricature*, 4 October 1832. Bibliothèque nationale de France, Département des Estampes et de la photographie.

at the Palais Royal in the 1820s and at the first Salon of the July Monarchy in 1831.[35] The caption conveys the crown prince's frustration as he contemplates these iconic images of his father's military career: "Philippe, my father, will leave me no more glory to acquire!"

Opponents of the monarchy seized on the princes' military pretensions with gusto. Republican and legitimist newspapers questioned their commands and suggested that they were given rank undue such young, inexperienced men. Satirists portrayed the expeditions of the early 1830s in infantilizing or feminizing terms as a gift from doting parents to spoiled children or as the fashionable accessory of ineffectual society dandies. As early as 1831, one the most influential publications of the early July Monarchy, Charles Philipon's satirical illustrated weekly *La Caricature*, suggested that the French had supported the Belgian revolt against the Netherlands solely to give the crown prince a "little Jemappes" of his own.[36] An

35. The Gallery of 1792 at Versailles contains copies by Vernet. The originals are now in the National Gallery, London.
36. Derville, "Commentaires de César-Poulot, surnommé le vainqueur des Gaules; ou relation véritable et non contrefaite des exploits remarquables qui viennent de placer Poulot à la tête des premiers capitaines du siècle," *La Caricature*, 1 September 1831.

FIGURE 14. "Have you lunched, Jacot?—*Valmy!* Have you lunched?—*Jemmapes!*—You always say the same thing—*Valmy! Jemmapes! Valmy! Jemmapes!*" In *La Caricature*, 25 August 1831. Bibliothèque nationale de France, Département des Estampes et de la photographie.

unsigned print from the following year's siege of Antwerp, which the Dutch had refused to turn over to the now-independent Belgians, incorporated many of the motifs common to satirical attacks on the duc d'Orléans's military career (fig. 16). The duke stands in full uniform, including a cartridge pouch adorned with a pear—Philipon's infamous icon of Louis-Philippe—surrounded by the instruments of war, transformed by the artist into what the caption describes as "little toy-toys" given by "his little Papa and little Mama" to their "sweetie" and "poulot" (poppet). The mockery is completed by sexualized references to his most important royal attribute, his blood, in the form of a suggestively placed sword and

FIGURE 15. "Philippe, my father, will leave me no more glory to acquire!" In *La Caricature*, 3 April 1834. Bibliothèque nationale de France, Département des Estampes et de la photographie.

a pennant reading "Who wants to marry me? I'm really Sweet!!!" The moniker "Grand Poulot" (Great Poppet) quickly caught on among opposition satirists, who adopted it as a standard nickname for the duc d'Orléans.

Satirists continued in this vein throughout the early 1830s, and eventually the monarchy began to take punitive action to stifle the harsh fun they poked at the expeditions and training camps in which the princes participated. Under draconian press laws instituted in September 1835, state prosecutors targeted not only the publishers of caricatures or newspaper articles criticizing the policy of "peace at all costs," but also those who questioned the courage, rank, or campaign service of the Orléans men.[37] At the same time, the royal family began to modify its rep-

37. Irene Collins, *The Government and the Newspaper Press in France, 1813–1881* (Oxford, 1959), 95–99; Goldstein, *Censorship*, 137–39, 156–57; Charles Ledré, *La presse à l'assaut de la monarchie* (Paris, 1960), 174–76; David Kerr, *Caricature and French Political Culture, 1830–1848: Charles*

FIGURE 16. *He Was Very Good.* "His little Papa and little Maman gave him little toy-toys. He's the Pussycat, the Poppet" [1835]. Bibliothèque nationale de France, Département des Estampes et de la photographie.

resentational strategies in response to critics' jabs. For example, Louis-Philippe reportedly stopped invoking Valmy and Jemappes after *La Caricature*'s 1831 parrot print spawned numerous imitators.[38] Most consequential, however, was their turn to the war in North Africa.

The Orléans family papers are silent about its origins, but the duc d'Orléans's first campaign in Algeria coincided closely with the political crisis of 1835, which saw the peak of violent opposition to the July Monarchy and the moment that the Orleanist compromise between royal and popular sovereignty began to collapse. Major republican uprisings in Lyon and Paris in April 1834, followed by the most serious of the eight attempts on Louis-Philippe's life in July 1835, marked a major turning point in the political culture of the period. They dramatically escalated the monarchy's sense of precariousness, prompting the September Laws' crackdown on the press and undermining the king's ability to represent the regime publicly. The new censorship law was relatively successful in muting visual attacks on the royal family, but as the imperatives of order took precedence over those of liberty, it became increasingly difficult to sustain the image of the meritorious citizen-king. Louis-Philippe's style became increasingly monarchical in the wake of the crisis. He claimed divine sanction for the first time after the Fieschi assassination attempt of 1835, for example, attributing his narrow escape to Providence. The physical accessibility that characterized his early reign came to an end as well, as fears for his safety led the king to withdraw from direct contact with his subjects. Official portraits and public festivals began to follow more traditionally royal models.[39]

It was in this context that Louis-Philippe's sons took to the battlefields of North Africa. Just two months after the passage of the September Laws, the *Moniteur universel* announced that the crown prince would join the Armée d'Afrique in its winter campaign against the capital of Algerian resistance leader, emir 'Abd

---

Philipon and the Illustrated Press (Oxford, 2000), 84 n. 44, 85; *Procès et acquittement du National, poursuivi pour avoir défendu l'égalité, les droits de l'armée, la loi contre le privilège et le régime des ordonnances...* (Paris, 1838).

38. Ledré, *La presse*, 142, 158; *La Caricature*, 18 April 1833 and 10 April 1834.

39. On the crisis of 1835 and the monarchy's response, see Robert Bezucha, *The Lyons Uprising of 1834: Social and Political Conflict in the Early July Monarchy* (Cambridge, Mass., 1974); Collingham, *July Monarchy*, chap. 13; Jill Harsin, *Barricades: The War of the Streets in Revolutionary Paris, 1830–1848* (New York and Basingstoke, 2002), chaps. 5 and 8; Corbin, "L'impossible présence du roi," 104–5, 109–16; Martin-Fugier, *La vie quotidienne*, 56–62; Marrinan, *Painting Politics*, 14–19. The September Laws instituted prior censorship for printed imagery, increased punishments for press offenses, and authorized prosecution of the publishers of hostile works. They particularly targeted caricaturists, who were held "morally" responsible for attempts on the king's life. Publisher Charles Philipon was charged with "moral complicity" in the Fieschi assassination attempt, and the public display of his prints was banned. Goldstein, *Censorship*, 149–51; Kerr, *Caricature*, 115–16.

al-Qadir, at Mascara.[40] The news was celebrated by administrators, soldiers, and settlers in Algeria as a sign of the government's commitment to the new colony. In France, it marked the advent of a new strategy for representing meritocratic monarchy that anchored the regime's symbolic foundations in a conquest seen by many as a political and economic burden.

Royal Citizen-Soldiers: The Orléans Princes in Algeria

The conquest of Algeria was the great exception to Louis-Philippe's pacifist foreign policy. Throughout the 1830s and 1840s, the French army fought to extend its hold, at least nominally, to most of Ottoman Algiers (map 1). Sustained resistance against the invaders drew an ever greater number of French troops into the "pacification" of the territory known first as the "former Regency," then as the "French Possessions in North Africa," and finally, from 1839, as "Algeria." The Armée d'Afrique swelled from thirty thousand to over one hundred thousand men (table 1), as the French sought to impose their authority and to end the armed resistance led by Ahmad, bey of the eastern province of Constantine; 'Abd al-Qadir, who built a powerful proto-state in western Algeria; and the Sufi *marabout* (holy man) Muhammad ben Abdallah, known as Bu Maza, who sparked a series of Mahdist uprisings in the Dahra mountains in 1845. After a failed siege in 1836, Constantine fell to the French in 1837, and a much-weakened Ahmad Bey fled into southern Algeria, whence he launched periodic raids on French forces until he surrendered in 1848. But 'Abd al-Qadir and Bu Maza led a guerilla-style struggle that lasted for years. Bu Maza eluded French forces until April 1847, and 'Abd al-Qadir, whose ability to evade capture made the "hunt for Abd-el-Kader" something of a parlor joke in France, did not yield until the end of that year. As the occupation grew, liberal lawmakers objected to its financial costs, while parliamentarians, journalists, and citizens of varied political stripes questioned the extreme violence that characterized antiguerilla warfare in North Africa.[41]

Louis-Philippe was deeply and personally invested in Algerian affairs. He insisted that his war ministers and Algerian governors general keep him abreast

---

40. *Moniteur universel*, 16 November 1835. I retain the French transliteration, "Abd-el-Kader," in translating French sources.

41. Julien, *La conquête* remains the authoritative account. Also useful, if uncritical of the colonial enterprise, is Paul Azan's *L'armée d'Afrique de 1830 à 1852* (Paris, 1936). More recently, see Antony Thrall Sullivan, *Thomas-Robert Bugeaud: France and Algeria, 1784–1849. Politics, Power, and the Good Society* (Hamden, 1983); Jacques Frémeaux, *La France et l'Algérie en guerre, 1830–1870, 1954–1962* (Paris, 2002); Benjamin Brower, *A Desert Named Peace: The Violence of France's Empire in the Algerian Sahara, 1844–1902* (New York, 2009).

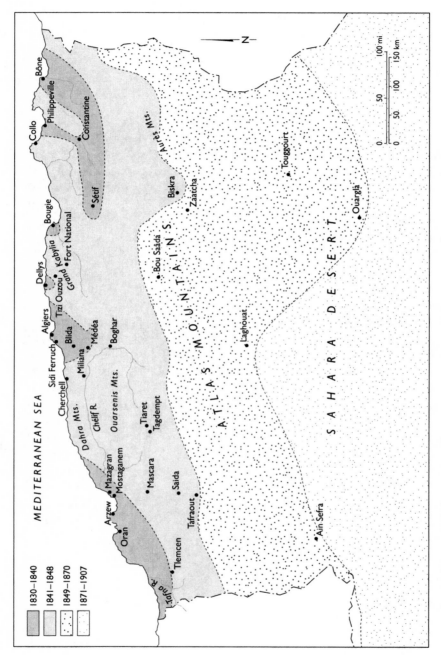

MAP 1. The French conquest of Algeria, 1830–1907. Adapted from John Ruedy, *Modern Algeria: The Origins and Development of a Nation*, 2nd ed. (Bloomington, 2005).

TABLE 1. SIZE OF THE ARMÉE D'AFRIQUE, 1830–51

Year	Troops
1830	37,000
1831	17,190
1832	21,511
1833	26,681
1834	29,858
1835	29,485
1836	29,897
1837	40,147
1838	48,167
1839	50,367
1840	61,263
1841	72,000
1842	70,853
1843	75,053
1844	82,037
1845	95,000
1846	99,700
1847	92,413
1848	77,789
1849	70,774
1850	71,496
1851	65,598

Source: Kateb, Européens, 'indigènes' et juifs, 38.
Note: Figures show year-end totals, which were often exceeded during the summer and fall campaign season.

of events in North Africa, and he corresponded extensively with his sons during their campaigns across the Mediterranean. The central preoccupation of his correspondence on Algerian matters, however, was their political utility and, in particular, the potential for his sons to answer the monarchy's critics by demonstrating their merits in battle. Compared to the tidy European confrontations of the early 1830s, the expanding Algerian conquest offered real action against a real enemy and, therefore, a chance for the princes to more convincingly show their mettle. And they could do so without upsetting the balance of power in Europe, despite English hostility to French expansion in the Maghreb. According to an 1841 Orleanist propaganda pamphlet, it was in "this African land that the prince, like the soldier, can prove [his] valor and capacity today without interrupting the European peace."[42]

All five princes campaigned repeatedly with the Armée d'Afrique. Despite concerns about their safety, especially after the duc d'Orléans's death in a carriage accident in 1842, there was only one year between 1835 and 1848 that one or more of Louis-Philippe's sons did not fight in North Africa (table 2). The duc

42. *Le duc d'Aumale et le 17e régiment d'infanterie légère* (Paris, 1841), 5.

TABLE 2. ALGERIAN CAMPAIGNS OF THE ORLÉANS PRINCES, 1835-48

Name	Campaigns
Duc d'Orléans	Capture of Mascara, Nov.–Dec. 1835 Crossing of the *Portes de Fer* (Bibans Pass), Oct.–Nov. 1839 Campaign to Médéah, Milianah, El Affroun, Mouzaïa (division commander), Apr.–Aug. 1840
Duc de Nemours	First Constantine expedition, Oct.–Dec. 1836 Second Constantine expedition, Sept.–Dec. 1837 Médéah and Milianah resupply expeditions, May–June 1841
Prince de Joinville (navy)	Second Constantine expedition (arrived after end of siege), Dec. 1837 Bombardment of Tangiers, landing at Mogador, Aug. 1844

Duc d'Aumale	Campaign to Médéah, Milianah, El Affroun, Mouzaïa
	  (orderly to Orléans), Apr.–Aug. 1840
	Commander, Seventeenth Light Infantry, Feb.–Aug. 1841
	Commander, Médéah subdivision (capture of *smalah*),
	  Oct. 1842–June 1843
	Commander, Constantine province, Nov. 1843–Oct. 1844
	Commander, Tittery province, Mar.–June 1846
	Governor general (submission of 'Abd al-Qadir),
	  Sept. 1847–Mar. 1848

Duc de Montpensier	Mchounech expedition (with duc d'Aumale), Mar. 1843 Pacification of Constantine province (with duc d'Aumale), Feb.–Mar. 1844 Pacification of Ouarensenis (with Bugeaud), May–June 1845

Sources: *Moniteur universel*; Martin-Fugier, *La vie quotidienne*, 228–33; *Galerie historique de l'Algérie*, vol. 1, *Les Princes en Afrique* (Paris, 1845).

d'Aumale, in particular, spent much of the 1840s in Algeria, where his successes, especially the capture of 'Abd al-Qadir's *smalah* (mobile tent capital) in May 1843, and his identification with the Armée d'Afrique earned him the nickname "Aumale l'Algérien." He was promoted from field commander to provincial commander in 1843, and then, after much discussion, named governor general in 1847, at age twenty-five.[43]

As the symbolic scaffolding that supported the image of the citizen-king began to collapse, Algeria moved to center stage in Orleanist representation. While the king distanced himself from the symbols of popular sovereignty, appearing less frequently in public and abandoning his association with the National Guard, the princes gained prominence as the public face of the regime. They began to travel more extensively in the provinces, and their affiliation with the Armée d'Afrique replaced Louis-Philippe's affiliation with the National Guard in royal

43. On Aumale's career, see Roger Huetz de Lemps, *Aumale l'Algérien, 1822–1870* (Paris, 1961); Raymond Cazelles, *Le duc d'Aumale* (Paris, 1984).

speeches, festivals, and iconography. Algerian battles took the place of Valmy and Jemappes in Orleanists' legitimating discourse, and the princes' "noble conduct" on North African battlefields supplanted their father's campaigns as the symbolic "seal [on] the pact of alliance . . . between the nation and the family of kings [that the nation] chose for herself" in 1830.[44] By 1841, the princes' role in the conquest of Algeria had become the central pillar of the Orleanist monarchy's meritocratic ideology and a new model of the royal citizen-soldier had emerged to bolster that of the citizen-king.

The Algerian turn in Orleanist representation was deliberate and carried out with remarkable self-consciousness by the members of the royal family. The crown prince, for example, wrote frequently of the Algerian war as an opportunity to prove his worth to his future subjects. In pursuing Algerian commands, he wrote to a friend, "My ambition is to claim my privilege as first French citizen only where there is physical or moral danger, . . . to obtain my political rank as a *premium laboris*, and to give my country and the cause I serve much more in devotion and services than I receive in honors and dignities."[45] When the king and the Council of Ministers refused in 1837 to grant him command of the second Constantine expedition out of fear for his safety, Orléans responded by reminding his father of "the importance of having the heir to the throne exercise a high command and a wartime command." His argument is worth citing at length, because it clearly articulates why the Algerian conquest became so important to the Orléans princes:

> I explained . . . my position, my obligation, in an era when labor is the common law, to make my career by the sweat of my brow, having neither the tribune, nor the press, nor any other occasion except my military duties to make myself known to France. I represented to him that I had to seize by the hair every occasion . . . to prove myself and to offer guarantees of not only bravery, but also capacity. . . . I explained to the King that he had remade the profession (*état*) of king over the last seven years; that I had to remake the status of prince for myself and my brothers; that today there is only one way of being forgiven for being a prince, which is to do more than others in all things.[46]

44. *Le duc d'Aumale et le 17e*, 6–7.
45. Orléans to Chabaud-Latour, 31 July 1837, in Ferdinand-Philippe, duc d'Orléans, *Lettres, 1825–1847*, ed. Philippe d'Orléans, comte de Paris, and Robert d'Orléans, duc de Chartres (Paris, 1889), 186–87.
46. AN 300 AP III 168, Orléans to général Damrémont, 31 August 1837. Also in Orléans, *Lettres*, 196–206, and Camille Rousset, *L'Algérie de 1830 à 1840: Les commencements d'une conquête*, vol. 2 (Paris, 1887), 230–41.

The need to earn their privileged status "by the sweat of their brows" was felt by all of Louis-Philippe's sons, whose letters to family and friends echo Orléans's belief that "it is only by the position that we must endeavor to make for ourselves in the army and by the support that we must strive to earn there that we can respond to the attacks that our enemies will make against us."[47] Especially after February 1840, when the Chamber rejected a law according the duc de Nemours a large annual endowment, the princes felt that the *point d'honneur* required their presence in Algeria, in order to "reconquer the terrain lost" to critics' accusations of their greedy self-interest.[48] They were similarly anxious to achieve military distinction without appearing to violate the meritocratic principles that governed advancement in the post-Napoleonic French army. Both Nemours and Aumale, for instance, resisted special promotions after notable North African battles out of concern that their advancement would be perceived as unwarranted. While acknowledging that the promotion of a prince was a special case, Nemours argued that it would be shameful to be given rank ahead of a more deserving comrade and that he should be judged "like a common martyr" on the basis of his battlefield contributions.[49]

Louis-Philippe was equally aware of the political significance of his sons' Algerian campaigns and sought to mobilize their exploits for public consumption. The king's personal correspondence testifies to his own desire to maximize the political potential of his sons' triumphs, while state officials carefully monitored the public response.[50] Engagements in which one of the princes distinguished himself prompted a flurry of letters in which the king and his political allies expressed their mutual pleasure at the impact on public opinion and, often, organized the publication of battlefield dispatches and reports. Louis-Philippe invariably wrote his son a letter of warm congratulations that noted the popular reaction to his conduct and, often, requested additional information for further publicity. Louis-Philippe's missive to the duc d'Aumale following the capture of 'Abd al-Qadir's *smalah* in May 1843 was typical: "My dear and beloved Son, the effect of your action is immense. The simplicity, so appropriate and honorable, of your Report, the narrative, so noble, so touching, so lucid on all the circum-

---

47. AN 300 AP III 102, Orléans to Nemours, 9 July 1834.
48. Duc de Decazes to baron de Barante, 22 March 1840, in *Souvenirs du baron de Barante de l'Académie française, 1762–1866*, ed. Claude de Barante, vol. 6 (Paris, 1897), 432.
49. AN 300 AP III 48, letter to [Orléans], 4 November 1837. Also Aumale to Soult, 25 September 1842, in Nicolas Jean de Dieu Soult, *Correspondance politique et familière avec Louis-Philippe et la famille royale*, ed. Louis and Antoinette de Saint-Pierre (Paris, 1959), 200.
50. See especially Louis-Philippe's correspondence with Soult in AN 300 AP III 41; AD Rhône 1M 164, préfet du Rhône to ministre de l'Intérieur, 19 December 1837; AD Côte-d'Or 1M 500, ministre de l'Intérieur to préfet de la Côte-d'Or, 19 August 1843.

stances, made a general impression on the Chambers and on the public. In truth, I can tell you that the Nation and the army are electrified by it."[51] The king then asked Aumale to have sketches made of the site, the troop movements, and the key episodes of the fighting for "a grand battle painting," which would become the focus of Horace Vernet's second African gallery at the Musée historique de Versailles.

The coordinated publicity surrounding the capture of the *smalah* is indicative of the comprehensive system developed to represent the princes' Algerian campaigns to French audiences as evidence of the Orléans family's fitness to rule. This system included not only the official government organ, *Le Moniteur universel,* and the highly politicized (and venal) private press, but also public speeches by members of the royal family, ceremonies honoring the princes during provincial voyages, public reviews, parades, and other displays of units from the Armée d'Afrique, as well as the galleries devoted to the conquest at Versailles.

Events involving the royal family were not the only ones in which the Algerian war appeared in the festive and ceremonial life of the July Monarchy, of course. From the early 1830s, the conquest was integrated into the three-day national holiday held on the anniversary of the July Days. The first day of the Fête de Juillet was devoted to a funeral ceremony commemorating those killed in 1830, but more joyous patriotic celebrations on 28 and 29 July often incorporated references to the Armée d'Afrique and the ongoing war in Algeria. Military parades held on the twenty-eighth frequently included famous African units, while scenes from the Algerian war were incorporated into the popular diversions offered on the twenty-eighth and twenty-ninth. Costumed "Bedouins" performed for Parisian festival-goers as early as 1831,[52] and in the 1840s scenes set in Algeria were featured among the military pantomimes presented on temporary stages erected around the city to entertain the populace (fig. 17). The conquest became a theme for the capital's elaborate pyrotechnic displays, as well. In 1836, the grand finale of the fireworks capping the three-day holiday simulated the siege of a "Moorish" fort designed to remind viewers of the capture of Mascara a few months earlier.[53] In the 1840s, public buildings were illuminated with "Oriental" or "Moorish" arches and even, in 1845, emblazoned with colored lights spelling out "Afrique française" (fig. 18). Although the exoticism of the war's setting explains much of its entertainment value, the July holiday also celebrated the Algerian conquest more seriously as one of the July Monarchy's great national achievements. As a

51. AN 300 AP III 48, Louis-Philippe to Aumale, 2 June 1843.
52. AN F7 3885, Bulletin de Paris, 28 July 1831.
53. AN F13 1022, A. Boulet, "Devis des fournitures des pièces d'artifices pour le feu qui sera tiré sur le Pont de la Concorde, le 29 juillet 1836 . . . ," 30 June 1836.

16ᵐᵉ ANNIVERSAIRE DES JOURNÉES DE JUILLET.

Dispositions générales.

Durant les Journées des 27, 28 et 29 Juillet, trois grands Mâts portant des bannières aux couleurs nationales, seront dressés sur le terre-plein du Pont-Neuf

LE LUNDI 27. --- Des distributions de secours seront faites à domicile dans les 12 arrondissemens de Paris.

LE MARDI 28. --- Des salves d'artillerie seront tirées à l'Hôtel des Invalides, à six heures du matin et à six heures du soir. -- Des Services funèbres, en mémoire des Citoyens morts en Juillet 1830, pour la défense des Lois et de la Liberté, seront célébrés dans les Édifices consacrés aux différens cultes. --- Un Service spécial aura lieu, à dix heures du matin, dans l'Église de la Paroisse Saint-Paul. Durant ce Service, les bannières du Pont-Neuf seront voilées de crêpe.

LE MERCREDI 29. --- Des Salves d'artillerie seront tirées à l'Hôtel des Invalides à six heures du matin et à six heures du soir.

DIVERTISSEMENTS.

Champs-Élysées.

Dans le grand carré des Champs-Élysées, deux grands Théâtres sur lesquels seront représentées des Pantomimes militaires à grand spectacle.

Quatre Orchestres de danse.

Un grand Mât de cocagne, garni de cinq prix.

Barrière du Trône.

A la barrière du Trône, il y aura un Théâtre de Pantomimes, deux Orchestres de danse et un grand Mât de cocagne garni de cinq prix.

Feu d'artifice.

Vers huit heures et demie, il sera tiré un Feu d'artifice à la barrière du Trône.

Fête sur le Bassin de la Seine.

A trois heures, Joûte sur l'eau dans le bassin de la Seine, entre le pont Royal et le pont de la Concorde.

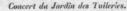

Concert du Jardin des Tuileries.

Un grand Concert d'harmonie sera exécuté dans le Jardin des Tuileries, à sept heures du soir.

Feu d'Artifice.

A neuf heures du soir, il sera tiré un grand Feu d'artifice sur le quai d'Orsay et le pont de la Concorde.

Illuminations.

Le grand carré, la grande avenue des Champs-Élysées, l'avenue d'Antin et le Cours - la - Reine, les berges de la Seine, l'arc de triomphe de l'Étoile, la colonne de Juillet, la place et la barrière du Trône, et tous les édifices publics et communaux seront illuminés.

Le Ministre de l'Intérieur arrête le Programme ci-dessus, qui sera publié et affiché à Paris et dans la banlieue, par les soins de M. le Préfet de la Seine.

Paris, le 16 Juillet 1846.   Signé DUCHATEL.

Gravure autorisée, le Dépôt ayant été fait à la Direction de la Librairie.

PARIS. — Imprimerie de CRAPELET, rue de Vaugirard, 9

FIGURE 17. Ministry of the Interior and Prefecture of the Seine, Program for the 16th Anniversary of the July Days, 1846. Bibliothèque nationale de France, Département des Estampes et de la photographie.

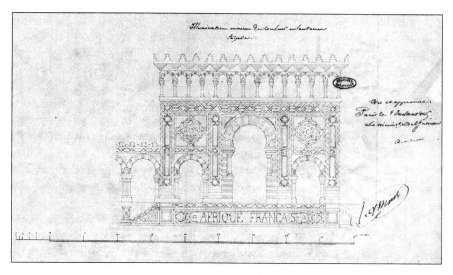

FIGURE 18. Louis Visconti, illuminations for the Quai d'Orsay, July 1845. Archives nationales, Paris, F21 719. Photo: Atelier photographique des Archives nationales.

public staging of the regime's legitimizing principles, the holiday set the conquest alongside the victims of the struggle against Bourbon despotism, the triumph of the Charter, and the restoration of the tricolor flag in the symbolic pantheon of Orleanism.

While the July Days holiday sought to glorify the regime by association with the Algerian war, Louis-Philippe was most invested in linking his own family to the Armée d'Afrique. The king himself took the lead in publicizing his sons' role in Algeria and set the tone for other Orleanist celebrations. He and his ministers encouraged press coverage of the princes' Algerian campaigns and provided the newspapers with copies of dispatches and reports detailing their exploits. Louis-Philippe was also the driving force behind his sons' provincial voyages, which served simultaneously to inform him about the situation in the kingdom, to demonstrate his concern for his subjects, and to familiarize the population with the new dynasty, "tighten[ing] the bonds of affection and gratitude" between the royal family and the people.[54] The emphasis placed on the Algerian war in these varied contexts reflects its central position in the royal family's legitimizing strategies of self-representation.

54. Proclamation of maire de Marseille, 10 November 1839, in *Procès-verbal de l'arrivée et du séjour à Marseille de S.A.R. Mgr le Duc d'Orléans* (Marseille, 1839), 8. On Louis-Philippe's provincial travels, see Alain Corbin and Nathalie Veiga, "Le monarque sous la pluie: Les voyages de Louis-Philippe Ier en province (1831–1833)," in *La terre et la cité: Mélanges offerts à Philippe Vigier*, ed. Alain Faure, Alain Plessis, and Jean-Claude Farcy (Paris, 1994), 217–30.

Although they often resented and occasionally dodged the receptions, speeches, banquets, balls, and military reviews that made up what they privately referred to as "la fonction"—"You can't imagine anything so boring," the duc d'Aumale wrote to a friend—the princes nonetheless, as the Orleanist historian and politician François Guizot noted, understood their duties as "servants of the country, . . . obliged to cultivate its interests and its grandeur."[55] Their military careers provided the primary means for them to do so, and public appearances were necessary to impress these services upon their future subjects. As the princes traveled around France, therefore, they listened and responded politely to flattering addresses from local authorities, reviewed and applauded garrison troops and National Guardsmen, and led parades of army units returning from North Africa.

Among the most notable of such events was the duc d'Aumale's triumphant return from Africa with the Seventeenth Light Infantry regiment in August of 1841, which combined the features of both the provincial tour and the Algerian military parade. Aumale had been promoted to lieutenant colonel and given command of the Seventeenth Light after his first Algerian campaign the previous year. The regiment was then one of the longest-serving units of the Armée d'Afrique, with six years of combat and over two thousand men lost in Algeria. Following a brutal expedition against 'Abd al-Qadir's stronghold in western Algiers province in the spring of 1841, the Seventeenth Light was finally ordered to return to France. At the end of July, Aumale and his men landed in Marseille, where they were met by cheering crowds and a week of festivities. The reception, Aumale reported to his father, was "much more brilliant than I could have hoped."[56] Then, on private instructions from the king himself, the regiment traveled slowly to Paris, stopping in a dozen major towns and cities along the circuitous route, and giving Frenchmen maximum opportunity to see the prince leading the tattered flag and battle-scarred faces of the Seventeenth Light's "old Africans" during the month-long march.

This voyage/parade encapsulated the delicate balancing act required by celebrations of the royal citizen-soldier. While the forms of royal ceremonial provided ample means to celebrate the Orléans princes' military accomplishments, overtly propagandistic royal rituals would belie the meritocratic underpinnings of the royal citizen-soldier model. To have the desired political effect, the princes had to play a prominent role and their actions had to be publicized. But obvious self-promotion also threatened to dispel the illusion that their careers were

55. Aumale to Couturié, c. 1841, and Guizot to princesse de Lieven, 18 July 1846, quoted in Martin-Fugier, *La vie quotidienne*, 235, 239.
56. AN 300 AP III 51, Aumale to Louis-Philippe, 30 July 1841.

governed by merit rather than inherited privilege. Aumale himself noted that it would be counterproductive for him to solicit or order ceremonies to mark his passage; even the appearance of attention-seeking might damage his reputation for honest soldiering, and spontaneous public enthusiasm would have greater political effect. He would accept any demonstrations offered but try to behave like a simple colonel, "albeit a colonel from a good house."[57] Throughout the trip, he responded to the effusive speeches of local officials and notables with deliberate modesty, deflecting praise onto his men and accepting compliments in the name of the entire regiment.[58]

This paradoxical logic of modest promotion governed all forms of Orleanist propaganda, which represented the princes simultaneously as exemplars of heroic courage and models of self-abnegating devotion to their comrades. The Orleanist press offers many examples of the way such accounts highlighted both their brilliance in combat and their selfless battlefield conduct, balancing praise for their exceptional heroism with a fiction that they were simple soldiers like any other. In 1840, for instance, the *Journal des débats* and the *Moniteur* printed a letter from an infantry officer describing the capture of the Téniah pass in the Mouzaïa mountains south of Algiers, in which both the duc d'Orléans and the duc d'Aumale had taken part. The letter praised the attack planned and led personally by Orléans, who commanded the expeditionary division, and Aumale's level-headed intrepidity in his first Algerian campaign. The latter showed his loyalty to his brothers-in-arms, the anonymous writer noted, by giving up his horse to a colonel stumbling with fatigue after the two-hour climb up to the pass.[59]

The royal family's public statements also emphasized the princes' identification with ordinary French soldiers, whose patriotic duties and physical hardships they were said to share. In the throne speeches that opened each parliamentary session, for example, Louis-Philippe invariably cited his sons' Algerian campaigns of the preceding year, but always described them as sharing in the sufferings of their comrades. After the duc d'Orléans's first Algerian campaign in December of 1835, for instance, Louis-Philippe proclaimed to the legislators his pride at seeing "the eldest of my line share in the fatigues and dangers of our

---

57. Ibid.
58. See speeches in *Moniteur universel*, 4 August–11 September 1841.
59. Ibid., 26 May 1840; *ordre de l'armée* in Henri Limbourg, *Le duc d'Aumale et sa deuxième campagne d'Afrique (février à septembre 1841)* (Paris, 1915), 1. The story was refuted by Colonel Changarnier, who wrote that it was "a fable from one end to the other." Quoted in Huetz de Lemps, *Aumale*, 39.

brave soldiers."[60] The next year, following the failure of the first Constantine expedition, he deplored the army's losses, while noting that his second son, the duc
de Nemours, had emulated his brother in sharing "the sufferings and dangers
of our brave soldiers."[61] Similar proclamations featured in each annual address
thereafter.

Equally important, Louis-Philippe insisted that his sons' place in the ranks
of the Armée d'Afrique was not accorded them because of their royal blood;
they were simply carrying out the civic duty imposed on all male citizens by
postrevolutionary conscription law.[62] Appealing to this ideal of the conscripted
soldat-citoyen, rather than to the ancient tradition of aristocratic military service,
Louis-Philippe affirmed that the royal family enjoyed no exemption from the so-
called blood tax of conscription. They had the same rights and obligations as all
French fathers and sons and, as he put it in the throne speech following the second siege of Constantine in 1837, "their blood belongs to France like that of all
her children."[63] The duc d'Aumale invoked the same principle in an 1843 speech
to a group of colonists, administrators and military officials in Algiers, claiming
that "the King has sent us, his sons, here to pay our debt to the *patrie* as citizens and soldiers, to show that our princely titles are those of the first servants
of France."[64] This argument was taken up and repeated by Orleanist officials
throughout France. The princes were met with statements like that of the subprefect of Semur (Côte-d'Or), who declared to Aumale as he passed through with the
Seventeenth Light in 1841 that, "you have, Monseigneur, inscribed your name on
the honor roll of the army and paid your primary debt to the *patrie*. This is one
more guarantee given to France by your august family."[65]

Algeria thus became the site on which the royal citizen-soldier was constituted
as the basis for the present and future legitimacy of the Orléans dynasty. As with
Bourbon celebrations of the expedition of 1830, the public response to festive as-
sertions of this legitimizing principle is difficult to determine. Officials tracking
esprit public noted "the keenest and most sincere sympathy," "the keenest interest," and "keen satisfaction" at news of the princes' most significant battles.[66]

---

60. Discours du Roi, 29 December 1835, *PVD* (1836), 1:vi.
61. Discours du Roi, 27 December 1836, *PVD* (1837), 1:v.
62. On the relationship between military service and citizenship, see Annie Crépin, *La conscription en débat, ou le triple apprentissage de la nation, de la citoyenneté, de la république (1798–1889)* (Arras, 1998).
63. Discours du Roi, 18 December 1837, *PVD* (1838), 1:v.
64. Toast at banquet organized by the maire d'Alger, 24 November 1843, in *Moniteur universel*, 5 December 1843.
65. AD Côte-d'Or 1M 500, address by sous-préfet de Semur at Saulieu, 30 August 1841.
66. AD Rhône 1M 164, préfet du Rhône to ministre de l'Intérieur, 19 December 1837; AN F7 3992, Bulletins de Paris, 29 August, 31 August, and 29 September 1844.

Police in the capital, always attentive to the efficacy of Orleanist propaganda, reported that the princes' reputation was "heightened by the modesty of [their] conduct" with the Armée d'Afrique.[67] At the same time, however, public exposure provided opportunities for the monarchy's opponents to express their dissatisfaction with the royal family. During the duc d'Orléans's 1839 visit to Lyon, for instance, the crowds that turned out to see him "manifested no enthusiasm on [his] passage." Municipal officials blamed the hostile local press for this cold welcome, but seditious placards posted in the Croix-Rousse recalled Orléans's role in repressing the *canut* revolt of 1831, suggesting that local memories of his earlier entry into the city, "drums beating, with fuse lit to forge our chains," overshadowed whatever enthusiasm Lyonnais workers may have felt for his subsequent exploits in Algeria.[68] A republican pamphlet circulated in Mâcon at the time of Aumale's stopover with the Seventeenth Light mocked the fuss being made over "the son of a king, colonel at 19 years of age" and the overblown rhetoric offered up for "a beardless young man," whose father wished only to crush the people with taxes, suffocate the press, and reign in unfettered despotism over France.[69]

The greatest threat, however, lay in the princes' physical vulnerability during and after voyages to Algeria. Authorities uncovered multiple plots or rumors of plots to assassinate them in or en route to North Africa,[70] and by the mid-1840s, efforts to forge affectionate bonds with the population by celebrating their Algerian campaigns were being counterbalanced by security measures. Urban police and the gendarmerie were ordered to exercise careful surveillance during princely visits, to prevent "all hostile manifestations," including seditious songs, cries, whistles, and boos, during their public appearances, and to provide armed protection along the routes they traveled.[71]

Aumale's entry into Paris with the Seventeenth Light offers a striking illustration of the mixed public response to the royal men's association with the Armée d'Afrique and the dangers attendant on its public demonstration. The prince and his regiment were met by large, cheering crowds as they entered the capital

67. AN F7 3889, Bulletin de Paris, 26 October 1837. See also F7 3992, Bulletin de Paris, 6 April 1844.
68. AD Rhône 1M 164, police reports from 19–22 November 1839. Quotes from report dated 9 p.m., 19 November 1839, and fragments of placard enclosed in report from the Brigade de la Croix Rousse, 22 November 1839.
69. *Le duc d'Aumale à Mâcon* (Chalon-sur-Saône, 1841), 3–4.
70. On suspected assassination plots, see AD Aude 1MD 410, doss. Fabrezan, "Affaire de prétendues révélations de la femme Poujade épouse Lignères du projet d'assassinat du duc de Nemours lors du siège de Constantine (1837–1841)"; APP Aa 426, sous-doss. "Attentat Quenisset et autres, 13 septembre 1841." There were also several purported conspiracies by soldiers and civilians in Algeria to assassinate the king himself.
71. AM Marseille 11 673, "Service à l'hôtel d'Orient et aux alentours," 21 April 1844.

in September 1841, and Parisians bought up some twenty thousand copies of a propaganda brochure lauding the valor of Aumale and his men. Republicans and "communists," however, staged antigovernment protests in advance of their arrival, raising official fears that radical elements would disrupt the regiment's entry into the city. The worst of these fears was realized when François Quénisset, an unemployed sawyer affiliated with the neo-Babouvist secret society, the Travailleurs Égalitaires, fired on Aumale as he led his troops and two of his brothers through the Faubourg Saint-Antoine. Quénisset's act itself drew contradictory reactions from the capital's residents. On the one hand, outraged spectators seized the would-be assassin, and police were barely able to extract him alive from their hands. Police spies reported outraged indignation among the Parisian working class about the attempt on Aumale's life. On the other hand, the assassination attempt had been an unplanned part of a larger republican conspiracy to break up the parade, and his arrest prompted several days of demonstrations by protesters waving red flags and shouting seditious slogans against the monarchy.[72]

This episode highlights the difficulties of interpreting public responses to the Algerian campaigns of Louis-Philippe's sons. If the planning and rhetoric of celebratory festivities make Orleanists' intentions clear, their efficacy in establishing the princes' personal merits and the legitimacy of the royal citizen-soldier as a model for postrevolutionary kingship is less so. For more explicitly articulated responses to Orleanist propaganda, we can look to the grandest and most enduring of the July Monarchy's celebrations of the princes' Algerian campaigns, the galleries dedicated to them in the Musée historique de Versailles. As the most significant public monument to the Algerian conquest and the primary representation of the Orleanist dynasty in the museum, Versailles' North African galleries are especially valuable for the response they elicited from political and cultural commentators. The dynamic interplay between patron, artist, and critics helps tease out the reception of the royal family's efforts to appropriate the Algerian conquest, revealing in the process Louis-Philippe's reaction to critics' views and the monarchy's limited ability to harness the colonial project to its own ends.

Algeria and the Orléans Princes at the Musée Historique de Versailles

When Louis-Philippe came to power in 1830, the famous château at Versailles stood largely empty. Europe's most spectacular royal residence had narrowly escaped demolition during the Revolution, and renovations begun during the

72. APP Aa 426, note for the procureur du Roi, "Attentat contre M. le duc d'Aumale," 13 September 1841; AN F7 3891, Bulletins de Paris, 8–16 September 1841; Harsin, *Barricades*, 198–207.

Empire and Restoration had been left unfinished. Louis-Philippe began to investigate possible uses for the site almost immediately, and in 1833, he settled on the idea of a pictorial museum of national history dedicated "to all the glories of France." The creation of the Musée historique de Versailles was a deeply personal project for the king, who covered almost all building costs from his Civil List and participated in all aspects of the museum's planning and construction. He made almost four hundred visits to the château between 1833 and 1848 to consult with the royal architect and the director of royal museums on everything from the choice and arrangement of artworks to the color of the paint on the walls. He bought, requisitioned, and commissioned thousands of painted battle scenes, along with sculpted and painted portraits of France's great men to fill the renovated palace, "literally replac[ing] the château's old structure of privilege with a vision of shared national pride."[73]

The Versailles museum was the July Monarchy's largest cultural and propaganda project, as well as one of a host of postrevolutionary historical spectacles that relied on visual means to simultaneously entertain and instruct increasingly democratic audiences about the national past. Like panoramas, phantasmagorias, and illustrated histories and magazines, the Musée historique was founded on the epistemological assumption that images not only made historical knowledge accessible to mass audiences, especially the young, uneducated, and semiliterate, but also spoke to viewers more directly, more truthfully, and more enduringly than words.[74] Visual pedagogy also had an important political function in the postrevolutionary period. By presenting French history in a realistic fashion, historical spectacles "interpolated viewers as part of a nation, helping to draw the boundaries around an emerging collective identity" that healed, or at least papered over, the rifts created by the political upheavals of the preceding decades.[75] This was precisely the goal at the Versailles museum, which was conceived as a kind of life-sized illustrated book to teach visitors about the achievements of earlier generations of Frenchmen and unite them around a glorious vision of their shared past.[76]

73. Michael Marrinan, "Historical Vision and the Writing of History at Louis-Philippe's Versailles," in *The Popularization of Images: Visual Culture under the July Monarchy*, ed. Petra ten-Doesschate Chu and Gabriel Weisberg (Princeton, 1994), 120. On the building of the museum, see Pierre Francastel, *La création du Musée historique de Versailles et la transformation du palais (1832–1848)* (Paris, 1930); Gaehtgens, *Versailles*; and Thomas Gaehtgens, "Le musée historique de Versailles," in Nora, *La Nation*, 3:143–68.
74. Maurice Samuels, *The Spectacular Past: Popular History and the Novel in Nineteenth-Century France* (Ithaca, 2004), 90–96. See also Martin Jay, *Downcast Eyes: The Denigration of Vision in Twentieth-Century French Thought* (Berkeley, 1993), chap. 2.
75. Samuels, *Spectacular Past*, 44.
76. Gaehtgens, *Versailles*, 74; Élisabeth Müller, *Plaisir et savoir: Huit jours au Musée de Versailles, entretiens familiers sur les faits les plus mémorables de l'histoire de France* (Paris, 1846).

When it first opened to the public in 1837, the heart of the museum was the grand Gallery of Battles, running the length of the château's south wing and hung with paintings of the French armies' great victories from the Middle Ages to the Napoleonic Empire. This was flanked by galleries dedicated to the revolutionary campaigns of 1792, the battles of the Empire, and the Revolution of 1830. The enormous battle and history paintings that lined these rooms amounted to a carefully edited, highly militaristic narrative designed to appeal to the martial tastes of popular Bonapartism and to present Louis-Philippe's reign as the ultimate expression of an age-old partnership between monarch and people for the defense and consolidation of the nation. The formula proved tremendously popular, and visitors flocked to the museum, which became a favorite destination for Parisians on a Sunday outing and an obligatory stop for visitors to the capital.[77]

Almost as soon as the original galleries were completed, Louis-Philippe gave orders to extend the museum into the château's north wing. The focus of the new spaces would be the events of his own reign, with a focus on the Algerian conquest. On the ground floor, the Crusades were presented as an historical allegory for the modern invasion.[78] On the second floor, a suite of three rooms constructed in the 1840s was devoted to the ongoing war. Unlike the better-known colonial exhibitions of the Third Republic, the primary purpose of these galleries was neither to put colonized peoples on display nor to valorize the civilizing mission on which France was ostensibly embarked in North Africa.[79] They more closely resembled the paintings of the 1798 Egyptian campaign commissioned by Napoleon, which put the conquerors themselves on display and sought to educate French viewers about the war while celebrating its leaders.[80]

The suite of African galleries positioned the Algerian conquest, and by association the Orléans dynasty, as the culmination of the museum's grand narrative of

---

77. Gaehtgens, *Versailles*, 247–315; Gaehtgens, "Le musée historique," 160–62; Marie-Claude Chaudonneret, *L'état et les artistes de la Restauration à la monarchie de Juillet (1815–1833)* (Paris, 1999), 211–12; AC Ms 1350, no. 103, 11 June 1837; AN F7 3889, Bulletin de Paris, 11 July 1837.

78. Kim Munholland, "Michaud's History of the Crusades and the French Crusade in Algeria under Louis-Philippe," in Chu and Weisberg, *Popularization*, 144–65.

79. There is a vast literature on the ideological workings of colonial exhibitions and museography. For France, see, among others, William Schneider, *An Empire for the Masses: The French Popular Image of Africa, 1870–1900* (Westport, 1982); Sylviane Leprun, *Le théâtre des colonies: Scénographie, acteurs et discours de l'imaginaire dans les expositions, 1855–1937* (Paris, 1986); Patricia Morton, *Hybrid Modernities: Architecture and Representation at the 1931 Colonial Exposition, Paris* (Cambridge, Mass., 2000).

80. On paintings of the Egyptian campaign, see Todd Porterfield, *The Allure of Empire: Art in the Service of French Imperialism, 1798–1836* (Princeton, 1998), 61–79; Darcy Grimaldo Grigsby, "Rumor, Contagion, and Colonization in Gros's *Plague-Stricken at Jaffa* (1804)," *Representations* 51 (1995): 1–46; Darcy Grimaldo Grigsby, *Extremities: Painting Empire in Post-Revolutionary France* (New Haven, 2002), chaps. 2 and 3.

nationalistic military glory. If the rest of the museum laid out the Orleanist vision of the national past, these new additions put Algeria at the center of the French present. As early as 1831, Louis-Philippe had begun buying and commissioning Algerian battle scenes, which were placed in the museum's original galleries as a bridge between the fallen Bourbons and the July Revolution. In the small gallery depicting the events of the Restoration, a series of five images of the bombardment and fall of Algiers hung, alongside several pictures of battles from the Greek War of Independence, between François Gérard's painting of Charles X's coronation and works depicting Louis-Philippe's assumption of power in July 1830.[81] This juxtaposition gave pictorial form to the claim that the Algerian invasion was the only worthwhile legacy of the Bourbons. In both scale and political significance, however, the images of the 1830 expedition paled beside the grand Algerian galleries added to the museum in the 1840s.

Louis-Philippe conceived of the first thematic gallery devoted to the Algerian conquest soon after news of the fall of Constantine reached Paris in October 1837. The city's capture evoked greater public reaction in France than any North African battle since 1830. A burst of prints, pamphlets, and books lamenting the failure of the first Constantine expedition in 1836 was now superseded by an outpouring of dozens of celebratory plays, poems, songs, and engravings, as well as the July Monarchy's first major public ceremonies dedicated to the Algerian war, a *Te Deum* and a state funeral for the expedition's commander, General Damrémont, and the soldiers killed in the siege.[82] The fall of Constantine was also a triumphant moment for the royal family. Louis-Philippe's second son, the duc de Nemours, had taken part in the first, failed expedition, and a year later, he commanded the assault columns that took the city. His role in leading the troops to victory was exhaustively reported in the press and earned him widespread praise.[83]

Louis-Philippe moved quickly to capitalize on the wave of public enthusiasm by commissioning a major painting of the siege from the famous battle painter, Horace Vernet.[84] Within days of the victory announcement, Vernet had left for Algeria to sketch the site and interview participants. On his return to France, Louis-Philippe asked the artist to fill a new gallery at Versailles with pictures commemorating the military highlights of the July Monarchy, of which the siege

---

81. Charles Gavard, *Galeries historiques de Versailles*, vol. 5, *Peinture*, pt. 1, *Tableaux historiques* (Paris, 1840), 165–93.
82. See chapter 3 of this book. The funeral is now best known for the premiere of Hector Berlioz's *Grande messe des morts*.
83. E.g. articles reprinted in *Moniteur universel*, 25–28 October 1837.
84. Louis-Philippe's private papers suggest that Vernet initiated the commission. *Moniteur universel*, 29 October 1837; AN 300 AP II 199, Louis-Philippe to Nemours, 27 October 1837.

of Constantine would be the centerpiece.[85] The commission included several non-Algerian subjects, but when the completed room opened to the public in 1842, its true theme was reflected in its name, the Constantine Gallery. Of the seven enormous battle paintings in the gallery, five were set in Algeria, including the huge central triptych depicting the three stages of the Constantine siege, which measures sixty-nine by sixteen feet.[86] Almost all of the paintings were exhibited at the annual Salons as they were finished and then installed at Versailles when construction of the gallery was complete.

Vernet was a logical choice for this important commission. Although largely ignored by modern-day art historians, he was at the time one of the most beloved living French painters and enjoyed close personal ties to the Orléans family. A prolific artist who made savvy use of new technologies to cultivate commercial and popular success, Vernet was considered by contemporaries to be "the *peintre ordinaire* of the French army." Even his many detractors acknowledged his extraordinary appeal to French viewers, who crowded around his works at the annual Salons and eagerly bought lithographed reproductions of his battle paintings. During the Restoration, he had gained a reputation as a leader of the liberal opposition, and his studio was a central gathering place for men who shared his militaristic tastes and republican-Bonapartist sympathies. As Alexandre Dumas later recalled, "Vernet was more than a celebrated painter: he was a national being responding as an artist to the same need for opposition that was beginning to make the reputation of Béranger and Casimir Delavigne as poets."[87]

The then duc d'Orléans was among those who frequented Vernet's studio during the Restoration, and his early commissions from the painter, including the famous battles of Valmy and Jemappes, were seen as a politicized attack on the king's prerogative as a patron of the arts.[88] When he assumed the throne, the two men had already forged one of the most politically significant

85. AC Ms 1350, no. 124, 1 March 1838.
86. In addition to the seven large battle paintings, the gallery included seven smaller over-door pictures of battles in Belgium and Algeria. For titles, see *Indicateur du palais et du musée de Versailles: Description complète des salles de Constantine, des Croisades, Galeries et Appartements* . . . (Paris, 1845) 3–4.
87. *Éloge de M. Horace Vernet par M. Beulé, secrétaire perpétuel de l'Académie des Beaux-Arts* . . . (Paris, 1863), 23; Dumas, *Mes mémoires*, vol. 9 (Paris, 1863), 22. On Vernet's politics, see Nina Maria Athanassoglou-Kallmyer, "Imago Belli: Horace Vernet's *L'Atelier* as an Image of Radical Miliarism under the Restoration," *Art Bulletin* 68, no. 2 (1986): 268–80; Elizabeth Fraser, *Delacroix, Art and Patrimony in Post-Revolutionary France* (Cambridge, 2004), 89–91.
88. Getty Institute, Los Angeles, Special Collections 850807, folder 1, notes from the duc d'Orléans to Pascalis, 1819–25; Étienne de Jouy and Antoine Jay, *Salon d'Horace Vernet: Analyse historique et pittoresque des quarante-cinq tableaux exposés chez lui en 1822* (Paris, 1822); Fraser, *Delacroix*, 92, 208 n. 43.

patronage relationships in modern French art. This relationship carried over into the July Monarchy, when Vernet received a number of large government commissions in addition to his work for Versailles. The artist had, moreover, firmly established his personal interest in Oriental and Algerian subjects by the time of the fall of Constantine. His well-known early works included *The Massacre of the Mamelukes in the Citadel of Cairo*, shown at the Salon of 1819, and he had traveled to Algeria in 1833 to research a painting of the capture of Bône (today Annaba).[89] The enormous new project at Versailles would draw upon Vernet's political and artistic reputation, and his longstanding relationship with his royal patron.

Iconographically, the completed Constantine Gallery glorified both the French colonial project and the military conquest on which it was predicated. The room's elaborate decorative program gave the room a didactic frame that depicted the French army as a civilizing force. A faux-frieze painted around the ceiling shows the "fruits of colonization": French sergeants drill Algerian troops; engineers construct roads; soldiers cultivate fields; merchandise is transported and exchanged; and French soldiers aid Algerian civilians.[90] The frieze is punctuated by gilded trophies (*trophées*) representing the spoils of war and allegories of the military virtues of Perseverance, Valor, Vigilance, Temperance, Fidelity, and Force (fig. 12).[91] The neoclassical style of these decorative elements invokes the Roman model of colonization that the French famously sought to emulate in Algeria.[92]

The decorative elements are visually overwhelmed, however, by the huge battle paintings that cover the walls. These were, according to one Orleanist art critic "destined to consecrate the memory of the glorious feats of arms of the first ten years of Louis-Philippe's reign . . . in which his sons . . . learned the soldier's trade from our veteran officers of land and sea."[93] The canvases trace the major expeditions in which the princes had taken part in the 1830s: the debut of the

89. On the 1833 trip, see SHD 1H 20, note dated Bône, 16 May 1833; Vernet to général Atthalin, March 1833, in Amédée Durande, *Joseph, Carle et Horace Vernet: Correspondance et biographies* (Paris, 1863), 96–102. *La Prise de Bône (Afrique)* was exhibited at the Salon of 1835 and purchased by the Maison du Roi. *Explication des ouvrages . . . exposés au musée Royal* (1833), no. 2108.

90. L. W[iesener], *Galeries historiques de Versailles: Description de la Salle de Constantine* (Versailles, 1842), 15. There are striking similarities between this frieze and that painted by Vernet's father-in-law, Alexandre-Denis Abel de Pujol, for the Musée d'Égypte installed in the Louvre in 1828 (Porterfield, *Allure*, 109–11).

91. Wiesener, *Galeries*, 15, 18, 23.

92. Patricia Lorcin, "Rome and France in North Africa: Recovering Algeria's Latin Past," *French Historical Studies* 25, no. 2 (2002): 295–329.

93. Étienne Delécluze, "Nouvelle salle du Palais de Versailles, dite de Constantine, décorée de peintures par M. Horace Vernet," *Journal des débats*, 3 April 1842.

FIGURE 19. Louis-François Lejeune, *The Battle of the Pyramids, 21 July 1798*, 1806. Réunion des Musées Nationaux/Art Resource, NY.

two eldest, the duc d'Orléans and the duc de Nemours, at Antwerp in 1832; a skirmish from the duc d'Orléans's first Algerian campaign in 1835; the 1837 siege of Constantine, where the duc de Nemours commanded the assault forces; and the occupation of the Mouzaïa pass, where both Aumale and the crown prince fought in May 1840. One other non-Algerian canvas depicted French naval forces in Mexico under the command of the prince de Joinville in 1838. It was clear to admirers and critics alike that the gallery's "historical unity . . . resides in the military training of the princes."[94]

As contemporaries understood, the Constantine Gallery was meant to bolster efforts to identify the princes with the army, and Horace Vernet faced the challenge of showcasing their valor in a way consistent with the ideals of the royal citizen-soldier. To balance the propagandistic functions of battle painting with the meritocratic ideology so dear to Louis-Philippe and his sons, Vernet modified the conventions of battle painting to simultaneously play up and play down the princes' presence. In traditional battle imagery, the commanding general (usually the king) and his general staff dominate the scene, while the decisive moment of the battle plays out behind them. Vernet abandoned this compositional logic for the "exacting and conscientious" style of *genre historique* and a combination of the "documentary" and "affective" modes developed by revolutionary battle painters confronted with a similar dilemma.[95]

94. Wiesener, *Galeries*, 23; AL VC2 (1834–42), Wiesener to Montalivet, 3 May 1842, marginal note 16 June 1842.
95. Susan Siegfried, "Naked History: The Rhetoric of Military Painting in Postrevolutionary France," *Art Bulletin* 75, no. 2 (June 1993): 238–42. On *genre historique*, see Marrinan, *Painting Politics*, 19–24.

FIGURE 20. Antoine-Jean Gros, *Napoleon Haranguing the Army before the Battle of the Pyramids, 21 July 1798*. Réunion des Musées Nationaux/Art Resource, NY.

The documentary style developed by François Lejeune in pictures such as *The Battle of the Pyramids, 21 July 1798* (fig. 19) used a disembodied, bird's-eye perspective to offer a clear view of the battlefield and the strategic disposition of the troops, and to attribute visual and political privilege to the spectator, a "radically democratic" move at the end of the eighteenth century.[96] Although Vernet gave relatively less space to large troop movements, he adopted the elevated viewpoint and painted similarly detailed landscape backgrounds based on army reports, topographical documents, and personal battlefield visits. Vernet also, however, drew upon the affective mode associated with Baron Antoine-Jean Gros, who celebrated the citizen-armies of the 1790s in vast pictures filled with detailed depictions of the courageous acts of ordinary soldiers. With Gros, he shared a tighter focus on the traditional group of commanding officers and an interest in moving "anecdotal" episodes, which can be seen in Gros's *Napoleon Haranguing the Army before the Battle of the Pyramids, 21 July 1798* (fig. 20). Vernet's creative combination of these two approaches presented the Orléans princes in traditionally heroic poses, but reduced their size within the overall composition of his canvases.

96. Siegfried, "Naked History," 240.

FIGURE 21. Horace Vernet, *The Siege of Constantine (10 October 1837): The Enemy Repelled from the Heights of Coudiat-Ati,* 1838. Réunion des Musées Nationaux/Art Resource, NY.

The Constantine triptych exemplifies this representational strategy. In the first of the three paintings, *The Siege of Constantine (10 October 1837): The Enemy Repelled from the Heights of Coudiat-Ati* (fig. 21), the duc de Nemours, silhouetted against the sky at the center of the canvas, leads the counterattack against a sortie by Ahmad's garrison, while in the foreground, other soldiers provide covering fire and care for the wounded. The central image, *The Siege of Constantine (13 October 1837, 7:00 a.m.): The Assault Columns Move Out* (fig. 22), offers a Lejeune-style overview of the final attack on the city three days later. The prince, leading the assault columns after commanding general Damrément was killed, stands slightly apart from his staff at the center of the picture, arm raised as he orders the columns into motion. Although this group is the painting's ostensible focus—it is highlighted by a puff of artillery smoke, and the prince is caught in the light raking in from the left—it is far from the dominant element. In the third and final image of the French army pushing over city walls breached by French artillery, the prince disappears entirely (fig. 23). The officers leading the troops into the breach were identified in the Salon *livret* and museum guidebooks as

FIGURE 22. Horace Vernet, *The Siege of Constantine (13 October 1837, 7:00 a.m.): The Assault Columns Move Out*, 1839. Réunion des Musées Nationaux/Art Resource, NY.

FIGURE 23. Horace Vernet, *The Siege of Constantine (13 October 1837): Fall of the City,* 1838. Musée national de Versailles. Réunion des Musées Nationaux/Art Resource, NY.

Colonel Combes, shown in the center waving the men forward, and Lieutenant-Colonel de Lamoricière, visible atop the wall on the right urging them into the city.[97]

Vernet's portrayal of Nemours in the first two paintings carefully followed the ideals of the royal citizen-soldier, as a guidebook and an outline facsimile (fig. 24) provided to museum visitors explained. The prince took an active part in the siege, putting himself in harm's way alongside his men, and played a leadership role without claiming all the viewer's attention for himself. Thus, in the first canvas, according to the text that accompanied the facsimile, the commander, General Damrémont, stands observing the battle with his general staff in the bottom right corner. Meanwhile, in the center, the prince, having been ordered to ri-

---

97. *Explication des ouvrages* (1839), no. 2052; Wiesener, *Galeries,* 14.

FIGURE 24. *Facsimile of the Paintings Exhibited at the Salon of 1839, under no. 2050, 2051, and 2052,* by M. *Horace Vernet, Representing the Siege of Constantine* (Paris: Impr. des musées royaux, 1839). Research Library, The Getty Research Institute, Los Angeles (2857–796).

poste against the enemy sortie, "throws himself forward at the head of a battalion of the Foreign Legion."[98] In the second picture, the bird's-eye view puts the prince and his general staff on an equal footing with the scenes dotting the fore- and middle ground, as the guidebook was careful to point out to visitors: "Ordinarily, in battle painting, the General Staff draws and holds almost the entire attention of the spectator at the expense of the rest of the army. Here, each is given a fair share; the simple soldier is in the foreground, while the crux of the action rests on the generals."[99]

When these works were first exhibited at the Salon of 1839, supporters of the regime saw them as Louis-Philippe and Vernet intended, as an affirmation of Nemours's courage and of his identification with the army. Étienne Delécluze, writing in the *Journal des débats*, applauded their "lifelike portrait of the entire Armée d'Afrique" and praised the fact that the prince and the simplest soldier "faced the enemy's fire with the same sang-froid and the same verve."[100] Opponents, however, were quick to seize on the prince's diminishing profile and especially on his absence from the third, decisive episode. Vicomte Walsh of the legitimist organ, *La Mode*, was the harshest of the hostile critics. Vernet had captured the "French nature" of the siege, Walsh claimed, but his depictions of Nemours (and by extension the prince himself) were far from heroic.[101] The first picture exaggerated Nemours's role, although command of a simple battalion was

98. The facsimile, which took its explanatory text from the Salon *livret*, was originally produced for the 1839 Salon, and later sold in the Constantine Gallery. See *Explication des ouvrages* (1839), no. 2050.

99. Wiesener, *Galeries*, 11.

100. "Salon de 1839 (Premier Article)," *La Mode*, 7 March 1839.

101. "La Mode au Salon de 1839," *La Mode*, 16 March 1839.

a disgracefully modest position for a prince. His commanding pose in the second painting struck Walsh as more appropriate, and the critic declared himself reassured that Nemours was no longer endangering himself at this point in the battle.

In a later review of the completed gallery, however, Walsh revised his opinion and suggested that Nemours had been given an unearned position in the central canvas. Louis-Philippe had pressured Vernet to focus on the prince rather than the expedition's commander-in-chief, General Damrémont, who had been killed in the battle:

> They have stolen from General Damrémont the place he earned with his blood, and there, at the outpost where he stood when the bullet hit him, they have put M. the duc de Nemours, whom they have made to run in paint all the dangers that General Damrémont ran in reality. . . . It is true that General Damrémont paid for the capture of Constantine with his life, but it is the Civil List that pays for the painting of it, and when the Civil List happens to pay for something, it must get its money's worth. So, they brushed out General Damrémont and substituted for him the duc de Nemours.[102]

Walsh's commentary on the third section of the triptych cut to the heart of Vernet's pictorial dilemma. In a work so clearly "consecrated to the glory of Monsieur the duc de Nemours," the prince's absence from the final act of the Constantine drama was surprising. His prominence in the first two paintings only made this subsequent disappearance more striking. Addressing himself to the artist, Walsh suggested caustically that "it would have been better not to show us Louis's son in your first two acts and to save him for the dénouement."[103]

Nemours's absence from this last picture was the result of two factors. The first, which Walsh exploited, was historical: the prince had not participated in the final assault because it was simply too dangerous for a member of the royal family to take part in the hand-to-hand fighting on the breached city walls. Indeed, members of the prince's entourage considered the risks Nemours had run earlier in the campaign, including at Coudiat-Ati, unnecessary and foolhardy.[104] Their caution in this regard was not unjustified; Damrémont was killed while inspecting the siege works on which Nemours stands in the

102. "Comment on peint l'histoire," *La Mode*, 25 June 1842.
103. "Petite Chronique: Salon." *La Mode*, 9 March 1839; "La Mode au Salon de 1839," *La Mode*, 23 March 1839.
104. AN 300 AP III, général Trézel to duc de Choiseul, 21 October 1837 (copy).

triptych's center panel, while Lamoricière, the officer on the right in Vernet's third painting, was badly wounded and Combes, in the center, died scaling the breach.

Historical fact was not necessarily an obstacle in such a case. Artists had long inserted rulers into unrealistically exposed positions or even into battles where they had not been present. Accuracy was one of the defining features of the historical spectacles that the Versailles museum emulated, however, and its pedagogical mission rested on convincing visitors that what they saw was the historical "truth." Indeed, this was partly why Louis-Philippe had chosen Vernet for this important commission. The painter owed much of his tremendous popularity and commercial success to the perceived truthfulness of his work.[105] Some critics condemned him for it—Baudelaire accused him of possessing an "almanac's memory" instead of an imagination—but to his many admirers, Vernet was the artist "whose works most faithfully reproduce this most curious quarter of our century."[106] The painter himself cultivated this perception, describing himself as "a slave to truth" and insisting that "painting . . . can represent only material facts."[107] He went to great lengths throughout his career to safeguard his reputation as the "faithful historian" of the French army.[108]

The political efficacy of the Versailles museum was thus dependent on the public's belief that it offered an accurate representation of past events. As Michael Marrinan has shown, a whole documentary apparatus was set up to reinforce this conceit. Visitors were provided with a host of documentation against which to check the artworks as they went through each gallery. Detailed guidebooks and prominent title plaques identified each painting and offered a key for identifying the events and figures depicted.[109] For the Constantine Gallery, pamphlets sold at the château gave a detailed account of the siege, and the facsimile engrav-

---

105. E.g. "Salon de 1839 (3e article.) Peinture historique et batailles," *Le Siècle*, 10 April 1839; "Salon de 1839," *Revue des deux mondes*, 4th ser., 18 (April–June 1839): 93–94; Walsh, "La Mode au Salon de 1839," *La Mode*, 16 March 1839; "Salon de 1845," *Le Siècle*, 1 April 1845; Théophile Gautier, "Salon de 1846," in *Voyage en Algérie*, ed. Denise Brahimi (Paris, 1997), 174. The large-scale lithographic reproduction of Vernet's battle paintings shows how far his popularity reached past the Salon and Versailles. Stephen Bann, *Parallel Lines: Printmakers, Painters, and Photographers in Nineteenth-Century France* (New Haven, 2001), 79–80.
106. Baudelaire, "Salon de 1846," in *Curiosités esthétiques* (Paris, 1868), 160; Etienne Delécluze, "Salon de 1839 (Premier Article)," *Journal des débats*, 7 March 1839.
107. CAOM 18X 89, Vernet to ministre de la Guerre (Saint-Yon), 1 May 1846; J. Bertholon and C. Lhote, *Horace Vernet à Versailles, au Luxembourg et au Louvre: Critique et biographie* (Paris, 1863), 7–8; Durande, *Joseph, Carle, et Horace Vernet*, 102–3.
108. *Album du Salon 1844, Collection des principaux ouvrages exposés au Louvre reproduits par les artistes eux-mêmes ou sous leur direction* (Paris, 1844), 4.
109. Marrinan, "Historical Vision."

ings available in the gallery allowed visitors to identify the individual figures in each picture.[110] The wide publicity given to dispatches from the Armée d'Afrique, which were reprinted in the political press as well as in popular illustrated broadsheets, or *canards*, provided another, external check on the museum's depictions of the Algerian war. Visual representations at Versailles could not contradict these heavily publicized accounts without undermining the museum's truth claims. The words of the *Moniteur universel* on Vernet's later work, *The Capture of the Smalah of Abd-el-Kader*, applied equally well to the Constantine triptych: "It concerns a recent feat of arms, of which accounts were too precise and for which we had too many eyewitnesses to make it possible or appropriate to sacrifice the representation's exactitude to those conventional arrangements and that laborious search for picturesque contrasts that inhere in the academic style. . . . The *Capture* of the famous *smala*, whose details [are] known to everyone, suffers no alteration."[111]

In addition to textual narratives like those cited by the *Moniteur*'s critic, the documentary record of the Constantine siege also included a different kind of eyewitnessing: widely circulated pictorial accounts that had already been seen by large numbers of French viewers. An excellent example is a lithograph by the Bonapartist printmaker Auguste Raffet, which appeared a year before Vernet's canvases were exhibited at the Salon (fig. 25). This print, and others like it, functioned as another index of veracity against which Vernet's works were measured, and Vernet's painting of the scaling of the breach bears a striking resemblance to Raffet's celebration of the faceless men who fought their way into the city. The choice made by the widely popular Raffet to focus on the anonymous rank and file also helps to explain why it was the third section of the Constantine triptych that was most appreciated by critics and by the public.

The third image, in which the duc de Nemours did not appear at all, was distinguished from its companions as a "masterpiece of its genre" and lauded by critics of all political stripes as a true representation of war. Even the legitimist vicomte Walsh was enchanted by the realism of the scene. So accurate and animated was Vernet's brush, he enthused, that the soldiers' greatcoats became real greatcoats, the shakos real shakos, the guns real guns; the whole scene "practically smells of gunpowder."[112] It was the dominant position accorded to the men of the rank and file, however, that critics saw as the main indicator of the paint-

110. Wiesener, *Galeries*, 4; *Fac Simile des tableaux.*
111. "Beaux-Arts: Salon de 1845. 2e article," *Moniteur universel,* 21 March 1845. Bann makes a similar point about images of "a political event of major importance, whose outcome was closely relevant to state policy, and whose visual description had to cohere to the received and acceptable version of how that outcome had been secured" (*Parallel Lines*, 45).
112. "La Mode au Salon de 1839," *La Mode*, 23 March 1839.

FIGURE 25. Denis-Auguste-Marie Raffet, *The Second Column Reaches the Breach*, lith. Gihaut frères (Paris), 1838. Author's collection.

ing's truthfulness, and it was precisely this quality that Vernet's painting shared with the Raffet print. The pamphlet guide to the Constantine Gallery praised this aspect of the work with particular warmth: "None can equal M. Horace Vernet in the art of capturing the noble truth of military scenes. Among so many men, there is not one whose features are insignificant or common; they each have an individual expression, heightened by that dignity that the approach of a glorious peril gives to the physiognomy."[113] It was the ordinary soldiers of the Armée d'Afrique, rather than the absent Orléans prince, that made the third panel of the Constantine triptych such a success with critics and the viewing public.

The critical response also points to the persistent difficulty of representing the royal citizen-soldier. Images that gave the duc de Nemours a central place were seen as too overtly propagandistic by the regime's opponents, but his absence opened the door to a vision of the military nation in which the royal family had no part, thereby sapping the Orleanist effort to legitimize the new dynasty by association with the army. The rooms added to the Constantine Gallery in the ensuing years would seek increasingly extreme solutions to this dilemma,

113. Wiesener, *Galeries*, 11.

as Vernet experimented with ever more spectacular modes of representing the princes' Algerian battles.

The second Algerian gallery was inspired by the duc d'Aumale's capture of 'Abd al-Qadir's *smalah* on 16 May 1843. After a period of negotiated peace under the 1837 Treaty of Tafna, 'Abd al-Qadir had reopened hostilities in 1839. Renewed warfare boosted the emir's legitimacy among the Algerian tribes, making him the undisputed leader of resistance against the invaders, but it also disintegrated the proto-state he had built up in western Algeria in the late 1830s. When the French occupied his capital, Mascara, in 1841, he formed the nomadic *smalah* to replace it. As 'Abd al-Qadir's military headquarters, administrative center, and primary instrument of authority over wavering tribes, the *smalah* immediately became a prime target for French forces.[114] According to Aumale's report on its capture, he had been dispatched with a column from Boghar to pursue the *smalah*, which was reportedly in the area. After three days' march, he and a detachment of five hundred French cavalry and indigenous cavalry (*spahis*) suddenly came upon their quarry at dawn on 16 May. With no time to wait for reinforcements, Aumale called for an immediate attack, and in just over an hour's fighting, they overcame the five thousand infantrymen protecting the *smalah* to take possession of the tent city. Although 'Abd al-Qadir himself was absent and his family managed to escape, the French captured the families of several of the emir's closest advisers, his administrative archives and treasury, and thousands of prisoners of war.[115] Louis-Philippe, eager to capitalize on the coup, immediately asked Vernet to paint "one grand battle painting and as many small ones as possible" for Versailles.[116]

The planning of this second gallery shows the easy slippage in Louis-Philippe's mind between his reign and the Algerian conquest, as well as a new approach to the representation of the royal citizen-soldier. *The Capture of the Smalah of Abd-el-Kader* was initially commissioned for a room being built next to the Constantine Gallery to commemorate the events of the king's own life. When Vernet suggested transforming this "Louis-Philippe Gallery" into a pendant to the Constantine Gallery, however, his patron immediately embraced the idea and ordered the museum's architect to begin removing the works already hung in the space.[117] Although the Smalah Gallery was left unfinished in 1848, museum

---

114. On 'Abd al-Qadir, see Raphael Danziger, *Abd al-Qadir and the Algerians: Resistance to the French and Internal Consolidation* (New York, 1977); Smaïl Aouli, Ramdane Redjala, and Philippe Zoummeroff, *Abd el-Kader* (Paris, 1994); Bruno Étienne, *Abdelkader: Isthme des isthmes (Barzakh al-barazikh)* (Paris, 2003).
115. *Moniteur universel*, 31 May 1843.
116. AN 300 AP III 48, Louis-Philippe to Aumale, 2 June 1843 (copy).
117. AC Ms 1351, no. 285, 3 August 1843.

planning documents show that it was intended, like its neighbor, to focus on the Orléans princes' military exploits, especially in Algeria.[118]

That Vernet never finished the gallery's other paintings seems to have made little difference to contemporaries, who were transfixed by its enormous centerpiece (fig. 26). Completed in February 1845, the *Smalah* was displayed at the Salon and then moved to Versailles, where the partly finished gallery opened to the public in September.[119] Measuring some sixty-six by fifteen feet and running the entire length of the room, the *Smalah* is truly spectacular in scale. As art historians have noted, Vernet's approach in this astonishing work owed more to the techniques of the panorama than to academic history painting.[120] One of the most popular historical spectacles of the nineteenth century, panoramas allowed viewers to "experience" a place or event by standing on a raised viewing platform while an elaborate light show animated a landscape painting wrapped around the circular room.[121] This was a format that had already been used with great success to bring Algerian battles to French audiences by Charles Langlois, whose *Panorama of Algiers*, a reenactment of the 1830 expedition, was viewed by thousands in Paris between March 1833 and November 1834.[122]

The panoramic character of Vernet's *Smalah* lay first and foremost in its sheer size, but its scale led the artist to adopt a compositional strategy that mimicked that of the boulevard spectacle as well. In the gallery space, it is impossible to take in the entire canvas at once (fig. 27), so the artist could not use a single figure group as the central focus of the composition. Instead, the picture is made up of a series of episodes arranged serially along its length: on the left, the French cavalry

---

118. AL V2 (1835–1848), sketches in Cailleux (directeur des Musées Royaux) note of 28 August 1844. The subjects included two scenes from Aumale's capture of the *smalah*, the duc d'Orléans's crossing of the Biban Pass (the Portes de Fer) in 1839, and one or more episodes from an 1844 campaign against tribes allied with 'Abd al-Qadir in the Ziban mountains in which Aumale and his youngest brother, the duc de Montpensier, took part. Joinville's naval career again provided the one non-Algerian theme, in this case the return of Napoleon's ashes to Paris in 1840.
119. AL V2C (1834–1846), Bouchemin to Cailleux, 13 September 1845.
120. Michael Marrinan, "Schauer der Eroberung: Strukturen des Zuschauens und der Simulation in den Nordafrika-Galerien von Versailles," in *Bilder der Macht, Macht der Bilder: Zeitgeschichte in Darstellungen des 19. Jahrhunderts*, ed. Stefan Germer and Michael F. Zimmermann (Munich and Berlin, 1997), 288–91; John Zarobell, *Empire of Landscape: Space and Ideology in French Colonial Algeria* (University Park, 2010), 45–46.
121. Stephan Oettermann, *The Panorama: History of a Mass Medium*, trans. Deborah Lucas-Schneider (New York, 1997); Vanessa Schwartz, *Spectacular Realities: Early Mass Culture in Fin-de-Siècle Paris* (Berkeley, 1998), chap. 4.
122. A. Jal, *Panorama d'Alger, peint par M. Charles Langlois . . .* (Paris, 1833); *Petites affiches du commerce*, 24 January 1834; Zarobell, *Empire of Landscape*, chap. 1. A version of the latter is also in John Zarobell, "Jean-Charles Langlois's Panorama of Algiers (1833) and the Prospective Colonial Landscape," *Art History* 26, no. 5 (2003): 638–68.

FIGURE 26. Horace Vernet, *Capture of the Smalah of Abd-el-Kader at Taguin, 16 May 1843*,
1844. Réunion des Musées Nationaux/Art Resource, NY.

charge into the tent city; in the center, a group of Algerian women beg the prince
for mercy in the middle ground, while the occupants of a collapsing tent scramble
to flee the attackers in the foreground; on the right, 'Abd al-Qadir's wives and
mother clamber into the camel-borne palanquins that will carry them to safety.
The viewer must physically move to see each vignette each in turn, making the
viewing experience a dynamic one and projecting the viewer into the scene.

Some critics found the extraordinary painting an outrage to artistic tradition
and good taste. Baudelaire, for one, condemned it as "a crowd of little interest-
ing anecdotes—a vast cabaret panorama" completely lacking in compositional
unity.[123] The critic for the legitimist *Quotidienne* accused the artist of "heedless
daring" and declared that the lack of central focus "results in a great malaise for
the spirit" as "the eye wanders, restless and unhappy, across this motley crowd
without knowing where to stop."[124] Others, however, deemed such criticism misplaced. "This kind of work must not be judged according to the rigor of the old
rules, which prescribe above all the unity of action and absolutely require that
one principal feat dominate all that surrounds it," the *Moniteur universel* declared. Given that its subject was such a recent and well-known event, "it sufficed
to stick to the simplicity of the truth and to put aside any idea of poetic fiction

123. "Salon de 1845," in *Curiosités esthétiques*, 11.
124. "Salon de 1845. 2e Article: M. Decamps.—M. Horace Vernet," *La Quotidienne*, 28 March
1845.

to make us admire the valor of the French soldier and his young general."[125] The leftist *Le Siècle* agreed that artistic and sentimental conventions were irrelevant to the painting of war. Real combat had no single focus; in battle, the action was "everywhere," so its truthful representation did not require a compositional focus. Critics who called for painterly poetry in battle scenes failed to recognize that the moral reflections inspired by war were far more serious than an artist's dreams. "The only poetic sentiment that one can demand of the Smala is the sentiment of truth," *Le Siècle* declared, which was more than adequately captured by "the clarity, verve, spirit, and *ingenuity*" of Vernet's canvas. The general public seems to have shared this view, for a "crowd filled with wonder" came in droves to see the picture at the Salon and later at Versailles.[126]

In portraying the duc d'Aumale as a royal citizen-soldier, the *Smalah* struck a more radical pictorial compromise than Vernet's Constantine triptych. The young duke appears near the center of the painting, seated on a white horse with his arm outstretched, as he orders the French cavalry to spare the pleading Algerian women before him (fig. 28). His is a typically royal gesture, but the episodic construction of the painting means that it is no more prominent than the other vignettes that make up the rest of the picture. Viewers were apparently quite conscious of this fact. *Le Siècle*'s critic was willing to designate the prince as

125. "Beaux-Arts: Salon de 1845. 2e article." *Moniteur universel*, 21 March 1845.
126. "Salon de 1845," *Le Siècle*, 1 April 1845.

FIGURE 27. Opening of the Smalah Gallery, in *L'Illustration*, 11 October 1845. Courtesy University of Iowa Libraries, Special Collections.

the painting's center, but only because of his location in the middle of the expanse of canvas.[127] In the viewer's dynamic interaction with the painting, however, the royal act of clemency stood as only one of a series of melodramatic, often violent, confrontations between French soldiers and the panicked inhabitants of the *smalah*, depicted in minute, quasi-ethnographic detail by the artist.[128]

A lengthy brochure published by the Musées Royaux and sold in the gallery attempted to impose some interpretive order on this mass of detail and to focus viewers' attention on the royal figure. The brochure provided information about the *smalah* itself, as well as a map of the French column's route, a fold-out facsimile naming each figure in the picture, and a lengthy narrative of the *smalah*'s capture highlighting Aumale's quick decision-making and élan.[129] Although in high demand with visitors, the guide seems to have been relatively ineffective in giv-

127. Ibid.
128. Jennifer Olmsted emphasizes the "ethnographic" detail and violence of these scenes. "The Sultan's Authority: Delacroix, Painting, and Politics at the Salon of 1845," *Art Bulletin* 91, no. 1 (2009): 96–98.
129. *Notice sur l'expédition qui s'est terminée par la prise de la Smalah d'Abd-el-Kader, le 16 mai 1843* (Paris, 1843).

FIGURE 28. Horace Vernet,
*Capture of the Smalah of
Abd-el-Kader,* detail of
fig. 26.

ing ideological coherence to Vernet's painting.[130] Visitors and critics of all political
stripes continued to remark on its episodic character, and once again, what they
appreciated above all was the attention that Vernet gave to each of the figures he
portrayed. The *Moniteur* declared of the painting, "there is not, among these in-
numerable figures . . . a single individual whose sentiments seem equivocal and
who does not take a heated part, as victor or vanquished, in the grand emotions
of the day."[131] *La Mode*'s vicomte Walsh admired this quality, too, writing, "all of
the soldiers that he shows us are so natural: it is the conscript making himself a
hero on the battlefield; these are our Angevins, our Bretons, our Vendeans, our
Perigordians, our Normans, our children of Paris, growing, earning their stripes,
wounds, and crosses amidst those burning sands upon which the soldiers of Saint
Louis once trod."[132]

These commentaries suggest that Vernet's new strategy for representing the
royal citizen-soldier had backfired. Rather than inspiring admiration for Aumale's
modesty in the midst of his heroics, the compositional logic of the *Smalah* allowed viewers to shift their attention almost entirely from the prince to the soldiers surrounding him. Despite Vernet's radical revision of the conventions of
battle painting, public responses to the Constantine Gallery and to the *Smalah*
made clear that the artist and his royal patron had failed in their collaborative

130. See AL VC2, notes from museum officials to directeur des Musées Royaux, 17 March 1845–12
May 1846; unsigned note, 11 March 1845; commandant de la 1re Division Militaire to Montalivet,
28 March 1845; Bugeaud to Montalivet, 3 May 1845. Ten thousand copies were printed, of which
thirty-seven hundred were distributed to the army.
131. "Beaux-Arts. Salon de 1845: 2e article," *Moniteur universel,* 21 March 1845.
132. "Livres—Tableaux—Statues: Les Beaux Jours de la Mode," *La Mode,* 6 April 1845.

effort to portray the duc d'Aumale and his brothers as simultaneously exemplary heroes and ordinary men doing their patriotic duty. This failure of representation helps to explain the wider failure of the Orléans family's efforts to claim legitimacy through military service. As Louis-Philippe sought new ways to valorize his sons in battle and in paint, opponents of the monarchy renewed their suspicions of the Algerian war and suggested more and less overtly that its only purpose was to provide the king's sons with a place to play at soldiering.[133] Even sympathetic critics found Vernet's depictions of the Orléans princes' Algerian campaigns to be most compelling not as a legitimizing new model of royal meritocracy, but as a collective portrait of the Armée d'Afrique's rank and file.

Louis-Philippe appears to have grasped the collapse of the royal citizen-soldier model even before the *Smalah* was completed. In ordering the creation of a third African gallery for the Musée historique de Versailles in 1844, he made it clear that this addition would be dedicated not to his sons but to "the feats of arms of the Armée d'Afrique."[134] Located at the south end of the Constantine Gallery, the new room was intended to commemorate the victory of French land and naval forces over 'Abd al-Qadir's ally, the sultan of Morocco, in August of 1844. A French naval squadron under the command of the prince de Joinville bombarded the port of Tangiers on 6 August and seized the fortified island of Mogador ten days later. On 14 August, Governor General Bugeaud decisively defeated 'Abd al-Rahman's army in the plain of Isly on the Algerian-Moroccan frontier. The double French victory forced the sultan to outlaw 'Abd al-Qadir, who had taken refuge in Morocco following the capture of the *smalah*, and to accept a redrawing of the border with Algeria. Louis-Philippe was particularly pleased that the victory came at the expense of the British, who systematically opposed any French intervention in Morocco.[135]

Plans to commemorate these events began barely two weeks after the Mogador landing. Louis-Philippe organized a military parade in Paris, where the flags captured at Isly were formally presented at a massive review of the local garrison and then escorted to the Invalides by the king, the available princes, Bugeaud, and the "vieux Africains" of the Second and Seventeenth Light and Twenty-Fourth Line infantry regiments.[136] The tent and parasol signaling the status of the Moroccan commander at Isly were set up in the Tuileries for the delectation of Parisian curiosity-seekers.[137] At the same time, Louis-Philippe gave

133. Margadant, "Gender, Vice," 1485.
134. AC Ms 1352, no. 316, 29 August 1844.
135. Louis-Philippe to Soult, 25 July 1844, in Soult, *Correspondance*, 238.
136. AN 300 AP III 48, Louis-Philippe to Soult, 10 September 1844.
137. *Moniteur universel*, 30 September and 1 October 1844; Marrinan, "Schauer der Eroberung," 290.

Vernet a budget of two hundred thousand francs to design a new gallery, even "richer and grander" than that of the *smalah*, at Versailles. Construction began immediately, but the project fell behind schedule and Vernet managed to complete only one painting, *The Battle of Isly*, before the Revolution of 1848 toppled the July Monarchy.[138]

Vernet's plans for the central painting of the Mogador landing suggest that he and Louis-Philippe had finally abandoned their effort to find a satisfactory means of representing the royal soldier-citizen. Unfinished preparatory work for the *Capture of Mogador* indicates a painting of the naval landing at Mogador on the scale of the *Smalah*. But where the *Smalah* had been deemed panoramic because of its size and composition, *Mogador* would adopt outright the "artificial resources" of the panoramist to produce "a more perfect illusion" in three dimensions.[139] Wooden columns, split vertically and set flush against the canvas, would divide it into three sections, while an openwork balustrade, also in three dimensions, ran along the base of the wall such that the viewer appeared to observe the landing from a balcony on the fortified island.[140]

We have seen how the place allocated to Louis-Philippe's sons had already begun to diminish in response to critics' identification with ordinary soldiers' sacrifices rather than princely heroics. This shift appears to culminate in the *Capture of Mogador*, where the scale and perspective of the panoramic conceit make it virtually impossible for the prince de Joinville, who had stayed on his ship during the landing, to hold a central position.[141] Vernet could have chosen to portray the prince on the deck of his flagship, as he had in *Attack on the Fort of Saint-Jean-d'Ulloa, 27 November 1838* for the Constantine Gallery, but this time he did not. Louis-Philippe appears to have given at least tacit approval for this choice. Indeed, the king was fully cognizant of the constraints imposed by the truth claims of both artist and museum, as his comments on one sketch for the *Smalah* demonstrate. Describing to Aumale his place in the middle distance, the king expressed "regret in some ways that you are not

---

138. AC Ms 1352, no. 316, 29 August 1844; no. 319, 26 October 1844. *The Battle of Isly* was shown at the Salon of 1846.
139. "Beaux-Arts. Salon de 1845: 2e Article," *Moniteur universel*, 21 March 1845. The two unfinished canvases are *La Prise de Mogador, 1844* (Musée nationale de Versailles, MV 8509) and *Un Épisode de la guerre du Maroc, 1844* (MV 8510). The latter has a mostly finished background showing a sunset sky, corresponding to Joinville's description of the scene (*Vieux souvenirs*, 265).
140. AC Ms 1352, no. 346, 4 October 1845; no. 376, 27 November 1846.
141. The incomplete center canvas of *La Prise de Mogador* shows the fortified island in the middle ground, and the buildings appear to be too close for a ship's deck to figure in the foreground. The archives are silent as to Joinville's appearance in this painting, but the king's congratulatory letter to the prince contains no request for documents to guide Vernet. AN 300 AP III 48, Louis-Philippe to Joinville, 29 August 1844.

in the foreground," but concluded that "I prefer you be where you were put, which, moreover, must be the truth."[142] In this case, the need to correspond to documented accounts of the event prevailed over the desire to give his son a more flattering position. The imperatives of historical truth thus converged with the public's manifest desire to see battle painting celebrate the rank and file of the French army at the expense of the Orléans princes. As the painter and his patron sought to maximize the visual and political impact of their last collaboration, they sought increasingly to popularize the monarchy by celebrating national glory rather than royal merits.

As the ordinary soldiers of the Armée d'Afrique gained pictorial predominance over the Orléans princes, Vernet abandoned the conventions of academic battle painting for what he considered more "truthful" forms of representation. Between the Constantine triptych and the Moroccan Gallery, Vernet had moved ever further into the mode of the panorama, which claimed not to represent the key moment of a battle but to transport the viewer directly into the event. Art historians have argued that Vernet's use of the panoramic vernacular backfired because it followed official reports too closely.[143] This was true of a certain number of hostile critics, who dismissed his work as "a bulletin that you see instead of hearing it read,"[144] but thousands more Salon-goers, museum visitors, and print buyers admired Vernet's paintings for just this quality. Théophile Gautier, the Romantic journalist and critic, found Vernet's art insufficiently poetic, but clearly understood that its references to viewers' prior cultural knowledge appealed to a broad audience:

> His paintings illustrate bulletins, and everyone knows in advance what he means. The text of his compositions is disseminated to thousands by a hundred newspapers; everyone has seen *chasseurs d'Afrique* and *zouaves* and, thanks to the frequent appearance of Arabs in Paris, there's not a street urchin who doesn't know his Bedouin like the back of his hand. It is entirely natural that the paintings of M. Horace Vernet enjoy a great popularity; even those least familiar with painting can see the accuracy of the reproduction of a kepi, a cartridge pouch, a pair of gaiters, or a burnoose.[145]

Although we cannot know how the finished Moroccan Gallery would have been received by museum visitors, the popularity of the Constantine triptych

---

142. AN 300 AP III 48, Louis-Philippe to Aumale, 6 April 1844.
143. Zarobell, *Empire of Landscape*, 45–46.
144. "Livres—Tableaux—Statues: Les Beaux Jours de la Mode," *La Mode*, 6 April 1845.
145. "Salon de 1845 (2e article): Horace Vernet.—Eugène Delacroix.—Théodore Chasseriau," *La Presse*, 18 March 1845.

and the *Smalah* made Vernet's step into the panoramic mode a logical one in light of both the monarchy's increasing anxiety and contemporary views on the pedagogical virtues of such spectacles. The more visually entertaining the museum could be made and the more "realistic" its representations, the more effective a teaching and propaganda tool it was believed to be. Even hostile critics like Gautier clearly saw this presumed "realism" as the source of Vernet's appeal to the mass of viewers more concerned with entertainment value than pictorial qualities. It made sense for Vernet and Louis-Philippe to adopt the techniques of popular entertainment as their priorities shifted from the glorification of the royal sons to glorifying the Algerian conquest as a whole. For the king, this representational shift was a double-edged sword. The African galleries at Versailles succeeded in inscribing the Algerian conquest in the museum's narrative of national military glory, but in doing so, they gradually dissociated the colonial venture from the royal family. Circumscribed by his own conception of meritocratic kingship and the fiction of historical truth that governed the Musée historique, the king could not ask Horace Vernet to give his sons a more prominent place without undermining the premise that they were soldiers like any other. Rather than resolving its paradoxes, celebrations of the princes' Algerian campaigns collapsed under the contradictions of the royal citizen-soldier model.

The princes themselves embraced the meritocratic ideal of kingship, but the public was never fully convinced of their sincerity. Until his accidental death in 1842, the duc d'Orléans managed to overcome a great deal of suspicion with personal charisma.[146] His death was a fatal blow to the dynasty. In his absence, it was the duc d'Aumale who came to best represent the ideal of the royal citizen-soldier, pursuing his military career with single-minded commitment and consistently crediting his successes to his troops and fellow officers. As a result, his professional rise was largely perceived in France as honestly earned.[147] "Aumale l'Algérien" was also the member of the royal family most closely associated with Algeria. During nearly a decade of service in the colony, he gained both the respect of the Armée d'Afrique and the affection of the European settlers, who saw his presence as a sign of a policy shift towards the civilian administration they desired. His appointment as governor general in September 1847 was greeted as a symbolic cementing of the bond between the royal family and the new French territory, which Ferdinand Barrot described as "the dynastic taking of possession of Algeria."[148] Even Aumale was unable to entirely overcome suspicions that he

146. Margadant, "Gender, Vice," 1483; Martin-Fugier, *La vie quotidienne*, 252.
147. Julien, *La conquête*, 266–68.
148. CAOM F80 1791, letter to François Guizot, 28 August 1847.

enjoyed special privileges because of his royal blood, however. The opposition press denounced as foolhardy his nomination to the governor generalship at age twenty-five, and even Orleanists, with some good reason, saw 'Abd al-Qadir's surrender three months later as a matter of lucky timing rather than Aumale's personal prowess.[149]

When news reached Paris on 2 January 1848 that the "hunt for Abd-el-Kader" had finally come to an end, the monarchy turned to its usual publicity measures to drum up public fervor. But the final defeat of France's Algerian enemy was overshadowed by a deepening political and economic crisis at home.[150] Louis-Philippe had become increasingly authoritarian in the 1840s and, by the last year of his reign, was imposing his views directly on the conservative government of François Guizot. As the liberal-minded Joinville wrote to Nemours late in 1847, the now elderly king had "erased the constitutional fiction," effectively seizing power from his ministers and making himself responsible for all government actions.[151] Pressure for electoral reform had been mounting since 1840, as the bourgeoisie gained in social power and began to clamor for political power to match. Accusations of monarchical corruption and decadence flew, fed by a series of government corruption scandals, a worsening industrial recession, and crop failures that undermined Louis-Philippe's claims to govern in the interests of the people. In the winter of 1847–48, a campaign of highly publicized protest banquets fixed public attention on these griefs, leaving 'Abd al-Qadir to languish, nearly forgotten, in the lazaret of Toulon.

A crowd of curiosity-seekers had gathered to see the emir land at Toulon, but there was little for the monarchy to celebrate in the defeat of the celebrated Algerian leader. What would, just months earlier, have occasioned major public festivities became instead a source of political embarrassment. General de Lamoricière, who negotiated 'Abd al-Qadir's surrender, had promised that he would be allowed to go into exile in Egypt or Syria, and Aumale had endorsed this commitment. The agreement caused outrage in France, however, where the press and opposition deputies accused the government of betraying the army by allowing its greatest enemy to go free. Guizot bowed to this pressure and disavowed the guarantees offered by Lamoricière and Aumale. 'Abd al-Qadir was imprisoned first in Toulon, then at Pau, and finally at the château of Amboise, where he was held in isolation until 1852.[152]

149. E.g. *Journal des débats*, 2–3 January 1848.
150. William Fortescue, *France and 1848* (London and New York, 2005), 55.
151. "Lettre du prince de Joinville au duc de Nemours," 7 November 1847, in *Revue rétrospective* 31 (1848): 482.
152. Julien, *La conquête*, 207–8.

FIGURE 29. Rousselot, *Now It's Your Turn!* Lith. Lordereau (Paris), 1848. Bibliothèque nationale de France, Département des Estampes et de la photographie.

Before the emir's fate had been decided, however, that of his captors was sealed. On 22 February 1848, reformers defied a government ban on political banquets, and the next day barricades went up in the streets of Paris. After two days of intense fighting, Louis-Philippe abruptly abdicated, and a provisional government was proclaimed to replace the monarchy. When the provisional government, pressed by the crowds, declared the republic, the royal family fled into exile in England. A few publishers, struck by the ironic parallels between the events of 1830 and those of 1848, revived the theme of the fallen French king meeting his erstwhile Algerian foe on the road to exile. "Well, well, well! We meet just as Charles X and the Dey of Algiers did in 1830," read the caption of one such print (fig. 29). Only a handful of publishers took up the simultaneous fall of 'Abd al-Qadir and Louis-Philippe, however, suggesting that the theme no longer had much resonance with French viewers. This loss of purchase must be attributed, at least in part, to the fact that the French image of 'Abd al-Qadir did not mirror opposition views of Louis-Philippe in the way that stereotypes of Hussein Dey as an Oriental despot had echoed liberal visions of the ultraroyalist Charles X. Widely seen as an ascetic warrior-priest, whose treasures had already been seized with his *smalah* in 1843, 'Abd al-Qadir offered few comic parallels to the secular greed and financial corruption of which republicans accused the Orléans regime. Most important, however, the French war in North Africa had acquired its own legitimacy since 1830. In eighteen years, as France sacrificed over a billion francs, nearly one hundred thousand soldiers, and an untold number of Algerian lives, critics had subjected the war's tactics and costs to intense scrutiny, but rarely questioned the overarching justice of the French cause. It is telling, in this respect, that criticism of Orleanist propaganda, such as Vernet's Algerian galleries, focused on its depiction of Louis-Philippe's sons, rather than on the conquest in which the princes were engaged.

Louis-Philippe's July Monarchy failed to forge a stable dynastic order on Algerian battlefields, but its symbolic investment in the conquest provided the political will to drive the war forward even when legislators balked at its expense. In seeking to shore up their own legitimacy through imperial expansion, Orleanists helped to create an imperialist dynamic independent of the monarchy itself. Thus, in 1848, regime change in France once again did not change French colonial domination in Algeria. Like the liberals of 1830, the republicans of 1848 rejected the previous regime's efforts to legitimize itself through the Algerian conquest but then committed significant resources to expanding its military and colonization work in North Africa. To understand why, we must turn now to the popular culture of the Algerian conquest, which offered a powerful counternarrative to the Orleanist vision of Algeria as a stage for enacting the ideals of meritocratic monarchy.

3

The Blood of Brothers

Bonapartism and the Popular Culture of Conquest

IN MARCH OF 1831, the Théâtre des Folies Dramatiques introduced Parisian theatergoers to Nicolas Chauvin, the young conscript character whose name gave rise to the term "chauvinism," the nineteenth-century neologism for a blindly aggressive patriotism. Chauvin had first appeared in a trio of songs in 1825, but it was the vaudeville stage that would make him a stock figure in French popular culture. The play in which Chauvin made his theatrical début, the Cogniard brothers' *La cocarde tricolore: Épisode de la guerre d'Alger*, revolved around the naïve conscript's initiation into battle and into manhood during the Algiers expedition of 1830. Under the tutelage of the title character, a Napoleonic veteran named La Cocarde, Chauvin learns to stand firm under enemy fire and to seduce the women of the dey's harem, before capturing the dey himself. Much of the play's great commercial success derived from its ribald plot devices and songs, which adapted for the stage the Orientalizing themes of comic engravings published the year before (fig. 4, chap. 1). Against the exotic backdrop of Algiers, represented on stage by palm trees and a minaret-dotted skyline, Chauvin and his comrades fall ill from eating undercooked camel, fumble as they chase the harem women, and blunder in their pursuit of Algerian fighters. But the heart of the play is Chauvin's transformation under the influence of La Cocarde, who teaches him the masculine virtues of virility, courage, and patriotism.[1]

---

1. Théodore Cogniard and Hippolyte Cogniard, *La cocarde tricolore: Épisode de la guerre d'Alger, vaudeville en trois actes: Représenté pour la première fois, à Paris, sur le théâtre des Folies Dramatiques,*

In both content and form, *La cocarde tricolore* highlights the importance of the postrevolutionary cult of Napoleon in popular representations of the Algerian conquest. It premiered amidst an "avalanche" of plays with Napoleonic themes that hit French stages after the July Revolution, and should be considered alongside these nearly thirty works that brought every aspect of Napoleon's life and career to life for French audiences in 1830 and 1831.[2] The Napoleonic frame of reference is set in the play's opening scene, where La Cocarde stands alone on stage and muses aloud about the memories of "le petit" that are triggered by the Algiers expedition. The landscape reminds him of fighting alongside the "Little Corporal" in Egypt thirty years earlier, inducing both a sense of rejuvenation and melancholy nostalgia for his former chief. As he sings to close the scene,

> *Each step recalls a success!*
> *I think I see once again all my days of glory.*
> *And yet, I feel regret . . .*
> *A memory clouds my happiness;*
> *As we find ourselves all reunited here,*
> *Aha! I feel it . . . something is missing,*
> *Only He, alas! is not among us."*[3]

In the absence of "Him," a codeword for Napoleon developed to evade Restoration censors, it falls to the faithful *grognard* La Cocarde to inspire the next generation of Frenchmen to the heights of glory and patriotic fraternity he associates with the Imperial past. It is the battlefields of North Africa that offer the opportunity to do so.

The linkages between the Algerian conquest and memories of the Napoleonic era were formal, as well as thematic. The primary vehicles that brought the North African war to French audiences were the vaudeville theater, patriotic poetry and song, and popular imagery that spread the Napoleonic legend in

---

le 19 mars 1831, 4th ed. (Paris, [1834]). On the history of the Chauvin character, see Gérard de Puymège, *Chauvin, le soldat-laboureur: Contribution à l'étude des nationalismes* (Paris, 1993); and Gérard de Puymège, "Le soldat Chauvin," in *Les lieux de mémoire*, ed. Pierre Nora, bk. 2, *La Nation*, vol. 3 (Paris, 1986), 45–80. Todd Porterfield discusses prints in the *victoires et conquêtes* genre in *The Allure of Empire: Art in the Service of French Imperialism, 1798–1836* (Princeton, 1998), 138–40.

2. Théodore Muret, *L'histoire par le théâtre, 1789–1851*, vol. 3, *Le gouvernement de 1830: la Seconde République* (Paris, 1865), 93. *La cocarde tricolore* does not appear in the lists of Napoleonic plays established by Louis-Henry Lecomte, *Napoléon et l'Empire racontés par le théâtre, 1797–1899* (Paris, 1900), and Maurice Samuels, *The Spectacular Past: Popular History and the Novel in Nineteenth-Century France* (Ithaca, 2004), 271–72.

3. Cogniard and Cogniard, *La cocarde tricolore*, 68.

postrevolutionary France. These were deeply conventional "minor" genres and commercial mass media that traded in repetitive themes, stock characters, and standardized narratives. In their search for profits, the authors, artists, and publishers who disseminated the myths of popular Bonapartism incorporated the Algerian conquest into established Napoleonic topoi, even as they drew explicit comparisons between the Armée d'Afrique and the Napoleonic armies. The illusionistic sets and elaborate stage combat in *La cocarde tricolore*, for instance, mimic the *mise en scène* of contemporary Napoleon plays. At the same time, it is praise from the Napoleonic veteran, La Cocarde, that kindles in Chauvin the bravery that results in the capture of Hussein Dey. "The whole army loves and esteems you!" he tells La Cocarde. "We all take you as a model. You have no rank, but your woolen epaulets that smell of powder are more respected than the golden ones" of the company's sergeant, a Bourbon loyalist who owed his position to patronage. When Chauvin and his comrades capture the dey, they fulfill Chauvin's earlier boast that French men remain the same despite the loss of Napoleon.[4] French audiences' eager embrace of such works—the script of *La cocarde tricolore* was reprinted at least nine times by five different publishers over the next thirty years, and the play was performed by the traveling troupes that served provincial towns without a permanent theater[5]—suggests that they, too, saw the colonial war as an opportunity to reprise the Napoleonic glories being celebrated on the same cultural stages.

The coincidence of Chauvin's military and patriotic education with his sexual initiation reflects the deeply gendered character of analogies between the Algerian conquest and the Napoleonic Wars. References to the Napoleonic precedent across a wide range of genres and media invoked a model of patriotic masculinity in which martial valor and civic virtue were intertwined. Grounded in an ideal of the self-sacrificing citizen-soldier introduced during the French Revolution and incarnated in Napoleon's armies, nineteenth-century images of the Armée d'Afrique cast the fight for domination in Algeria as the enactment of a kind of active male citizenship defined by military service. Despite its obvious resonance with the vision of the royal citizen-soldier elaborated by the Orléans royal family, the citizen-soldier enshrined in the gendered idioms of popular Bonapartism implicitly challenged the limitations imposed on citizenship and political participation under the July Monarchy.

In *La cocarde tricolore*, Bonapartist patriotism is equated with the founding values of the July Monarchy. When the royalist sergeant arrests La Cocarde for

---

4. Ibid., 74, 78.
5. AD Haut-Rhin 4T 99, Charles Desrochers, "Répertoire de la troupe du 9eme arrondissement théâtral," n.d. [c. 1834–35]. Maurice Ordonneau adapted the play as an operetta in 1892.

wearing a tricolor cockade given to him by Napoleon himself, the loyal veteran is saved from the firing squad by news of the revolution in Paris. "No more tyranny! No more oppressors!" the protagonists cry as they wave the tricolor flag and celebrate La Cocarde's release in the final scene; "Liberty has returned to France!" "Vive la liberté! vive la Charte!" As Louis-Philippe distanced himself from the revolutionary origins of his throne, however, references to Napoleon regained the oppositional connotations they had carried between 1815 and 1830. A hint of their radical potential can be found in the closing song of the vaudeville, whose chorus paraphrases the *Marseillaise* to declare the characters' shared determination to defend the new revolution:

> *Citizens, soldiers, to arms! . . .*
> *Friends, let us close our ranks,*
> *And form our battalions against our enemies.*"[6]

Imbued with these revolutionary echoes, the Bonapartist interpretation of the conquest laid out in popular culture created a powerful counternarrative that implicitly challenged the vision of the Algerian war offered in Orleanist royal propaganda. In the tensions between popular and official representations of the conquest, we can see the extent to which the postrevolutionary politics of empire were a matter not only of French power over Algerians, but also of power, citizenship, and sovereignty within France itself.

At the same time, there were limits to patriotic equations between the Armée d'Afrique and the Napoleonic armies, as the brutal realities of colonial warfare challenged the conceptions of honorable combat that underpinned the Napoleonic legend. These limits were most strikingly demonstrated by the failure of efforts to build a national monument to the Armée d'Afrique, which were derailed by revelations about the nature of the guerilla war being fought in North Africa. Public fundraising for a memorial commemorating the 1840 defense of Mazagran collapsed under the scrutiny it drew to the conduct of the French army in Algeria and the "total war" strategy implemented by Governor General Thomas-Robert Bugeaud in the 1840s. The extraordinary violence of Bugeaud's war neither displaced the Napoleonic citizen-soldier as a model of masculine civic virtue, nor undermined the political will in France to carry on with the conquest, however. Popular representations of the conquest began to change in the second decade of the war, as producers modified Bonapartist conventions to focus on the triumphs and sacrifices of the ordinary soldier instead of on heroic general officers. Rather than discrediting French domination, this

6. Cogniard and Cogniard, *La cocarde tricolore*, 90.

shift provided new arguments for expanding French domination in Algeria and completing it with civilian colonization. The suffering of French soldiers in the course of the unconventional war of conquest was cast as a patriotic debt that the nation could only repay by completing the imperial project for which they had died. Tensions between colonial warfare and Napoleonic militarism thus produced not a repudiation of imperial expansion but the political impetus for the settlement of thousands of French citizens on land confiscated from its Algerian occupants.

Popular Bonapartism and the Popular Culture of Conquest

The boulevard theater that produced *La cocarde tricolore* was only one of many cultural venues in which French citizens could follow the Algerian conquest during the July Monarchy. Alongside the official accounts publicized by the government, descriptions of combat and military life in North Africa reached literate metropolitans through private letters, published campaign narratives, and histories of the ongoing war. The bulletins printed in the *Moniteur universel* were reproduced by other Parisian and provincial newspapers, many of which had their own correspondents in Algeria as well. Army dispatches also provided content for *canards*, cheap, crudely illustrated news broadsheets hawked on the streets of Paris and other major cities. Criers singing out their sensational titles were a common sight and sound to urban residents, especially the semiliterate men and women of the lower middle and artisanal classes, who were enjoined to hand over one sou for "Detailed and official accounts of the most Remarkable events that have taken place in Africa," "Official news from Algiers . . . on the brilliant new Victory achieved by the French Army in Africa," or "Accurate details on the operations of the French Army in Algeria: Terrible lesson given to the Arabs by our brave soldiers."[7] The same reports were recycled yet again by the publishers of the almanacs and chapbooks of the famous *bibliothèque bleue*, sold by itinerant peddlers to peasants and other rural dwellers.

The arts also brought the Algerian war to a wide range of French reading, viewing, and listening publics in this period. The literate enjoyed adventure stories and sentimental novels featuring officers of the Armée d'Afrique. City dwellers and those in provincial towns visited by traveling players cheered dramatic

---

7. These examples are from *canards* printed by Antoine Chassaignon of Paris, in BNEst Qb1 (1830–1848). See also BNEst, coll. De Vinck, vol. 102, "Nouvelles d'Afrique." On the practices of *canard* sellers, see Jean-Pierre Séguin and Julie-Emilie Adès, *Les canards illustrés du 19e siècle: Fascination du fait divers* (Paris, 1982), 4–5.

reenactments of Algerian battles in local theaters and fairground stages. Members of bourgeois literary *cercles* and singing societies; working-class patrons of cabarets, *goguettes*, and *ginguettes*; the audiences of urban street musicians; and artisans and peasants who bought peddlers' songbooks for their *veillées* could hear and join in the performance of poems and songs celebrating the Armée d'Afrique. Bourgeois Salon-goers crowded around Algerian battle paintings hung at the Louvre each year, while booksellers, print shops, street criers, and *colporteurs* across France offered images of the war for all budgets, from artists' lithographs to illustrated newspapers, copperplate engravings, and woodblock prints. The conquest could be consumed even more intimately by both men and women in the form of everyday objects and household decorations, such as calendars, liquor labels, plates, or wallpaper, adorned with Algerian scenes; personal items and clothing, from handkerchiefs, pipes, and fans bearing Algerian scenes to elegant ladies' "Algerian coats" and morning cloaks inspired by the Arab *burnous*; and comestibles, including oranges, Barbary figs, couscous, and patent medicines bearing names like "Eau d'Afrique." The market for Algerian-themed goods extended even to children, for whom *imagiers* produced board games, kites, and the first *petits soldats*, cut-out paper dolls of both French and Algerian soldiers.

This vast array of Algerian-themed goods had three critical features. First, they were commercial. As such, their makers sought to appeal to the perceived demands of French consumers, while identifying profitable new themes and creating new tastes. The proliferation of such goods should not be taken as a straightforward reflection of public opinion, but these commercial media can reasonably be considered more attuned to the preferences of contemporary audiences than official celebrations. Second, largely as a result of their commercial character, there was considerable exchange and repetition across these media. Just as bulletins from the Armée d'Afrique were reproduced by the publishers of newspapers, *canards*, and almanacs, as well as carefully consulted by battle painters like Horace Vernet, so too compositions and themes introduced by elite painters and lithographers were appropriated by dramatists, writers, and the producers of the nascent illustrated press, *imagerie populaire*, and other Algerian-themed objects. Finally, these were largely the same media and genres that served as the primary vectors of the Napoleonic legend after 1815. Operating clandestinely during the Restoration and openly after 1830, entrepreneurs following a combination of ideological and economic imperatives deluged France with items celebrating the Emperor and his military glories. When the Algerian war began, these preexisting forms were adapted to represent the Armée d'Afrique's battles. As Théophile Gautier observed of military plays set in Algeria, they differed little from those depicting the Napoleonic Wars: "it's always the same dialogue of gunshots, the same racket, the same smoke. Only the losers, instead of being Prussians or Kinserlicks [Austrian soldiers], are Bedouins."[8]

The commercialism, intertextuality, and Bonapartist associations of the media that brought the Algerian conquest to French audiences were interrelated, and together they gave the popular culture of conquest wide social and geographical reach. Commercial success depended largely on entrepreneurs' ability to respond quickly to current events, making reproduction and reuse common. Conventions were further solidified by the caution of producers who often preferred to imitate proven models rather than to create untested new ones. The far-flung distribution networks through which texts, images, and objects circulated spread generic conformity as well, since provincial publishers and manufacturers frequently copied items created in Paris or other major cities.[9] The public served by these networks grew significantly in the early nineteenth century as a result of changes in printing technologies, which lowered the price of printed works, and literacy rates boosted by the Guizot Law, which introduced free public primary education in 1833. These technological and sociological shifts produced a visual, oral, and, increasingly, textual "popular culture that encompassed a social continuum ranging from the privileged class of landlords and urban capitalists to the petty bourgeoisie and upper crust of the laboring class," and had further echoes among even the lowest ranks of French society.[10]

The fact that the Emperor had proved one of the most reliably popular— and profitable—themes in postrevolutionary culture made Napoleonic motifs especially attractive to the cultural entrepreneurs of the July Monarchy. During the Restoration, when representations of Napoleon were legally prohibited, images, objects, and texts celebrating the Emperor had nonetheless been clandestine bestsellers. Imperial emblems, especially tricolor cockades and flags, coins

8. "Feuilleton de la Presse," *La Presse*, 27 April 1840.
9. These circuits of emulation and imitation are best known for print imagery. See Stephen Bann, *Parallel Lines: Printmakers, Painters, and Photographers in Nineteenth-Century France* (New Haven, 2001); J.-M. Garnier, *Histoire de l'imagerie populaire et des cartes à jouer à Chartres . . .* (Chartres, 1869), 283–84; Pierre-Louis Duchârtre and René Saulnier, *L'imagerie parisienne: L'imagerie de la rue Saint-Jacques* (Paris, 1944), 7–8; François Blaudez, "L'histoire de l'imagerie d'Épinal,"in *Épinal et imagerie populaire*, ed. Jean Mistler et al. (Paris, 1961), 104–6, 115; René Perrout, *Trésors de l'image d'Épinal* (1910–12; Paris, 1985), 116–19; Jean-Pierre Séguin, *Antoine Chassaignon: Imprimeur, libraire et canardier parisien, 1810–1854* (Paris, 1955), 120; Séguin and Adès, *Les canards*, 5–7; *Images de Metz, 1835–1892* (Saint-Julien-lès-Metz, 1999), 14; Dominique Lerch, "Recherches sur les mentalités au XIXe siècle, l'apport de l'imagerie populaire provinciale: L'imagerie Wentzel de Wissembourg" (thèse de 3e cycle, Université de Strasbourg, 1978), 1:85.
10. Petra ten-Doesschate Chu and Gabriel Weisberg, introduction to *The Popularization of Images: Visual Culture under the July Monarchy*, ed. Petra ten-Doesschate Chu and Gabriel Weisberg (Princeton, 1994), 4. See also Maurice Agulhon, "Le problème de la culture populaire en France autour de 1848," *Romantisme* 9 (1975): 50–64.

and medals, engravings and song lyrics, and a dizzying variety of busts and other bric-a-brac depicting Napoleon, his armies, and his family circulated by the hundreds of thousands in a flourishing black market. Napoleon's death in 1821 did nothing to dampen demand for such goods among French consumers, many of whom refused to believe that he was truly dead. The sudden lifting of the ban on Bonapartist symbols in 1830 prompted a renewed outpouring of goods devoted to the Emperor's life and career. In addition to the plays that invaded French stages in the first year of the July Monarchy, the cultural marketplace was flooded with now-licit imagery, literature, and collectibles commemorating the Napoleonic years. Louis-Philippe's embrace of the Bonapartist legacy, especially in monumental projects like the Arc de Triomphe and the Musée historique de Versailles, only gave official sanction to this thriving trade.[11] Given their well-tested commercial success, it is little surprise that many producers turned to the forms of popular Bonapartism to represent the Algerian conquest and made the Napoleonic precedent a central point of reference for the nineteenth-century war.

The adoption of Bonapartist forms to represent the Algerian war had important political ramifications. The market for Napoleonic goods in postrevolutionary France had as much to do with the political messages they carried as with the aesthetic tastes of French consumers. The political aspirations expressed in popular Bonapartism were diverse and inchoate—popular Bonapartism must be carefully distinguished from the "Imperialism" that sought to restore the Empire—but they were clearly oppositional. Generally speaking, after 1815, the Emperor paradoxically came to represent the revolutionary principles of liberty, equality, and fraternity. The legend of Napoleon, Sudhir Hazareesingh writes, "blended the 1789 ideal of individual self-realization with the inclusive and rallying nationalist language of 1792, when the Republic defended French sovereignty against foreign invasion. More menacingly, it also drew on the imagery of the 1793 Terror, which focused on the elimination of the 'enemies of the people.'" In the "language of liberation" that defined the Bonapartist cult, Napoleon became "the proud symbol of the humble man's stubborn resistance against social and economic exploitation," and political oppression and exclusion.[12] The vibrant traffic in Napoleonic wares not only spread these ideals, but also constituted a

11. On the trade in Napoleonic objects, see Jean Lucas Dubreton, *Le culte de Napoléon* (Paris, 1960); Bernard Ménager, *Les Napoléon du peuple* (Paris, 1988); Barbara Day-Hickman, *Napoleonic Art: Nationalism and the Spirit of Rebellion in France (1815–1848)* (Newark, Del., 1999); Sudhir Hazareesingh, *The Legend of Napoleon* (London, 2004), chap. 3.
12. "Memory and Political Imagination: The Legend of Napoleon Revisited," *French History* 18, no. 4 (2004): 469–70. See also Robert S. Alexander, *Bonapartism and the Revolutionary Tradition in France: The* Fédérés *of 1815* (Cambridge, 1991), chap. 3.

form of "unofficial" political practice that challenged the legitimacy of the constitutional monarchies.[13]

Restoration officials saw popular Bonapartism as a serious threat and worked
assiduously to prevent the circulation of "seditious" Napoleonic objects, images, and practices. Its status was less certain under the July Monarchy. In many
respects, the Orleanist regime was itself a creature of popular Bonapartism.
The crowd that helped bring Louis-Philippe to power in 1830 was "in a word,
Bonapartist." The men on the barricades during the July Days fought in the name
of a distinctly Bonapartist form of economic and political liberty, brandished the
tricolor flag, and raised cries of "Long Live Napoleon I" and "Long Live Napoleon
II!" alongside those of "Long Live the Charter!", "Long Live Liberty!", and "Long
Live the Nation!"[14] After 1830, as we have seen, Louis-Philippe incorporated
Bonapartist themes into the Orleanist symbolic order. As his efforts at national
reconciliation faltered and the new model of citizen-kingship began to lose its
legitimacy, however, Napoleonic references once again became a political threat,
aided by the Imperialist pretender, Louis-Napoleon Bonaparte, who twice attempted, however feebly, to seize power during the July Monarchy.

Nowhere was the renewed radical potential of the Napoleonic legend more
evident than in discourses about war and the army. A deeply militaristic nationalism was the predominant feature of popular Bonapartism, although this remains, ironically, the feature of postrevolutionary political culture least carefully
analyzed by historians. Nostalgia for the military glory of the Empire represented
more than simple chauvinism, although chauvinism itself carried significant political valences in this period. To celebrate the Napoleonic armies as the apogee
of national grandeur and harmony was implicitly to criticize the pacifism of the
July Monarchy and to challenge the limited conception of citizenship enshrined
in the Charter of 1830. We have seen how opponents of the monarchy espoused
aggressive militarism and attacked the military valor of the Orléans men to challenge their right to rule. Such criticism resonated with many Frenchmen. Riots
broke out following the government's refusal to intervene in Belgium and Poland
in 1830, and Louis-Philippe's capitulation to Great Britain in the Eastern Crisis
of 1840, when France and Britain came to the brink of war over Egypt's struggle
for independence from the Ottoman Empire, provoked both strikes and an assassination attempt against the king. In both cases, the protesting crowds invoked
Napoleon as the man who would have adopted a policy of action rather than

13. Sheryl Kroen, *Politics and Theater: The Crisis of Legitimacy in Restoration France, 1815–1830*
(Berkeley, 2000), chap. 4.
14. Edward Leon Newman, "What the Crowd Wanted in the Revolution of 1830," in *1830 in France*,
ed. John Merriman (New York, 1975), 19, 28–29, quote 30.

passivity.[15] These sentiments were widely shared within the army itself, where vaguely Bonapartist and often-radical republican sympathies predominated.[16] Indeed, the Orléans princes' military service was partly intended to ensure the loyalty of these men to the royal family.

Equally insidious for the monarchy was the egalitarian vision of citizenship inherent in Bonapartist militarism. The Napoleon beloved by the people of post-revolutionary France was not the Emperor in his opulent regalia, but the military leader clad in simple grey coat and bicorne hat. The "Little Corporal," according to popular mythology, lived and fought alongside his men, sharing their privations and triumphs in the service of liberty, national unity, and the defense of the *patrie*.[17] This affectionate vision required a convenient forgetting of the aggressive nature of Napoleonic warfare, as well as of the resentment of conscription that had boiled over into widespread draft evasion during the Empire. These erasures, however, allowed postrevolutionary popular culture to represent the Napoleonic armies as the epitome of a democratic form of citizenship that stood in stark contrast to the restricted political rights of the July Monarchy. As Michael Marrinan points out, Louis-Philippe tried to neutralize the political threat posed by the image of the Little Corporal by "institutionalizing it within the closely cropped historical frame of past military glory" in the Musée historique de Versailles and other Napoleonic monuments.[18] But at a time when military service was the only civic duty (besides taxation) that was shared, at least in theory, by all adult French men, the political symbolism of Napoleon's citizen-armies had a broad appeal that could not be successfully co-opted by the Orleanist regime.

The army of nineteenth-century France was governed by the revolutionary ideal of the nation in arms, which established a fundamental equivalence between citizenship and conscription, and by the Napoleonic principle of "careers open to talent."[19] Under the Gouvion-Saint-Cyr Law of 1818 and the Soult Law of 1832, every French male was required to enter the recruitment lottery at age twenty and, if chosen, to serve for a period of seven years. Conscription law

15. Michael Marrinan, *Painting Politics for Louis-Philippe: Art and Legitimacy in Orleanist France, 1830–1848* (New Haven, 1988), 147–48; H. A. C. Collingham with Robert S. Alexander, *The July Monarchy: A Political History of France, 1830–1848* (London, 1988), 234–35.
16. Collingham, *July Monarchy*, 241–43; William Serman, *Les officiers français dans la nation* (Paris, 1980), 45–63.
17. Marrinan, *Painting Politics*, 148–50, 158; Day-Hickman, *Napoleonic Art*, chap. 5; Sudhir Hazareesingh, "Memory, Legend and Politics: Napoleonic Patriotism in the Restoration Era," *European Journal of Political Theory* 5, no. 1 (2006): 71–84.
18. Marrinan, *Painting Politics*, 160.
19. Annie Crépin, *La conscription en débat, ou le triple apprentissage de la nation, de la citoyenneté, de la république (1798–1889)* (Arras, 1998); Paddy Griffith, *Military Thought in the French Army, 1815–1851* (Manchester, 1989), esp. chap. 1.

was less egalitarian in practice—the purchase of replacements was allowed, and those who could afford to pay for a substitute usually did so—but the basic principle of *recrutement* was, in the words of deputy Destutt de Tracy, "that every Frenchman . . . is a soldier and a soldier-citizen."[20] While the prospect of drawing a "bad" lottery number hung heavy over many French youths during the July Monarchy, especially after the Soult Law doubled the size of conscription classes, the military also provided young men from the lower strata of society an unparalleled avenue for social advancement. The nineteenth-century army retained the Napoleonic tradition of meritocratic promotion, and the Soult Law allowed any soldier to advance to the rank of marshal, regardless of birth, estate, or education. Few of modest origins reached the very highest levels of command, but men promoted from the ranks made up nearly two-thirds of the July Monarchy's officer corps, where they benefited from wage guarantees, job security, and pensions unavailable to peasants or workers in any other profession.[21] The Orleanist regime itself endorsed the ideals of the citizen-army. Indeed, the monarchy sought to reinforce the political significance of military service by reviving the revolutionary tradition of celebrating the departure of new conscripts with elaborate public ceremonies and civic banquets.[22] But in doing so, it also reinforced the idea, central to the Napoleonic legend, that conscripted citizen-soldiers were the true representatives of the national will and the staunchest defenders of national liberty.

It was this principle of contemporary popular Bonapartism that underpinned representations of the Algerian conquest in French popular culture. To the few outspoken anti-imperialists in postrevolutionary France, the "vaudeville patriotism" of popular Bonapartism endangered the nation's interests by sapping its resources and revived the international "hatreds" stirred up by Napoleon's warmongering.[23] Amédée Desjobert, the Norman deputy who was the most vocal

20. Speech to the Chamber of Deputies, quoted in Crépin, *La conscription*, 76. A quarter of French soldiers were substitutes during the July Monarchy, and companies selling insurance to pay a replacement flourished despite efforts to abolish them. See Raoul Girardet, *La société militaire dans la France contemporaine, 1815–1939* (Paris, 1953), 22; Douglas Porch, "The French Army Law of 1832," *Historical Journal* 14, no. 4 (1971): 758; Crépin, *La conscription*, 71, 84–88, 178–79; Nuria Sales de Bohigas, "Some Opinions on Exemption from Military Service in Nineteenth-Century Europe," *Comparative Studies in Society and History* 10, no. 3 (1968): 286–87.
21. David Hopkin, *Soldier and Peasant in French Popular Culture, 1766–1870* (Woodbridge, UK, and Rochester, N.Y., 2003), esp. 146–50, 174–85; Jean Delmas, "Les militaires et leur place dans la nation," in *Histoire militaire de la France*, vol. 2, *De 1715 à 1871*, ed. Jean Delmas (Paris, 1992), 446–52; Griffith, *Military Thought*, 15–20; Serman, *Les officiers*.
22. Crépin, *La conscription*, 130–31.
23. Henri Boyer-Fonfrède, "Un mot sur la colonisation d'Alger," *Mémorial bordelais*, 12 December 1835, quoted in Marwan Buheiry, "Anti-Colonial Sentiment in France during the July Monarchy: The Algerian Case" (Ph.D. diss., Princeton University, 1973), 148.

parliamentary opponent of the conquest, repeatedly castigated the hypocrisy of
elite colonialists who could afford replacements for their own sons but enthusiastically sent the sons of others to die in North Africa.[24] But to the creators and
consumers of popular culture, celebration of the Armée d'Afrique was a statement of democratic principles. Framing the colonial force as a reincarnation of
the Napoleonic armies appealed to and perpetuated the idea that conscripted
soldiers were full citizens, despite their disenfranchisement under the censitary
monarchy, and that they, not the ruling royal family, embodied the legitimate
sovereign power in France.

Grognards and *Conscrits*: The Armée d'Afrique as Napoleonic Revival

Links between the Armée d'Afrique and the Napoleonic armies were established
from the very first days of the conquest, when liberals seeking to reclaim the Algiers
expedition from the Bourbon monarchy lauded the men of the Armée d'Afrique
not, as ultraroyalists did, as the descendants of Louis IX, but as "the worthy successors of the soldiers of Marengo, the Pyramids, and Austerlitz."[25] Whereas legitimists applauded the fall of Algiers as evidence of divine sanction for Charles X
and the Bourbon cause, opposition journalists and publicists asked, "Are not the
victors of Algiers the children of the veterans of Marengo and Austerlitz? Is it
not our blood that flows in their veins? Is it not France that triumphs?"[26] As the
possibility of a third Bourbon restoration faded away in the 1830s, references to
the past became less partisan, and authors began to highlight a more generalized
conception of the army as a national institution that transcended regime change.
Thus a legitimist chaplain writing in 1840 recalled the expeditionary force of 1830
as unifying multiple generations of French fighting men: "There were old warriors, standing upright on the ruins of the Empire, like pillars around which our
young soldiers clustered, avid for danger and for glory, happy to prove to their
predecessors that they were worthy of marching in their footsteps."[27] An 1847 history of the French armies similarly described the Armée d'Afrique in terms that
drew the Bourbon, republican, Imperial, and Orleanist armies into a single national tradition: "One sees in these African feats the moral bond that unites the old

24. Amédée Desjobert, *L'Algérie en 1846* (Paris, 1846), 106–8; Buheiry, "Anti-Colonial Sentiment,"
183–84.
25. Aristide-Michel Perrot, *La conquête d'Alger, ou relation de la Campagne d'Afrique . . .* (Paris,
1830), 2.
26. *Le Constitutionnel*, 11 July 1830.
27. Abbé M. Dopigez, *Souvenirs de l'Algérie et de la France méridionale* (Douai, 1840), 27.

monarchical army to our current army. The same blood that flowed in the veins of the soldiers of Bouvines, Agnadello, and Wagram flows still in that of the soldiers of Constantine and Sidi-Brahim."[28] References to the royal armies of the Old Regime were relatively rare, however, and it was the armies of the Revolution and, above all, the Empire that served as the primary point of reference for authors praising the Armée d'Afrique. The conscripts who sang an early song entitled "Le Bataillon d'Afrique" referred to themselves as "a living memory / Of the veteran of the Republic,"[29] but the Napoleonic armies were the most common referent for celebratory writing which hailed the Armée d'Afrique as the heir of the Imperial legacy and proof that modern French men were "worthy" of their forefathers.

Throughout the July Monarchy, representations of the conquest in popular culture insisted that the glory and patriotic devotion of the Grande Armée, betrayed at Waterloo and made bereft by Napoleon's death on St. Helena, could be revived in Algeria. A few writers even transposed to the Algerian theater messianic rumors of Napoleon's return from the dead, suggesting, however figuratively, that the Algerian war could bring the Emperor back to lead a new generation of French soldiers to glory. In one poem celebrating the capture of 'Abd al-Qadir's capital Mascara in 1835, for instance, the spirit of France (la génie de la France) appears over the battlefield in the form of Napoleon to inspire the French troops to victory.[30] Others presented the Algerian war as a kind of incantation for the resurrection of the Emperor, who could now "rise up" and return to lead France with the help of the Armée d'Afrique:

> Here, on the African shore
> Find the men you need, immortal Captain,
> Your Frenchmen of yesteryear! . . .[31]

Most important, however, was the example of patriotic masculinity that Napoleon's loyal troops set for new generations of French men. The revival of French military glory was a matter not merely of winning more battles, but of forging nineteenth-century men in the Napoleonic mold. New victories,

28. Adrien Pascal, *Histoire de l'armée et de tous les régiments depuis les premiers temps de la monarchie française jusqu'à nos jours* . . . (Paris, 1847), 3.
29. Charles Gille, "Le Bataillon d'Afrique" (c. 1835), in *Que la France était belle au temps des colonies* . . . *Anthologie de chansons coloniales et exotiques françaises*, ed. Alain Ruscio (Paris, 2001), 49.
30. Th. Corbet, *Mascara: Les Français en Afrique. Poème en huit Chants, suivi d'un Aperçu sur le Koran* (Lyon, 1837).
31. Vicomte Henri de Callias, "Les héros de Mazagran" (15 March 1840), in *Néoprytanée Central, société du progrès, Pièces dites par les auteurs* . . . *surtout à sa grande solennité littéraire et musicale du Dimanche, 31 mai 1840* (Paris, 1840), 2.

Bonapartist authors insisted, could only be achieved if the soldiers of the modern army recognized and worked consciously to emulate their forefathers-in-arms. To earn renewed glory, the men of the July Monarchy had to *prove* themselves worthy of their predecessors. Thus a popular song of 1846 called explicitly upon new conscripts to follow the example of the *grognards*, the ragged but devoted veterans of the Grande Armée who, according to a famous contemporary lithograph, "grumbled, and followed him [Napoleon] always"[32]:

> *Conscripts who brave the fates,*
> *On Algerian fields,*
> *Imitate the grognards in all things:*
> *Serve the patrie well.*
> *Be French and . . .*
> . . . .
> *March always forward,*
> *Like an old soldier of the old [army]!*[33]

Many officers shared this view of Algeria as "a military gymnasium" for young soldiers, who could be trained and battle-hardened in North Africa without threat to the continental balance of power.[34] An 1840 military history of France written for noncommissioned officers to read to new recruits insisted that what the men should know about the Algerian War was that it had "singularly enlarged the circle of military knowledge, taught [us] to triumph over any obstacle the terrain may offer, accustomed our young soldiers to all kinds of fatigues, kindled and matured in them the military spirit, opened a field of experience to new officers, and produced a nursery of generals worthy of replacing the illustrious men who are passing away."[35] Military enthusiasm was not what it had been under the Empire, some officers argued, but the discipline, regimental fraternity, and "true patriotism" of the Napoleonic armies could be revived in Algeria. The guerilla tactics of colonial warfare increased Algeria's value as a training ground for modern wars in which tactical mobility, and thus discipline and fitness, were expected to be more important than sheer numbers or heavy armaments.[36]

32. Auguste Raffet, *Ils grognaient, et le suivaient toujours* (Paris, 1836).
33. Justin Cabassol, "Le vieux de la vieille," in *La chanson au XIXe siècle: Recueil de chansons populaires et contemporaines . . .*, vol. 1 (Paris, 1846), 8.
34. Eugène Lerminier, "De la conservation d'Alger," *Revue des deux mondes*, 4th ser., 6 (1 June 1836): 607.
35. Théodore Touchard, *Histoire pittoresque et militaire des Français, racontée par un Caporal à son Escouade*, vol. 2 (Paris, 1840) 669–70.
36. L. de V*** [Thomas-Robert Bugeaud], *La Guerre d'Afrique: Lettre d'un lieutenant de l'Armée d'Afrique, a son oncle, vieux soldat de la Révolution et de l'Empire* (Paris, 1838), 8.

To ambitious junior officers, Algeria offered a unique arena for professional advancement. Under the regulations governing promotion during the July Monarchy, each year of active campaigning in Algeria was counted twice in calculating seniority, and battlefield citations could further hasten ascent through the ranks. Career-minded young officers thus sought out Algerian postings.[37] Although we have no aggregate data on the officer corps of the Armée d'Afrique, careerist attitudes are evident in the writings of many individual "Africain" officers. Charles Julien de Bourguignon, a young lieutenant from Aix, was appalled by conditions in Algeria, but wrote to his family that "if I wish to remain here for a while, it is because I believe advancement must be more rapid [than in France]."[38] The future hero of the siege of Paris, Colonel Denfert-Rochereau, likewise wrote upon entering the army's engineering academy in 1845, "What is most clear now that I am a soldier is that I must make every effort to advance. Thus I intend to go to Africa once I leave the Academy and to remain there until the age of 30. I think that the great variety of work [and] the country's difficulty are things that must count for officers and procure for them occasions for advancement."[39]

Denfert-Rochereau would not get to Algeria until 1860, but others who made careers in Algeria during the July Monarchy shared his view. For example, Lucien-François de Montagnac, a graduate of Saint-Cyr who served in Algeria from 1837 until he was killed in 1845, believed "that my whole military future depends on these few years of campaigning."[40] His letters home celebrated each engagement with the enemy as an opportunity for decoration and assessed each new posting in terms of its potential for advancement. Positive developments were reported immediately as "another step forward" on his career path. These hopes were well rewarded: Montagnac left for Algeria as an infantry captain and, through savvy politicking and aggressive pursuit of front-line duties, had been promoted to lieutenant colonel by the time of his death. He had reached the rank of colonel in only twenty-four years, compared with an average of thirty years for his peers. Younger men who entered the service after the invasion of Algiers could advance even more rapidly: an officer leaving Saint-Cyr in 1830 who served exclusively in Algeria could become a colonel in twenty years or fewer.[41]

37. Charles-André Julien, *Histoire de l'Algérie contemporaine*, vol. 1, *La conquête et les débuts de la colonisation (1827–1871)* (Paris, 1964), 273, 303–4.
38. Letter c. 1836, excerpted in Marie-Claire Grassi, "La conquête de l'Algérie: Lettres inédites (1837–1849)," *Les Carnets de l'Exotisme* 14 (1994): 107.
39. Letter to his uncle, 16 January 1845, no. 203a, in Aristide Denfert-Rochereau, *Lettres d'un officier républicain (1842–1871)*, ed. William Serman (Vincennes, 1990), 40.
40. Letter to Bernard de Montagnac, 8 January 1837, in Lucien de Montagnac, *Lettres d'un soldat: Algérie, 1837–1845* (Vernon, 1998), 17.
41. E.g. letters to Bernard de Montagnac, 24 July 1838 and 22 March 1841, in Montagnac, *Lettres*, 39 and 85. On promotion rates, see Girardet, *La société militaire*, 51; Delmas, "Les militaires," 454.

While the meritocratic values embraced by young officers were reflected in popular representations of the Armée d'Afrique, contemporary literature and imagery suggested that there was more to be gained in Algeria than battlefield honors or promotions. For new conscripts, in particular, it was manhood itself that was to be won on North African battlefields. This was the lesson of military vaudevilles in which the young conscript heroes demonstrate their worth and enter into the company of French men by following the example of Imperial veterans. As a genre, military vaudeville had been defined by its celebration of the Napoleonic armies, and the relationship between young conscripts and the veterans of the Empire became a central theme of plays set in Algeria. Some playwrights linked the "Oriental" Algerian setting with Napoleon's 1798 invasion of Egypt by pairing the young conscript character with a veteran of the Egyptian campaign, as the Cogniard brothers did in *La cocarde tricolore*.[42] But exoticism was less important than patriotism in making Napoleonic veterans a model for nineteenth-century French men.

A vaudeville produced in Metz in 1845, for example, set its celebration of the virilizing powers of the conquest in the context of an exchange between the young conscript Rataplan and Lavaleur, an elderly Imperial veteran who now keeps a café in Nancy. On his return from Algeria, Rataplan recounts his experience to the retired sergeant and explains that he had been inspired in battle by the old man's patriotic example: "I thought of you and your campaigns, father Lavaleur. Of old, veteran soldiers covered themselves in glory. The young army can do as much, and our descendants will do the same. There is nothing miraculous about it, it is enough to be French." To drive home the point, Rataplan then repeats it in song:

> And in our ranks, every young warrior
> Often praises the immortal laurels
> Of the veterans who made our glory.
> But each, too jealous of this noble heritage,
> Owes it to your memory
> To show, like you, true courage,
> And to his country prove that he can die.[43]

42. See also *Sous Constantine: À-propos-vaudeville en un acte, mêlé de couplets, par MM. E. Delmerlière et Duflot. Représenté pour la première fois à Lyon, sur le théâtre du Gymnase, le 8 novembre 1837* ... (Lyon, 1837).

43. J. B. Lombard, *Rataplan, ou le petit tambour, vaudeville en un acte, représenté pour la première fois le 4 novembre 1827, modifié depuis la guerre d'Afrique* (Metz, 1845), 7.

Rataplan's own bravery under fire earns him not only the cross of the Legion of Honor and Lavaleur's respect, but also the love of the veteran's daughter and her hand in marriage. Lavaleur had rejected other, wealthier suitors, but Rataplan's conduct in Algeria shows that he possesses the qualities of "a true husband," "a soldier husband" who has shared the dangers and travails of his fellows.[44] By demonstrating that he, like Lavaleur and his comrades, is willing to die for his country, Rataplan has shown himself to be a "real" French man, capable of reproducing the Napoleonic nation both militarily and sexually.

Implicit in songs and plays like these was the assumption that the Napoleonic decades marked the zenith of French national unity and glory, and that the Imperial armies represented the standard of patriotic and masculine virtue against which men of the July Monarchy were to be measured. To many, however, Louis-Philippe's cautious diplomacy and laissez-faire domestic policies made it difficult, if not impossible to meet this standard. Critics of the monarchy believed that pacifism was a product of its ties to the bourgeoisie, whose interests in expanding trade and manufacturing would be threatened by war. The cowardice of the "bourgeois monarchy" thus went hand in hand with its greed and corruption. These criticisms underpinned widespread anxieties about the impact of the long European peace on French virility. If battle hardened men and taught them the values of fraternity and patriotic sacrifice, the comforts of peacetime encouraged selfishness and sloth. In this context, the conquest of Algeria offered French men a unique opportunity to demonstrate their patriotism and virility, just as it offered the Orléans princes a chance to show their merits as royal citizen-soldiers.

Frustration with the monarchy's foreign policy was evident in plays, songs, poems, and other works that lauded the Algerian war as an opportunity for action in an age of diminished patriotic possibilities. "It is [in Algeria] that one must seek the few examples of the patriotism that is daily dying out in the *mère-patrie*," wrote a republican journalist from Dijon in an article that perfectly captured the sentiments implicit in Bonapartist celebrations of the conquest.[45] A poem written in 1840 offers an unusually explicit example of this view. "'It's over,' they said,—'Oh France! that family of giants/has faded'" since the fall of Napoleon, but the exploits of the Armée d'Afrique give the lie to the pessimism of France's domestic and foreign critics. The Algerian conquest shows that

---

44. Ibid., 5.
45. *Le Proletaire de Poitiers* (5 March 1847), quoted in Philippe Darriulat, *Les patriotes: La gauche républicaine et la nation, 1830–1870* (Paris, 2001), 72.

> *Forever inexhaustible in her fecundity*
> *France, on its day of anger,*
> *Has only to strike the soil with her menacing foot*
> *To raise up a people of soldiers . . .*
> *If the fathers are dead, the sons are not!*
> *Let the Trumpet sound . . . —at the hour of carnage*
> *You will see them, rivals of paternal courage,*
> *March with the same step to vanquish or to die . . .*[46]

"These are indeed France's sons!" another song from the same year declared. Thanks to their "manly courage," "the foreigner sees that from age to age / The Frenchman knows how to vanquish or die."[47] As the anticolonialist Henri Boyer-Fronfrède bitterly noted, the "bellicose rhymes of vaudeville" and its literary cousins—"*gloire et victoire* (glory and victory), *laurier et guerrier* (laurels and warriors), *succès et français* (success and French)—were a universal dithyramb against cowardice" during the July Monarchy.[48]

Equally important, the conquest offered an antidote to the moral and physical degeneration perceived to threaten the men of an increasingly urban, commercial society. This was the message of one sentimental novel, whose young hero rejects a lucrative career as a merchant to volunteer for the Armée d'Afrique. Although unafraid of hard work, Oscar's refined character meant that "his tastes did not incline him to embrace the commercial career" of the kindly but weak merchant who had offered him a position. He chooses the army instead, the narrator explains, because of his conviction "that he would be more worthy of the love of [his beloved] Aline when he had received the baptism by fire that opened to heroes the glorious career in which he burned to distinguish himself."[49] The moral of Oscar's tale, which ends with his marriage and retirement to France, seemed to apply collectively to the nation as well. By reviving the warrior ethos of the Republic and Empire, a wide range of texts argued, the Armée d'Afrique renewed the vitality of an entire nation corrupted by the bourgeois materialism that drove the July Monarchy's pacifist policy. Victories in Algeria "proved that our soldiers had not degenerated and that the brave men of the Republic and the Empire had worthy successors."[50]

46. Th. Wains-des-Fontaines, "Mazagran: Fragment d'un poème couronné par l'Association-Lionnaise, le 18 juin 1840," *Affiches, annonces judiciaires, avis divers du Mans, et du département de la Sarthe*, 28 August 1840. Manuscript copy, dated 28 March 1840, in CAOM 1E 87.
47. "Chant de Mazagran: Air de l'Attaque du Convoi," in *Les héros de Mazagran: Relation de la sublime défense de 123 Français contre 12,000 Arabes* (Lyon, 1840), 4.
48. Quoted in Buheiry, "Anti-Colonial Sentiment," 150.
49. Émile La Martinière, *Les Amours dans le désert, ou les aventures d'un officier de l'armée française en Afrique* (Paris, 1846), 16–17, 6.
50. F. Caze, *Notice sur Alger* (Paris, 1831), 23.

For, despite the slumber of corruption
That bastardizes the great nation,
Despite that selfish, terrible bird of prey
That holds us 'neath its talon and gnaws our guts,
From time to time, still, in our venal heart
We feel the ferment of national pride,

. . . .

In reading the immortal bulletin
We returned to the distant past
With all our mind, and we could believe
That, disinherited children of former glory,
We could someday soar again
And under sacred fire grow young again.[51]

The war in North Africa thus appeared to many to offer a field on which the Bonapartist virtues of military glory, patriotic service, and individual self-realization could be reclaimed, when the pacifism, materialism, and increasing authoritarianism of Louis-Philippe's constitutional monarchy denied French men the opportunity to fully express themselves as men and citizens. For all of the analogies drawn between the Armée d'Afrique and the Napoleonic armies in the popular culture of the July Monarchy, however, important differences did emerge in the ways that the two forces were represented. The soldiers of the Empire were a powerful symbol of patriotic masculinity, but the Napoleonic cult was still focused around the Emperor himself and, to a lesser extent, his most trusted lieutenants. By contrast, popular representations of the Algerian war rarely took the Armée d'Afrique's highest-ranking general officers as their subject. Instead, they focused on its junior officers and rank-and-file soldiers. In this regard, popular culture reflected the preferences expressed by critics of the Algerian galleries at the Musée historique de Versailles, who saw the ordinary French soldier as the true hero of the Algerian conquest. This critical shift in the conventions of popular Bonapartism can be seen in the case of the two French expeditions against Constantine in 1836 and 1837.

---

51. L., "Mazagran," *Le Courrier de la Côte-d'Or* (4 April 1840), reprinted in Pierre-Jacques Derainne, "L'idée coloniale en France au XIXe siècle: Le regard de la presse dijonnaise sur la conquête de l'Algérie (1830–1848)" (mémoire de maîtrise, Université de Bourgogne, 1986), 94. I thank the author for sharing this work with me.

From Moscow to Constantine

In the first years of the conquest, Ahmad Bey of Constantine was one of the most dogged opponents of French expansion, refusing any submission to the invaders' authority as "contrary to our faith and our religion" and insisting on the legitimacy of Ottoman sovereignty over the regency of Algiers.[52] The French government, still uncertain about its long-term plans for Algeria, was reluctant to extend its occupation into the eastern province and refused to provide the commander of the Armée d'Afrique, General Clauzel, with reinforcements for an expedition against Ahmad's capital. Despite the lack of government support, Clauzel decided to attack Constantine in November of 1836. Undertaken with great fanfare, the expedition was a disaster. Drastically insufficient forces, poor intelligence, and terrible winter weather in the mountainous terrain turned the expected "military promenade" into a catastrophe.[53] Slowed by snow, sleet, and freezing rain, and running out of food after losing its supply convoy in muddy mountain passes, the French column retreated after a token attempt to enter the city. As Clauzel's initial reports informed the government, with significant understatement, "the Constantine expedition has not been a total success." Of the eighty-seven hundred men who had marched out from Bône on 8 November, only four thousand returned a month later, although only a handful were killed by enemy fire. The rest, weakened by hunger, perished of disease, cold, and drowning in mountain streams so swollen that they had to be swum rather than forded.[54] The journal kept by the duc de Nemours, who accompanied the expedition, describes in gruesome detail the state of the retreating column, which abandoned the sick and wounded, and left the road behind it "literally strewn with white corpses."[55] The debacle provoked public outrage, and attacks from the opposition pushed the government to publicly disavow the expedition. The ministry placed full responsibility for the disaster on the shoulders of Clauzel, who was immediately recalled from the governor-generalship.[56]

Despite its humiliating outcome, Clauzel's expedition was the first Algerian battle since 1830 to capture the French imagination, which found in the wintry catastrophe resounding echoes of Napoleon's failed 1812 invasion of Russia.

52. *Les mémoires d'Ahmed, dernier bey de Constantine* (Paris, 1949), quoted in Julien, *La conquête*, 95.
53. Charles de Rémusat, quoted in Julien, *La conquête*, 133. On the expedition, see Camille Rousset, *L'Algérie de 1830 à 1840: Les commencements d'une conquête*, vol. 2 (Paris, 1887), 105–75.
54. Dépêche télégraphique to ministre de la Guerre, in *Moniteur universel*, 13 December 1836; "Rapport sur l'expédition de Constantine," 1 December 1836, in *Moniteur universel*, 16 December 1836.
55. AN 300 AP III 102, "Journal du Duc de Nemours, Constantine, 1836," entry for 24 November.
56. *La Charte de 1830*, in *Moniteur universel*, 18 December 1836.

Clauzel himself provided the language for subsequent discussions of the failed expedition as a new retreat from Moscow. Although he had not taken part in the Russian campaign himself, his report on Constantine proclaimed that the "unprecedented sufferings" of the soldiers at the hands of weather and topography recalled "all the rigors of a Saint Petersburg winter, at the same time that the totally rutted fields represented, for veteran officers, the mud of Warsaw."[57] The Russian analogy was taken up by many other writers, who described Clauzel's retreat from Constantine as "a kind of retreat from Moscow transported to Africa" and lamented that "Constantine has become a new Moscow for us."[58] Although hardly triumphant, comparisons between Constantine and Moscow reinforced the idea that the Armée d'Afrique was a worthy heir to Napoleon's Grande Armée. As one writer claimed, the sons of the soldiers of Moscow had also struggled against the elements in their painful retreat and emerged, as their fathers had done, battered but undefeated.[59]

This emphasis on the shared sufferings of French soldiers against the Russian and North African winters was given graphic form in the few images devoted to the 1836 expedition. Most notably, Auguste Raffet, the master lithographer best known for his Napoleonic imagery, took the failed expedition as his first major Algerian subject in an album of six lithographs published in February 1837.[60] The best-known of these, *The Second Light Under Changarnier Covering the Retreat from Constantine*, depicted one of the few glorious moments of the expedition, in which Commandant Changarnier and his light infantry regiment defended the ambulance wagons that trailed behind Clauzel's retreating column (fig. 30). Although Raffet's lithographs sold for one franc and had an essentially bourgeois clientele, the Metz firm of Dembour copied *The Second Light* in a woodblock broadsheet that was sold to a much broader audience by peddlers and print merchants for only one sou. Raffet had not witnessed the event—although he made many images of the Algerian war, he never went to North Africa—so he based his portrayal of the retreat on reports from participants, his own knowledge of military tactics which was drawn primarily from the Napoleonic Wars, and his imagination. The resulting image combines well-known details from contemporary narratives of the retreat with compositional elements from his own earlier Napoleonic works.

57. Clauzel, "Rapport sur l'expédition."
58. "Nouveau désastre en Algérie," *La Mode*, 25 January 1846; CAOM F80 1162; Poirel, *De la colonisation militaire, agricole et pénale d'Alger* (Nancy, 1837), 46.
59. Dopigez, *Souvenirs*, 365.
60. Gabriel Esquer, *Iconographie historique de l'Algérie depuis le XVIe siècle jusqu'à 1871*, vol. 1 (Paris, 1929), xviii–xix; Dominique Bernasconi, "L'image de l'Algérie dans l'iconographie française (1830–1871)" (mémoire de maîtrise, Institut d'Études Politiques–Paris, 1970), 18.

FIGURE 30. Denis-Auguste-Marie Raffet, *The Second Light under Changarnier Covering the Retreat from Constantine*, Carmer frères (Paris), 1837. Author's collection.

From accounts of the Constantine disaster Raffet took, in particular, reports of the mutilation of French bodies by Ahmad's forces. The focal point of the image is the severed head of a French soldier brandished on the point of an Algerian horseman's sword; several more heads, taken from the corpses visible in the foreground, can be seen dangling from the hands and saddles of Algerian cavalrymen. These details leave the viewer with no doubt as to the intended fate of the French wounded crowded into the ambulance wagon in the lower left corner of the image, and they explain the urgency of the defense being mounted by Changarnier and his men. Not surprisingly, these sensational, bloody details were the elements incorporated most directly into Dembour's copy (fig. 31). Raffet's composition, however, was drawn from a lithograph he had made two years earlier of the retreat of Napoleon's *bataillon sacré* at Waterloo (fig. 32). The contrast in *The Second Light* between orderly French formations and the indistinct cloud of Algerian cavalry reflects a classic representational strategy of Orientalist battle imagery, but the central defensive square around a second ambulance also mirrors this earlier depiction of the last desperate moments of the Empire. In this, Raffet drew symbolic analogies between the Second Light and the *bataillon sacré*, a unit of the Imperial Guard composed solely of officers that protected the Emperor personally, as well as between those they protected: the wounded of the Armée d'Afrique and Napoleon himself. The dead horses lying in the snow in the foreground of *The Second Light* offer a further echo not only with the *Retreat of the Bataillon Sacré*, whose middle ground is strewn with

FIGURE 31. *Constantine Expedition: Heroic Feat of Commandant Changarnier*, Dembour (Metz), 1837. Réunion des Musées Nationaux/Art Resource, NY.

dead horses, but also with familiar images of the retreat from Moscow by Raffet and others.

Raffet's Constantine lithographs elicited from viewers a combination of admiration and empathy that reinforced calls from French policymakers to avenge the humiliating failure of the expedition. Parliamentary demands for an inquiry into the causes of the disaster were matched by a royal proclamation of sympathy for the army's "painful losses" and admiration for the "valor, perseverance, and admirable resignation" with which they "upheld the honor of our flag." Louis-Philippe concluded his throne speech of 1837 with a call for the Chambers to spare the Armée d'Afrique further suffering by providing the resources for a second attack on Ahmad's capital.[61] The parliament acquiesced, and a second expedition was planned for the fall of 1837. Its success allowed the king to open the following year's legislative session with the announcement that "The French flag floats over the walls of Constantine."[62]

The second Constantine expedition gave rise to a veritable outpouring of popular works, which cemented the Armée d'Afrique's place in the French collective imagination. According to a petition addressed to the Chamber of Deputies by a Parisian shawl merchant on behalf of the men wounded in the expedition, "the African war and above all the glorious capture of Constantine have revived

61. "Discours du Roi," 27 December 1836, *PVD* (1837) 1:v.
62. "Discours du Roi," 18 December 1837, *PVD* (1838) 1:v.

FIGURE 32. Denis-Auguste-Marie Raffet, *Retreat of the Bataillon Sacré at Waterloo, 18 June 1815*, lith. Gihaut frères (Paris), 1835. Bibliothèque nationale de France, Département des Estampes et de la photographie.

all the memories of our old glory [and] rejuvenated all the traditions of national heroism."[63] The authors of a Lyonnais vaudeville reenacting the siege had one character declare that the victory provided decisive evidence that "the Gallic cock, our emblem/Of the eagle is the worthy heir."[64]

The fall of Constantine not only inspired the first Algerian gallery at Versailles, but it also marked the full entry of the Algerian conquest into the popular culture of the July Monarchy. To take popular imagery as an index, printers, who had produced a handful of images of the failed siege of 1836, made the second Constantine expedition the single most celebrated battle of the July Monarchy. In the six months following Ahmad's defeat, government censors registered no less than forty prints representing the victory by publishers from Paris, Lyon, Dijon, Marseille, Bordeaux, and centers of *imagerie populaire* in eastern France. These popular images offer an ideal source for examining more closely the ways that the Algerian war was incorporated into, but also challenged the representational conventions of popular Bonapartism. In particular, the cheap, colorful woodblock

63. AN C2157, no. 129, Fichel, "Demande que des pensions soient accordés aux blessés de Constantine," n.d. [February 1838].
64. Delmerlière and Duflot, *Sous Constantine*, 20–21.

prints known as *images d'Épinal* were one of the key vectors for the Napoleonic legend and, beginning in 1837, took on a similar role in shaping popular conceptions of the Algerian conquest.

Imagerie d'Épinal took its name from the Pellerin printing house in the town of Épinal (Vosges), but there were a number of printers in eastern France competing for the sous of provincial and rural consumers. Pellerin, Dembour and Gangel of Metz, Deckherr Frères of Montbéliard, and Wentzel of Wissembourg all designed their products for the most modest consumers and distributed them through sophisticated, nationwide networks of itinerant peddlers (*colporteurs*). Whereas even the most popular of the Parisian printmakers concentrated in the rue Saint-Jacques charged a franc or more for framed copperplate engravings to decorate urban households, peddlers sold the poster-sized *images d'Épinal* for one sou to be pasted directly onto the walls, armoire doors, or chest lids of cottages and ateliers in the farthest reaches of the French countryside.[65] Although we do not know how many of them were Algerian battle scenes, *images d'Épinal* were nearly ubiquitous in nineteenth-century France. As a Metzian journalist observed in 1837, "however poor he might be, the peasant, the artisan, the simple laborer buys images. Workshops, market stalls, cottages are plastered with them." This made *images d'Épinal* one of the most effective means of communication in nineteenth-century France, and they served both as a powerful means both to transmit ideas about Algeria and "to sow ideas of war and of conquest among the people" across the country.[66]

As historians of popular imagery have long recognized, the eastern *imagiers* were intimately associated with the construction and dissemination of the Napoleonic legend. Although religious images, especially portraits of saints, made up the vast majority of their business, the medium was defined by Bonapartist imagery, especially the Pellerin company's masterpiece, a series of illustrated broadsheets commemorating the glorious victories and key defeats of Napoleon's career. Produced by master printmaker François Georgin under the direction of Nicolas Pellerin's son-in-law and partner, Germain Vadet, the fifty-nine prints in the series traced Napoleon's rise and fall from the siege of Toulon in 1793 to his death in 1821. Printed and sold by the hundreds of thousands, these images gave

65. On the production, distribution, and consumption of *imagerie populaire*, see the works cited in note 9 above, as well as Dominique Lerch, *Imagerie populaire en Alsace et dans l'Est de la France* (Nancy, 1992); Nicole Garnier with Marie Christine Bourjol-Couteron and Maxime Préaud, *L'imagerie populaire française*, 2 vols. (Paris, 1990–96); Daniel Bernard, *Coureux et gens d'étrange en Berry: Essai sur l'itinérance dans une région du Centre de la France* (Paris, 1984); Gérald Guéry, ed., *Les colporteurs de Chamagne: Étude d'après leurs passeports, 1824–1861* (Chamagne, 1990), 29–30.
66. François Blanc, "Rapport sur les images de M. Dembour," *Mémoires de l'Académie royale de Metz* (1837–38), in *Images de Metz*, 71, 90.

the Napoleonic legend a visual and material form that was accessible to even the poorest, most remote of French consumers.[67]

The Pellerin series was meant to provide a visual documentary of the Napoleonic campaigns for semiliterate and provincial audiences, or, in the words of one early commentator, to "introduce all to the most remarkable episodes in our military history."[68] It also functioned, as Barbara Day-Hickman argues, as an implicitly oppositional political statement. Pellerin and Vadet, the latter himself an Imperial veteran, were both involved in local republican organizations, and the artist Georgin was a passionate follower of the cult of Napoleon thanks to a veteran uncle. The images that these men produced reflected their political leanings, as well as Pellerin's astute business sense. Populist and millenarian in tone, they depicted Napoleon as a paternal figure, father to his troops, friend of the common man, and harbinger of a more egalitarian political system. As a "graphic enactment" of Napoleon's messianic resurrection, the Épinal prints became a key element in the popular political culture that connected France's spiritual and political renewal with the return of the Emperor.[69] They also provided the visual context, as well as the business model, for Pellerin and the other *imagiers* as they began to produce images of the key battles in the war for domination in Algeria.

The example of the fall of Constantine shows the simultaneously informative and celebratory nature of popular imagery, as well as the way in which Pellerin and his artists began to modify the conventions of Napoleonic imagery to represent the new colonial war. As descriptive documents, the Algerian prints follow the strict formulae laid out in earlier military imagery, including Georgin's Napoleonic series. The brightly colored image depicting a key moment of the battle occupies most of the surface; a caption running down the left and right margins, across the bottom, or around all three sides fills the remaining space. The captions are composed of the same elements as those of the Imperial battle prints: a statement of the day's glory, a staccato chronicle of the battle, and an estimate of the casualties sustained by the enemy. We can compare, for example, the captions from Pellerin's *Battle of Wagram*, created by Georgin in 1835, and the same company's *Fall of Constantine*, published in January of 1838 (figs. 33 and 34). Both captions follow the standard conventions, down to the

67. On *imagerie d'Épinal* and Bonapartism, see, among others, Perrout, *Trésors*, 131–34, 151–59; Jean Mistler et al., *Épinal et imagerie populaire* (Paris, 1961), 113–20; François Roth, "Nation, armée et politique à travers les images d'Épinal," *Annales de l'Est*, 5th ser., 32, no. 3 (1980): 199; François Lotz, *Images profanes des Wentzel et de leurs successeurs au XIXe siècle* (Pfaffenhoffen, 1997), 4; Day-Hickman, *Napoleonic Art*.
68. Sabourin de Nanton, *Épinal et l'imagerie dans les Vosges* (Strasbourg, 1868), 9.
69. Day-Hickman, *Napoleonic Art*, 19.

dashes used to separate the phases of the narrative, which inform the reader when the action took place and outline the two sides' principal tactical moves. Both highlight the bravery of the French troops in the face of sensational dangers, such as the "hail of shot and bullets" that Drouot's artillery withstood at Wagram, or the "awful mêlée" and "terrible explosion" that met the brave men of Lamoricière's Seventeenth Light on the breach at Constantine. The Austrians lost forty thousand men at Wagram, while six thousand Arabs were "massacred" at Constantine. Finally, each caption explains the strategic significance of the battle. Wagram was "decisive" in the French recovery from the earlier defeat at Aspern-Essling, while "France's domination [found] itself solidly established in Africa" after the fall of Constantine.

Despite their structural similarities, there are subtle, but important differences between the two prints. In *Battle of Wagram*, both image and text reserve agency for Napoleon. The battle, the print implies, is the work of the Emperor and his general staff, who visually dominate the scene. Napoleon's pointing finger suggests that what we see is the moment in which he orders that support be sent to the left flank. Beyond a few dead and wounded men sprawled in the immediate foreground, however, lower-ranking officers and ordinary soldiers appear only in faceless ranks ranged across the plain in the distance. *Constantine*, by contrast, devotes much greater attention to the actions of individual soldiers and officers. Here, the central command group of *Wagram* is reduced to the passive figures of General Damrémont, who lies dying in the foreground, and his chief of staff, General Perregaux, falling beside him after a fatal shot to the head. Lieutenant-General Valée, who assumed command after Damrémont was killed, is nearly indistinguishable among the staff officers crowded up against the right margin in the middle ground. The duc de Nemours, reported by the caption to have command of the vanguard, is simply invisible. Instead, the action in this print rests with the ordinary soldiers grouped across the paper: in the lower left, infantrymen prepare for the final assault; an artillery unit at the center generates clouds of smoke as it pounds the city walls; a team carries a wounded comrade out of the line of fire in the right foreground; on the horizon, another artillery unit and a pair of cavalrymen rush about their business. Only a tiny fragment of the rigid ranks of infantry remains on the far right of the image, and even they have individual faces, unlike their Napoleonic counterparts.

Constantine's caption reflects a similar shift in emphasis. It recounts the strategic preparations of Damrémont and Perregaux, as well as their deaths, but the majority of the text is focused on the men who did most of the actual fighting. Lower-ranking officers, including several colonels, two captains, and a commander, are mentioned by name, and the anonymous soldiers of the rank and

FIGURE 33. Jean-Baptiste Thiébault, engr. after François Georgin, *Battle of Wagram*, Pellerin (Épinal), 1835. Bibliothèque nationale de France, Département des Estampes et de la photographie.

file engage in distinct, identifiable tasks. Rather than presenting a battle of large movements, as at Wagram, the narrative of the siege of Constantine includes the detailed actions of ordinary soldiers, who are described "reloading" in preparation for the final assault, rushing forward on their colonel's command, and "advanc[ing] foot by foot and house by house" through the streets of Constantine in "two hours of butchery by bayonet and knife."

These contrasts do not sever the ties inherent in the depiction of the Algerian battle in a medium that had become so closely associated with the Napoleonic Wars. The visual distinctions between the two images were likely due in part to the personal styles of their respective artists; the faceless ranks of infantrymen are characteristic of François Georgin's work and appear less often in that of the unknown artist responsible for most of Pellerin's Algerian images, including the *Fall of Constantine*.[70] The song that accompanied the latter encouraged viewers to link the Armée d'Afrique with its Napoleonic predecessors, describing the soldiers at Constantine in now-familiar terms as "children of the soldiers of the Loire," marching under "the old flag from Marengo." Like so many contemporary authors, the anonymous songwriter concluded by urging France's European rivals to recognize the renewed grandeur of the nation.

70. See examples of Georgin's work in Garnier et al., *Imagerie populaire*, 2:200–20. The only known artist of Pellerin's Algerian battles is Charles Pinot, who designed *La prise de Mascara* (1836) and *La soumission d'Abd-el-Kader* (1848).

FIGURE 34. *Fall of Constantine*, Pellerin (Épinal), 1837. Réunion des Musées Nationaux/Art Resource, NY.

But taken together, the differences in visual and textual description of the siege of Constantine amount to a significant shift in the understanding of war as an enactment of sovereignty and citizenship. Whereas Napoleonic imagery tended to view soldiers as the anonymous instruments of the Emperor's strategic genius, a conception given visual expression in Georgin's stiff rows of faceless men, representations of the Algerian war privileged the heroic deeds of individual soldiers within a larger strategic context. In this regard, images like Pellerin's *Fall of Constantine* hewed closer to the political values of popular Bonapartism, which cast combat as the expression of an active male citizenship denied to most French men under the July Monarchy. At the same time, the shift of attention to ordinary soldiers and officers laid the groundwork for reconciling serious discrepancies that began to emerge between the ideals of popular Bonapartism and the brutal realities of colonial warfare in North Africa. In the final verse of the song from Pellerin's *Constantine*, the author calls on the French nation to raise a monument to the Armée d'Afrique that would complement the Colonne de Vendôme, the "urbanite column" commemorating Napoleon's victory at Austerlitz. Two years later, this appeal was answered, and a public effort begun to build a Napoleonic-style monument to the heroes of the Algerian war. The fate of this project reveals the challenges that the war posed to easy equations between the Armée d'Afrique and the citizen-soldiers of the Napoleonic army.

The Mazagran Monument and the
Limits of the Napoleonic Model

Public enthusiasm for the Algerian conquest subsided during the period of relative calm that followed the capture of Constantine. In 1840, however, the threat of war with Britain over the Eastern Question ratcheted nationalist fervor to heights unprecedented for the July Monarchy. In the absence of action in Europe, a minor incident in Algeria became the focus of pent-up patriotic energies. In February of 1840, at the moment that the Soult government was being handed a vote of no confidence for its mishandling of the Eastern Crisis, the garrison of a small redoubt outside of the Oranais town of Mostaganem was besieged by forces under the command of 'Abd al-Qadir. The story, as it was quickly standardized in the French press, went as follows: from 2 to 6 February, 123 soldiers of the Tenth Company of the First Battalion of the Fifteenth Light Infantry, under the orders of Captain Lelièvre, were assailed in the redoubt of Mazagran. Despite the numerical odds, they held off four assaults from ten or twelve thousand Arab infantrymen for four days before a sortie from the main garrison at Mostaganem drove off the attackers and rescued the men.

News of the siege reached France a few weeks later, and the public, frustrated by French impotence in the Middle East, seized upon the story of victory against overwhelming odds by a handful of ordinary soldiers. A flood of imagery—*images d'Épinal, liqueurs* (decorative liquor labels) (fig. 35), and fine lithographs—prose, verse, and song, and at least six plays appeared celebrating the "heroes" of Mazagran. "Nothing else was talked of for many weeks," an English magazine reported; "a huge mimic Mazagran was got up in the Champs Elysées; it was stamped upon paper-hangings, pocket-handkerchiefs, painted upon the scenes of theaters, engraved in every variety of style; and Mazagran pantaloons, hats, gloves, shawls, &c, became instantly and universally the vogue."[71] The king immediately promoted Lelièvre and the other officers of the Tenth Company and, with great fanfare, awarded the cross of the Legion of Honor to all of its 123 members. Later that spring, the "heroes of Mazagran" were "given the full pyrotechnic treatment" in the fireworks display that capped the Fête du Roi at the Tuileries.[72] No fewer than three bronze medals were struck to commemorate the event, and several cities offered Lelièvre a sword of honor in recognition of

71. "The War in Algeria," *Chambers's Repository of Instructive and Amusing Tracts* 3, no. 18 (Philadelphia and London 1854), 25.
72. Alfred-Auguste Cuvillier-Fleury to his wife, 3 May, 1840, in *Journal et correspondance intimes de Cuvillier-Fleury*, vol. 2, *La famille d'Orléans aux Tuileries et en exile, 1832–1851*, ed. Ernest Bertin (Paris, 1903), 190.

FIGURE 35. Label for liquor bottles showing the defense of Mazagran, 1840. Bibliothèque nationale de France, Département des Estampes et de la photographie.

a feat that seemed to conform perfectly to Bonapartist ideals of the heroic rank and file.[73]

The triumphalist narrative presented in these works quickly achieved mythical status and was repeated with minor variations in a variety of media. Lelièvre showed selfless leadership and the defenders boundless patriotic devotion in vowing to use their last munitions to blow up themselves and their post rather than allow their bullet-riddled flag to fall into enemy hands. When ammunition ran low, they beat off the attackers by hand with bayonets and stones. Despite being so enormously outnumbered, "the 123" still escaped alive after inflicting over five hundred casualties on the enemy and putting their Arab besiegers to flight. Hailed as "models of valor" in the classical tradition,[74] the defenders of Mazagran were cited in song and verse as living proof that the warrior ethos of the Napoleonic era lived on in contemporary French men. So powerful was their devotion said to be that several cultural entrepreneurs presented Mazagran as the final seal on the developing colonial ties between France and Algeria. Several prints, like one engraving from 1841, literally carved "the 123" into the foundations of an Algeria "forever French" (fig. 36), while poems and songs celebrated

73. On the celebrations, see Julien, *La conquête*, 258; Charles Dejob, "La défense de Mazagran dans la littérature et les arts du dessin," *Revue d'Histoire Littéraire de la France* 19 (1912): 318–40.
74. "Victoire de Mazagran," in Louis Boutet, *Chansonnier nouveau pour 1840* . . . (Paris, 1840), 6. The ribald epigram on the cover of this songbook suggests that it was intended for one of the bourgeois singing societies that combined music with epicurean entertainments. The same volume contained three other songs on the theme: "Mazagran," "Le pas de charge des Français sur les Arabes," and J.-E. Aubray, "Défense de Mazagran." For other examples, see *Les héros de Mazagran*; Jules Ladimir, *Mazagran, ode au Capitaine Lelièvre et à ses soldats. Précédée d'une Notice historique* (Paris, 1840).

Mazagran as the cement that bound France and Algeria together into "a single *patrie*."[75]

Almost immediately, the idea was put forward to erect a national monument commemorating the defense of Mazagran. The city and garrison of Algiers opened a subscription to raise such a monument, and the Orleanist press took up the initiative, volunteering to collect funds from metropolitan donors. The government gave its approval for the project, and a commission led by Marshal Gérard, a distinguished veteran of the Napoleonic Wars, was appointed to select a design and a site for the memorial. After two years of planning, the commission proposed a grand column that would stand at the foot of the Champs-Elysées as a pendant to the great Napoleonic monuments of the capital. From this central location, the column would enjoy axial views of two iconic Napoleonic monuments, the Arc de Triomphe and the Hôtel des Invalides. The design selected by the commission further reinforced the connection to the Napoleonic armies by imitating that of the Colonne de Vendôme. Just as the Vendôme monument was made from cannons captured at Austerlitz in 1805, the Colonne de Mazagran would be made of marble columns salvaged from Roman ruins in Algeria and bronze from guns taken at Algiers in 1830. Constructed in a "Moorish style," it would bring the symbols of French colonial domination to the heart of Paris and give material form to the analogies drawn between the Algerian and Napoleonic armies in popular culture.[76]

By the time the Gérard commission completed its deliberations, however, it had become evident that the monument could not be built as planned. Despite the earlier public fervor over "the 123," the subscription had raised only forty-one thousand francs, far less than the amount necessary to carry out the elaborate plans.[77] Faced with this shortfall, the commission suggested that the scale of the monument be reduced. Instead of a grand column on one of the central points of the capital, a smaller, more affordable column, stone, or pillar could be erected in some other location.[78]

75. J.-E. Aubry, "Le Joyeux Villageois," in Boutet, *Chansonnier*, 10.
76. CAOM 1E 187, Cubières to Gérard, 10 April 1840; Gérard to Soult, 4 May 1842. I have been unable to locate any visual record of the design. The only architectural plans in the archives are for a column on Algiers's Place du Gouvernement. CAOM 1E 187, Architecte de la ville [d'Alger], "Projet d'une colonne triomphale à élever sur la place du Gouvernement à Alger," 1 October 1840.
77. CAOM 1E 187, Gérard to Soult, 4 May 1842. On the subscription's organization and the identity of the subscribers, see CAOM 1E 187, doss. 3, "Souscriptions (1840–1841)." Most of the first donations came from members of the Paris National Guard, likely on orders from their officers. Lists of subscribers printed in *La Presse* and *Le Constitutionnel* show that politicians, bankers, noblemen, military officers, and a few magistrates, notaries, legal clerks, and schoolboys accounted for most of the money raised. Dejob, "Défense," 327.
78. CAOM 1E 187, Gérard to Soult, 10 June 1842.

FIGURE 36. Charles de Mamotte, *Algeria Forever French*, lith. Kaeppelin (Paris), 1840. Bibliothèque nationale de France, Département des Estampes et de la photographie. "123 against 10,000" is carved on the rock in the lower left of the image.

Given the acclaim that greeted the defense of Mazagran in February of 1840, why did the subscription fall so short? If thousands of French citizens were willing to open their pockets for images, songs, or plays celebrating Captain Lelièvre and the men of the Tenth Company, why did so few contribute to the monument fund? One possible interpretation is that popular enthusiasm for the Algerian war was essentially superficial and could not sustain the costs of a massive project like the Mazagran Column. The enduring popularity of the conquest in contemporary culture suggests that this view would underestimate Algeria's significance in postrevolutionary France. An early historian of Mazagran's commemoration points out that leftist journals actively opposed the subscription, claiming that the monument was just one more piece of Orleanist propaganda and that good republicans should reserve their donations for the relief of poverty.[79] The deliberations of the Gérard commission, however, point to another explanation, which acknowledges the political importance of the Algerian conquest and emphasizes the ways that the conduct of the war itself challenged the cultural frameworks through which contemporary Frenchmen understood it. By 1842, when the monument commission was forced to abandon its plans for a monument on a grand, Napoleonic scale, questions had begun to arise about the commensurability with Bonapartist ideals of both the heroes of Mazagran and the conflict in which they were involved. The answers to these questions, brought to public attention by the monument-building process, caused the collapse of the commemorative project.

The first concerns raised within the Gérard commission itself had to do with the long-term import of the defense of Mazagran. The redoubt itself had little strategic value; it was only a small outpost of the nearby fortified town of Mostaganem. Moreover, the struggle with 'Abd al-Qadir had actually escalated since February 1840. Two years later, it was evident that the 123's feat of self-preservation had had only minimal impact on the emir's fighting capacities. Gérard reported that his colleagues were also worried that commemorating a single engagement of questionable importance would be an injustice to the Armée d'Afrique, which deserved the nation's recognition as a whole.[80] The Council of Ministers, to which the commission submitted its plans and concerns, shared the commissioners' doubts and ultimately decided to reject even the scaled-down proposal: "however glorious the defense of Mazagran, the importance of this feat of arms cannot be considered great enough to justify the necessarily considerable costs."[81] There should be therefore "no monument of any kind." Instead, the most appropriate course, and "a great enough honor," would be to inscribe the

79. Dejob, "Défense," 324, 326–27.
80. CAOM 1E 187, Gérard to Soult, 4 May 1842.
81. CAOM 1E 187, Soult to ministre des Travaux Publics, 20 June 1842.

name "Mazagran" on the Arc de Triomphe, and then use the forty-one thousand francs raised to pay the pensions or family benefits owed to those wounded or killed in the battle.[82]

The Gérard commission's questions about Mazagran's impact on the course of the war reflected broader strategic changes taking place in Algeria in 1840. With the fall of Constantine, France had gained control of the country's major towns and cities, and the war with 'Abd al-Qadir had come to resemble the unconventional conflicts that European strategists called *la petite guerre* (small war) rather than a "big war" between regular armies.[83] Having used the ceasefire instituted in 1837 under the Treaty of Tafna to consolidate his power in western Algeria, the emir resumed hostilities in 1839 with a new, offensive strategy and guerrilla-style tactics designed to disrupt French communications, cut off supplies, and terrify enemy soldiers and colonists with constant attacks.[84] The rapid success of this strategy forced the French to escalate their troop levels and to adopt new counterguerrilla tactics of their own. The growing number and operational importance to the Armée d'Afrique of light infantry units like that to which the Mazagran garrison belonged is indicative of this shift. Although more sustained than many engagements that followed, the siege of Mazagran was nonetheless indicative of the cumulative, rather than decisive battles that were becoming the norm in North Africa. The many minor engagements of this "small war" did not fit with the Napoleonic tradition that reserved grand memorials for great, decisive victories that turned the tide of war. The defense of Mazagran could not be treated like the battle of Austerlitz.

Even the ministerial decision to reduce the monument to an inscription on the Arc de Triomphe raised objections, however. The head of the War Ministry's Algerian bureau responded to this new proposal by pointing out that the Arc de Triomphe was specifically dedicated to the victories and conquests of the Revolution and Empire, and that Mazagran fell outside those parameters. Poetic analogies notwithstanding, the Armée d'Afrique was not the army of the Republic or Napoleon, and therefore did not belong on a monument to their victories. Furthermore, he continued, if one were to open the Arc de Triomphe to more recent feats of arms, there were other "military memories" in the history of France since 1815 more deserving of commemoration.[85] Gérard, president of the monu-

<hr/>

82. CAOM 1E 187, Fellmann, "Note pour le Ministre" and marginal response, 17 June 1842.
83. On nineteenth-century theories of "small war," see Walter Laqueur, *Guerrilla Warfare: A Historical and Critical Analysis* (1976; New Brunswick, N.J., 1998), chap. 3.
84. Raphael Danziger, *Abd al-Qadir and the Algerians: Resistance to the French and Internal Consolidation* (New York, 1977), 224; Bruno Étienne, *Abdelkader: Isthme des isthmes (Barzakh al-barazikh)* (Paris, 2003), 183–87.
85. CAOM 1E 187, Fellmann, "Note pour le Ministre," 17 June 1842.

ment commission, also protested the council's suggestion that the subscription money be used for something other than its original purpose. Doing so, he argued, would require the subscribers' permission and obtaining that permission might require uncomfortable explanations on several counts, including the weak public support for the monument fund, the questionable significance of Mazagran's outcome, even the very existence of the events of February 1840. "The publicity given to these explanations could have unfortunate consequences," he wrote.[86]

The "unfortunate consequences" became evident a few months later, when London's *Morning Chronicle* proclaimed that the defense of Mazagran had been a hoax, and asked if there had been any progress on the monument or if Lelièvre still enjoyed the honors that had been lavished upon him two years before.[87] In December of 1842, the opposition journal *Le National* printed a short summary of the *Morning Chronicle*'s allegations and demanded a denial or an explanation from the Ministry of War: "If we have been fooled by imposters, we must not allow ourselves to become complicit in such an unworthy distortion, but if on the other hand the English paper is slandering the soldiers of Mazagran, we must immediately condemn it."[88] Although few in France believed the claim that the whole affair had been a hoax, some observers did note that the French garrison had sustained few casualties, suggesting that their heroism had at least been exaggerated.[89] The parliamentary opposition began to pressure the government to do something with the subscription money and to answer the questions that had been raised about the siege.[90]

If government officials were well aware of the secondary importance of the Mazagran redoubt in strategic terms, they were equally conscious that there was an uncomfortable degree of truth behind the *Morning Chronicle*'s allegations. The Ministry of War responded to the new pressure by sponsoring the publication of an eyewitness account by the chief engineer at Mostaganem that reiterated the standardized, heroic narrative of the siege.[91] The Ministry could not, how-

---

86. CAOM 1E 187, Gérard to Soult, 25 June 1842.
87. *Morning Chronicle* (London), 25 November 1842.
88. CAOM 1E 187, extract from *Le National* of 4 December 1842, Soult to chef de la division des Affaires d'Algérie, "Extrait de la feuille d'analyse des Journaux, soumise au Ministre le 4 décembre 1842."
89. Eugène Pellissier de Reynaud, *Annales algériennes*, new ed., vol. 2 (Paris, 1854), 429. The French reported three killed and sixteen wounded and estimated Algerian losses at five or six hundred dead. *Moniteur universel*, 2 March 1840.
90. CAOM 1E 187, chef du 1er Bureau, "Note pour le Ministre," 18 May 1843. Complaints about the monument's slow progress had begun to arise within several months of the event. E.g. Auguste Barthélemy, *La colonne de Mazagran* (Paris, 1840).
91. [Joseph-Auguste] Abinal, *Relation de l'attaque et de la défense de Mostaganem et de Mazagran au mois de février 1840* (Paris, 1843).

ever, entirely deny the aspersions cast on its heroes, as the *Morning Chronicle* was well aware when it published the original article as a riposte to French criticism of the British army's conduct in Afghanistan. Not only had there been little progress on the Mazagran monument, but Lelièvre and his subordinates in the Tenth Company had also turned out to be far from models of patriotic dedication and virtue.

Captain Lelièvre himself was a known drunkard, whose annual inspections consistently characterized him as an ignorant, incompetent, and undisciplined officer, prone to gambling, debt, and "much frivolity" in his private affairs.[92] Neither his conduct nor his standing with his superiors was improved by the events of 1840. During an inspection tour the following year, General d'Hautpoul was appalled to find the celebrated captain "an object of scandal," having "giv[en] himself over to all possible excesses" and pawned his epaulets and Legion of Honor cross to pay his debts.[93] So serious were his personal and professional failings that he was indefinitely suspended from active duty in October of 1841 on Hautpoul's recommendation. The comportment of Lelièvre's men largely mirrored that of their captain. The *bataillon d'Afrique* to which the Tenth Company belonged would later become one of the iconic units of the French colonial army, but the so-called *bat' d'Af* was originally created in the 1830s as a disciplinary unit to which soldiers and officers were assigned as punishment for misconduct elsewhere. The Mazagran garrison had a particularly sordid reputation, even for the *bataillon d'Afrique*, and was known both within the army and publicly for its card games, smoking, and drinking, rather than for its sober attention to duty.[94] Indeed, the "heroic" defenders were transferred away from Mazagran shortly after the siege because of their violent mistreatment of the local population. The Tenth Company, military authorities discovered, had taken to attacking and robbing Algerians traveling to and from the Mostaganem market. They had killed several who resisted, and terrorized local people had responded by avoiding the market, cutting off the town's food supplies. Only when the "cutpurses" of the Tenth were replaced by a regular infantry unit were food supplies restored to Mostaganem.[95]

It was these embarrassing facts that Gérard had wished to avoid publicizing through any public inquiry into the status of the Mazagran monument. By

92. General Bernell, inspection of 1837, quoted in Robert Launay, "Mazagran (février 1840), d'après des documents inédits," *Le Correspondant* 81 (10 February 1909): 556.

93. *Mémoires du général marquis Alphonse d'Hautpoul, pair de France, 1789–1865* (Paris, 1906), 234.

94. Julien, *La conquête*, 311; Launay, "Mazagran," 554; *La nouvelle gloire française: Récits des combats et hauts faits militaires de l'Armée d'Afrique . . .* (Paris, 1840), 133.

95. François-Charles Du Barail, *Mes souvenirs*, vol. 1, *1820–1851*, 12th ed. (Paris, 1897), 96–97.

1842, however, changes in French tactics in Algeria had begun to draw attention on their own, and it was becoming clear in France that the Tenth Company was representative of much broader problems in the Armée d'Afrique, both off the battlefield and on. The alcoholism and indiscipline reproached in Lelièvre and his unit were rampant among the French forces in Algeria as a whole, and the conduct of the Armée d'Afrique overall led colonial officials to try to distance soldiers as much as possible from the colonists. Such behavior, however, was often a symptom of the horrors involved in soldiering in North Africa, as new tactics adopted in the 1840s drove men to epidemic levels of alcoholism, insubordination, even suicide in their efforts to escape the atrocious violence of the war.[96]

The success of 'Abd al-Qadir's offensive in 1839–40 had pushed the French back into a few fortified towns, and Governor General Valée had proved incapable of much more than resupplying these beleaguered garrisons. He was replaced at the end of 1840 by General Thomas-Robert Bugeaud, who instituted an antiguerrilla strategy of "total war" predicated on the idea that complete domination was the only way to guarantee French power in Algeria and that victory could only be won by terrorizing the Algerian population into submission. Abandoning the existing system of fortified outposts and large expeditionary columns, Bugeaud created light, mobile flying columns to pursue 'Abd al-Qadir's forces, to punish rebellious tribes, and to ensure the quiescence of groups that had recognized French authority. The "total war" strategy was successful, in that the emir's allies began to desert him out of fear of French reprisals, but its terrorist tactics put tremendous psychological pressure on French troops and growing political pressure on the conduct of the war. The forms of physical, social, and cultural violence institutionalized in the 1840s took a shocking toll on the local people. By the mid-1850s, war and economic disruption had reduced the Algerian population to almost half its precolonial size, from about 4 million to 2.3 million.[97] What Benjamin Brower calls the "multiple logic of violence" also shaped French responses to colonial warfare.[98]

---

96. Julien, *La conquête*, 288–89, 296–97.
97. Kamel Kateb, *Européens, "indigènes" et juifs en Algérie (1830–1962): Représentations et réalités des populations* (Paris, 2001), 16, 30.
98. Benjamin Brower, *A Desert Named Peace: The Violence of France's Empire in the Algerian Sahara, 1844–1902* (New York, 2009), 6. On Bugeaud's strategy, see also Julien, *La conquête*, 174–78, 315–23; Antony Thrall Sullivan, *Thomas-Robert Bugeaud: France and Algeria, 1784–1849. Politics, Power, and the Good Society* (Hamden, 1983), chap. 4; Thomas Rid, "Razzia: A Turning Point in Modern Strategy," *Terrorism and Political Violence* 21 (2009): 617–35; Jennifer Sessions, "'Unfortunate Necessities': Violence and Civilization in the Conquest of Algeria," in *France and Its Spaces of War: Experience, Memory, Image*, ed. Patricia Lorcin and Daniel Brewer (New York, 2009), 29–44.

The primary tactical weapon in Bugeaud's "total war" was the *razzia*, a scorched-earth raid designed to simultaneously destroy the enemy's economic resources and feed the French army. His predecessor had condemned the first French *razzias* as inexcusable "wars of savages,"[99] but "cut," "burn," "devastate," "ravage" became the orders of the day after 1841. Officers soon coined the verb *razzier* to describe the routinized activity of burning grain silos, trees, villages, and whatever crops and animals they could not carry away.[100] Regulations according the troops a portion of the booty exacerbated the *razzia*'s violence by giving soldiers further incentive to pillage.[101] The atmosphere of unrestrained violence gave rise to other horrific practices, as well, and French troops "[took] on a savagery that would make an honest bourgeois' hair stand on end," according to one officer.[102] Algerian soldiers were decapitated and their heads displayed on bayonet points, flagstaffs, saddles, and camp walls as a warning to local people.[103] Cash rewards were distributed for each pair of ears taken from the enemy, and one commander ordered that any man who brought in a living prisoner be beaten.[104] Officers' accounts rarely mention rape specifically, but scattered references to "insulted women" leave no doubt that sexual violence was part of the French repertory of terror.[105] Most horrific to French observers were the *enfumades* of the mid-1840s, in which French forces trapped hundreds of Algerian civilians inside caves and smoked them to death by setting bonfires at the cave entrances. Characterized by metropolitan legislators as an "act of premeditated murder of a defenseless enemy," the *enfumade* became the ultimate symbol of the barbaric nature of Bugeaud's war.[106]

To many military men and metropolitan observers, such atrocities were deeply at odds with the ideals of the citizen-soldier enshrined in contemporary

99. SHD 1H 62, Valée to General Guingret, 19 May 1839.
100. Colonel de Saint-Arnaud to Leroy de Saint-Arnaud, 31 October 1842, in *Lettres du maréchal de Saint-Arnaud, 1832–1854*, 2nd ed., vol. 2 (Paris, 1858), 436.
101. SHD 1H 83, Bugeaud, circular, 18 June 1843. On the regulations, see "Arrêté qui détermine les règles suivant lesquelles doit s'opérer la répartition des prises faites sur l'ennemi," 26 April 1841, in *RAGA*, 160; SHD 1H 76, Bugeaud to General Baraguay d'Hilliers, 12 May 1841.
102. Montagnac to Bernard de Montagnac, 31 March 1842, in Montagnac, *Lettres*, 118.
103. Smaïl Aouli, Ramdane Redjala, and Philippe Zoummeroff, *Abd el-Kader* (Paris, 1994), 338–39.
104. Louis Blanc, *History of Ten Years, 1830–1840*, vol. 2 (London, 1845), 482; Montagnac to Elizé de Montagnac, 15 March 1843, in Montagnac, *Lettres*, 152–53; Colonel Tartas to General Castellane, 15 November 1843, in *Campagnes d'Afrique, 1835–1848: Lettres adressées au Maréchal de Castellane . . .* (Paris, 1898), 332; Stephen d'Estry, *Histoire d'Alger, de son territoire et de ses habitants . . .* , 2nd ed. (Tours, 1843), 346; AN AP 1^A, Alfred Chanzy, "Journal, Algérie: Octobre 1845–Février 1846," entry for 18 November 1845.
105. E.g. Colonel de Mirbeck to Castellane, 24 May 1847, in *Campagnes d'Afrique*, 513.
106. Prince de la Moskowa, speech to Chamber of Peers, 11 July 1845, in *Moniteur universel*, 12 July 1845.

culture. Victor Destutt de Tracy, a persistent critic of the conquest and himself a veteran of the Napoleonic Wars, declared to the Chamber of Deputies in 1846 that he "would never have consented to enter the ranks of the army had [he] known that [he] might one day have been given duties as revolting as those being imposed on our brave African soldiers."[107] It is telling that Bugeaud himself, already hated by the left and the right for his role in repressing republican and legitimist unrest, was rarely portrayed in popular media and never appeared on French stages or in *imagerie populaire* as a modern incarnation of the Napoleonic generals who received such attentions in this period.[108] If "statues were an immediate and apparently unmediated way of communicating political values" in nineteenth-century France,[109] neither the French state nor potential contributors wished to spread these particular values by enshrining them in the Mazagran monument.

Yet the horrors of *razzia* warfare alone cannot account for the failure of the Mazagran monument to garner broad public support. Violence as such posed little problem to French audiences, who eagerly consumed cultural goods devoted to the conquest that were soaked in virtual blood. Poets and songwriters, as well as the authors of the captions of *images d'Épinal* and other popular texts, were happy to report the disproportionate casualties of French and Algerian forces in combat, and to describe the defeat of Algerian troops as an asymmetrical "massacre." *Canards* provided crude but graphic illustrations of combat in Algeria and enumerated in detail the booty seized in *razzias*, which were described in similar detail in the illustrated histories and newspapers intended for wealthier, bourgeois readers. In popular plays, including *La cocarde tricolore*, the protagonists sang cheerful songs about "beat[ing] on the Bedouin" and their shared desire to "by gunshots, kicks, or the butt of my rifle/Break ['Abd al-Qadir's] snout."[110] Spectators roared for realistic fight scenes, resulting in such fierce stage combat that the extras playing Algerian soldiers had to be paid twice as much those who portrayed French troops.[111] These and other entertainments invited French civilians to identify with the Armée d'Afrique and to participate vicariously in the violence of colonial warfare. One popular fairground attraction captured in an engraving from the 1840s, for instance, asked fairgoers to test their strength by

---

107. Speech to the Chamber of Deputies, 9 June 1846, in *La Presse*, 10 June 1846.
108. He was known on the right as "the jailer of the duchesse de Berry" and as "the butcher of the rue Transnonain" to the left.
109. William Cohen, "Symbols of Power: Statues in Nineteenth-Century Provincial France," *Comparative Studies in Society and History* 31, no. 3 (1989): 495.
110. Cogniard and Cogniard, *La cocarde tricolore*, 84; Louis Péricaud, *Le Théâtre des Funambules: Ses mimes, ses acteurs, et ses pantomimes* (Paris, 1897), 201.
111. Théophile Gautier, "Feuilleton de la Presse," *La Presse*, 27 April 1840.

hitting an effigy of 'Abd al-Qadir's head (fig. 37), striking a blow simultaneously for their own and the nation's power and virility. The *petits soldats* printed by the *imagiers* of eastern France were likewise designed to engage children in paper battles between cut-out French and Algerian armies (figs. 38 and 39). The open, even enthusiastic acknowledgement of colonial violence in popular culture suggests that, while the controversies surrounding Bugeaud's methods may have discouraged donations from the newspaper-reading middle classes, the popular rebuff of the Mazagran monument was rooted elsewhere.

Where Algerian colonial warfare came most significantly into conflict with the patriotic ideals associated with popular Bonapartism was in its aggressive character. In the popular Bonapartism of the mid-nineteenth century, patriotic war was essentially defensive. The equation of soldiering with citizenship derived from the revolutionary tradition of mass mobilization against foreign invasion, established with the volunteers of 1792 and the *levée en masse* of 1793 which demanded that French men take up arms in defense of home, family and *la patrie en danger*. After 1815, Bonapartist rituals and iconography tied military glory to the defense of liberty and national sovereignty. In this context, the claim that the Armée d'Afrique had inherited the courage and revived the glory of their Imperial predecessors signified not the renewal of Napoleon's quest for world domination, although this was its result, but revitalization of the national defense force. An early Bonapartist account of the 1830 expedition beautifully captures this paradox in concluding that by invading Algiers, modern French soldiers had shown themselves capable of defending their borders: "Let the foreign hordes dare to cross our frontiers: we can proudly say that they would find there worthy successors to the soldiers of Marengo, the Pyramids, and Austerlitz."[112] That this author illustrated French soldiers' fierce defense of their homeland with the iconic battles of Napoleon's Egyptian and European conquests only emphasizes the extent to which the Bonapartist legend had sanitized the Emperor's image, stripping his wars of their expansionist character and conflating them with the earlier defensive wars of the Republic.

Such misremembering of Imperial aggression, and the importance of defending the *patrie* in popular conceptions of Napoleonic military glory, together provide the final key to the collapse of the Mazagran project. In the context of the Eastern Crisis of 1840, when the threat of war with Britain revived memories of the foreign occupation of 1814, the defense of Mazagran had demonstrated that French men had the courage and military prowess to fight off the "foreign hordes" once again if necessary. The explosion of enthusiasm for Lelièvre and his men reflected this conviction, which was expressed most clearly in texts

112. Perrot, *La conquête*, 2.

FIGURE 37. Andrew, Best, and Leloir, "Dynamometer," in *Le Messager parisien: Almanach de l'Illustration,* 1844. Bibliothèque nationale de France, Département des Estampes et de la photographie.

that lauded them not only as the heirs of their Imperial fathers, but as "new Leonidases" at a "new Thermopylae."[113] Inexpensive prints and other consumer items continued to celebrate the heroes of Mazagran into the fall of 1840. In the two years required to plan a grand monument, however, the discrepancies between defensive ideals and the realities of the brutal war of aggression in Algeria became all too apparent.

With a monumental linkage to the Napoleonic past off the table, the Gérard commission began in the spring of 1843 to discuss ways to "dissimulate the questionable importance of the feat of arms of Mazagran" by moving the monument from Paris to Algeria.[114] An initial suggestion for a commemorative fountain in Algiers was rejected in favor of an even more discreet option, a fountain in Mostaganem bearing no identifying marks so as to avoid antagonizing the town's residents.[115] What began as a popular initiative to erect a massive triumphal column on Paris' Champs-Elysées had devolved into a governmental effort to bury memories of Mazagran in an anonymous structure in a small Algerian town that served primarily as an army resupply depot. Even the fountain plan came to naught, however, and the subscription funds were finally used a de-

113. E.g. Puységur, "En France," *Annales de la Société Académique de Nantes et du Département de la Loire-Inférieure* 12 (1841): 88; Callias, "Les héros," 3; Noël Morel, *Mazagran: Épisode lu au Théâtre du Panthéon* (Paris, 1840), 3; Wains-des-Fontaines, "Mazagran."
114. CAOM 1E 187, Gérard to ministre de la Guerre, 24 May 1843; 1er Bureau de la Division des Affaires d'Algérie, "Rapport au Ministre," 3 June 1843.
115. CAOM 1E 187, Fellmann, "Rapport fait au Ministre," 1 July 1843.

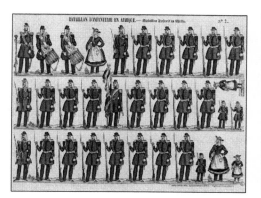 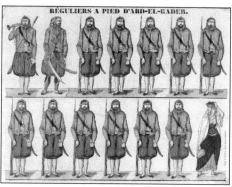

FIGURE 38. *Infantry Battalion in Africa*, Pellerin (Épinal), 1847. Réunion des Musées Nationaux/
Art Resource, NY.
FIGURE 39. *Abd-el-Kader's Regular Foot*, Pellerin (Épinal), 1846. Réunion des Musées Nationaux/
Art Resource, NY.

cade later to raise a column topped with a statue of Victory on the site of the
Mazagran redoubt.[116]

Although the column was eventually built in Algeria, the checkered history
of efforts to build a national monument to the heroes of Mazagran reveals the
challenges posed by colonial warfare to the Bonapartist ideals that shaped public perceptions of it. Three years after the siege of Mazagran, neither its strategic importance, the personal honor of its defenders, nor the glory of the war
itself were secure enough to allow a national monument on a Napoleonic scale
to go forward. To raise such a monument as a pendant to the Invalides or to
inscribe Mazagran on the Arc de Triomphe was deemed an insult to the memory of France's "true" military heroes, of whom the defenders of Mazagran were
ultimately deemed unworthy. Temporary "monuments" to Algerian events,
such as parades of victorious units, state funerals for officers killed in action,
and the public display of trophies captured from Algerian forces, appeared in
France between 1830 and 1848, but no national memorial to the war was erected
in France in the nineteenth century. The few public monuments to the Armée
d'Afrique built in this period were raised by municipalities to honor native sons
who took part in the conquest. The only metropolitan memorial to the defenders

116. *La Presse*, 23 September 1847. The archives are silent on this column, which seems to have
been built between 1851 and 1853. André Pierre Fulconis, *Louis Guillaume Fulconis, 1818–1873, stat-
uaire: Une vie d'amitié (Provence, Algérie, Normandie, Paris)* (n.p., n.d.), 207; "Chronique du mois:
Novembre et décembre 1851," *Revue de l'Orient, de l'Algérie et des colonies . . .* 10 (1851): 343; Jean
Barbier, *Itinéraire historique et descriptif de l'Algérie . . .* (Paris, 1855), 240.

of Mazagran, for instance, was erected in Lelièvre's hometown of Malesherbes in the Loiret.[117] The Musée historique de Versailles remained the most prominent national monument to the conquest until 1931, when the Maison des Colonies was built in Vincennes for the International Colonial Exposition. Otherwise, the most common and enduring commemorations of the Algerian war were streets named after North African battles, a rapid and inexpensive form of commemoration that avoided the scrutiny and fundraising entailed in major statuary monuments. The rue de Mazagran was one of half a dozen Parisian streets named for events of the war between 1830 and 1848, when the names "Algiers," "Constantine," "Mazagran," and "Isly" blossomed on the maps of many French towns and cities.

The failure of the Mazagran monument, and the absence of any other national monument to the conquest, are largely explained by the gap that emerged between the defensive ideals of Bonapartist militarism and the atrocities that were institutionalized in the Algerian war of conquest. But revelations about the defenders of Mazagran and the nature of colonial warfare did not entirely drain the political and cultural power from comparisons between the Armée d'Afrique and the Napoleonic armies. Alongside criticism of Bugeaud's unconventional tactics, there emerged in the 1840s a new emphasis on the sacrifices of the Armée d'Afrique that served to reconcile the violence of the Algerian war with the ideal of the Napoleonic citizen-soldier. While the vices of Lelièvre and his men were incompatible with Bonapartist models of patriotic manhood, such misconduct was increasingly seen as the consequence, rather than the cause, of French atrocities. From this perspective, French soldiers appeared as the victims, not the perpetrators of a strategy imposed by the high command. Bugeaud had his defenders, including Alexis de Tocqueville who claimed that practices like the *razzia* were "unfortunate necessities which cannot be escaped by any people at war with Arabs."[118] But others in both the Chambers and the Armée d'Afrique lamented their effects on French soldiers. "I have often had to shudder," the future General Canrobert wrote to a superior in the mid-1840s, "at the profound demoralization that [the *razzia*] casts into the heart of the soldier who slits throats, steals, rapes, and fights for himself under the eyes of officers often powerless to stop him."[119] Ordinary soldiers left few traces of their thoughts on the war, but officers noted their growing "repugnance" for *razzias* that could only be overcome by increas-

---

117. This monument had its own complex history, as it was destroyed and replaced twice in the following century. AD Loiret O suppl. 509 5M 5–7; *Moniteur universel*, 27 February 1842.

118. "Essay on Algeria" (1841), in Alexis de Tocqueville, *Writings on Empire and Slavery*, ed. and trans. Jennifer Pitts (Baltimore, 2001), 70.

119. Chef de bataillon Canrobert to Castellane, 18 July 1845, in *Campagnes d'Afrique*, 413.

ing their allocation of booty.[120] Troops returning to France brought with them memories and, perhaps, stories to confirm and spread elite criticism of the war.

As public criticism of the Algerian war mounted during the Bugeaud years, the hardships of soldiering in Algeria became an increasingly common theme in popular culture. The celebrated caricaturist Cham (Amédée de Noé), for instance, published a series of satires of military life in Algeria that highlighted the suffering of the men in Bugeaud's flying columns, as their superiors force-marched them through arid landscapes. With black humor, Cham depicted the poor water supplies, short rations, extreme heat and damp, disease, and fatigue that plagued soldiers pushed to their physical limits by "the hunt for Abd-el-Kader" (fig. 40). Such detail, however, was most characteristic in works intended for the newspaper-reading middle classes, who also followed political debates about conditions within the Armée d'Afrique. In genres with a broader, mass audience, the sacrifices of ordinary soldiers were represented by heroes from the lower ranks of the army.

Two figures, in particular, gained fame in the 1840s: Sergeant Blandan, who refused to surrender when his small detachment was ambushed near Boufarick in April of 1842 and continued to encourage his men despite being fatally wounded; and Bugler Escoffier, a young bugler captured by 'Abd al-Qadir in 1843 after giving his own horse to his company's captain, whose mount had been killed. Both Blandan and Escoffier earned public recognition from the army and the king, as well as popular renown for their self-sacrifice. Blandan, according to Bugeaud's widely publicized order of the day, "preferred to die rather than capitulate before a multitude of Arabs,"[121] while Escoffier was reported to have declared to his captain, "You are more useful to the squadron than I; take my horse and save yourself. It is of no consequence if I am taken."[122] While Blandan's death was commemorated with a flurry of engravings and a monument near the site of the fatal ambush,[123] Escoffier's eighteen months of captivity provided fodder for sensational *canards* and engravings, as well as a lengthy serial in the *Journal des débats* and a painting exhibited at the Salon of 1845.

The popular appeal of these figures lay, as Ernest Alby, author of *La captivité du Trompette Escoffier* explained, in the sufferings they endured for the sake of their comrades and the nation: "These events excite our feelings to the

120. SHD 1H 105, "Rapport sur l'ensemble des opérations de la colonne de Médéah pendant les mois d'Avril, Mai, Juin et Juillet 1845 chez les Ouled Naïl, au Dira et au Jurjura, Monsieur le Général Marey, commandant," [15 July 1845].
121. AM Lyon 469WP 006, "Ordre général à l'armée et aux Français de l'Algérie," 6 July 1842.
122. BNEst, coll. De Vinck, vol. 102, *Captivité du Trompette Escoffier et de ses Camarades chez Abd-el-Kader* (Paris, [1843]).
123. Fulconis, *Fulconis*, 104–8.

FIGURE 40. Cham [Amédée de Noé], *There's Sixty Leagues Down!* "Only thirty leagues left, and then we'll rest. . . . Abd-el-Kader will have to get tired sometime, the devil! . . . . . . ," in Cham, *A la guerre comme à la guerre* (Paris: Aubert et Cie., 1846). Courtesy Library of Congress, Rare Books and Special Collections Division.

highest degree because [they] recount to us the misfortunes and heroism of our soldiers."[124] Alby's equation of misfortune with heroism was reiterated in other accounts, like a *canard* published on the occasion of Escoffier's release in 1845, whose headlines, sung out by colporteurs to potential buyers, promised "details of the unprecedented sufferings endured by the French prisoners during their captivity" and the "atrocities committed on these unfortunates who were beaten black and blue, loaded down with chains, and led into a wood where they were left for six days to suffer the atrocious pains of hunger." The accompanying illus-

124. Ernest Alby, *Histoire des prisonniers français en Afrique depuis la conquête*, 2 vols. (Paris, 1847), 1:vii. *La Captivité du Trompette Escoffier* was published separately in 1848.

trations set a depiction of a gaunt, ragged Escoffier being physically menaced by his captors alongside an image meant to represent the selfless action that had led to his capture (fig. 41). The collapse of suffering into heroism in such textual and visual narratives implied that the former was as deserving of public recognition as the latter. "If we have songs of triumph and national rewards for the heroes who win renown on the battlefields of Algeria," Alby argued in his introduction to Escoffier's story, "we must also have words of consolation and goodwill for the children of our camps and towns who have been subjected to all the miseries of captivity."[125] These same sentiments underpinned the transformation of the troops' sacrifices into an object of patriotic veneration.

Some opposition legislators, especially deputy Amédée Desjobert and conservative peer General de Castellane, used the travails of the Armée d'Afrique to argue against Bugeaud's war, but few in the 1840s dared to suggest that the way to end that suffering was to withdraw from Algeria. As Tocqueville wrote in 1841, "in the eyes of the world, such an abandonment would be a clear indication of our decline."[126] Solutions were instead found in the expansion of colonial settlement, which, it was argued, would allow France to occupy Algeria peacefully. Ironically, this was the very argument behind Bugeaud's "total war" policy, as he made clear shortly after taking over the governor-generalship. "The army can only be liberated by strong colonization," he wrote, but since colonization required security, the "imperious necessity" to defeat 'Abd al-Qadir as quickly as possible justified the most extreme forms of violence.[127] A parliamentary commission, sent to investigate French brutalities to Algeria in 1846, recommended that the size of the army be reduced by setting firm boundaries on the French-occupied area and returning nonpolitical administrative functions to Algerians. These measures would bring the fighting to an end and allow France to achieve "the peaceful domination and rapid colonization of Algeria."[128]

Yet war and colonization could not be so easily disentangled. Indeed, to many, the war itself and, particularly, the sacrifices of French soldiers constituted not only the means to colonization, but also its very reason for being. Colonization, Ferdinand Barrot explained to the Chamber of Deputies in 1846, was "the true means of completing the conquest begun by the war."[129] Cultural and colonial politics converged as Bonapartist celebrations of heroic, self-abnegating soldiers came to provide the ideological foundations for a new, patriotic argument for

---

125. Alby, *Histoire des prisonniers*, 1:3.
126. Tocqueville, "Essay on Algeria," in *Writings*, 59.
127. CAOM F80 1674, Bugeaud to Soult, 26 November 1841.
128. Tocqueville, "First Report on Algeria" (1847), in *Writings*, 133, 138, 167.
129. Speech to the Chamber of Deputies, 9 June 1846, in *La Presse*, 10 June 1846.

FIGURE 41. *Captivity of Bugler Escoffier and His Comrades with Abd-el-Kader,* Chassaignon (Paris), 1845. Bibliothèque nationale de France, Département des Estampes et de la photographie.

colonization. Settlers should be sent to Algeria, according to an anonymous petition received by the minister of war in 1845, "to use a conquest acquired by fifteen years of combat and sacrifice" and to give meaning to the suffering of French conscripts.[130] Only if the nation committed itself to colonization, another petitioner wrote, would it "no longer be in vain that so many brave soldiers, so many brave officers have . . . spilled their generous blood on the Algerian soil."[131] The failure of efforts to build a national monument to the Armée d'Afrique in the 1840s could be compensated, according to this logic, by the construction of a flourishing colony that would constitute "another monument to French glory, more eloquent, more durable, and above all more fecund" than any of marble and bronze.[132]

This emotional appeal, grounded in the Bonapartist identification between the army and the nation, proved nearly impossible for French lawmakers to refuse. As one colonial advocate demanded as early as 1836, "we have expended so much, money and men, for France's honor and strength; discharge your debt to us. Who would dare refuse to pay the debt of victory and to pass a law

130. CAOM, F80 1790, "Colonisation de l'Algérie" (Paris, 1845).
131. AN C2152, no. 133, Société Coloniale d'Alger, petition to the Chamber of Deputies, 23 February 1838.
132. CAOM F80 1671, "Rapport soumis au Roi par le Président du Conseil, Ministre Secrétaire d'Etat de la Guerre sur les mesures à prendre pour assurer l'avenir de l'occupation et de l'administration de l'ancienne Régence d'Alger," July 1834.

indemnifying the blood gloriously spilt?"[133] The answer, it appeared in the following decade, was very few. By 1840, the French state had spent over 340 million francs in Algeria, and the army had lost more than thirty-five thousand men.
Government expenses skyrocketed over the next decade to an estimated 1.5 billion francs, while combat and, primarily, disease killed another sixty thousand
French soldiers.[134] Despite these mounting financial and human costs, and the
anxieties provoked by Bugeaud's antiguerrilla tactics, French lawmakers proved
unwilling to refuse the budgetary requests of the Armée d'Afrique's commanders
or to reject plans for colonization. Instead, they endorsed a colonization policy
that enlisted thousands more French men to take up the struggle for domination in Algeria by the plow, rather than the sword. If the Bonapartist vision of
masculine citizenship helped to undermine the Orléans royal family's claims to
power, it also provided the legitimizing foundation for a large-scale project of settler colonialism in Algeria. Settlers and soldiers would become partners in making Algeria the jewel in the French imperial crown.

133. Eugène Lerminier, "De la conservation d'Alger," *Revue des deux mondes*, 4th ser., 6 (1836):
615.
134. Brower, *Desert Named Peace*, 33; Kateb, *Européens, "indigènes" et juifs*, 38; *Discours prononcé
par M. Desjobert, représentant du peuple (Seine-Inférieure) dans la discussion du projet de loi tendant
à régler le régime commercial en Algérie* . . . (Paris, 1850), 3.

PART II

By the Plow

4

The Empire of Virtue

Colonialism in the Age of Abolition

The French invasion of Algiers in 1830 was followed immediately by widespread calls to colonize the Ottoman regency. Even liberal opponents of the attack on Algiers suggested that creating a colony there could offer the nation some useful compensation for the despotic machinations behind the expedition. What it would mean to colonize Algiers was subject to debate, however. The first enthusiastic responses to the fall of Algiers are emblematic of the uncertainty that reigned around the very terms "colony" and "colonization" at this moment. Petitions and plans for colonization sent to the king, the Chamber of Deputies, and various ministers in the months after the July Revolution proposed that the conquest be used for the creation of model farms, the resettlement of orphans, army veterans, or unemployed paupers, and the deportation of convicts and Charles X's supposed Jesuit allies. The benefits—often fanciful—of such schemes, according to their authors, included new military strongholds on the Mediterranean, expanded markets for French manufactured goods, and, above all, a potential new source of expensive tropical goods and a nearby outlet for France's surplus population.

Two petitions received by the Chamber of Deputies in the fall of 1830 are representative of the contrasting visions that prevailed among colonization advocates at the dawn of the Algerian conquest. A certain Polin, self-styled "Philanthropist, friend of social Virtues, Prosperities & national Glories," proclaimed that Algiers could replace the islands of Asia and the Americas by providing "all Kinds of precious Exotics that make us Dependent for several hundreds of millions per year on those distant stations, and are made excessively onerous by their overly great

Distance from France and unfavorable to commerce by their too High prices in addition to the dangers of long maritime crossings."[1] Another "simple citizen" named Goubot, however, suggested that if the government would "make concessions of land taken from the deserted part of the territory," "numerous French families [would] hurry to go settle there." Given the "fertility of its soil, doubtless left uncultivated in many places" by its inhabitants, Algiers "will become henceforth one of our granaries of abundance."[2] While Polin and Goubot shared a belief in the potential agricultural wealth of the conquered regency, their visions of a future Algerian colony otherwise reflected a momentous shift underway in French thinking about empire. Polin's assumption that colonies were primarily maritime, commercial entities devoted to the production and export of tropical crops was slowly giving way to the ideal of European settlement outlined by Goubot.

To the average Frenchman in 1830, the term *colonie* was associated with the New World and characterized by three features: the restrictive commercial regime of the *exclusif* that allowed overseas possessions to trade only with France, political subordination to the metropole, and dependence on slave labor to produce "colonial crops," such as tobacco, coffee and sugar. Used with the definite article, "the colonies" still referred in the early 1830s to the sugar islands of the Caribbean and a political economy of monopoly trade and plantation slavery.[3] The "philanthropist" Polin viewed the colonization of Algiers through this Atlantic lens, which was shared by champions of Algerian colonization who focused on the new conquest's potential to replace the West Indies as a source of colonial commodities. General Clauzel, who replaced Bourmont as commander in chief of the Armée d'Afrique after the July Revolution, was a firm believer in Algeria's suitability for tropical agriculture, and one of his first acts was to create a model farm "to introduce into the territory of Algiers colonial and exotic crops for which France pays tribute to foreigners."[4] Clauzel's Ferme expérimentale d'Afrique quickly collapsed, but adapting tropical cash crops to the Algerian climate and soil conditions remained a concern of French colonial agronomists. Subsequent administrators established a system of nurseries and experimental gardens that continued to work towards this goal throughout the July Monarchy.[5]

1. AN C 2107, Polin, petition to the Chamber of Deputies, 15 September 1830.
2. AN C 2104, Goubot, petition to the Chamber of Deputies, 12 October 1830.
3. *Dictionnaire de l'Académie française*, 6th ed. (1832–35), s.v. "Colonie," http://colet.uchicago.edu/cgi-bin/dico1look.pl?strippedhw=colonie&dicoid=ACAD1835.
4. AM Marseille 13F 1, B. Cadet de Vaux, commissaire du Roi près la municipalité d'Alger, to maire de Marseille, 20 September 1830; CAOM F80 1161, "Statuts de la Société anonyme pour l'exploitation de la Ferme Expérimentale d'Afrique," 1 October 1830.
5. Michael Osborne, "The System of Colonial Gardens and the Exploitation of French Algeria, 1830–1852," *Proceedings of the 8th Annual Meeting of the French Colonial Historical Society* (1982):

By contrast, the "simple citizen" Goubot imagined a future Algerian colony as an extension, rather than a commercial appendage, of the metropole. His vision of Algeria as a province of France reflected the tremendous political and ideological pressure that had come to bear on the existing conception of colonies by 1830. The *exclusif* and servile labor were increasingly seen as morally repugnant and incompatible with the "modern" virtues of personal, economic, and political liberty. Few postrevolutionary Frenchmen were willing to repudiate empire altogether, but many sought to construct a new colonial system more in keeping with these values. Instead of seeking to reproduce the slave-based plantation agriculture of the Caribbean and Indian Ocean islands, mid–nineteenth-century colonialists imagined a new kind of settler colony, a society of European farmers that quickly came to embody what they called "serious," "true" or "veritable" colonization.

The French were not alone in embracing settler colonialism in the mid-nineteenth century. The redefinition of empire had its roots in the cosmopolitan intellectual world of the Enlightenment, when influential thinkers attacked colonial rule, monopoly trade, and slavery as symptomatic of European monarchs' absolutist tyranny.[6] The Revolutionary and Napoleonic wars reinforced this connection between imperial domination abroad and despotism at home.[7] The identification of empire with tyranny fed criticism of European domination over settler colonies in the Americas at the end of the eighteenth century, but "settlerism" was revived after 1815 by a transnational movement that reached its apogee in the middle decades of the century. Like the antislavery movements that arose in Britain, France, and the United States at the same time, the colonial settlement movement was sustained by an international network of thinkers and advocates, whose influence had global ramifications. The "settler revolution" of the nineteenth century was, as James Belich argues, an overwhelmingly "Anglo" phenomenon,[8] and this made British classical economists and the reformers

---

160–68; Charles-André Julien, *Histoire de l'Algérie contemporaine*, vol. 1, *La conquête et les débuts de la colonisation (1827–1871)* (Paris, 1964), 76–77; Adolphe Blanqui, *Algérie: Rapport sur la situation économique de nos possessions dans le nord de l'Afrique* (Paris, 1840), 76; A. Cochut, "Ressources agricoles de l'Algérie (*Colonisation et agriculture de l'Algérie*, par M. Moll)," *Revue des deux mondes*, n.s., 16 (1 October 1846): 142–70; Louis Moll, *Colonisation et agriculture de l'Algérie*, 2 vols. (Paris, 1845). Despite these efforts, Algeria remained an importer of *denrées coloniales*. *TEFA* (1837), 330.

6. See Anthony Pagden, *Lords of All the World: Ideologies of Empire in Spain, Britain and France, c. 1500–c. 1800* (New Haven, 1995); Sankar Muthu, *Enlightenment against Empire* (Princeton, 2003); Jennifer Pitts, *A Turn to Empire: The Rise of Imperial Liberalism in Britain and France* (Princeton, 2005), chap. 2–3.

7. This argument was made most explicitly by Benjamin Constant in *De l'esprit de la conquête et de l'usurpation* (1814; repr., Geneva, 1980).

8. *Replenishing the Earth: The Settler Revolution and the Rise of the Angloworld, 1783–1939* (Oxford, 2009).

known as the Theorists of 1830 a powerful model for French promoters of settler colonization, much as British abolitionists influenced the French antislavery movement.[9] French writers and policymakers were inspired by British settlement efforts in Canada, Australia, and New Zealand. But they also found instructive examples of colonial emigration and settlement in Russia, Austria, Germany, Latin America, and the United States, as well as in France's own colonial past and in ancient history.[10]

What united the settler movement and distinguished its vision of empire from other colonial formations was the relationship it posited between land and labor. As Patrick Wolfe argues, "settler colonialism seeks to replace the natives on their land rather than extract surplus value by mixing their labor with a colony's natural resources. . . . Thus the primary object of settler colonialism can be characterized as one of elimination."[11] This goal was never fully realized in French Algeria. The military conquest took a devastating demographic toll on the indigenous people, and the French war belongs firmly within the bloody pantheon of "settler genocides" to which it has been assigned.[12] But Algerian military strength and disease resistance, European settlement patterns, and principled opposition in France combined to prevent the extermination of Algerians for which some colonization advocates called. The disruptions caused by the war increased the incidence and mortality of disease, but long-standing commercial and diplomatic relations, as well as environmental links between Europe and North Africa,

9. On British influence on French antislavery, see Lawrence Jennings, *French Reaction to British Slave Emancipation* (Baton Rouge, 1988); Seymour Drescher, "British Way, French Way: Opinion Building and Revolution in the Second French Slave Emancipation," *American Historical Review* 96, no. 3 (1991): 709–34; Lawrence Jennings, *French Anti-Slavery: The Movement for the Abolition of Slavery in France, 1802–1848* (New York, 2000).
10. Although the transnational dimensions of the settler movement have yet to be examined in depth, there are many national and, more recently, comparative studies. See, among others, Fred Hitchens, *The Colonial Land and Emigration Commission* (Philadelphia, 1931); Donald Winch, *Classical Political Economy and Colonies* (Cambridge, Mass., 1965) chaps. 5–8; C. A. Bayly, *Imperial Meridian: The British Empire and the World, 1780–1830* (London, 1989), 196–221, 238–52; H. Oppenheimer, *Le libéralisme français au début du XIXe siècle (Jean-Baptiste Say) et la colonisation* (Paris, 1930); Marcus Hansen, "German Colonization Schemes before 1860," *Smith College Studies in History* 9 (Northampton, Mass., 1924), 1–65; Willard Sunderland, *Taming the Wild Field: Colonization and Empire on the Russian Steppe* (Ithaca, 2004); Jeffrey Ostler, *The Plains Sioux and U.S. Colonialism from Lewis and Clark to Wounded Knee* (Cambridge, 2004); John Weaver, *The Great Land Rush and the Making of the Modern World, 1760–1900* (Montreal, 2003); Belich, *Replenishing the Earth*.
11. Patrick Wolfe, "Land, Labor, and Difference: Elementary Structures of Race," *American Historical Review* 106, no. 3 (2001): 867. See also Patrick Wolfe, *Settler Colonialism and the Transformation of Anthropology: The Politics and Poetics of an Ethnographic Event* (London, 1999).
12. Ben Kiernan, *Blood and Soil: A World History of Genocide and Extermination from Sparta to Darfur* (New Haven, 2007).

meant that local populations were less susceptible to European-borne diseases than indigenous peoples in Australia and North America.[13]

For the same reasons, germs did not give Algeria's conquerors the deadly advantages they offered elsewhere. Food shortages, famine, and epidemics followed close on the heels of war between 1830 and 1870, but the biggest killers— cholera, typhus, and smallpox—were already present in North Africa. Although the French invasion and confiscation of Algerian lands spread these diseases and raised mortality rates to horrific levels, foreign pathogens did not wipe out entire populations as they did elsewhere.[14] When the war of conquest came to an end and the large-scale expropriation of land slowed in the 1870s, the Algerian population rebounded.[15] At the same time, European emigrants settled primarily in the cities and towns of the Mediterranean littoral. Hundreds of thousands of hectares were given over into European hands, but colonial agriculture remained dependent on Algerian labor.[16] In this respect, Algeria did not become a "pure" settler colony, but one of what Jürgen Osterhammel terms the "African" subtype, like Southern Rhodesia and South Africa.[17]

None of this was foreseen, however, by the French colonial theorists and planners gazing avidly across the Mediterranean in the 1830s and 1840s. To these men, Algeria promised a brilliant future as a land of mass European settlement. For all those who dreamed of "civilizing" the "natives" through trade and agricultural example, there were an equal number who fantasized about an Algeria "civilized" by the replacement of its existing inhabitants with French farms and families. Such fantasies vastly overestimated the power of the colonial state to clear and occupy land, just as they underestimated the power and determination of the land's inhabitants not to be displaced. But the aspiration to replace the indigenous people with European colonists, however shortsighted and appalling, fixed the aims of French colonialism in Algeria within the global settlement movement of the mid-nineteenth century.

13. Philip Curtin, *Death by Migration: Europe's Encounter with the Tropical World in the Nineteenth Century* (Cambridge, 1989), 93–94.
14. Kiernan, *Blood and Soil*, 244–45. On disease and contact in the Americas and Pacific, see David Stannard, *American Holocaust: The Conquest of the New World* (New York, 1992); Judy Campbell, *Invisible Invaders: Smallpox and Other Diseases in Aboriginal Australia, 1780–1880* (Melbourne, 2002).
15. Kamel Kateb, *Européens, "indigènes" et juifs en Algérie (1830–1962): Représentations et réalités des populations* (Paris, 2001), 62–66, 119–23.
16. Julien, *La conquête*, 402. On the expropriation of land, see John Ruedy, *Land Policy in Colonial Algeria* (Berkeley, 1967); chapter 5 of this book.
17. Jürgen Osterhammel, *Colonialism: A Theoretical Overview*, 2nd ed., trans. Shelley Frisch (Princeton, 2005), 12. Wolfe calls these, along with the plantation colonies of Southeast Asia, "so-called settler colonies" ("Land, Labor," 868 n. 7).

Despite great variation in local conditions, especially in the mode and consequences of land expropriations, the international settlement movement was
driven by a set of common concerns about the condition of European societies
in the early industrial age. Guided by interlocking fears of overpopulation, revolutionary political strife, and the destabilizing impact of industrialization and
urbanization, European social reformers embraced emigration as a panacea for
these manifold social ills. This was most evident in Great Britain, where the ties
between social dislocation and emigration made charitable societies and poor law
boards key agents of recruitment for the settler colonies. British theorists derided
the crudest version of this system as "little more than shoveling out your paupers," but the phrase captures the central importance of poverty and social unrest
in shaping attitudes towards settler colonization.[18]

The need to reimagine empire was felt with particular urgency in July
Monarchy France, where the collapse of the colonial Old Regime remained fresh
in mind. Those few colonies that remained to France after 1815 were tropical islands whose commodity agriculture was dependent on slavery and the *exclusif,*
the moral, political, and economic legitimacy of which was fatally undermined
during and after the Revolution. Abolitionists condemned slavery as both a cause
and a symptom of a bankrupt imperial system, while major slave uprisings and
a British-imposed ban on the slave trade cast doubt on the continued viability
of colonies dependent on slave labor. At the same time, the growing influence
of free trade doctrines posed a serious challenge to mercantilist restrictions on
colonial commerce, without which colonial sugar production was presumed to
be unsustainable. These same pressures were at work elsewhere, to be sure. In
Britain, the Colonial Reformers of the 1830s condemned the "systematic tyranny"
of mercantilism and the "black and inexcusable crime" of slavery, while calling for
"a reconstruction and great extension of the British dominion beyond the seas, on
principles of internal self-government and commercial freedom."[19] But in France,
the territorial losses of the preceding half-century greatly increased the imperative
for reform. Without a drastic rethinking of imperial structures, the few remaining
French colonies seemed poised to go the way of New France, Louisiana, and Saint-
Domingue. "In the nineteenth century," the liberal economist Jean-Baptiste Say

---

18. Charles Buller, speech to the House of Commons, 6 April 1843, in *The Collected Works of
Edward Gibbon Wakefield,* ed. Muriel Lloyd Pritchard (Auckland, 1969), 1023. See also Robin
Haines, *Emigration and the Labouring Poor: Australian Recruitment in Britain and Ireland, 1831–
1860* (London, 1997).
19. Herman Merivale, *Lectures on Colonization and Colonies, Delivered before the University of
Oxford in 1839, 1840, & 1841, and Reprinted in 1861* (1861; repr. Oxford, 1928), 8, 303, vi.

predicted in 1814, "the old colonial system will fall apart everywhere."[20] Imbued with this conviction, postrevolutionary French thinkers and policymakers came to believe that imperial restoration would entail full-scale colonial reconstruction: "[the colonial system] of the sixteenth, seventeenth and eighteenth centuries has become outdated; . . . a new system of colonization is therefore necessary."[21]

Nineteenth-century impulses for colonial reform presented important continuities with eighteenth-century critiques of empire, but they were given new impetus by the rise of the so-called social question as an object of intellectual and governmental concern in the 1830s. The prospect that colonial emigration could offer a solution to acutely felt domestic social problems converged with calls for colonial reform to produce decisive pressure towards settlement overseas. In the imperial circuit of virtue imagined by postrevolutionary thinkers, European immigrants would provide free labor to the colonies, the growth of settler societies would increase the scope of global trade, and colonial emigration would provide an outlet for elements that posed a threat to public order at home. Equally important, the new colonial emigrants were expected to settle not in cities, but on the land. The resulting colonial society would be essentially rural, and agriculture and civic virtue would flourish in place of the corruptions of urban, industrial life. The goal of this kind of agrarian colonization was summed up in the phrase that would be applied to French policy in Algeria throughout the nineteenth century: "peuplement et fertilisation" (settlement and fertilization).

The invasion of Algiers in 1830 offered French imperialists a fortuitous opportunity to put the new settler ideal into practice. Because the Ottoman regency had no recent history of Western colonization, it was seen as a blank slate for colonial experimentation, a "country where everything remains to be done" and a "testing site" for new models of European settlement, in the words of the Saint-Simonian leader, Prosper Enfantin.[22] Implementation of the settler ideal followed a hesitant, experimental path during the July Monarchy, but it nonetheless set in motion the process that would define the French presence in Algeria. Proponents of Algerian colonization claimed that the new conquest "must not be called a colony," with all that the term connoted, but rather must be made "one of the most beautiful provinces of France."[23] By the end of the July Monarchy, projects for

---

20. Jean-Baptiste Say, *De l'Angleterre et des Anglais* (Paris, 1815), 55.
21. Jean-Gustave Courcelle-Seneuil, "Colonie," in *Dictionnaire politique: Encylopédie du langage et de la science politiques*, ed. Louis-Antoine Garnier-Pagès (Paris, 1842), 235.
22. Prosper Enfantin, *Colonisation de l'Algérie, par Enfantin, membre de la Commission Scientifique de l'Algérie* (Paris, 1843), 116, 448.
23. Alexandre de Laborde, speech to the Chamber of Deputies, 29 April 1834, *AP* 89:490; Abbé Landmann, *Exposé sur la colonisation de l'Algérie adressé à MM. les pairs de France, lors de la discussion des crédits supplémentaires 1846* (Paris, 1846), 10.

assimilating the settled areas of Algeria were well underway, and the desire to make
the colony part of France was brought to fruition by the republicans of 1848.

The Colonies of the Ancients and the Moderns

At the heart of postrevolutionary debates about Algerian colonization lay a rejection of the colonial Old Regime. Building on well-known Enlightenment critiques
of empire, the leading political, moral, and social economists of Restoration and
July Monarchy France, along with many of their lesser-known compatriots, constructed their vision of *véritable colonisation* against the history of European
domination in Asia and the Americas. By the end of the eighteenth century, as
Anthony Pagden argues, European thinkers had come to see the colonial experiences of the early modern period as an object lesson in "what successful empires
should *not* attempt to be."[24] Slavery and commercial monopolies, in particular,
were repudiated as economically inefficient and morally corrupting, and held up
as a foil for a new model of settler colonialism. Although some critics did attack large-scale overseas settlement, especially in the wake of the settler revolution that made Britain's North American colonies into the independent United
States, their criticisms were historically specific. Moral and political arguments
for the possibility of virtuous forms of settler colonization, however, survived the
anticolonial onslaught of the eighteenth century relatively intact. The most influential eighteenth-century thinkers exempted "true" settler colonies from their
condemnations of empire, and their postrevolutionary followers embraced settlement colonization as an imperial form that could prosper without the cardinal
sins of commercial, political, or personal servitude.

It is difficult to trace with precision the intellectual genealogy of French colonial thought in the mid-nineteenth century. The relative obscurity of many of the
writers involved, the heterogeneity of their political allegiances, and the indirect
nature of their influence on policymaking all hinder the historian's task. We can,
however, identify a striking set of common themes in writings on empire during
the Restoration and July Monarchy, which transcended the otherwise virulent
political disputes between liberals, conservatives, and radicals. In their shared
concerns with the political and moral economy of empire lie the broad outlines of
a colonial consensus that underpinned the development of Algerian colonization
policy. Framed in terms of an opposition between "the colonies of the moderns"
and "the colonies of the ancients," this new understanding simultaneously condemned the dangers of empire as practiced under the Old Regime and embraced

24. Pagden, *Lords of All the World*, 6.

the possibility of a new kind of empire compatible with new political and social values.

One key figure in postrevolutionary French colonial thought was Jean-Baptiste Say, disciple of Adam Smith and leader of the French liberal school of economics. Best known for popularizing Smith's ideas and the new discipline of political economy in France, Say was interested in colonial problems from the beginning of his career in the 1790s until his death in 1832.[25] As a young man, he joined the revolutionary abolitionist group, the Société des amis des noirs, and contributed articles and reviews on colonial issues to the Ideologue journal, *La Décade philosophique*, which he edited from 1794 to 1800. After keeping quiet on colonial matters during the procolonial Napoleonic Empire, he returned to the question during the Restoration in his major treatises on political economy and the pages of the left-leaning *Revue encyclopédique*, published by the abolitionist Marc-Antoine Jullien. During the Restoration and early July Monarchy, Say became the leading economist in France, appointed in 1820 to a new chair in "industrial" economy at the Conservatoire des arts et métiers and then to the first chair in political economy at the Collège de France in 1831.

Although classical political economists were "institutionally isolated and rather unpopular in official circles" in France until the mid-1840s,[26] Say's Restoration-era writings on empire develop the two essential assumptions on which the postrevolutionary colonial consensus rested. First, Say combined the *philosophes'* moralizing critique of colonial societies with an economic argument against colonial slavery. In this regard, he was as much a student of Diderot as of Smith and Turgot, and his work provided the critical bridge between Enlightenment ideas about empire and those of postrevolutionary economists. Second, Say condemned slavery and colonial monopolies without entirely rejecting imperialism. Instead, he found in settlement colonies an alternate form of virtuous empire. Working from a damning comparison between the "colonies of the moderns" and the "colonies of the ancients," his two-pronged argument contrasted the evils of European imperialism since the discovery of the Americas with the virtues of colonization as practiced by the ancient Greeks and Romans.

25. Say is one of the few early nineteenth-century French thinkers whose views on empire have received scholarly attention. See Oppenheimer, *Le libéralisme*; Philippe Steiner, "Jean-Baptiste Say et les colonies, ou comment se débarrasser d'un héritage intempestif," *Cahiers d'économie politique* 27–28 (1996): 153–73; Bernard Gainot, "*La Décade* et la 'colonisation nouvelle,'" *Annales historiques de la Révolution française* 339 (2005): 99–116; Anna Plassart, "'Un Impérialiste Libéral'? Jean-Baptiste Say on Colonies and the Extra-European World," *French Historical Studies* 32, no. 2 (2009): 223–50. The Ideologues were a group of liberal philosophers, scientists, and economists of the revolutionary and Napoleonic eras.
26. Katherine Lynch, *Family, Class, and Ideology in Early Industrial France: Social Policy and the Working-Class Family, 1825–1848* (Madison, 1988), 49.

The basic distinction drawn by Say between the colonies of the ancients and the moderns was simple, and lay in the motives for their founding. The *système colonial des anciens* was based upon necessity, and colonies were founded only when population growth or persecution forced some part of the inhabitants to seek a new home in unoccupied or thinly peopled lands elsewhere. The *système colonial des modernes*, by contrast, was motivated by commercial greed. Armed with new navigational technologies, the moderns "went as far as another hemisphere and into inhospitable climates not to settle themselves and their descendents, but to gather precious commodities and to bring back to their *patrie* the fruits of a hasty and extensive production."[27] Where the ancients had created permanent settlements that harmed no one, the moderns' commercial colonies entailed violent conquest and coercive means of exploitation, including slavery.

The main thrust of Say's attack on the colonies of the moderns focused on the economic results of the trade monopolies intended to maximize the colonies' profitability to the metropole. Here, he closely followed the argument of Adam Smith's *The Wealth of Nations*, claiming in the influential *Cours complet d'économie politique pratique* (1828–29) that mercantilist trade restrictions actually held little economic value.[28] Using the example of sugar, he argued that tariffs designed to protect producers in the French West Indies from Spanish and British Caribbean competitors actually increased the cost of this essential product to French consumers by some 30 percent. At the same time, colonial markets for French exports were steadily shrinking. Colonists' purchasing power declined as they indebted themselves to finance the purchase of more slaves, and slaves themselves, the vast majority of the colonial population, had no money at all to purchase goods imported from France. Thus the monopoly relationship between colony and metropole, which Say referred to as "asservissement" (enslavement), was economically inefficient and ultimately unsustainable.

Say's analysis of the economics of sugar production reflected his free trade principles, as well as important shifts in the colonial economy in the postrevolutionary period. Great Britain and the United States had instituted a ban on the slave trade in 1807, which was extended to France and the other European powers after the Congress of Vienna. Illicit slaving met part of the colonies' ongo-

27. Jean-Baptiste Say, *Traité d'économie politique, ou simple exposition de la manière dont se forment, se distribuent et se consomment les richesses*, 6th ed., ed. Horace Say (1803; Paris, 1841), 223–24.

28. Jean-Baptiste Say, *Cours complet d'économie politique pratique* . . . , 2nd ed., ed. Horace Say, 2 vols. (Brussels, 1840), 1:248–50, 627–28, 632–33; Adam Smith, *An Inquiry into the Nature and Causes of the Wealth of Nations* (3rd ed., 1784), ed. R. H. Campbell and A. S. Skinner, Glasgow Edition of The Works and Correspondence of Adam Smith, vol. 2 (Oxford, 1976), bk. 4, chap. 7, c, 594–96. Smith's views are discussed in Winch, *Classical Political Economy*, chaps. 1–2. See also Say, *Traité*, 228.

ing demand for labor, bringing some 77,300 additional captives to the French Caribbean between 1817 and 1831, when a Franco-British mutual search treaty curtailed the illegal trade. At the same time, metropolitan beet sugar production, introduced by Napoleon, expanded rapidly after 1815. The "sugar war" between colonial and "indigenous" French producers turned against the colonies in the mid-1830s, when prices dropped dramatically and domestic beet sugar captured a third of the French market.[29] By 1838, representatives of the Caribbean plantocracy were crying that "the colonial system was shaken to its foundations."[30] Say himself cited competition from beet sugar refineries in northern France as one of the developments that would force an end to colonial monopolies. "The nature of things is too strong," he argued, to ignore this new economic reality: "We will everywhere be obliged, even without political commotions [i.e. slave revolts], to abandon the old colonial system and to cede to the influence of the price of things."[31] While relatively few in France—including the Orleanists who presided over the foundation of the Algerian colony—shared Say's absolute commitment to free trade, they did accept his argument that the existing imperial economy was no longer profitable to France.

The greatest danger to the colonial order, however, lay in slave emancipation, which appeared to most observers in the 1830s and 1840s to be imminent. Unrest in the slave colonies and the renewal of abolitionist activity in France combined to pose a deadly threat to the existing system. The abolitionist movement of the July Monarchy was admittedly weak. The efforts of the main antislavery group, the Société française pour l'abolition de l'esclavage, were diluted by its legalistic strategy, elitist composition, and gradualist approach. As a result, the French colonial lobby was successful in fending off abolitionist legislation under the Orleanist regime with arguments that slave labor was necessary to the French sugar supply and that slaves were not yet sufficiently prepared for freedom.[32] Louis-Philippe

---

29. Jennings, *French Anti-Slavery*, 32–33, 117–18.
30. Henri Gratien Bertrand, *Sur la détresse des colonies françaises et de l'île Martinique en particulier; et de la nécessité de diminuer le taxe exorbitant établie sur le sucre exotique* (Paris, 1838), 31. See also Say, *Cours complet*, 1:257 n. 1; Michel Chevalier, review of Adolphe Guéroult, *De la Question coloniale en 1842*, in *Le Courrier français*, 2 April 1842. On the "sugar wars," Christian Schnackenbourg, "La disparition des habitations-sucreries: Guadeloupe (1848–1906). Recherche sur la dégradation des structures préindustrielles de la production sucrière antillaise après l'abolition de l'esclavage," *Revue française d'histoire d'outre-mer* 75, no. 276 (1987): 257–331; Roland Treillon and Jean Guérin, "La guerre des sucres," *Culture Technique* 16 (1986): 224–35.
31. Say, *Cours complet*, 1:636, quote 1:250.
32. Jennings, *French Anti-Slavery*, 76–82. Parliamentary commissions recommended emancipation in 1838 and 1839, and the Soult government accepted the proposal in 1839. These plans were put aside during the ministerial upheavals of 1840–41, but the colonial commission presided over by the duc de Broglie continued its work and decided in 1845 that, in principle, slavery in the French colonies would be abolished over a ten-year period.

was himself committed to protecting the interests of the powerful plantocracy, and only after the February Revolution of 1848 were radical abolitionists able to push through an emancipation bill.[33]

Nonetheless, by the time of the invasion of Algiers, both opponents and defenders of colonial slavery were convinced that emancipation was inevitable. The violence of the Haitian Revolution had left deep scars in the French collective imagination, and the injustices that had led the slaves to revolt returned to the public eye in sentimental and lurid narratives of slavery and the slave trade that appeared in fiction, theater, and art during the Restoration and July Monarchy.[34] Major slave uprisings in Martinique (1822 and 1831) and Jamaica (1831), along with the passage of the British Emancipation Act in 1833, confirmed to most French observers that slavery's days were numbered. The French state was not overwhelmingly concerned with the impact of British emancipation, but the liberation of slaves by the leading European colonial power still appeared to be a sign of changing times. In 1838, when the British abandoned the apprenticeship regime that had been meant to slow the liberation process, even the colonial council of Guadeloupe conceded that "emancipation is henceforth an inevitable fact."[35] The only tactic remaining to the planters was to delay abolition as long as possible, while pushing to be indemnified for the loss of their human property. Unless "France resigns herself to sacrifice her tropical possessions," the liberal colonialist André Cochut argued in 1845, "the point of departure for the inevitable reform [of the colonies] must be the abolition of slavery."[36]

With emancipation looming on the horizon, French colonial officials and interest groups turned to European emigrants as a new source of colonial labor. Abolitionists expected that emancipated slaves would continue to provide the islands' labor force, working for their former masters as paid employees, but many colonial actors—administrators and planters alike—were concerned that below-replacement birthrates among slaves could not sustain the labor supply even after abolition. This concern became more acute in the late 1830s, as tensions arose over the British right to search French trading vessels for clandestine slaving. An external source would have to be found to replace the workers formerly imported from West and Central Africa.[37]

---

33. Ibid., 70, 105, 146–47, 270.
34. On contemporary images of slavery, see among others, Léon-François Hoffmann, *Le nègre romantique: Personnage littéraire et obsession collective* (Paris, 1973); Doris Kadish, *Translating Slavery: Gender and Race in French Women's Writing, 1783–1823* (Kent, Ohio, 1994); Christopher Miller, *The French Atlantic Triangle: Literature and Culture of the Slave Trade* (Durham, N.C., 2008).
35. Quoted in Jennings, *French Anti-Slavery*, 126. See also Jennings, *French Reaction*, 7–26.
36. "De la colonisation de la Guyane française," *Revue des deux mondes*, n.s., 11 (August 1845): 520.
37. Drescher, "British Way," 716; Jennings, *French Reaction*, 145–48.

In colonial circles, debate focused on whether the new flow of imported labor should be made up of European emigrants or nonwhites transported from other French colonies.[38] Practical difficulties and the doubtful legality of transferring African workers between colonies, deemed too similar to the banned slave trade, shifted the momentum towards European migration. French colonialists pinned their hopes, at least temporarily, on schemes that more closely resembled the recruitment of Irish, Scottish, and German emigrants by colonial governments in the British Caribbean than the systems of "coolie" or indentured labor being developed in British territories in the Indian Ocean, in Latin America, and in the United States in this period.[39] An inquiry commissioned by the Chamber of Deputies' colonial committee in 1838 concluded that poor or working-class European immigrants would resolve the colonial labor problem and provide the basis for a new "empire without slaves."[40] The Ministry of the Navy and Colonies acted on this recommendation, creating a commission to settle French workers in Guiana in 1842 and subsidizing emigration under an 1845 law that provided passage to Martinique and Guadeloupe for European farmers.[41]

If the transition from slave to free labor in the Caribbean had as much to do with economics as with humanitarian concerns, the moral authority of the abolitionist argument made the institution of slavery in any new colony impossible to imagine. Like most French abolitionists of his day, Jean-Baptiste Say was a gradualist and advocated liberating slaves in stages designed to overcome their

38. Marwan Buheiry, "Anti-Colonial Sentiment in France during the July Monarchy: The Algerian Case" (Ph.D. diss., Princeton University, 1973), 14–18; Commission de Colonisation de la Guyane Française, *Extrait du procès-verbal de la séance du 4 mars 1842: Explications présentées par M. Jules Lechevalier* (Paris, 1842); Victor Schœlcher, *Des colonies françaises: Abolition immédiate de l'esclavage* (1842), in *Esclavage et colonisation*, ed. Émile Tersen (1948; repr., Paris, 2007), 87–89. British colonists shared this concern. Catherine Hall, *Civilising Subjects: Metropole and Colony in the English Imagination, 1830–1867* (Chicago, 2002), 71–72.
39. European labor recruitment was particularly extensive in Jamaica. See Carl Senior, "Irish Slaves for Jamaica," *Jamaica Journal* 42 (1978): 104–16; Carl Senior, "German Immigrants in Jamaica, 1834–38," *Journal of Caribbean History* 10–11 (1978): 25–53.
40. François Manchuelle, "Origines républicaines de la politique d'expansion coloniale de Jules Ferry (1838–1865)," *Revue française d'histoire d'outre-mer* 75, no. 279 (1988): 188–90. Proposals for black African workers were later renewed by colonists seeking to develop cotton cultivation in Algeria. Roland Villot, *Jules du Pré de Saint-Maur, colon oranien*, 2nd ed. (Oran, 1955), 83. I borrow the phrase "empire without slaves" from Christopher Brown, "Empire without Slaves: British Concepts of Emancipation in the Age of Revolution," *William and Mary Quarterly*, 3rd ser., 56, no. 2 (April 1999): 273–306.
41. AD Yvelines 4M 2/24, ministre de la Marine et Colonies, Circular "Application de la loi du 19 juillet en ce qui concerne l'introduction des travailleurs libres aux Antilles," 9 January 1845. This law providing 120,000 francs to subsidize emigration and was renewed in 1849. "Nouvelles des Antilles," *Annales de l'extinction du paupérisme*, 1 September 1849.

supposedly natural indolence and to ready them for life as free men. But he also shared the postrevolutionary belief that slavery was "a system of vicious corruption" symptomatic of the essential moral failings of modern colonies.[42] The heritage of Diderot and the *philosophes* weighed heavily in Say's moral assessments of empire. To Enlightenment thinkers, European expansion since the discovery of the Americas had presented a "terrible spectacle of so many vast regions pillaged, ravaged or reduced to the most cruel servitude," in Diderot's words.[43] Such injustices were understood to have a dehumanizing impact not only on their victims, but also on their perpetrators. In the eyes of critics from Montesquieu to Condorcet and beyond, the corruption of empire transcended the boundaries between metropole and colony, sapping the moral fiber of individuals engaged in imperial ventures and the nations that spawned them.[44] This was most true of slavery. As Say argued, the corruption it engendered affected all those party to the system: "A slave is a depraved being, and his master is no less so; neither one nor the other can become completely industrious, and they deprave the free man who has no slaves."[45] This intellectual heritage, in conjunction with the structural changes in the colonial economy outlined above, made it clear to those involved in colonial issues that any legitimate new colony would require a free alternative to enslaved labor, even as abolition languished in the Chambers.[46]

When attention turned to Algeria after 1830, French colonialists departed from the assumption that slavery was "a monstrous production of the barbarian customs of the Middle Ages,"[47] incompatible with postrevolutionary political values. Outmoded in the era of liberty, this sin of the past could not be given new life in the new colony. As Navy Minister Rigny argued before the Chamber of Deputies in the first major debate on Algerian colonization in 1833, "the sugar colonies could be colonized in certain epochs; [but] they were colonies of forced labor; today we can create only colonies of free labor."[48] Indeed, much of Algeria's significance in contemporary eyes lay in the fact that it offered an alternative to the slave colonies of the Old Regime and an opportunity to redefine the term "colonization" altogether. Advocates of Algerian colonization deemed it a "possession that much more precious and secure because its, inordinately prodi-

---

42. Say, *Cours complet*, 1:249.
43. In Guillaume-Thomas Raynal, *Histoire philosophique et politique des établissements et du commerce des Européens dans les deux Indes*, 10 vols. (Geneva, 1780), 2:268.
44. Pagden, *Lords of All the World*, esp. chap. 6; Muthu, *Enlightenment*, 104–11.
45. Say, *Cours complet*, 1:251.
46. E.g., H . . . de B . . . , *De l'Algérie et de la colonisation* (Paris, 1834), 7–10.
47. V. H. D[uteil], *Nécessité de la colonisation d'Alger et des émigrations* (Paris, 1832), iii.
48. Discussion of the budget de la guerre, 4 April 1833, *AP* 82:275.

THE EMPIRE OF VIRTUE

gal soil, can be productive without slavery, which is dying out all over."[49] Even defenders of Caribbean slavery felt the long reach of the idea that new colonies must be free colonies. An 1834 brochure, entitled *Coup d'œil sur les colonies, et en particulier sur celle d'Alger* drew on Montesquieuean climatological theory to argue that European colonization was not feasible in Algeria, since whites born in temperate Europe could not withstand the physical burdens of agricultural labor in hot climates. But even the author of this venomous defense of slavery could not bring himself to support extending the institution to North Africa, on the grounds that "the new direction of ideas that is sometimes characterized as the progress of Enlightenment absolutely forbids [us] to think of making of this magnificent country [Algeria] a slave colony in the style of Saint-Domingue."[50] The philosophical and political repudiation of slavery, so powerful that even its defenders could not condone its extension to North Africa, demarcated the "old" sugar colonies of the Caribbean from the "new" colony in Algeria.

That free labor would mean European emigration and settlement was assumed by nearly all participants in the ensuing debates on Algerian colonization. The liberal *Revue des deux mondes* articulated the link between abolition and settlement colonization in 1836, in one of its first articles on the topic. Celebrated jurist Eugène Lerminier argued that the new colony should be made up of European emigrants working their own land, thereby overcoming the shameful and unjust violence of slavery. He described Algeria as unmarked by the original sin of earlier European empires and insisted that France could not allow itself to repeat the mistakes of the past in this virgin territory. A member of the Société française pour l'abolition de l'esclavage, Lerminier expressed this prescription in the abolitionist movement's language of enlightened humanitarianism.

49. F. P., "Avant-propos," *L'Afrique française*, July 1837. The glaring exception was preexisting "Algerian" slavery. The French colonial administration resisted abolitionist pressure to interfere with indigenous slavery throughout the July Monarchy. Military officials claimed that it would antagonize powerful indigenous slave owners but also took pains to differentiate Muslim slavery from the chattel slavery practiced in European colonies. Military reports described Algerian slaveholding as a form of domesticity, in which slaves were incorporated into Muslim families and enjoyed comfortable conditions. Although political concerns about the possible consequences of meddling with wealthy Algerians were clearly paramount here, it is significant that French authorities felt obliged to argue for the "Oriental" rather than colonial character of Algerian slavery. Charles d'Assailly et al., *Pétition aux Chambres: Esclavage en Algérie* (Paris, [1846]). CAOM, Fonds Bugeaud, 2EE 7, "Observations sur l'abolition de l'esclavage en Algérie," 2 May 1847. TEFA (1842–43), 58–59. See also Drescher, "British Way," 718, 723–24; Jennings, *French Anti-Slavery*, 254–56; Benjamin Brower, *A Desert Named Peace: The Violence of France's Empire in the Algerian Sahara, 1844–1902* (New York, 2009), pt. 3.
50. AN C2132, Benjamin, *Coup-d'œil sur les colonies, et en particulier sur celle d'Alger* (Paris, 1833), 20, pamphlet enclosed with petition to Chamber of Deputies, 27 April 1834.

Here is a vast colony without slaves that offers itself to us; without slaves, do you hear? Here we need neither debase nor torment humanity. Here the planter's cane will not strike the slave before the sugar cane. No, on African soil, everything can take place nobly; free men will cultivate the land, French and European colonists will live by work under the protection of our arms, and the new colony will see flourish three of the most noble, humane things: liberty, agriculture, and war.[51]

The addition of "war" may seem incongruous in this otherwise passionate condemnation of colonial violence, but the author's ardent Bonapartism, conjoined with a Romantic conception of war as "*the* way to enforce justice and as *the* occasion for self-expression," made combat commensurate in his eyes with the peaceable virtues of liberty and agriculture.[52] Widely held views of the Algerian conquest as a crusade against Oriental despotism and fanatical Islam only reinforced Lerminier's assertion that war was among the noble undertakings possible in Algeria. Both the just war of conquest and the eradication of slavery's unjust violence therefore lay fully within what he considered "the new spirit, the spirit of the nineteenth century."[53] War's inclusion in the list in no way diminished the larger argument that a noble form of modern colonialism could be imagined under a free labor regime untainted by the moral stain of slavery.

Without recourse to a servile labor force, settlement by European emigrants became a necessary feature of the Algerian colonial enterprise. "There is no longer any question of slavery, it is therefore citizens who are called to become colonists [and] owners of the Algerian soil," wrote the author of one colonization project in 1845.[54] This was partly a matter of necessity. Algerians responded to the French invasion with a combination of flight and armed resistance that made a local work force difficult to recruit.[55] Military officers proposed that Kabyles, supposed to be more

---

51. Eugène Lerminier, "De la conservation d'Alger," *Revue des deux mondes*, 4th ser., 6 (1 June 1836): 612.

52. Nancy Rosenblum, "Romantic Militarism," *Journal of the History of Ideas* 43, no. 2 (1982): 249. On Lerminier's hero worship of Napoleon, see Bonnie G. Smith, "The Rise and Fall of Eugène Lerminier," *French Historical Studies* 12, no. 3 (1982): 379, 382.

53. Lerminier, "De la conservation," 611.

54. CAOM, GGA L4, Hersant-Desmares, "Affrique [sic] Française. Projet de Colonnie [sic] Général en Algérie, ayant pour base La Nationalité et Composée de divers Eléments," 27 December 1845.

55. On emigration, protest, and jihad as responses to the French invasion, see Julia Clancy-Smith, *Rebel and Saint: Muslim Notables, Populist Protest, Colonial Encounters (Algeria and Tunisia, 1800–1904)* (Berkeley, 1997), 70–91; Kateb, *Européens, "indigènes" et juifs*, 49–58.

dexterous, hardworking, and reliable than Arabs, might provide a labor source, but insurrection in Kabylia soon put paid to this idea.[56] A few early colonists were able to recruit Algerian laborers; most notable was the Polish Prince de Mir, whose Rassauta farm was lauded for employing some eight hundred Arabs alongside three hundred Europeans.[57] But negative views of Arab Algerians' work ethic carried the day among French colonists and officials, especially after even Mir's farm was attacked in the Hadjoutes' 1839 offensive against settlers in the Mitidja. Even though Algerian workers commanded lower wages than Europeans, politicians, administrators and theorists considered them "so indolent in body and spirit" as to be more costly in the long run.[58] Ignoring the fact that declining Algerian output was largely due to the disruptions caused by the French invasion and seizure of land, French writers interpreted the uncultivated territory they observed as proof that Algerians were unsuited to modern, European-style agriculture.

European emigration was more than an economic solution to the problem of colonial labor in the age of abolition, however. As an alternative to chattel slavery, it became the defining feature of a new vision of empire to be inaugurated in Algeria, where social virtue could flourish to the benefit of both metropole and colony. The economists who assumed Jean-Baptiste Say's mantle during the July Monarchy declared that it would be a terrible mistake to "confuse this conquest and this colony with the things that we in Europe ordinarily understand by these two words."[59] Adolphe Blanqui, Say's student and successor to his chair at the Conservatoire, argued in no uncertain terms that "this new colony has nothing in common with all those that have preceded it, and it would be unreasonable to apply systems incompatible with its original and unorthodox nature," such as plantation slavery.[60] Without this corrupting force, July Monarchy colonialists argued, empire could be morally rejuvenated in North Africa. Settled and cultivated by Europeans, Algeria would have none of "those human creatures transformed into beasts of burden, and in consequence, none of those odious tortures under which humanity has only too often groaned." French settlers would have no need to fear revolt or massacre—as long as the French army instilled a salutary fear in Algerians. The new colony would

56. Patricia Lorcin, *Imperial Identities: Stereotyping, Prejudice and Race in Colonial Algeria*, (1995; repr., London, 1999), 46–47.
57. E.g. Ch[arles] Solvet, *Voyage à la Rassauta: Lettre à M. A . . . député* (Marseille, 1838).
58. A. Cochut, "De la colonisation de l'Algérie.—Les essais et les systèmes," *Revue des deux mondes*, n.s., 17 (February 1847): 502.
59. Eugène Buret, *Question d'Afrique: De la double conquête de l'Algérie par la guerre et par la colonisation, suivi d'un examen critique du gouvernement, de l'administration et de la situation coloniale* (Paris, 1842), 16.
60. Blanqui, *Algérie*, 65.

"not be a cursed land," but "the sister of France, she will be a new France."[61] It is no coincidence that the membership of the Société française pour l'abolition de l'esclavage, while it included the leading opponents of Algerian colonization, leftist deputies Amédée Desjobert and Hippolyte Passy, also counted some of its staunchest advocates, among them Gustave de Beaumont, François de Corcelles, Alexandre de Laborde, Alphonse de Lamartine, Eugène Lerminier, and Alexis de Tocqueville.

In promising a solution to the economic and moral problem of slavery, European settlement also offered an alternative to the second feature of "modern" colonies condemned by nineteenth-century thinkers: the character of the European colonists themselves. Drawing once again from Enlightenment critiques, especially that of Diderot, nineteenth-century French thinkers interpreted the corruption of modern colonies largely as the product of the corrupt individuals who created, ran, and populated them. Slavery and trade monopolies were, in this analysis, symptoms of the essential selfishness of colonists and administrators who saw the colonies purely as a source of personal enrichment. Say attributed the persistence of modern colonies to private interests, in particular those of colonial officials and planters who sought enormous wealth without regard for the effect of their actions on society as a whole. In the venal colonial administration, bureaucrats advanced by means of "favors," rather than the intelligence and hard work on which "industrious" careers were based. Taken as a whole, the governing apparatus of empire sought to extend its own power at the public expense.

Colonists, for their part, were equally self-interested and wished only to enrich themselves as quickly and as easily as possible, according to Say. In their single-minded pursuit of personal fortune, they built a society devoid of civic virtue. They went overseas only temporarily to seek wealth by whatever means possible and then returned to Europe to enjoy their ill-gotten gains, without ever developing a long-term stake in the colonial community. "One goes there only with the *esprit de retour*," Say wrote, "that is to say, to return to Europe to enjoy a fortune acquired for better or for worse." In the cases of both administrators and

---

61. L[ouis] F[rançois] L'Héritier (de l'Ain), "Importance de l'Algérie sous le rapport de ses produits agricoles," *L'Afrique française* 1 (July 1837): 11. The link between colonial settlement and slavery was equally clear to the leading British theorist of colonial emigration, Edward Gibbon Wakefield, whose *A Letter from Sydney, The Principal Town of Australasia* (1829) argued that slavery was the only practical alternative to assisted emigration to the colonies. In Wakefield, *Collected Works*, 112–13. This aspect of "systemic colonization" was also the focus of Marx's discussion of "The Modern Theory of Colonization," which celebrated settlement colonization for allowing the small colonist to resist reduction to the status of wage-laborer at the hands of the capitalist landowner. *Capital*, vol. 1, pt. 3, chap. 33 (Marxists Internet Archive, 1999), http://www.marxists.org/archive/marx/works/1867-c1/ch33.htm.

colonists, individual greed perpetuated a system that ran counter to reason and to humanity, creating "an order of things vicious in itself, contrary to the interests and well-being of a large number of men, and which the progress of the human race must reject sooner or later, such as slavery."[62] Although mobility had long been an object of suspicion, and migrants, like other travelers, were perceived as a threat to social order in Europe,[63] transience carried even greater dangers in the colonial world, where there were few established institutions to provide continuity to social life and stability to the moral order.

Nineteenth-century French thinkers across the political spectrum shared Say's views on the linkage between slavery and selfish, transient colonists. The convergence on this point between liberal economists like Say and the romantic socialists who occupied the far left of contemporary intellectual life indicates the strength of the colonial consensus of the day. Socialists like Prosper Enfantin, Charles Fourrier, and Étienne Cabet are well known for their embrace of Algeria as a site for utopian community building, but socialist critiques of early modern empire are equally revealing.[64] Say's great rivals, the socialist historian and economist Jean-Charles-Léonard Sismonde de Sismondi and his student Eugène Buret, the editor of *Le Courrier français*, both wrote at length on precisely the question of slavery and the *esprit de retour*. They disagreed with Say on the question of free trade, but the three men concurred on the evils of slavery. Although he maintained a cautious, gradualist position on emancipation, Sismondi had been one of the few French thinkers to speak out openly against the slave trade in the first decades of the century, and he devoted much of his 1837 essay *Les colonies des anciens comparées à celles des modernes* to demonstrating the connections between slavery and the *esprit de retour* of greedy colonists.[65] Buret also saw these as the defining features of modern colonies:

62. Say, *Cours complet*, 1:293–94.

63. On attitudes towards mobility, see Daniel Roche, *Humeurs vagabonds: De la circulation des hommes et de l'utilité des voyages* (Paris, 2003).

64. On romantic socialists' views of empire, see Marcel Emerit, *Les saint-simoniens en Algérie* (Paris, 1941); Lorcin, *Imperial Identities*; Osama Abi-Mershed, *Apostles of Modernity: Saint-Simonians and the Civilizing Mission in Algeria* (Stanford, 2010); Fernand Rude, "Les Fourriéristes lyonnais et la colonisation de l'Algérie," *Cahiers d'histoire* 1 (1956): 41–63; Naomi Andrews, "Romantic Socialists Theorize and Promote the *Mission civilisatrice*" (paper presented at the 35th Annual Meeting of the French Colonial Historical Society, San Francisco, 30 May 2009).

65. Jennings, *French Anti-Slavery*, 6; Marcel Dorigny, "Sismondi et les colonies: Un maillon entre Lumières et théoriciens du XIXe siècle?" in *Rétablissement de l'esclavage dans les colonies françaises, 1802: Ruptures et continuités de la politique coloniale française (1800–1830)*, ed. Yves Bénot and Marcel Dorigny (Paris, 2003), 472–75; Jean-Charles-Léonard Sismonde de Sismondi, *Les colonies des anciens, comparées à celles des modernes, sous le rapport de leur influence sur le bonheur du genre humain* (Geneva, 1837).

We ordinarily mean by "colony" the exploitation of a distant country by adventurous men who emigrate for a few years in hopes of making a rapid fortune. Colony and slavery are just about synonymous because the European requires inexpensive labor, docile hands to rip from the soil the riches that he covets. Do you think Saint-Domingue, the West Indies, Île Bourbon, Mauritius, and the Dutch islands would have been so promptly cultivated if the colonists had had to cultivate the coffee, sugar, and spice lands themselves or using Europeans?[66]

Prosper Enfantin, "father" of the Saint-Simonian movement, drew a similar connection between colonists' selfishness, transience, and dependence on slave labor, which he attributed to the masculine character of colonial societies. From Roman military settlements in North Africa to the English, Dutch, and Spanish plantations in the Atlantic world, Enfantin argued, "adventurous men" who traveled alone to the colonies had no incentive to settle permanently or to cultivate and develop the land for the long term. Only emigration with more balanced sex ratios, "the transplantation of a *male and female* population, forming *families, villages, and towns*," could constitute "a considerable *civilian* population, an *agricultural, commercial,* and *industrial* population." Despite the radicalism of his larger belief in sexual freedom, Enfantin here shared the views of many of his contemporaries, who were convinced that the presence of women was both an index of and a recipe for the health and stability of colonial society.[67] As Baron Jean-Jacques Baude, former prefect of police of Paris and *commissaire du roi* in Algeria, wrote about the same time, "it is [women] who constitute families where there were only individuals: spouses, mothers, daughters, they become the social bond; they fix what was only passing and give long life to that which was only ephemeral. Only when we see by their number that this condition has been met can we have faith in the strength of colonies and the future of the institutions we found."[68] Of the promise of family colonization Enfantin concluded, "a single fact suffices to prove it: *we will have no more slaves.*"[69]

Slavery was not the only evil that could be attributed to colonists' selfishness and *esprit de retour*. European colonial society also suffered from the domination of men whose values were fundamentally hostile to the development of social good and civic virtue. As Talleyrand argued in 1797, greed was an individualistic trait,

---

66. Buret, *Question d'Afrique*, 19.
67. Enfantin, *Colonisation de l'Algérie*, 10–11. On Enfantin's views of sexuality, see Claire Moses, *French Feminism in the Nineteenth Century* (Albany, 1984), 46–50.
68. Jean-Jacques Baude, *L'Algérie*, vol. 2 (Paris, 1841), 234.
69. Enfantin, *Colonisation de l'Algérie*, 35.

and individualism was accentuated in those who went to the Americas in search of wealth: "The more avid they were, the more isolated they became."[70] Since human nature was disposed to prefer a stable social life, long-distance travel such as that required by empire either attracted individuals lacking the normal social inclinations or loosened the social bonds of those who engaged in it. The pursuit of imperial wealth had "given birth to a new species of nomadic savages" whose travels rendered them rootless and fundamentally antisocial, according to Diderot, with "neither fathers, nor mothers, nor children, brothers, relations, friends, fellow citizens."[71] Such men were, by definition, incapable of the virtuous social and civic sentiments necessary to a stable community, and to postrevolutionary commentators, symptomatic of "all the jealousies, all the worry, all the miseries, all the vices of old Europe" that were as anachronistic as colonial slavery.[72]

Say, Sismondi, and their contemporaries, however, did not reject empire entirely. Instead, they looked to the ancient past for examples of colonization that contributed to the general good and the development of human society. "When we seek to understand the causes that have contributed to spreading among men all the advantages of social life," Sismondi wrote, "the first [and] most important signaled to us by the study of Antiquity is the foundation of colonies."[73] Populated permanently by free families who identified with the colony and recognized their collective interests as a community, such colonies might constitute real markets for their metropoles, as well as societies in which the public good was respected. Under these conditions, Say argued, colonies could be considered "favorable to the progress of the human race and to its happiness."[74] Unlike Sismondi, liberal economists believed a certain degree of self-interest was necessary among colonists. "Pecuniary interest" had been critical, along with religion, language, culture, and family, in maintaining the ties between the colonies of antiquity and their metropoles, even after the colonies had reached economic and political maturity.[75] Now, modern colonies could not recruit permanent settlers except "with the lure of a remuneration that guarantees the future, whether this remuneration consists of property titles, a share in profits, or very high wages."[76] Without slaves,

70. Charles Maurice de Talleyrand, "Essai sur les avantages à retirer des colonies nouvelles, par le citoyen Talleyrand, lu à la séance publique du 15 messidor an V," in S. Dutot, De l'Expatriation, considérée sous ses rapports économiques, politiques et moraux (Paris, 1840), 330.
71. Raynal, Histoire . . . des deux Indes, 10:474–475; Jean-Charles-Léonard Sismonde de Sismondi, Études sur l'economie politique, vol. 2 (Paris, 1838), 152.
72. Sismondi, Les colonies des anciens, 7.
73. Ibid., 1.
74. Say, Cours complet, 1:401.
75. Ibid., 1:297.
76. Cochut, "De la colonisation de l'Algérie," 502.

however, such rewards could only be reaped through hard work on the part of the colonists themselves, making them committed members of their local societies and productive contributors to the larger good, rather than parasites profiting at others' expense. The self-interest of permanent settlers was thus presumed to be a source of social virtue that stood in sharp contrast to the corrupting self-interest of slave-holding Caribbean planters.

Evidence of settlement colonization's virtues could be found, according to postrevolutionary economists, in the colonies of ancient Greece and Rome, and their modern incarnation, the United States. Both Adam Smith and Jean-Baptiste Say had cited the Greek and Roman republics as owners of empires whose colonies strengthened the metropole without imposing undue financial or moral burdens. First, they had avoided the pitfalls of exclusive trade. Although Smith, like most liberal economists, preferred the Greek colonies to the military empire of the Romans, he claimed that the imperial expansion of both "derived their origin either from irresistible necessity or from clear and evident utility." This in contrast to the European colonies in the Americas and West Indies, which had no such reasonable social motives and were driven entirely by the "human avidity" of individuals. This greed propped up the company rule and commercial monopolies that maintained the colonies in a dependent relationship to their metropoles, constrained the scope for productive forms of self-interest among colonists, and facilitated the development of slavery.[77] The Greeks and Phoenicians, Say similarly argued in his defense of settler colonies, had not created dependent colonies subject to metropolitan monopolies, but had founded flourishing, independent societies on the coasts of Africa, Sicily, and Spain.[78] Indeed, Pellegrino Rossi, Say's student and successor at the Collège de France, would later argue that Greek expansion could hardly be called a "colonial system" as the term was commonly understood in France, because it was driven not by the desire for military or commercial domination, but by "the force of things" that pushed part of the population to emigrate.[79]

For both Smith and Say, as for many nineteenth-century French thinkers who read them, Anglophone North America embodied these virtuous qualities for the modern age. Although Smith invoked the pre-1776 British colonies and Say the western frontier of the independent United States, their ideals were the same: freed from company rule and trade restrictions, North American settlers had de-

77. Smith, *Wealth of Nations*, bk. 4, chap. 7, b, 2:567; bk. 4, chap. 7, a, 2:558; bk. 4, chap. 7, a, 2:563; bk. 4, chap. 7, b, 2:570–71, 587.
78. Say, *Cours complet*, 1:294.
79. Pellegrino Rossi, "Fragments d'histoire de l'économie politique chez les Grecs," in *Mélanges d'économie politique, d'histoire et de philosophie publiés par ses fils*, vol. 1 (Paris, 1857), 72–74.

veloped the productive self-interest that resulted in agricultural prosperity, social cohesion, and an increase in the public good.[80] The socialist Sismondi was less concerned about trade monopolies, although he did condemn modern colonies' enforced dependency on commerce designed to enrich their metropoles. And he was less convinced that the contemporary United States embodied the virtues of the ancients. Strangely, for a committed abolitionist, he did not mention slavery, nor did he highlight the treatment of Native Americans, despite lengthy denunciations of settler violence against aboriginal peoples in Australia and the Cape Colony. It was the "solitary, brutal, violent" existence of the "backwoodman" and the environmental damage done by clear-cutting farmers that Sismondi counted as black marks on the American record. He did agree with Say, however, that the young nation was "much closer to the ideas and sentiments of the Greeks and Romans" than any other modern European colony. The Pilgrims had emigrated for irreproachable reasons (the search for religious freedom) and "proposed above all to create for themselves a new *patrie* as the Greeks did in the past." It was later arrivals, who came from Europe with nothing more than the love of gain and the desire to expand trade, that had "sowed the germs of dissolution."[81] In sum, in the words of August Blanqui, the United States exemplified "the true principles of all colonization, in the current state of economic science and the civilized world."[82]

It was this understanding that defined *véritable colonisation* in debates about Algerian colonization after 1830. The influence of political economists like Smith, Say, and Sismondi can be seen in the footnotes and citations that littered works on Algeria. Buret's 1842 treatise on the "Algerian question" echoed Smith and Say in insisting that "the African colony can only resemble those of the Ancients."[83] Five years later, publicist Jean Brunet called on French colonial officials to imitate both the ancients, including the Phoenicians, Carthaginians, Greeks, and Romans, and the English in North America.[84] For Buret, Brunet, and their contemporaries, however, emigration and colonial settlement were more important than free trade in defining the ancient and North American colonial systems. Brunet was typical in this regard, and his call to emulate the ancients and the Anglo-Americans focused on the creation of a permanent colony of European emigrants, protected by French armies and settled on land distributed

80. Smith, *Wealth of Nations*, bk. 4, chap. 7, b, 2:567–81; Say, *Cours complet*, 1:297–99, 402. For Say, as for Tocqueville later, the notable, yet somehow not fatal exceptions to the United States' admirable virtue were its treatment of Native Americans and its toleration of slavery.
81. Sismondi, *Les colonies des anciens*, 12, 15, 8–9.
82. Blanqui, *Algérie*, 77.
83. Buret, *Question d'Afrique*, 19. See also Enfantin, *Colonisation*, 27–32.
84. Jean Brunet, *La question algérienne* (Paris, 1847), 143–44.

by the state. This type of colonization was expected to extend the social progress enjoyed in the metropole by offering property to emigrants and civilization to native Algerians. The result would be a colonial society that shared in the virtues of individual liberty and public solidarity that were seen as the birthright of post-revolutionary Frenchmen. A New France in Algeria would thus reproduce the best aspects of the metropole while avoiding the moral excesses and corruption of the old colonial empire.

Emigration, Settlement, and the Social Question

An Algerian colony would also, another group of reformers hoped, ameliorate dangerous changes taking place within France itself. Population growth, urban-ization, and revolution loomed large in the collective imagination of postrevolu-tionary elites, who feared their destabilizing consequences. According to census figures, the nation's population had increased by almost 20 percent between 1801 and 1831, and it grew another 10 percent in the next two decades. During the July Monarchy, the locus of population growth shifted from rural areas to cities, however. The number of urban communes of over 3,000 residents doubled in the 1830s and 1840s, while France's largest cities, led by Paris, exploded. The capital had 547,000 inhabitants in 1801 and passed the one million mark at the 1846 census. Other large cities lagged far behind in total population, but experienced dramatic expansion nonetheless, primarily through internal migration: Marseille grew 75 percent, from 111,000 to 195,000, between 1801 and 1851; Lyon grew by 62 percent to 177,000; and Bordeaux by 44 percent to 130,000.[85]

Earlier thinkers had seen large populations and urban life as sources of wealth and human progress, but nineteenth-century social critics began to see them as potential sources of social and political unrest. Seemingly endemic crime, dis-ease, and increasingly visible social and political protest convinced them that the growth of cities was a sign of pathological disorder rather than prosperity. Cities were not flourishing, but overcrowded with immigrants whose ignorance, im-morality, and poor hygiene made working-class quarters a breeding ground for crime and disease. Contemporary statistics and fiction alike painted portraits of working-class criminality that sent chills down the spines of middle- and upper-class readers. Balzac, for example, estimated that one in ten Parisians was a crook, a category that included confidence artists, petty thieves, burglars, prostitutes, and kept women. Crime seemed to go hand in hand with social maladies, such as infanticide, suicide, and madness, as well as biological disease. The deadly cholera

---

85. Figures from Charles Pouthas, *La population française pendant la première moitié du XIXe siècle* (Paris, 1956), 22, 75, 98–99.

epidemic that struck France in 1832 provided striking confirmation to anxious elites that the urban poor were a pathological element, as mortality rates in insalubrious working-class neighborhoods far outpaced those in wealthier areas.[86]

Most terrifying to observers, however, was the perceived violence of the urban poor. The life of the "laboring classes" was pervaded by brutality, from domestic violence to the bare-knuckle fighting known as the *savate*, according to elite discourse. Such everyday violence largely affected working-class communities themselves, but political violence by artisans and workers took the privileged classes as its target. The Revolution of 1830 was followed by major workers' uprisings in Lyon (1831 and 1834) and Paris (1834), as well as waves of machine-breaking, strikes, and the rise of illegal mutual aid societies. These events evidenced the growth of an increasingly militant and organized working-class movement that struck fear into the hearts of property-owning elites. The term *paupérisme*, introduced into French from English in 1823, connoted the extent to which the poor "conjured up fear of socio-political chaos and moral disorder" in the minds of middle-class observers, who saw pauperism as "a social plague—a stealthy contagious disease . . . undermining the health and vigor of the body politic— that manifested a quintessential characteristic of the modern nineteenth-century world."[87]

Intertwined concerns about uncontrolled population growth, urban overcrowding, and revolution provided new arguments for colonial emigration and settlement, which seemed to many observers to offer a panacea for a wide range of domestic ills. Whereas those who advocated Algerian colonization on economic and moral grounds were situated primarily on the left of the political spectrum, interest in colonial emigration transcended political differences. From conservative social Catholics and moral economists to radical romantic socialists, reformers concerned about the changes occurring around them recast colonization in terms of poverty and revolution, and tied the "Algerian question" to what had become known in the 1820s as the "social question."

According to participants in the debate over the social question, the root cause of urban pathology was poverty. The French state had, of course, long been concerned with indigence, but the translation of Thomas Malthus's *Essay on the*

---

86. The classic work on perceptions of the urban working class remains Louis Chevalier, *Laboring Classes and Dangerous Classes in Paris During the First Half of the Nineteenth Century* (1958), trans. Frank Jellinek (New York, 1973). See also, among others, Jill Harsin, *Policing Prostitution in Nineteenth-Century Paris* (Princeton, 1985); William Coleman, *Death Is a Social Disease: Public Health and Political Economy in Early Industrial France* (Madison, 1982).
87. André Gueslin, *Gens pauvres, pauvres gens dans la France du XIXe siècle* (Paris, 1988), 94–109; Frances Gouda, *Poverty and Political Culture: The Rhetoric of Social Welfare in the Netherlands and France, 1815–1854* (Lanham, 1995; repr., Amsterdam, 1995), quote 36.

Principle of Population into French in 1809 linked poverty to overpopulation and gave both questions unprecedented importance in intellectual and governmental discourse.[88] Mobilizing new forms of social statistics, economists, reformers, and administrators sought to identify the causes of urban "misery" so that it could be controlled. These men often disagreed about the specific mechanisms driving the phenomenon, but they shared a conviction that unmeasured population growth was the prime source of pressure on national resources. Adopting Ricardo's dim view of working-class sexuality, middle-class observers claimed that workers undercut their own earnings by producing large numbers of children who flooded the labor market and upset the wage equilibrium.[89] Mechanization and the reorganization of labor to fit industrial processes aggravated the situation by reducing the number of jobs available. Private charity, critics argued, could not keep up with poverty on the scale that resulted from these structural changes. At the same time, however, French social reformers were deeply suspicious of state involvement in charity and poor relief.[90] The foundation of overseas colonies seemed to be one of the few ways to relieve the suffering of the poor and to protect the security of the propertied without recourse to what reformers of all stripes saw as demoralizing, impersonal, and poverty-aggravating public welfare.

Almost every proponent of Algerian settlement during the July Monarchy shared the presumption that colonial settlement constituted a useful remedy for growing social ills. In the simplest terms, the social interpretation of colonial settlement focused on emigration as means of combating overpopulation without recourse to Malthus's "positive checks" on reproduction. Fifty years before natalism became a national obsession, advocates of settlement colonization dismissed the idea that emigration might weaken France by depopulating the countryside. Rapid population growth posed a much greater danger, they argued.[91] Malthus himself was skeptical about the efficacy of emigration as a long-term check on population growth—he believed that immigrants and newlyweds would quickly replace departing emigrants—although he supported British colonization efforts

88. On the reconfiguration of poverty, see Gouda, *Poverty*, 17–23, 35–38; Gueslin, *Gens pauvres*; Giovana Procacci, *Gouverner la misère: La question sociale en France (1789–1848)* (Paris, 1993). On population, Joshua Cole, *The Power of Large Numbers: Population, Politics, and Gender in Nineteenth-Century France* (Ithaca, 2000).

89. E.g. Eugène Buret, *De la misère des classes laborieuses en Angleterre et en France . . .* , vol. 1 (Paris, 1840), 43.

90. On French suspicion of state-run welfare during the July Monarchy, see Timothy Smith, "The Ideology of Charity, the Image of the English Poor Law, and Debates Over the Right to Assistance in France, 1830–1905," *Historical Journal* 40, no. 4 (1997): 1000–1008.

91. E.g. Say, *Cours complet*, 1:401. A vulgarized version of this argument can be found in A[drien] R[ognat], *Hermès, ou le génie colonisateur: Essai politique contenant les principes fondamentaux en matière de colonisation* (Paris, 1832), 24–25.

as a means of temporarily relieving the population crisis of the 1820s and 1830s.[92] Most French Malthusians, however, embraced emigration as part of a comprehensive solution to overpopulation. Say, for example, lauded settler colonies as a safeguard against overpopulation, which he believed to be the cause of colonial expansion in the ancient world, as we have seen. Emigration by the indigent, he argued, helped to prevent poor families from turning to abortion or infanticide to limit the number of mouths they had to feed. When population began to outstrip food supplies, the excess would find an outlet overseas.[93]

Algeria offered a seemingly ideal site for combating pauperism and overpopulation. Its proximity to Europe, reputedly fertile soil, and Mediterranean climate made it quite different from and more suitable to European habitation than tropical island colonies. These perceptions were critical in shaping French colonization plans, as we will see in the next chapter. The point here, though, is that advocates of Algerian colonization presumed that French emigrants would transition easily to life in North Africa, where they would embark on healthy, agricultural lives and prosper from the work of their own hands. Hundreds of petitions and colonization plans submitted to parliamentary and ministerial officials during the July Monarchy reflect this conviction. One pamphleteer, a certain V. Duteuil, suggested in 1832 that domestic security would be much increased by the emigration of the "frightening mass of agitated, hungry individuals" and ambitious youth "idle and worrisome to the friends of order and peace."[94] The letter accompanying a copy of the brochure that Duteuil sent to Casimir Périer, president of the Conseil d'État, declared that settlement in Algeria was "the only way to reestablish public peace in all those old States overburdened with population and to consolidate the thrones shaken by the effects of the general malaise of a society whose needs increase daily and whose resources have remained static following the misfortunes of the age."[95] As another colonial advocate put it a decade later, Algerian colonization would constitute "a great step towards the extinction of mendicity, even of pauperism, and thus would contribute a great deal to the security of the social order. Afterwards, there would be almost no more vagabonds or any of those lazy and penniless men always ready to sell [their] services to those seeking to disturb public tranquility."[96]

---

92. R. N. Ghosh, "Malthus's Views on Emigration and Colonization: Letters to Wilmot-Horton," *Economica*, n.s., 30, no. 117 (1963): 45–62.
93. Say, *Cours complet*, 1:400, 382.
94. Duteuil, *Nécessité de la colonisation*, 9.
95. CAOM F80 1161, Duteuil to président du Conseil, 10 January 1832.
96. A. Amaury, *Colonisation de l'Algérie: Observations, pour appendice et à l'appui d'un plan d'établissement en Algérie de Colonies Agricoles, proposé comme un d'entre les moyens les plus efficaces de parvenir à une diminution sensible de la mendicité et même du paupérisme en France . . .*

The relationship between the North African colonial project and the domestic social question was not always stated this explicitly. For many political economists and social reformers, it was simply assumed, and the very prevalence of this assumption suggests how deeply ingrained the idea had become in intellectual and political circles.[97] It was no coincidence that many of the men who wrote and advocated most forcefully for the colonization of Algeria during the July Monarchy came to the question by way of inquiries into the organization and prosperity of Western societies. Among the first to envision Algeria's advantages from a social perspective was Sismondi, who in May 1830 published a lengthy article on the Algiers expedition that concluded, "This will not be just a conquest; this will be a colony, a new country in which the surplus of the French population and energy will be able to spread out."[98] Buret became interested in Algerian colonization after completing a prize-winning work on the causes of *la misère* in modern Europe. He spent two years following the publication of this work writing *La question d'Afrique*, a four-hundred-page tome on Algerian colonization. At the far left, the utopian socialist Prosper Enfantin turned to Algeria in the wake of his famous series on the Saint-Simonian religion in the *Globe* (1831–32) and a voyage to Turkey and Egypt in search of the female messiah and plans for what would become the Suez Canal. In 1839, he petitioned to join the scientific commission being sent by the government to explore its new conquest, and the hefty volume based on his observations appeared in 1843.[99] Alexis de Tocqueville, the leading liberal thinker in nineteenth-century France, began studying Algeria shortly after returning from the North American trip that would result in *Democracy in America*. He traveled twice to the colony, beginning while he was still working on *Democracy*—which was itself read as an analysis of the world's most successful settler colony[100]—and went on to become one of the

(Paris, 1842), 11. Also, AN C2199, Amaury, "Établissement de colonies agricoles en Algérie, proposé comme moyen des plus puissants pour arriver à l'extinction de la mendicité en France," 5 January 1844; AN C 2226, Amaury, *De l'Algérie et du paupérisme en France* (Algiers, 1847).

97. By the late 1820s, French social reformers and their audiences took for granted that wage competition and working-class immorality went hand in hand. William Reddy, *The Rise of Market Culture: The Textile Trade and French Society, 1750–1900* (Cambridge, 1984), 145–46.

98. Sismondi, *De l'expédition contre Alger* (Paris, 1830), 12. Sismondi was appalled by the cruelty of the war of conquest and by the grasping nature of the early settlers, and *Les colonies des anciens* includes an impassioned plea for a civilizing French presence rather than exploitation by greedy speculators.

99. On Enfantin's role in the Commission Scientifique, see his file in CAOM F80 1596; Monique Dondin-Payre, *La Commission d'exploration scientifique d'Algérie: Une héritière méconnue de la Commission d'Egypte* (Paris, 1994).

100. CAOM F80 1162, Poirel, *De la colonisation militaire, agricole et pénale d'Alger* (Nancy, 1837), 11.

Chamber of Deputies' foremost experts on Algerian affairs in the 1840s, as well
as a significant landowner in the colony. Tocqueville's fragmentary writings on
Algeria have been analyzed in depth elsewhere, and do not require extensive discussion here.[101] It is worth noting, however, that his views on the importance of
Algerian colonization were quite conventional for the time and that he shared the
assumption, "universally admitted" in the 1840s, that colonization meant settlement by European emigrants. "The future of our domination in Africa depends
on a single event," Tocqueville declared in 1846, "the arrival on African territory
of a European population . . . whose greatness contains the entire future of our
greatness in Africa."[102]

The conviction that emigration would improve the fortunes of poor French
families and restore social order at home fostered support for Algerian colonization. Settlement schemes promised to help the poor earn a living they could no
longer make in France. In September of 1830, for example, a M. Fabien from
Cambrai, petitioned the deputies to create a colony in North Africa, claiming that
"at this moment a large number of unemployed workers ask nothing better than
to go to Algiers."[103] Clauzel, a determined advocate of colonization, insisted in
1831 that emigration was the sole desire of "the part of the population that hopes
to find in Algeria the work and bread that it can no longer find in France."[104]
An Alsatian cleric, Abbé Landmann, whose proposals for associative agricultural
colonies were seriously considered in the 1840s, explained that his project targeted "poor families happy to find steady bread that they might not have on the
continent."[105] Similar sentiments were expressed in dozens of unsolicited plans
sent to the legislative Chambers, Ministry of War, and Algerian Government
General in the 1830s and 1840s. Despite differences in their details, most of these
shared the belief that settlement on Algeria's rich arable plains would aid those
buffeted by the shifting winds of the new industrial economy.

101. See, among others, Mary Lawlor, *Alexis de Tocqueville in the Chamber of Deputies: His Views on Foreign and Colonial Policy* (Washington, D.C., 1959), esp. chap. 6–7; Melvin Richter, "Tocqueville on Algeria," *Review of Politics* 25 (1963): 362–98; Pitts, *Turn*, chap. 7.
102. Speech to the Chamber of Deputies, 9 June 1846, in *Writings on Empire and Slavery*, ed. and trans. Jennifer Pitts (Baltimore, 2001), 118–19.
103. E.g. CAOM F80 1161, "Pétition à la Chambre des députés au sujet de la colonisation," 7 September 1830. Fabien had written a month earlier demanding that Algiers be occupied perma-nently. AN C2103, "Demande que le Gouvernement prenne des mesures pour conserver Alger à la France," 18 August 1830.
104. CAOM F80 1161, Clauzel to ministre de la Guerre, 31 May 1831.
105. CAOM F80 1128, Procès-verbaux des séances de la Commission de colonisation de l'Algérie, 9 February 1842. Landmann's plans were laid out in *Les Fermes du Petit Atlas, ou colonisation agri-cole, religieuse et militaire du nord de l'Afrique* (Paris, 1841); *Mémoires au Roi sur la colonisation de l'Algérie* (Paris, 1845); and *Exposé.*

Colonization also offered a productive alternative to repressive forms of poor relief. In the eyes of nineteenth-century social reformers, punitive measures that clapped debtors and vagrants into prisons and *hospices* merely spread criminality. Cash handouts were also viewed with suspicion and considered both ineffective in stemming the tide of pauperism and encouraging of laziness. Reformers and economists thus advocated more "productive" remedies for poverty, among which a return to the land figured prominently.[106] Agriculture offered the poor a better future only on the condition that they work for it and, unlike the makework of metropolitan poorhouses, contributed to the national economy. As one anonymous advocate of colonization wrote in the mid-1830s, "the colonies are a great resource for offering work to industrious individuals by granting them land; they cultivate it themselves, become farmers in their turn, and contribute later to the prosperity of the mother country."[107]

This view of settlement colonization—and its agrarian underpinnings—not only mirrored the logic of contemporary British colonial theorists but also fit into a continental rural colonization movement in the early nineteenth century. Dutch reformers had created *colonies agricoles* to rehabilitate the impoverished in the Low Countries in the 1810s, and similar establishments were founded on this model in France during the July Monarchy.[108] A plan drawn up by the legitimist social Catholic Baron Pierre-Marie-Sébastien Bigot de Morogues, one of the early proponents of domestic agricultural colonies, made clear the goals of such settlement projects. According to Bigot de Morogues, the small farm alone could guarantee the worker an adequate and fair wage for his labor. "It is in the sufficient salaries that agriculture and small-scale industry promise so much more than manufacturing that we have found the remedy for the evils that weigh on the richest and most civilized countries in the world," he wrote.[109] In keeping with contemporary distinctions between the "deserving" and "undeserving" poor, however, rural colonies should serve those members of society whose indigence was not of their own making. Admission was to be limited to "intelligent, honest, hardworking and able-bodied men," who found themselves unable to support their families on wages constrained by "commercial stagnation,

106. Gouda, *Poverty*, 118–25, 207–15.
107. H . . . de B . . . , *De l'Algérie*, 5.
108. Gouda, *Poverty*, 235–43; Gérard de Puymège, *Chauvin, le soldat-laboureur: Contribution à l'étude des nationalismes* (Paris, 1993), 147–56. For their influence on thinking about Algeria, CAOM F80 1161, général Cubières to baron Pelet, "Note sur la colonisation d'Alger," 6 April 1831.
109. *Trois opuscules sur les moyens de prévenir les misères des ouvriers* (Paris, n.d.), 7. Bigot's principal works on the social question and *colonies agricoles* are *De la misère des ouvriers et de la marche à suivre pour y remédier* (Paris, 1832); and *Du paupérisme, de la mendicité, et des moyens d'en prévenir les funestes effets* (Paris, 1834). On Bigot more generally, see Reddy, *Rise*, 147–49.

the mutations of trade, the effects of large industry's encroachments on small, or the [encroachment of] machines' fictional [i.e. false] work upon that of hands."[110] Virtuous workers who had fallen victim to changes in the international economy or in the prevailing modes of production, rather than to their own bad judgment or vices, were those targeted by colonization schemes.

The precedent of domestic colonization shows there was far more to the social reformers' support for settlement colonization than merely "shoveling out paupers." Since pauperism was closely associated with cities and proletarianized industrial labor, rural settlement offered the possibility of rehabilitating the poor and permanently reversing the social, moral, and political evils propagated by urbanization and industrialization. Transforming the urban proletariat into peasant farmers would "regenerate the poor classes and . . . reform their morals by developing their intelligence and by restoring, at the same time, their physical strength."[111] This promise echoed the "antimodernist consensus" of the mid-nineteenth century, which glorified rural life and peasant agriculture as the antithesis of urban corruption and the essence of a purified French nation.[112] Settlement colonies were a practical measure of poor relief, but they also aimed to make this mythical image a reality.

The same nostalgic fantasies informed plans for the colonization of Algeria. A system in which poor emigrants from France were settled on the rich Algerian land would multiply the number of small farmers who constituted the ideal citizens of this stable, agrarian society. Self-sustaining agriculture would replace uncertain wage labor, and working-class tendencies towards laziness, improvidence, and revolt would be transformed into laboriousness, thrift, and docile patriotism. Advocates claimed that the man who was "miserable in France, will become [in Algeria] the owner of field, vine, home, farmyard, and, soon, of beast, in sum, of an assured means of subsistence and independence for himself and his family. He will have created for himself a new *patrie*, all while remaining attached to France, and he will bless the government that has procured for him such unexpected bliss."[113] This was the model for the *véritable colonisation* that French policymakers sought to implement in Algeria, simultaneously laying the foundations for a new, morally virtuous empire and mitigating the social changes threatening the French body politic.

110. Pierre-Marie-Sébastien Bigot de Morogues, *Projet de colonies agricoles libres, fondées par maisons dispersées dans les campagnes et y formant de petites propriétés* . . . (n.p., [1833]), 2.
111. De Raineville, *Colonies agricoles, considérées comme moyens de venir au secours des indigens* (Amiens, [1841]), 1.
112. Gouda, *Poverty*, 125. Also James Lehning, *Peasant and French: Cultural Contact in Rural France during the Nineteenth Century* (Cambridge, 1995), 12–18; Puymège, *Chauvin*, 146. Images of the peasant were unstable, as Raymond Grew argues. "Picturing the People: Images of the Lower Orders in Nineteenth-Century French Art," *Journal of Interdisciplinary History* 17, no. 1 (1986): 203–31.
113. CAOM F80 1161, Gouré, *Considérations sur Alger* (Paris, 1830), 15.

5

Selling Algeria

Speculation and the Colonial Landscape

The very idea of an Algerian settler colony assumed that the newly conquered territory was suitable for European settlement and European-style agriculture. Whether favorable or hostile to the colonization in North Africa, policymakers and publicists, as well as many ordinary citizens, viewed the matter largely in terms of its potential to repay the efforts of "serious colonists . . . who devote themselves with their families to the cultivation of the land."[1] Consequently, debate about Algerian colonization was premised on observers' beliefs about the nature of the Algerian soil and couched in the sexualized language of fertility and sterility. Advocates of settlement argued from an almost blind faith in Algeria's fabulous fecundity, while opponents denounced the soil as barren. The arguments of anticolonialists quickly lost traction, however, and colonialists' claims about the great beauty and fertility of the land gained a nearly unimpeachable position in the French imagination.

The myth of Algeria's great fertility had long roots in the classical texts and early modern travel accounts that were the main sources of French knowledge of the region in the early nineteenth century. In works like that of Thomas Shaw, an English doctor whose 1738 travel account was reprinted in a new French translation on the eve of the invasion, French military planners, legislators, and other readers found profuse praise for the apparently infinite agricultural bounty of

1. Report on a *projet de loi* for extraordinary credits for colonization in 1843, cited in *TEFA* (1842–43), 157.

the former regency. In the 1830 edition of Shaw's *Travels*, the enumeration of Algeria's many and varied crops ran to over ten pages detailing everything from staples, such as wheat, barley, and rice giving higher yields than their European counterparts, to garden vegetables (turnips, carrots, and cabbages of prodigious size), all of the fruit trees of Europe, and more exotic items such as date palms and the *sidra* tree, which Shaw claimed was the lotus of the ancients.[2] This and other travelers' accounts confirmed what educated nineteenth-century Frenchmen read in classical histories and geographies about the productivity of the Algerian land, especially under the Roman Empire. Greek and Roman authors lauded the abundant harvests, vegetation, and game of North Africa, and modern writers like Shaw reported that "the general fertility of the soil, so celebrated by the ancients, is still the same."[3] Together these texts underpinned a widespread belief in what one Frenchman enthusiastically described in 1833 as "the beauty of the soil, the fertility, and the abundance that derives from the territory of Algiers and from all this vast kingdom."[4] Subsequent explorations by French military men, savants, and amateurs sought out further evidence of past prosperity, which they found in archaeological, botanical, and climatological research.[5] The mythical status of Algeria's rich soil was grounded in this history and reinforced by maps and landscape imagery that depicted the North African territory as a picturesque land overflowing with natural bounty.

Opponents of the occupation contested such visions, but to little avail. Deputy Hippolyte Passy, for example, ridiculed his colleagues' "vast and magnificent hopes" for Algeria's fertility,[6] while the Chambers' African Commission of 1834 cautioned that the soil was predominantly "either sandy and arid, or clayey and

---

2. Thomas Shaw, *Voyage dans la régence d'Alger, ou Description géographique, physique, philologique, etc., de cet état*, trans. and ed. J. MacCarthy (Paris, 1830), 9–19. Shaw's *Travels, or Observations relating to several parts of Barbary and the Levant* appeared in English in 1738 and was first translated into French in 1743. On the sources of French knowledge, see Denise Brahimi, *Les voyageurs français du XVIIIe siècle en Barbarie* (thèse de 3e cycle, Université de Paris III, 1976); Ann Thomson, *Barbary and Enlightenment: European Attitudes towards the Maghreb in the 18th Century* (Leiden, 1987), esp. pt. 2, chap. 1; Patricia Lorcin, *Imperial Identities: Stereotyping, Prejudice and Race in Colonial Algeria* (1995; repr. London, 1999), 105–8; Patricia Lorcin, "Rome and France in North Africa: Recovering Algeria's Latin Past," *French Historical Studies* 25, no. 2 (2002): 297–99; Diana Davis, *Resurrecting the Granary of Rome: Environmental History and French Colonial Expansion in North Africa* (Athens, Ohio, 2007), 16–23, largely parallels my own analysis.
3. Shaw, *Voyage*, 21.
4. CAOM F80 1670 (2), Sarda père to ministre de la Guerre, 28 July 1833.
5. The most notable of these was the Scientific Commission of 1839. See Monique Dondin-Payre, *La Commission d'exploration scientifique d'Algérie: Une héritière méconnue de la Commission d'Égypte* (Paris, 1994); Lorcin, "Rome and France," 302–5.
6. "Rapport de la commission du budget du ministère de la guerre," 9 April 1834, *Moniteur universel*, 10 April 1834.

swampy." The African Commission nonetheless concluded that there was much
to be gained from expanding French domination into the interior. Abandoning
the conquest would "offend the nation's legitimate pride" and sacrifice the economic advantages promised by the areas beyond the coastal towns then occupied
by the French army.[7] Despite anticolonialists' ongoing objections, the Algerian
fertility myth proved irresistibly seductive. Advocates of colonial settlement continued to invoke it to promote colonization to lawmakers, the French public, and
potential settlers, and when early colonization efforts failed to realize the land's
legendary wealth, they blamed the inhabitants, rather than the soil itself: indigenous Algerians' ignorance and indolence prevented them from cultivating the
land properly, while early European immigrants' shortsighted greed led them to
eschew agricultural labor in favor of speculative investment in petty commerce
and land.

The fertility myth and what Diana Davis calls the "declensionist narrative"
of environmental degradation are familiar justifications for the expropriation
of land by colonial states. From the time of Columbus, Europeans continually
"misread" the land stewardship of indigenous peoples around the globe and presumed that territories not cultivated by European methods were "empty" and
available for settlement.[8] More surprising is the conviction of French policymakers and observers that the Europeans themselves constituted a serious obstacle to
"fertilizing" the Algerian soil. Many early visitors to Algiers were appalled by the
destruction wrought by the Armée d'Afrique in its seemingly endless appetite for
firewood, forage, and food supplies. Members of the African Commission were
"struck on first glance by the denuded state of the soil." "The French occupation
had carried devastation behind it," the African Commission's agriculture subcommittee concluded; whatever trees and fields "the ignorance and the character
of the Turkish Government had not destroyed have almost entirely disappeared
from the areas where we are masters."[9] Later, the destruction of woods and crops
became a central aim of Governor General Bugeaud's "total war" strategy.

French officials and commentators could debate indigenous agricultural
practices and regret the destruction caused by the army, but there was no question about Europeans who failed to cultivate the lands they had acquired. To

7. "Rapport général sur l'occupation des divers points de la Régence, sur l'organisation du gou-
vernement et sur les dépenses de 1834 et 1835," 7 March 1834, *Procès-verbaux et rapports de la
Commission d'Afrique instituée par ordonnance du Roi du 12 décembre 1833* (Paris, 1834), 400, 405.
8. James Fairhead and Melissa Leach, *Misreading the African Landscape: Society and Ecology in a
Forest-Savanna Mosaic* (Cambridge, 1996). On land and law in settler colonies, see Henry Reynolds,
The Law of the Land (Ringwood, Australia, 1987); Stuart Banner, *Possessing the Pacific: Land,
Settlers, and Indigenous People from Australia to Alaska* (Cambridge, Mass., 2007).
9. CAOM F80 10, Commission d'Afrique, rapport de la 1ère commission, "Question agricole," 1834.

know that agriculture was the bedrock of civilization and yet leave one's land fallow could only be explained as a deliberately antisocial choice by men who had purely speculative intentions. Such behavior threatened to introduce into the new colony the evils that slave-owning planters wreaked in the old ones. In the context of the postrevolutionary rethinking of empire, Algerians were assigned a position analogous to that of emancipated slaves, who could not be trusted to provide labor and would best be replaced by emigrant settlers, while European speculators were seen as latter-day planters who put their own short-term desires before the well-being of society as a whole. The struggle to reconcile suspicions of speculation and the agricultural imperatives of colonization with settlers' property proved far more troublesome to French policymakers than the decision to expropriate Algerians. If the fertility myth shaped the basic assumptions about Algeria's suitability for *véritable colonisation*, "the settlement of Algeria and the putting into production of the soil" required the recruitment of "good" colonists and keeping land out of the hands of "bad" ones.[10]

The Politics of Colonial Landscape

Between 1830 and 1834, known as "the period of uncertainty," the French Chambers debated whether to continue the occupation of Algiers in part, in whole, or indeed at all. In the parliamentary struggle, the nature of the land became one of the essential points of argument. Algerian policy was set by ministerial decree and, after July 1834, by royal ordinance, and then implemented by the Ministry of War, which held administrative jurisdiction over the territory occupied by the army. Legislative influence over Algerian matters was therefore limited to the power of the purse strings, and the annual debate over the Ministry of War's budget became a kind of yearly referendum on Algerian affairs. While debate focused primarily on military and diplomatic matters, the fertility of the Algerian soil was regularly invoked in these arguments. When colonization came to the forefront of budget discussions in the early 1830s, the fertility myth itself became an object of debate.

Anticolonial deputies denigrated the quality of the Algerian soil in order to combat any expansion of colonization or of the occupation itself, while their opponents leaned heavily on the country's fertility to argue for continued occupation and investment in further colonization. Amédée Desjobert, for example, insisted

---

10. Thomas-Robert Bugeaud, *L'Algérie. Des moyens de conserver et d'utiliser cette conquête* (Paris, 1842), 65–66.

that rosy visions of Algerian cornucopias were "complete illusion."[11] Procolonial legislators like the Marseillais deputy André Reynard maintained conversely that Algeria was "ready to become a very useful agricultural colony." Its mild climate, abundant water supplies, and fertile soil would lend themselves to the cultivation of a host of foodstuffs and industrial crops, from lemons and olive trees to almonds, figs, oranges, rice, cereals, tobacco, hemp, linen, silk, and cotton. Justin Laurence cited the historical fertility of Roman Numidia and argued that "the soil . . . is of a fertility that calls only for the hand of man."[12] These views were reiterated by representatives of the small but growing European community in Algiers, landowners, functionaries, and merchants who sent emissaries and petitions to lobby the Chambers for support of colonization efforts with claims that "the conquest of Algiers offers France infinite resources."[13]

Arguments that Algeria was unsuited to European settlement confronted an image of agricultural wealth that was too well established to be overcome, such that the nature of the soil began to fade from parliamentary discussion by the late 1830s. Skeptics continued to point to the insalubrity of specific areas and high mortality rates among French troops and European colonists, especially in the Mitidja plain, but discussions within the Ministry of War's Algerian bureaus focused on how to combat disease rather than withdrawal from infertile or malarial areas. Anticolonial members of the Chambers turned their attention to the conduct of administrative and military matters by the colony's successive governors general, in an attempt to limit France's financial engagements and to prevent the expansion of colonial settlement. With the nomination of the *doctrinaire* duc de Broglie as President of the Conseil d'État in March 1835, the procolonial but *laissez-faire* views espoused by François Guizot became the quasi-official government position.[14] Guizot and other colonialist liberals argued that the state should limit its involvement to protecting colonists against Arab attackers and disease, but agreed that Algeria should be retained and settled by Europeans. This view obtained through the ministerial upheaval of the late 1830s, until the right-center Soult-Guizot government adopted an active colonization policy in 1840.

Under these generally *coloniste* governments, the myth of Algeria's fertility was given new forms to meet new challenges. While opponents within the

11. Speech to the Chamber of Deputies, 7 June 1838, in *Moniteur universel*, 8 June 1838.
12. Speeches to the Chamber of Deputies, 30 April 1834, *AP* 89:612, 624.
13. AN C2112, no. 1562, Joseph Choveton, petition to the Chamber of Deputies, 28 December 1831.
14. The *doctrinaires* were a small but influential group around François Guizot, known for their support for the Charter of 1830, intellectual and academic pretensions, and penchant for British liberalism. H. A. C. Collingham with Robert S. Alexander, *The July Monarchy: A Political History of France, 1830–1848* (London, 1988), 113.

Chambers began to focus increasingly on the brutal tactics of Bugeaud's "total war" strategy, the treatment of Algeria's indigenous population, and conditions within the Armée d'Afrique, the legislature continued to seek ways to control the costs of the occupation. The economic crisis that struck France in 1837, combined with large budget deficits from war preparations during the Eastern Crisis of 1840 and the construction of Thiers's Paris fortifications, begun in 1841, worried fiscal conservatives who sought to limit the Ministry of War's Algerian budget. The successive war ministers and governors general were thus forced to defend the conquest and to reassure legislators of the rewards that would result from the successful prosecution of the war. As these men pushed to expand the area under French occupation after 1837, they regularly turned to affirmations of the land's fertility to justify the conquest of each successive point.

Persistent accusations of "illusion," "chimera," or "fantasy" in the legislative debates of the 1830s were partly based on an acutely felt absence of reliable information on Algeria and its occupation by the French army. Each time the Algerian question came before the Chambers, lawmakers protested that their deliberations were hampered by "uncertainty [and] ignorance founded on the lack of authentic, official documents."[15] In 1835, the deputies addressed this lack by requiring that the Ministry of War provide them with a full annual report on the situation in North Africa.[16] Composed in the ministry's Algerian bureaus from documents provided by officials in Algiers, the *Tableau de la situation des établissements français dans l'Algérie* (Picture of the situation of the French establishments in Algeria) became the primary source of official information about the colony and an important vehicle for the Algerian fertility myth from the time the first one was published in 1837. Presented to the Chambers each year along with the ministry's proposed Algerian budget, the *Tableaus* served to justify these funding requests. The ongoing war of conquest and Algerians' active subversion of French information-gathering efforts meant their data were often only approximations, as the *Tableaus'* authors recognized, but the supposedly scientific, corporately authored reports became an institutionalized work of colonial propaganda.[17]

15. Baron Mounier, speech to the Chamber of Peers, 19 April 1833, *AP* 82:668.
16. "Loi portant fixation du Budget des dépenses de l'exercise 1835," 23 May 1834, in *Bulletin des lois du Royaume de France*, pt. 1, 9th ser., vol. 6 (Paris, 1834), no. 126.
17. On the difficulties of data gathering, see *TEFA* (1838), 127; ibid. (1839), 51; [Henri] de Peyerimhoff, *Enquête sur les résultats de la colonisation officielle de 1871 à 1895. Rapport à Monsieur Jonnart, Gouverneur Général de l'Algérie*, vol. 1 (Algiers, 1906), 6; Kamel Kateb, *Européens, "indigènes" et juifs en Algérie (1830–1962): Représentations et réalités des populations* (Paris, 2001), chap. 1. On the *Tableaus*, see Jules Duval, "Tableaux de la situation des Établissements français dans l'Algérie," *Bulletin de la Société de Géographie*, 5th ser., 2 (1865): 49–170.

The Ministry of War's goal, according to the first *Tableau*, was "to consolidate French power in Algeria [and] to consecrate on that land torn from pirates the foundations of a durable establishment that will repay the sacrifices made by France to settle the civilization of old Europe on African soil."[18] To this end, the annual reports presented the Chambers with an enticing vision of an Algerian landscape ideally suited to agricultural exploitation and crying out for technologically sophisticated European colonists "to people and to fertilize" it.[19] "Ease of defense, healthiness, proximity to springs and running water, fertility of environs [were] the primary conditions sought" in sites for colonization, and few places failed to fulfill these criteria.[20] External signs of the soil's current or previous fertility were cast in terms of the information they provided about the land's potential for settlement. In Blidah, for example, impressive hedges of wild olive trees were said to "give an idea of what competent cultivation could produce with little effort on this favored land." Cherchel's surroundings boasted fruit trees and vines that "promise[d] a brilliant future to cultivation." At Médéah, the ministry's writers found mulberry bushes, pear and cherry trees, and poplars, as well as vines producing excellent grapes. Where current productivity disappointed, the *Tableaus*' authors looked for evidence of past fertility onto which to plot future colonization efforts. Archaeological traces of Roman occupation offered particularly compelling proof of former prosperity. At Guelma, "the Roman ruins that one meets at every step . . . sufficiently prove the advantages . . . that this part of Algeria once offered and would offer again to a sedentary population." In some places, only the Roman ruins marked promising spots for settlement, as in the villages of Douéra, Boufarick, Koléah, Philippeville, Sétif, and Rachgoun, which were established in 1841 on sites where the "remains of former towns . . . attest to the importance the Romans attached to these positions."[21]

Throughout the July Monarchy, the *Tableaus* invoked the fertility myth to support the expansion of settlement in North Africa. Yet their relentless enumeration of the progress of colonization, from the size of the European population to the number of hectares under European cultivation, also made it evident that the Algerian colony was largely failing to meet the hopes that had been pinned on it. Inherent in the fertility myth was the presumption, highly gendered and sexualized, that the marriage of European agriculture with the fecund Algerian

18. "Exposé des motifs," *TEFA* (1837), xii.
19. Ibid. (1843–44), 220.
20. Ibid. (1838), 137; (1840), 84.
21. Ibid. (1837), 42; (1841), 33; (1840), 18; (1842–43), 196; (1841), 19. On the Roman precedent, see Davis, *Resurrecting*; Lorcin, "Rome and France."

soil would produce magnificent harvests; one had only to *peupler* in order to *fertiliser*. Algeria's was "a soil that awaits only the plow" or "awaits only hands to once again produce rich harvests," according to the *Tableaus*.[22] Accounts of the progress of Algerian agriculture under French domination, however, told a less encouraging story. Simply put, French conquest was failing to make the fertility myth a reality.

The initial culprit appeared to be the native inhabitants of the former Ottoman regency. Their failure to properly cultivate the land was a long-standing feature of European thinking about North Africa. Since the eighteenth century, Western commentators had conjoined praise for the great fertility of the Algerian soil with negative assessments of local agriculture. According to the narrative of decline that emerged in this period, the agricultural wealth of Roman Mauretania had fallen into sterility with the Arab invasions of the seventh century.[23] The Ottoman state was a destructive force that had despoiled the land by razing Roman improvements and displacing the agricultural population. According to the *Tableau* of 1840, for example, the Turks had "overturned the walls [of Sétif] and strewn the land with the debris of its monuments; the insecurity of the sedentary inhabitants of its soil ruined its agriculture and left it with only its former renown for fertility."[24] Nineteenth-century French observers increasingly blamed the supposed ignorance, indolence, or nomadism of the Arab "race" as a whole for the desertification, deforestation, and sterilization said to have ruined the former "granary of Rome." In 1833, the Algerian Commission claimed that Arabs plowed the land only superficially and abandoned land once the soil had been exhausted.[25] The Ministry of War's *Tableaus* concurred in the following years that the unfulfilled potential of the soil was attributable to mismanagement by absent, imprudent, or vicious natives. Parts of the province of Oran, for instance, were found to be entirely deforested, and "the nomadic peoples who wander the country [to be] the cause of this desolation." Rather than planting, pastoralist groups "without any worry for the future" destroyed the land by driving their herds through fields and burning pastures.[26]

Algerians would hardly have recognized themselves in such descriptions, which misrecognized the finely tuned systems of crop rotation and soil enrich-

22. *TEFA* (1842–43), 195, 189.
23. Thomson, *Barbary and Enlightenment*, 42–44, 100–102; Davis, *Resurrecting*, 20–23.
24. *TEFA* (1840), 31.
25. CAOM F80 10, Commission d'Alger, "Question agricole," [1834].
26. *TEFA* (1837), 50. Deforestation, an ongoing concern for the French state, was also attributed to Algerian pastoralists. See also ibid. (1842–43), 258; David Prochaska, "Fire on the Mountain: Resisting Colonialism in Algeria," in *Banditry, Rebellion and Social Protest in Africa*, ed. Donald Crummey (London, 1986), 229–52.

ment that characterized precolonial agriculture.[27] Light, maneuverable plows had real advantages in fields studded with dwarf-palm roots, and both shallow tilling and pasturing herds helped preserve the soil. A few military officials recognized the logic of local agriculture, but most observers agreed "that [productivity] could be much greater and that the lands of the plains could compare with our good French lands. But to achieve this, sedentary colonists must replace the nomadic tribes, and we must necessarily introduce European methods; these are the *sine qua non* conditions" for restoring Algeria's former fecundity.[28]

Over the course of the July Monarchy, however, it became increasingly evident to French policymakers, observers, and publicists that the new settlers were doing little to fertilize the land. First, they were simply too few to cultivate the vast areas presumed to be lying fallow. The European population grew steadily (table 3), but migrants did not flood in at the fantastic rates predicted by enthusiastic colonialists. Second, and more confounding, those who did come were not settling on the land. The vast majority of Algeria's Europeans lived in cities throughout the colonial period, and this concentration in urban areas was particularly acute in the first decades of the occupation. During the July Monarchy, Algiers alone was home to over half of the settler population, and the five largest towns, Algiers, Oran, Bône, Philippeville, and Boufarick, each with a population of 4,000 or more, together accounted for 80 percent of European residents. By the end of 1846, the first year in which colonial authorities collected such data, just 16,422 of Algeria's 109,400 Europeans were making a living from agricultural pursuits.[29] Explaining and reversing these troubling patterns became as pressing a task for French colonial policymakers as preventing the destruction they attributed to the indigenous population.

Recruiting Colonial Emigrants

The slow growth of the European population posed a persistent, but fairly straightforward challenge to colonial advocates and policymakers throughout the nineteenth century. Overcoming it was believed to hinge simply on informing suitable individuals of the fertility of the Algerian soil, whose seductive power would then entice striving French cultivators to take passage for North Africa. From the early 1830s, representatives of colonial interests called for greater publicity to attract new settlers. "Let [the Government] only conserve, protect and organize Algiers; above all, let it make [Algeria] known," wrote one group of

27. André Nouschi, *Enquête sur le niveau de vie des populations rurales constantinoises de la conquête jusqu'en 1919: Essai d'histoire économique et sociale* (Paris, 1961), 54–57, 65–69.
28. CAOM F80 10, Commission d'Alger, "Question agricole," [1834].
29. *TEFA* (1845–46), 87, 189.

TABLE 3. EUROPEAN POPULATION OF ALGERIA, 1830–51

Year	French	Foreign	Total
1830			602
1831	1,230	1,998	3,228
1832			4,858
1833	3,478	4,334	7,812
1834	4,349	5,401	9,750
1835	4,888	6,363	11,251
1836	5,485	9,076	14,561
1837	6,592	10,154	16,746
1838	8,034	12,044	20,078
1839	9,526	13,497	23,023
1840	11,322	16,756	28,078
1841	15,497	20,230	35,727
1842	19,056	25,475	44,531
1843	28,163	30,523	58,686
1844	38,646	37,221	75,867
1845	44,305	51,016	96,321
1846	47,274	59,894	109,400
1847	53,696	50,197	103,893
1848	63,540	51,561	115,101
1849	58,005	54,692	112,697
1850	62,044	64,704	125,748
1851	66,050	65,233	131,283

Source: TEFA (1837–55).

colonists to commander in chief Clauzel in 1833.[30] Fifteen years later, publicist Jean Brunet repeated that "only an official publicity as widespread as possible can overcome [the] obstacles" facing colonization, an argument that became a standard refrain among the Algerian settlers throughout the colonial period.[31] In response to these calls, both the colonial administration and settler interest groups mobilized the fertility myth to recruit new emigrants to work the Algerian soil.

30. CAOM F80 1161, "Un group de colons" to général Clauzel, Algiers, 9 July 1833.
31. Jean Brunet, La question algérienne (Paris, 1847), 151; Peyerimhoff, Enquête, 1:219; Seth Graebner, "'Unknown and Unloved': The Politics of French Ignorance in Algeria, 1860–1930," in Algeria and France, 1800–2000: Identity, Memory, Nostalgia, ed. Patricia Lorcin (Syracuse, 2006), 49–57.

The most direct of such efforts took the form of guides and handbooks intended to explain the colony's advantages to prospective emigrants and to provide logistical assistance to Europeans planning to travel to the colony. Emigrant handbooks were relatively few in the 1830s but began to appear more regularly and with official endorsement in the 1840s, especially after a pair of royal ordinances expanded the distribution of colonial land grants in 1841 and 1842. Early guidebooks were meant primarily for leisure travelers and wealthy landowners, but in the late 1830s and especially in the early 1840s, as settlement began to accelerate, publishers began to address a more socially diverse audience of potential emigrants.

From the first, these volumes served as mouthpieces for the fertility myth, which framed the "topographical" descriptions with which most opened. The first French guidebook to Algeria, published to coincide with the departure of the expeditionary force in the spring of 1830, was addressed to an elite readership of politicians, fashionable society, and army officers. The *Guide des Français à Alger* offered practical information about the climate, geography, and economy of the regency, followed by a discussion of the "advantages that France could gain from the conquest of Algiers" that exemplifies the fertility myth at work:

> Africa has always been represented as a beautiful woman whose head is crowned with ears of wheat, symbol of abundance; France could not, therefore, make a more important conquest that that of its northern shores. None of the colonies so far established on any point of the universe at all can compare with this coast, either for its climate or its natural output; in no area do the people of Europe meet the inexhaustible resources of this beautiful country. . . . The Romans put their principal glory into colonizing Africa, so justly called by them the garden of nature. And she never ceased to furnish them with wheat, wine, and oil, and to provide for the needs of their overabundant population. It is a curious and true fact that during the years least favorable to harvests in Europe, there were always abundant harvests in Barbary, and an even more competent agriculture would make this country even more productive.[32]

This guide was aimed at a wealthy audience of military men and armchair travelers, but works intended specifically for settlers or potential settlers soon followed. The earliest of these was published in 1833 by the Société coloniale of Algiers, a group founded the previous year to "look after the agricultural, industrial, and commercial interests of the Colony."[33] Written in the self-congratulatory tone of

32. *Guide des Français à Alger* (Marseille, 1830), 143–45.
33. "Statuts de la Société coloniale de l'état d'Alger," in *Annuaire de l'état d'Alger, publié par la Commission de la société coloniale* (Marseille and Paris, 1832), 74.

civic boosterism, the *Annuaire de l'état d'Alger* offered the small European community and their metropolitan correspondents a directory of the administrative services, commercial outlets, and cultural amenities available in the colony, as well as agricultural information to aid the "large number of colonists, attracted by the beauty of the climate, the fertility of the soil, and the proximity of the *patrie*, who will soon flood into this new colony."[34] New arrivals would find in the book detailed descriptions of seasonal precipitation patterns, the chemical composition of the water supplies, the trees that could be naturalized in Algeria, and the crops for which France was partially or wholly reliant on foreign trade that could be grown there. Similar handbooks for humbler emigrants began to appear in the second half of the 1830s. By 1839, for instance, an Avignon publisher was offering a cheap, pocket-sized manual for farmers in the French Midi and in Algeria, which were considered to have similar growing conditions.[35]

At about the same time, the French state began to appeal actively to potential emigrants, using the press, local officials, and subsidized handbooks to disseminate the fertility myth on a mass scale. These publicity efforts fell under the purview of the Ministry of War's Direction of Algerian Affairs, whose Second Bureau was responsible for matters concerning colonization, including "bringing to the public's knowledge the conditions imposed on and the advantages offered to emigrants."[36] The fragmentary record of the Second Bureau's propaganda activities suggests that it provided logistical, informational, and financial aid to authors whose work was judged helpful to colonization.[37] Most notably, in 1843, the Bureau purchased twelve hundred copies of a *Guide du colon et de l'ouvrier en Algérie*, which were distributed to prefects, subprefects, and mayors across France and made available to citizens interested in settling in Algeria.[38]

34. Ibid., 35–37, 67.
35. *Manuel de l'agriculteur du Midi de la France et de l'Algérie, ou la petite maison rustique méridionale* (Avignon, 1839). The publisher's note suggests that this is not the first edition of this work (v–vi).
36. CAOM F80 1588, chef du 3e Bureau de la Direction d'Algérie, "Note pour le 1er Bureau," 20 July 1843. The serial restructurings of the Algerian administration mean that there is no coherent archival record of the 2e Bureau's activities.
37. E.g. CAOM F80 1568, 2e Bureau de la Direction d'Algérie, "Analyse de deux brochures sur l'Algérie, par M. Raimond Thomassy," n.d. [c. 1840]; directeur des Affaires de l'Algérie to M. de Hocqueville, 18 February 1841; CAOM F80 1588, chef du 3e Bureau de la Direction de l'Algérie, "Note pour le 1er Bureau," 20 July 1843; Bugeaud to directeur des Finances, 3 September 1843; Martineau to directeur des Finances, 24 August 1843; directeur des Finances to ministre de la Guerre, 15 September 1843.
38. CAOM F80 1804, Fellmann, minute du rapport au Ministre, 11 August 1847; AD Loire-Atlantique, 1M 1783, ministre de l'Intérieur, "Envoi d'une brochure intitulée: Guide du colon et de l'ouvrier en Algérie," 24 November 1843.

Since official publications, such as the Ministry of War's *Tableau de la situation des établissements français en Algérie*, remained out of reach of "that part [of the public] that includes the primary and indispensable elements for realizing [the government's colonization plans], *the cultivators and the workers*," subsidized handbooks sought to make their messages more widely available.[39]

Like the "literature of colonial promotion" produced by emigrant aid societies, settlement agencies, and railroad companies in the United States, Australia, New Zealand, and South Africa, French emigrant handbooks combined practical advice on administrative formalities, packing, and agricultural techniques with landscape descriptions showing Algeria's suitability for settlement.[40] Invariably focused on the great, near-spontaneous fertility of the soil, these handbooks maintained that Algeria was eminently proper for cultivation by Europeans. It was "not only cultivable, but fertile, wooded, and watered by several streams," said one guide; "villages will not be long in arising in this country, so well disposed [is it] by nature for rapid colonization."[41] "Without claiming that Algiers is *the promised land*," another declared, "we can guarantee that with a little [financial] advance, intelligence, and perseverance, any hard-working man will be able to create an easy life for himself in the colony."[42] The view of such volumes was summed up in a handbook issued by a Parisian company established to assist emigrants in the early 1840s: "French Africa is one of the most beautiful and most fertile countries in the world. A pass of the plow has never been unfruitful for the colonist, and it will always be thus as long as the plowman is patient and intelligent."[43]

Promotional literature, however, had the disadvantage of being addressed primarily to those already interested in emigration, and it was open to accusations that it sought to "delud[e] public opinion" for the benefit of "interested parties."[44]

39. *Guide du colon et de l'ouvrier en Algérie . . . Rédigé d'après les documents officiels du Ministère de la guerre et du Ministère de l'intérieur, et les renseignements puisés près des autorités locales à Alger* (Paris, 1843), 9–10 (emphasis in original).
40. G. Malcolm Lewis, "The Rhetoric of the Western Interior: Modes of Environmental Description in American Promotional Literature of the Nineteenth Century," in *The Iconography of Landscape: Essays on the Symbolic Representation, Design and Use of Past Environments*, ed. Denis Cosgrove and Stephen Daniels (Cambridge, 1988), 179–93; Folke Dovring, "European Reactions to the Homestead Act," *Journal of Economic History* 22, no. 4 (1962): 466–68; Robert Grant, *Representations of British Emigration, Colonisation and Settlement: Imagining Empire, 1800–1860* (Houndsmills, UK, 2005).
41. *Guide du colon*, 27.
42. Armand Pignel, *Conducteur, ou Guide du voyageur et du colon de Paris à Alger et dans l'Algérie, avec carte itinéraire* (Paris, 1836), v.
43. AD Bas-Rhin 3M 685, *Le guide des colons et des commerçants en Algérie (Afrique française)* (Paris, n.d. [c. 1843]). The company claimed to have offices in Paris, Marseille, and Toulon, as well as agents in the principal Algerian towns to assist emigrant clients.
44. Amédée Desjobert, *L'Algérie en 1846* (Paris, 1846), 40.

Generalist works, such as travel accounts, parliamentary reports, and scientific studies, were considered by many colonial officials better suited to spread credible knowledge of Algeria to a wider reading public. In 1842, Governor General Bugeaud lauded "the savants, deputies, magistrates, [and] travelers [who] have come to study Africa and make it known to the world," and whose work had persuaded "well-off families to come inhabit" the colony.[45] But like the Ministry of War's *Tableaus*, works produced by men of letters for a relatively elite audience did not reach a broad enough readership to truly expand the pool of prospective settlers. When a new type of inexpensive illustrated weekly magazine emerged in the 1830s, it offered colonial propagandists the mass, popular audience they sought.

The first such journal, *Le Magasin pittoresque*, was founded in 1833 by Édouard Charton, a social reformer with Saint-Simonian and republican sympathies who saw popular education as an essential means of improving the working-class life. Like the English *Penny Magazine* on which it was modeled, the *Magasin pittoresque* was intended to provide the rapidly growing ranks of modest readers with improving materials to replace frivolous works in their small libraries.[46] A decade later, Charton helped to found *L'Illustration*, which mixed its predecessor's generalist approach with coverage of current events for a more comfortable, bourgeois readership.[47] As their titles suggest, the two journals were distinguished by their rich illustrations, reflecting Charton's conviction that "without drawings, it is impossible to arrive at the complete education of men, great and small."[48] Numerous engravings and low prices made them "the best-selling journals of popularized knowledge" in nineteenth-century France.[49] Within a year of its founding, the *Magasin pittoresque* was reported to have sixty

45. Bugeaud, *L'Algérie*, 64.
46. Frontispiece, *Magasin pittoresque*, 1 (1833); Édouard Charton, *Projets de sociétés* (Paris, n.d.), 9.
47. Charton left *L'Illustration* in 1845 because of ideological differences with his collaborators. Marie-Laure Aurenche, "Charton, Édouard," in *Dictionnaire biographique du mouvement ouvrier français*, ed. Claude Pennetier, rev. ed., CD-ROM (Paris, 1997), n.p.
48. "Des moyens de l'instruction. Les livres et les images," *Magasin pittoresque* 13 (1833): 98. Although lithography was less expensive, woodcuts were preferred for illustrating texts because of their compatibility with contemporary printing presses. Stephen Bann, *Parallel Lines: Printmakers, Painters and Photographers in Nineteenth-Century France* (New Haven, 2001), 33; Pierre Gusman, *La gravure sur bois en France au XIXe siècle* (Paris, 1929), 27.
49. Theodore Zeldin, *France 1848–1945*, vol. 1, *Ambition, Love and Politics* (Oxford, 1973), 88. The *Magasin pittoresque* cost two sous per issue, or six francs for a year's subscription, compared with the two to five sous charged by republican journals aimed at the same working-class, artisan, and petty bourgeois readers. *L'Illustration*'s annual subscription of thirty to thirty-two francs put it beyond the reach of working-class consumers, but it still cost half as much as the leading political papers of the period, which ranged from forty to eighty francs per year. Irene Collins, *The Government and the Newspaper Press in France, 1813–1881* (Oxford, 1959), 78, 88–91.

thousand subscribers, and mid-century circulation figures suggest that the two weeklies together reached more than twice as many readers as the most popular political daily.[50] Their illustrations enjoyed an even wider audience. Enlarged copies of the engravings were hung outside the magazines' offices and at newspaper or print shops to attract buyers, and thousands came to see the posted samples.

Given their popularity and the important role they assigned to visual communication, the two illustrated weeklies offered colonial officials an attractive platform from which to reach a large pool of potential colonists. Administrators in Paris and Algiers had long used the press in their efforts to shape the public perception of Algerian affairs, both by inserting articles in newspapers and through the official organs of the French state and the colonial administration.[51] The *Moniteur algérien* was created in 1832 partly to publicize colonial life to metropolitan readers, and colonial officials corresponded directly with French departmental authorities to counter negative press reports about the colony.[52] Although the *Magasin pittoresque* and *L'Illustration* were lauded by contemporaries as "a source of news that the government had neither created nor favored,"[53] both appear to have joined willingly in the Ministry of War's campaign to promote the Algerian colony, which resonated with their founder's views on colonial questions. Charton himself belonged to the abolitionist Société de la morale chrétienne, and his collaborators supported Algerian colonization on "national and moral" grounds.[54]

Although surviving records from the Second Bureau of Algerian Affairs do not discuss the illustrated press explicitly, there is evidence of significant ties between the Charton weeklies, especially the *Magasin pittoresque*, and colonial administrators in Paris. One key link lay in the person of Félix Mornand, an em-

---

50. The *Magasin pittoresque* had a print run of 40,000 in 1834, and subscriptions to *L'Illustration* grew from 12,000 to 35,000 by 1848. The highest circulating political daily, *Le Siècle*, had a run of 41,000 in 1841. Marie-Laure Aurenche, *Édouard Charton et l'invention du* Magasin pittoresque *(1833–1870)* (Paris, 2002), 191; Jean-Noël Marchandiau, *L'Illustration 1843/1944: Vie et mort d'un journal* (Paris, 1987), 325; Collins, *Government*, 88.
51. Placing articles or buying editorial support was widespread in the July Monarchy. Collins, *Government*, 86. Lawrence Jennings shows that subventions from both government agencies and private interest groups played a significant role in coverage of colonial issues. "Slavery and the Venality of the July Monarchy Press," *French Historical Studies* 17, no. 4 (1992): 957–78.
52. "Arrêté du 8 février 1832," *Moniteur algérien*, 27 January 1832; AD Bas-Rhin 3M 685, correspondence between Bugeaud and préfet du Bas-Rhin, 8–22 January 1845; préfet du Bas-Rhin to maires, "Notes sur la colonisation de l'Algérie," January 1845.
53. George Sand, quoted in Aurenche, "Charton, Édouard."
54. Marchandiau, *L'Illustration*, 18, 54; Jean Reynaud to Édouard Charton, 15 December 1838, 20 December 1842, and 6 January 1843, in Jean Reynaud, *Correspondance familière* (Paris, 1886), 137, 157–58, 161–62.

ployee in the Ministry of War's Algerian bureau who was also one of the *Magasin pittoresque*'s most energetic early collaborators and later a major contributor to *L'Illustration*. Mornand had served as secretary to the African Commission of 1834 and was subsequently hired as a clerk in the Ministry of War's Algiers Bureau.[55] Throughout his time at the ministry, Mornand contributed regularly to the *Magasin pittoresque*, and he was commissioned in 1837 to write a history of the French occupation in Algeria for a new series of inexpensive books by the journal's subject experts.[56] With Mornand as a probable link to the Ministry of War's Algerian bureaus, both the *Magasin pittoresque* and *L'Illustration* gave the colony a privileged place in their pages, which were regularly filled with accounts of the Armée d'Afrique's heroic exploits, ethnographic portraits of Algeria's indigenous inhabitants, and picturesque descriptions of the landscape. *L'Illustration*, which covered current events, paid more attention to military affairs than did its sister publication, but both journals offered readers a mythical vision of Algeria's fertile soil that mirrored that put forth in ministerial sources.

Both journals drew much of their information about Algeria from documentation produced by the Ministry of War. Their descriptions of Algerian sites were often reproduced verbatim from the *Tableau de la situation des établissements français dans l'Algérie*. In one especially striking example, a description of Milianah initially published in the *Tableau* of 1840 was incorporated into a *Magasin pittoresque* article in November 1840, and then reappeared, slightly reorganized, in *L'Illustration*'s first article on Algeria in March 1843. The woodcut illustrations that were so critical to the weeklies' popularity also often came from the Ministry of War. General Jean-Jacques Pelet, director of the army's documentation service, provided landscapes by military artists affiliated with the Armée d'Afrique to illustrate the *Magasin pittoresque*'s articles, in particular. Together, these texts and images helped bring the Algerian fertility myth to prospective emigrants from the lower ranks of French society.

The illustrated weeklies drew the same connections between Algeria's natural beauty and its potential for colonization as the government documents on which they were based. The thrice-repeated account of Milianah, for example, described the town as "the key to the interior of these lands, [which] will open access to the rich plains and fertile valleys situated between the Chélif and Mazafran" rivers. The success of the town's French garrison in establishing a tannery, pottery, tal-

---

55. SHD 5Yg 62 (Mornand). After resigning from the ministry in 1844, Mornand went on to an active career as a travel writer and journalist, contributing to *L'Illustration* and serving briefly as editor of the *Courrier de Paris*.
56. The projected history was to be one of the first works in the *Bibliothèque du Magasin pittoresque* but was never published. Only four works in the series ever appeared. *Magasin pittoresque* 5 (1837); Aurenche, *Édouard Charton*, 413–15.

low factory, and distillery testified to its commercial possibilities, "proving of what importance Milianah could become, envisaged from an industrial point of view." Finally, "under Roman domination, Milianah, the ancient *Maniana*, by its central position in the midst of a rich country became a seat of civilization, a flourishing city, [and] home to a host of families from Rome," which provided conclusive evidence of its present-day suitability for colonization by the French.[57]

The illustrations that accompanied such articles reinforced their visions of future prosperity with picturesque landscape views that laid symbolic territorial claims while incorporating Algeria into French conceptions of habitable space.[58] Following the conventions of the picturesque genre, these images featured a town set against a backdrop of hills. A road or stream crosses the foreground to provide visual movement, and a few human figures give a sense of scale. Although usually identifiable as native Algerians, these figures are almost uniformly engaged in some peaceable activity, such as tending livestock, leading a camel loaded with trade goods, or, as in the engraving that illustrated the *Magasin pittoresque*'s article on Milianah, smoking a pipe (fig. 42). The mood of such images is one of pastoral tranquility and is quite different from the distancing exoticism usually associated with Orientalist imagery, including works being produced by French painters in Algeria at this time. Images of colonists, their lands, and their homes that characterized contemporary representations of Anglo-American settlements are conspicuously absent from the pages of the French weeklies, although articles did explain the state assistance being offered to emigrants.[59] But paired with texts that emphasized the land's suitability for colonization, landscapes cast in the picturesque mode helped to familiarize

57. *TEFA* (1840), 22; *Magasin pittoresque*, 48 (November 1840); *L'Illustration*, 11 March 1843.

58. Mary Louise Pratt, *Imperial Eyes: Travel Writing and Transculturation* (London, 1992), 61; Michael Edney, *Mapping an Empire: The Geographical Construction of British India, 1765–1843* (Chicago, 1997), 59; W. J. T. Mitchell, "Imperial Landscape," in *Landscape and Power*, ed. W. J. T. Mitchell (Chicago, 1994), 19–27.

59. On art and settler colonialism, see Angela Miller, *Empire of the Eye: Landscape Representation and American Cultural Politics, 1825–1875* (Ithaca, 1993); Elizabeth Johns, "Landscape Painting in America and Australia in an Urban Century," in *New Worlds from Old: 19th Century Australian & American Landscapes*, ed. Elizabeth Johns et al. (Canberra, 1998); Rob McNeil, "Time After Time: Temporal Frontiers and Boundaries in Colonial Images of the Australian Landscape," in *Colonial Frontiers: Indigenous-European Encounters in Settler Societies*, ed. Lynette Russell (Manchester, 2001), 47–67. On the estate view in France, Nicholas Green, *The Spectacle of Nature: Landscape and Bourgeois Culture in Nineteenth-Century France* (Manchester, 1990), 101. Views of European estates in Algeria likely circulated privately, but one view identified as such appeared at the Salon between 1830 and 1851: "Propriété de M. le comte d'Esparbès de Lussan, près d'Alger," by a student of Horace Vernet, Emile Lambinet. *Explication des ouvrages . . . exposés au musée Royal* (1846), no. 1057.

FIGURE 42. *View of Milianah, after a Drawing from the Dépôt Général de la Guerre,* in *Magasin pittoresque* 8, no. 48 (November 1840). Courtesy University of Iowa Libraries, Special Collections.

Algeria in the eyes of potential emigrants and to domesticate the conquered territory as a site of future French settlement.

Landscape illustrations also served the fertility myth by effacing the violent conflict that hung over the real Algerian landscape and was recounted in the articles they accompanied. Although many were based on the work of military artists, few signs of war marred their picturesque calm, especially in the *Magasin pittoresque*. Two views engraved from drawings by the Dépôt de la guerre's soldier-artists, one of Mazagran by Alexandre Genet and one of Mostaganem by Théodore Jung, are representative of this kind of imagery (figs. 43 and 44). The absence of military activity is especially striking since the original images were produced for operational purposes. As Anne Godlewska notes, French military authorities saw cartography and landscape as interdependent forms of intelligence-gathering and strategic documentation. Along with surveyors' descriptive notices, landscape views were meant to help officers interpret sketched reconnaissance maps of the terrain in which they were operating. Later, in the Dépôt's Paris offices, landscape drawings provided a resource for military cartographers preparing a new map of Algeria and for artists preparing battle paintings, often watercolors, used in officer training courses and displayed publicly at the Salons or the Musée histo-

FIGURE 43. *View of Mazagran, after a Drawing Transmitted to the Dépôt de la Guerre by Captain Genet*, in *Magasin pittoresque* 8, no. 17 (April 1840). Courtesy University of Iowa Libraries, Special Collections.

rique de Versailles.[60] Although Genet and his fellow officer-artists often worked "amidst musket fire,"[61] the images that appeared in the illustrated press gave little indication of their battlefield origins. Even in *L'Illustration*, where battle scenes appeared more frequently than in its sibling, landscape imagery obscured the violence that made possible the presence of the French artist, as well as of future French emigrants.

This erasure can be seen in a *L'Illustration* article describing an 1844 expedition into the northern Sahara, where tribes allied with 'Abd al-Qadir had taken refuge from the French. The long textual account of the expedition to the town of Biskra is illustrated by two images, a map of the expeditionary column's route and a view of the village of Mchounech (figs. 45 and 46). The map offers a bird's-eye view of the region between Constantine and the oases. Annotated with schematic representations of key towns and topographical features mentioned in the text, it

60. Anne Godelewska, "Resisting the Cartographic Imperative: Giuseppe Bagatti's Landscapes of War," *Journal of Historical Geography* 21, no. 1 (2003): 27; Anne Godlewska, Marcus Létourneau, and Paul Schauerte, "Maps, Painting and Lies: Portraying Napoleon's Battlefields in Northern Italy," *Imago Mundi* 57, no. 2 (2005): 151. On the artists of the Armée d'Afrique, see Isabelle Bruller, *L'Algérie romantique des officiers de l'armée française, 1830–1837* (Vincennes, 1994).
61. SHD 3M 547, général Pelet, "Instruction pour M. le capitaine Genet," 28 October 1835.

FIGURE 44. *View of Mostaganem in the Province of Oran.—Drawing by Yung*, in *Magasin pittoresque* 12, no. 17 (April 1844). Courtesy University of Iowa Libraries, Special Collections.

allows the reader to follow the complex narrative of the column's march. The article itself describes the commercial and agricultural importance of the region in the usual laudatory terms. The valley of the Oued-el-Abïadh, for example, is described as "full of palm trees, well-cultivated gardens, and stone houses" according to "official sources."[62] The accompanying illustration provides a view of the valley's rich vegetation from the perspective of soldiers seated tranquilly on the promontory overlooking the river and oasis below. The French column marching into the frame from the lower right appears almost as an afterthought, rather than as the protagonist of the narrative. The line of troops blends into the strong horizontals and diagonals that define the hills and river, while the shapes of men, beasts, and materiel dissolve into the palms silhouetted against the middle ground. There is little here to suggest that the column's mission was to spread terror among the people of the desert, nor that the garrison of indigenous troops they left behind at Biskra would rise up just a month later and kill their French officers.[63]

62. "Algérie: Expédition de Biskarah," *L'Illustration*, 13 April 1844.
63. Benjamin Brower, *A Desert Named Peace: The Violence of France's Empire in the Algerian Sahara, 1844–1902* (New York, 2009), 37–40.

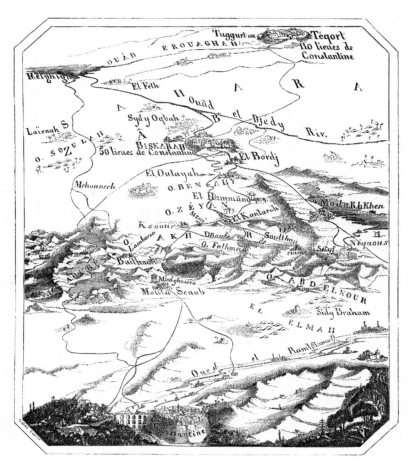

FIGURE 45. *Bird's-Eye Map of the Biskarah Expedition*, in *L'Illustration*, 13 April 1844. Courtesy University of Iowa Libraries, Special Collections.

The dissonance between war and the picturesque that pervades this image highlights one of the key difficulties faced by those seeking to encourage mass emigration to Algeria. While the monarchy and others glorified the battlefield exploits of the Armée d'Afrique, colonial officials and colonization advocates sought to promote a pastoral vision grounded in the Algerian fertility myth. The ongoing war for territorial control complicated this task. Even in the pages of the illustrated journals, representations of a fertile, peaceful landscape awaiting new, European inhabitants could not be separated from accounts of the terrible

FIGURE 46. *View of Mchounech, after an Original Drawing,* in *L'Illustration,* 13 April 1844.
Courtesy University of Iowa Libraries, Special Collections.

violence of the fight to seize those lands from their Algerian occupants. The few images of French colonial migrants to appear in these journals emphasized the paternal solicitude of the French state towards its citizens striking out for the "New France" across the Mediterranean, especially in comparison with the misery of emigrants awaiting departure for the United States (figs. 47 and 48). But the weeklies' efforts to "pacify" the Algerian landscape were challenged by the representations circulating in contemporary popular culture, which depicted colonial warfare in sensational detail.[64] One of the only popular engravings of settler life produced in France in this period was a gruesome scene of European families being massacred by 'Abd al-Qadir's Hadjoute allies in an 1839 attack on settler farms in the Mitidja plain, reputed to be Algeria's most superlatively fertile region (fig. 49). Set alongside melodramatic narratives of colonists taken captive by 'Abd al-Qadir, such images posed a significant challenge to state propaganda efforts to reassure French citizens that their future prosperity would be assured by migration to North Africa.

The widespread perception of Algeria as a theater of war was seen by colonization advocates as a major obstacle to the recruitment of emigrants. Not without reason, representatives of settler interests insisted that dispelling Algeria's reputation for insecurity was one of the first conditions necessary to attract a steady flow

64. See chapter 3 of this book.

FIGURE 47. *Embarkation of Colonists for Algeria,* in *L'Illustration,* 19 December 1846. Courtesy University of Iowa Libraries, Special Collections.

of migrants to the colony.[65] "The spectacle of this continual struggle . . . against the Arabs; the accounts, sometimes exaggerated but often all too true, of individual catastrophes that fill the colony's martyrology in such a deplorable manner; the inevitable vexations attendant on continuous troop movements . . . , all this must frighten many minds," warned Algiers's Interior Director in 1842.[66] The fragmentary archive of early French colonial emigration suggests that prospective colonists were in fact discouraged by the ongoing violence. Authorities in Alsace, for example, noted a "panic" around Colmar in 1843, when returning emigrants spread rumors about the colony's "insecurity," prompting several families to turn back from their voyage to Algeria.[67] Another prospective emigrant from southwestern France sought assurances from his prefect that he and his family could be settled in a safe location, "so as not to be sacrificed to the rage of the unsubdued" Algerians.[68] These few examples only hint at the anxieties that must have been raised by representations of the ongoing war of conquest in official and popular

65. *Opinion émise par M. Urtis, propriétaire à Alger, devant la Commission de Colonisation de l'Algérie à la séance du 12 mars 1842* (Paris, [1842]), 5.
66. CAOM F80 1674, Guyot, "Plan de colonisation pour la province d'Alger," 12 March 1842.
67. AD Bas-Rhin 3M 689, maire d'Erlenbach to sous-préfet de Schelestadt, 17 December 1843.
68. AD Ariège 10M 18/1, Jean François Delaunay to préfet de l'Ariège, [1845].

FIGURE 48. Ernest Charton, engr. Andrew, Best and Leloir, *Emigrant Families Camped in the Port of Le Havre*, in *Magasin pittoresque* 12, no. 47 (November 1844). Courtesy University of Iowa Libraries, Special Collections.

culture. The full scope of the problem is reflected in the Ministry of War's emigration figures for 1846, when controversy over Bugeaud's brutal tactics and the outbreak of Bu Maza's mahdist insurrection led nearly two-thirds of those accorded free passage on government ships to renounce their plans.[69]

The tensions between representations of conquest and colonization laid bare the violent essence of settler colonialism: the dispossession of indigenous peoples and their replacement on the land by the invaders.[70] There were observers and officials in France who recognized this basic fact, as well as its consequences for Algerians. The "Arabophile" indigenous affairs officers of the Bureaux arabes, in particular, sought to preserve Algerian land rights, and the French never adopted a systematic policy of extermination or expulsion against the precolonial

69. *TEFA* (1845–46), 183.
70. Patrick Wolfe, *Settler Colonialism and the Transformation of Anthropology: The Politics and Poetics of an Ethnographic Event* (London, 1999), 163.

FIGURE 49. *Burning of the Mitidja*, engr. Léotaud (Paris), 1839. Bibliothèque nationale de France, Département des Estampes et de la photographie.

population. Colonial authorities focused their energies less on preventing the displacement of Algerians, however, than on protecting colonists with fiercer prosecution of the war against 'Abd al-Qadir and on building a defensive barrier, the so-called *obstacle continu*, around the main zone of European settlement. Those formulating colonization policy, meanwhile, turned to the character of the growing settler population to explain the land's failure to produce in accordance with the expectations set up by the fertility myth. Shifting attention from the nature of the land to the nature of European emigrants, however, raised fundamental questions about the principles underlying the ideals of *véritable colonisation*, the ways that these ideals should be implemented, and France's ability to do so successfully.

Bad Colonists

Tens of thousands of Europeans emigrated to Algeria in the first decades of the conquest, but they failed to "fertilize" the soil as the promoters of settlement colonization expected. By 1844, the state had distributed nearly 7,500 parcels of land in official settlements, but only 3,400 hectares had been cleared and sown by their new owners.[71] Six years later, the area under European cultivation had quadrupled but still amounted to less than a third of the 50,000 hectares granted within government "population centers."[72] The slow growth of colonial agriculture signaled to many that there were serious deficiencies in the sort of emigrants arriving in the colony, of whom officials in Paris and Algiers complained that "only a very tiny fraction engage or plan to engage in agricultural work."[73] Simply put, those migrating to Algeria were not the "true colonists" called for by settler colonization theory. Instead, most appeared to contemporaries to be speculators interested only in rapid profit.

Observers and colonial administrators identified two types of speculation in particular as a threat to the ideals of *véritable colonisation*: speculation in petty commerce, especially café and tavern keeping, and speculation in land. What united the two activities in the eyes of contemporary critics was the shared disdain of those who engaged in them for economically and socially healthy agricultural labor. An 1846 travel guide gave voice to the widely held view that "the colonization of Algeria . . . is making less progress than we should be able to expect from the victorious march of our armies, because most of the emigrants who go there are not cultivators: they are mostly speculators who are trying to make a fortune with some establishment like those of the great cities of Europe, either by keeping a boarding house, cafés, restaurants, or by buying land to sell at a profit without making the necessary expenditures to put them into cultivation."[74] Louis de Baudicour, one of the first historians of Algeria's settlers, summed up midcentury disdain for the first emigrants as "nothing more than petty tradesmen [and] a certain number of *cantiniers* [who] had followed the army." "[Algeria] needs *agriculteurs* above all," Baudicour lamented, but "it is precisely this class of workers, the most numerous in France, that has furnished the fewest colonists for Algeria."[75]

Postrevolutionary critiques of the slave-holding Caribbean planter were echoed in attacks on speculators, whose greed threatened to infect Algeria with the ills of the colonial Old Regime. Like their early modern homologues, both petty entrepreneurs and land speculators were understood to profit at society's expense

71. *TEFA* (1843–44), 242–43.
72. Ibid. (1846–49), 226–33. *Centre de population* was used interchangeably with *village colonial* for settlements created with state funds where public land was distributed to European (and some Algerian) colonists.
73. CAOM F80 1672, "Chronologique de 1831," [1836].
74. [E. Quétin], *Guide du voyageur en Algérie: Itinéraire du savant, de l'artiste, de l'homme du monde et du colon*, 2nd ed. (Paris, Algiers, and Poitiers, 1846), 87.
75. Louis de Baudicour, *La colonisation de l'Algérie: Ses éléments* (Paris, 1856), 146–47.

and to be possessed of the *esprit de retour* that had proved so damaging to earlier colonies. They were presumed to have no "serious thoughts of expatriation,"[76] but instead took advantage of others—the honest colonists and self-sacrificing soldiers who frequented cafés and *cabarets*, and poor emigrants trying to buy or rent land—in their pursuit of a rapid fortune, with which they then planned to return to France. Officials, travelers, and commentators on both sides of the Mediterranean saw dangerous similarities between these men and the slaveholding "adventurers" of the early modern period. Thus economist André Cochut warned that the accumulation of land in the hands of a few speculators would create an exploitative system in which rich proprietors would sit idle, "surrounded by their white slaves, like the planters of the Antilles with their negroes."[77]

To most French observers, however, the greatest danger of Algerian speculations lay in new forms of corruption associated with modern urban-industrial capitalism. The hospitality trades enumerated in the guidebook above were, as the author remarked, urban activities identified with Europe's growing industrial metropolises. Taverns, cafés, inns, and other establishments in which strangers gathered to drink had long been viewed as potential sites of seditious or criminal activity, and these traditional suspicions were augmented in the nineteenth century by new fears of social and moral disorder. Urban administrators, moral economists, and Malthusian demographers identified alcohol and café sociability as important causes of pauperism and family breakdown in the emerging industrial order. Drinking was said to loosen the sexual inhibitions of the poor, encouraging unplanned pregnancies and overly large families, and the attractions of café or tavern to lead men to neglect their domestic responsibilities. The cabaret, according to the examples chosen for the *Grand dictionnaire du XIXe siècle*, was "the terror of the energetic and hardworking mother of a family," "a leper that attaches itself like vermin to the miserable populations."[78] The proliferation of such establishments in Algeria introduced these dangers into the nascent colony, threatening not only the welfare of honest emigrants but also the moral stability of settler society as a whole.

---

76. *Notes sur l'Algérie, par un ancien officier de l'armée d'Afrique, en retraite* (Niort, 1841), 25.
77. Cochut, "De la Colonisation de l'Algérie.—Les essais et les systèmes," *Revue des deux mondes*, n. ser., 17 (1 February 1847): 537.
78. S.v. "Cabaret," in *Grand dictionnaire universel du XIXe siècle*, ed. Pierre Larousse, vol. 3 (Paris, 1866–77), 9. The words are quoted from Fourrierist anti-Semite Alphonse Toussenel, *Les juifs, rois de l'époque: Histoire de la féodalité financière* (Paris, 1845), 147–48. See also William Sewell, *Work and Revolution in France: The Language of Labor from the Old Regime to 1848* (Cambridge, 1980), 229–33; Scott Haine, *The World of the Paris Café: Sociability Among the French Working Class, 1789–1914* (Baltimore, 1996), chap. 1, 106–17; Rebecca Spang, *The Invention of the Restaurant: Paris and Modern Gastronomic Culture* (Cambridge, Mass., 2000), 213–14.

Concerns about the influence of petty trade in food and drink in Algeria were prompted by the not inaccurate perception that alcohol held a disproportionately large place in colonial life. Cafés, inns, taverns, and wine shops had arrived in Algiers with the invasion force, and they followed the Armée d'Afrique into other towns and forward posts around the edges of French-occupied territory. Drinking establishments quickly become the most numerous European-run businesses in Algeria. In 1837, wine and brandy accounted for almost a quarter of the colony's imports, and there were 631 licensed European alcohol vendors, 1 for every 26 of the 16,770 settlers in French-occupied territory. By comparison, Paris, which had the highest per capita concentration of cafés and taverns in Europe, had approximately 1 such establishment per 100 inhabitants at this time. The number of licensees climbed to 874 in 1841 and continued to rise thereafter.[79] According to visitors and officials, many of the colony's outlying villages were nothing but "an agglomeration of taverns," inhabited by publicans, *débitants* (alcohol vendors), and *marchands de vins* who could not "be taken for colonists."[80] To contemporary observers both inside and outside the colonial administration, such settlements more closely resembled the seamy fringes of French cities than the healthy agrarian communities towards which the ideals of true colonization aspired. For example, the commune of Mustapha, in the Mitidja plain, was described by the author of one sentimental novel as "at once the Belleville, Romainville, and Saint-Mandé of the regency," because its many *ginguettes* (open air cafés–dance halls) recalled the Parisian suburbs known for the rowdy bars and carnivalesque entertainment they offered the capital's working classes.[81] Like the *cabarets* of the Paris *banlieue*, those of the Algerian countryside were associated with drunken debauchery, sexual disorder, violence, and crime.

79. *TEFA* (1837), 332, 343, 298–99; *Rapport fait au nom de la quatrième sous-commission par M. Magnier de Maisonneuve, le 15 février 1843: Régime commercial, impôts directs et indirects, organisation des services financiers* (Paris, 1843), 16. Thomas Brennan, "Towards the Cultural History of Alcohol in France," *Journal of Social History* 23, no. 1 (1989): 82–83. Drinking establishments continued to play an outsized role in Algerian colonial society, and café keeping remained the largest trade among Europeans at the end of the century. David Prochaska, *Making Algeria French: Colonialism in Bône, 1870–1920* (Cambridge, 1990), 118–19.
80. AN 82AP 5, "Copie de la dénonciation faite à M. l'intendant civil contre le général Bro. Avec notes marginales du général Bro," 3 March 1836.
81. A.G. Malessart, *Le colon: Esquisses algériennes* (Paris, 1845), 258. On the *barrières*, see Louis Chevalier, *Laboring Classes, Dangerous Classes in Paris During the First Half of the Nineteenth Century* (1958), trans. Frank Jellinek (New York, 1973), 101–7; Green, *Spectacle*, 76–80; James Cuno, "Violence, Satire, and Social Types in the Graphic Art of the July Monarchy," in *The Popularization of Images: Visual Culture under the July Monarchy*, ed. Petra ten-Doesschate Chu and Gabriel Weisberg (Princeton, 1994), 10–36.

Close linkages in the contemporary imagination between drinking establishments and prostitution meant that Algeria's European women were also associated with thinly veiled forms of commodified sexuality. These intimations were
encapsulated in the figure of the *dame de comptoir* (the lady behind the bar),
who was established as a colonial social "type" in an 1835 play of the same name.
First performed in Algiers and then published in France, *La dame de comptoir*
presented its title character, the lover of a rural innkeeper, as the epitome of this
new type. Dallying with a second suitor while scheming to land a rich husband,
Elisa represented a form of sexual speculation that was both identified with and
facilitated by her role in her lover's tavern.[82] There was some basis for such stereotypes of European women in Algerian colonial society, as there was with the
number of cafés. Indeed, Algiers police shut down *La dame de comptoir* after
only eight performances because a woman in the audience claimed that the Elisa
character satirized her personally. Government records reveal a disproportionate number of prostitutes among European women in the colony, where sex ratios within the settler population were, as on colonial frontiers the world over,
deeply imbalanced (table 4). While there were nearly twice as many European
men as women throughout the July Monarchy, registered *filles publiques*—
the majority of them French—accounted for more than one of every hundred
European women, more than five times the proportion in Paris itself.[83] Given the
importance attached to women as an index of colonial society's moral health, the
apparent predominance of "loose women" over "well-composed" families was a
worrying sign.[84]

By the mid-1830s, the inn or café keeper had become a standard figure of
suspicion in official and public portraits of Algerian colonial society. Not all of
these men and women were considered immoral. Administrators found some,
such as a couple that started two cafés in Cherchel in the 1840s, to "enjoy a good
reputation,"[85] and representatives of the settler community praised the elegant,
Parisian-style hotels and restaurants that sprang up in the new European quarter of Algiers. Popular literature also occasionally portrayed honest *hoteliers*, like
a Breton emigrant in Christian Pitois's *L'Algérie de la jeunesse* (The youngster's

82. *La dame de comptoir, ou le colon extravagant: Comédie en un acte* (Algiers and Toulon, 1835).
83. Calculated from figures in E.-A. Duchesne, *De la prostitution dans la ville d'Alger depuis la conquête* (Paris, 1853), 58; Christelle Taraud, *La prostitution coloniale: Algérie, Tunisie, Maroc (1830–
1962)* (Paris, 2003), 56, 73; A. Trebuchet and Poirat-Duval, "État de la prostitution en France," in
A.-J.-B. Parent-Duchâtelet, *De la prostitution dans la ville de Paris . . .* , 3rd ed., ed. A. Trebuchet and
Poirat-Duval, vol. 1 (Paris, 1857), 59.
84. *TEFA* (1842–43), 182.
85. AD Ariège 10M 18/1, directeur de l'Intérieur (Guyot) to préfet de l'Ariège, "Réponse à une demande de renseignements sur le Sr. Portet," [c. April 1845].

TABLE 4. MEN AND WOMEN AMONG ADULT EUROPEAN POPULATION IN ALGERIA, 1833–47

Year	Men	Women
1833	4,596	1,545
1834	5,594	2,255
1835	6,237	2,270
1836	7,736	3,089
1837	9,014	3,418
1838	10,549	4,129
1839	11,948	4,655
1840–41	11,381	7,149
1842	22,738	9,764
1843	25,393	14,585
1846	51,547	29,160
1847	44,674	30,129

Source: TEFA (1837–49).

Algeria), who kept a reputable inn that stood out among the seedy *cabarets* of the surrounding countryside.[86] Such upstanding individuals were exceptional, however. For the most part, cafés and *cabarets* were depicted as havens of "idleness and debauchery" that set "a bad example" for serious colonists.[87] As Adolphe Blanqui reported to the Académie des sciences morales et politiques in 1839, the "frightful manner" in which alcohol was sold and consumed by the settler population gave "a fair idea of the nature of the social progress at work in our colony."[88]

The association with cafés and other purveyors of alcohol largely defined the poorer sort of Algerian colonist in the French imagination in the first decades of the conquest. Although there were relatively few images of settlers in this period, the few that did appear resembled Benjamin Roubaud's satirical portrait of "what is called a colonist" (fig. 50). Printed in *Le Charivari* in early 1845, the caricature portrays the settler lounging idly in the doorway of a liquor and tobacco shop, hands crammed in the pockets of his white suit in a pose mirroring that of the drunkard in contemporary images of metropolitan social types. A colonist, according to the caption, is someone "who has come to Africa to

86. P. Christian [Christian Pitois], *L'Algérie de la jeunesse* (Paris, [1847]), 79.
87. CAOM GGA L4/1, Achard, *Algérie: Projet de colonisation présenté par M. Achard, membre du Conseil Général du Département du Bas-Rhin* (Paris 1842), 9–10.
88. Adolphe Blanqui, *Algérie: Rapport sur la situation économique de nos possessions dans le nord de l'Afrique* (Paris, 1840), 79–80.

FIGURE 50. Benjamin Roubaud, *What Is Called a Colonist*, in *Le Charivari*, 1845. Bibliothèque nationale de France, Département des Estampes et de la photographie.

plant billiard cues and harvest the *boudious* [coins] of Cognac lovers." This sort of "agriculture," it continues, is encouraged by drinking rather than more productive forms of trade. Similarly revealing was the fictional voyage to Algeria of Monsieur Mayeux, the satirical, hunchbacked figure of bourgeois greed who stalked the stages and pages of July Monarchy France. In an 1846 story, Mayeux takes his wife and children to Algeria to make "a brilliant fortune." After much discussion about which trade will most rapidly parlay the family's small savings into the greatest profits, he decides to become a *cantinier*, and sells wine and beer to soldiers at an army post until the inevitable series of misadventures leads him back to France.[89]

89. Emile Krako, *Vies et aventures surprenantes de M. Mayeux et de sa nombreuse famille: Ses relations avec les personnages les plus haut placés, son Voyage en ALGÉRIE et dans le MAROC, ses Visites à ABD-EL-KADER et à l'Empereur* . . . (Paris, 1846), 179–80.

FIGURE 51. Cham [Amédée de Noé], caricature of a self-proclaimed colonist, in *Mœurs algériennes: Chinoiseries turques. Nouvel album de Cham (de N.)* (Paris: Aubert et Cie., 1846). Courtesy Library of Congress, Rare Books and Special Collections Division.

Petty speculators' supposed transience, laziness, and distaste for agricultural labor challenged not only the goals of *véritable colonisation*, but also the racialized assumptions on which the settler colonial order was based. Like "poor whites" in other colonial contexts, speculators bore a disturbing resemblance to the colonizers' stereotypes of the indigenous people.[90] Drawn to outlying villages and military posts by the presence of French troops, they threw up temporary shelters, then abandoned them "like a nomadic tribe" when the soldiers moved on, according to one colonial official.[91] Another humorous

90. The classic work on "poor whites" is Ann Laura Stoler, "Rethinking Colonial Categories: European Communities and the Boundaries of Rule," in *Colonialism and Culture*, ed. Nicholas Dirks (Ann Arbor, 1992), 319–52. On the particularities of the "poor white problem" in settler colonies, see Dane Kennedy, *Islands of White: Settler Society and Culture in Kenya and Southern Rhodesia, 1890–1939* (Durham, 1987), chap. 9.
91. CAOM F80 1674, undated, untitled, anonymous report, [c. 1843].

portrait of a self-proclaimed "colonist" represents petty European traders as blurring racial and cultural boundaries (fig. 51). One of a series of lithographs in which the external markers of identity—religion, costume, and language— are confused by the "Arabo-French" population, this 1837 cartoon shows a Frenchman in "Oriental" costume who appears, to a properly attired country-man, to have become a seller of dates or "seraglio pastilles." The man indignantly insists that he has become a *colon*, but the visual evidence clearly belies his claim.[92]

Colonization advocates and colonial officials sought to maintain cultural boundaries and reduce the depredations of café keepers, *cabaretiers*, and others on "good" colonists and soldiers. Emigrant handbooks, for instance, warned new arrivals against the fraudulent practices of hotel and inn keepers, suggesting that "sober and essentially thrifty" readers carefully verify prices and conditions before taking accommodations or meals.[93] Medical authorities recommended that settlers "abstain from excess of all kinds . . . and remain sober, especially with alcoholic liquors."[94] To "reduce among our soldiers, who are its principal consumers, the occasions for debauchery, which has been shown to be the all too real cause of disease and mortality," military officials banned the sale of alcohol to junior officers and soldiers outside of approved establishments. So that "the colonial population [might] grow under good conditions of hygiene, labor and morality," authorities also imposed steep fees on liquor licenses. By limiting the number of cafés and taverns, they hoped "to return to their agricultural work the first colonists recruited by the Government to clear the land."[95] These restrictive measures seem to have had little impact, however, as the profitability of these businesses allowed their proprietors to cover the climbing costs of licenses and caution money.

Underlying much of the suspicion of petty commerce was the assumption among bourgeois officials and observers that only property, especially landownership, rooted the individual permanently in society and brought self-interest into line with the general interest. This was the logic of citizenship in mid-century France, where property ownership was equated with investment in society's well-being, and its significance was compounded in the Algerian context.

92. *Mœurs algériennes, chinoiseries turques: Nouvel album de Cham (de N.)* (Paris, [1837]), pl. 1, 6, 8.
93. *Guide du colon*, 73.
94. "Instruction hygiénique pour les colons récemment arrivés en Algérie," 2 April–10 May 1847, in *RAGA*, 506.
95. Magnier de Maisonneuve, *Rapport . . . de la quatrième sous-commission*, 15–16; "Arrêté relatif à la police des débits de boissons," 6–29 March 1842, in *RAGA*, 186; "Ordonnance qui régularise l'imposition du droit de licence à Alger," 31 January–20 March 1847, in *RAGA*, 475–77.

Speculators' *esprit de retour*, in particular, was understood to be a function of their lack of ties to the land, which posed especially grave dangers in a nascent colony under precarious French control. As General Duvivier explained, "in a country surrounded by so many constant and indefinite dangers, we cannot afford to burden ourselves with a floating population . . . who would not be morally chained to the colony's existence by the vigorous bonds forged by the love of property, especially when the cultivator cultivates it with his own hands."[96] It is telling that the couple of Cherchel café owners mentioned above for their good reputation were specifically praised for housing their second café in a house they had built "with the fruit of their savings," in other words, for owning property.[97]

Rampant speculation in land, however, suggested that property alone was an insufficient guarantee of either permanence or morality. Land speculation posed a different kind of danger than petty commerce, but it struck both practically and ideologically at the heart of French colonization efforts. Land was both the object and the means of colonial settlement, and speculative investment in property was therefore of the utmost social and moral consequence. Speculators' activities impeded the realization of the fertility myth, and their dishonesty and selfishness cast a moral cloud over the entire colonial enterprise. They undermined the claims to economic, cultural, and moral superiority that justified French domination, and belied the promise of national regeneration held out by advocates of agricultural colonization.

Like café keeping and prostitution, land speculation appeared in Algiers with the invasion force in 1830. French and European buyers immediately began a massive "land grab" for the urban and rural properties of Algerians fleeing the invading army.[98] Fraud was endemic in these early transactions. Europeans unfamiliar with complex local land tenure systems, which were based on use-rights obtained through the collectivity rather than individual ownership, were sold properties that the sellers had no legal right to alienate.[99] The Algerian landholding regime did not require what the French considered "regular" property titles, and European buyers lacked the language skills to read documents they

96. CAOM F80 1674, "La Colonisation d'Afrique (1er article)," *Le National*, 14 February 1842.
97. AD Ariège 10M 18/1, directeur de l'Intérieur (Guyot) to préfet de l'Ariège, "Réponse à une demande de renseignements sur le Sr. Portet," [c. April 1845].
98. Prochaska, *Making Algeria French*, 65.
99. In general, land could be held by individuals (*melk*), tribal communities (*'arsh*), or religious corporations (*hubus*). See John Ruedy, *Land Policy in Colonial Algeria* (Berkeley, 1967), 1–12. On the question of titles, see Isabelle Grangaud, "Prouver par l'écriture: Propriétaires algérois, conquérants français et historiens ottomanistes," *Genèses* 74, no. 1 (2009): 25–45.

obtained from Algerian sellers. One oft-repeated anecdote tells of sales contracts drawn up for properties described simply as *haouch* ("farm") or *trab* ("land"), located in *outhans* ("country"), being sold by *oulid* or *ben* ("son"). Other sales concerned land that had already been bought or that did not exist at all. The limited reach of French military control meant that European buyers often could not inspect or verify the land they purchased, either. Fraud by Algerian sellers raised an outcry among early settlers and colonial officials, but Europeans behaved with even greater lack of scruple. Both private individuals and colonial officials took advantage of the chaotic postinvasion situation to pressure Algerian property holders into selling. Using the threat of expropriation by the French authorities, they pushed landholders to sell rather than settle for the minimal indemnity paid by the army for confiscated property. Colonial officials bought buildings they knew the administration planned to purchase or gambled that they could protect their acquisitions from expropriation. Others simply refused to pay for their purchases.[100]

The scope of the European land grab was tremendous, although the surface area concerned is impossible to determine with certainty. Government record keepers were more concerned with the monetary value than the extent of the land changing hands, and many transactions were undervalued or went unrecorded altogether to avoid taxation. The existing sources show that between 1831 and 1837, some 5,307 private property transactions were registered with the French authorities, totaling approximately 5.3 million francs in outright sales and 1.1 million francs of annual *rentes*.[101] Initially sales affected primarily rural properties in the countryside around Algiers, but urban real estate soon became an object of intense traffic, as well. As French control expanded beyond Algiers and its *banlieue*, speculation followed in its wake with often devastating consequences for the Algerian tribes. André Nouschi has found that in Constantine province, which was relatively protected in the first years of the conquest, the transfer of land to Europeans seriously disrupted agriculture and trade. Patterns of crop rotation and pasturage were upset, and speculators began to export goods normally consumed locally. The emptying of local markets, in conjunction with environmental crises and outbreaks of disease, especially cholera, gave rise to famine or near-famine in the area in the 1840s.[102] French observers, however, were less concerned about the impact on Algerians than with

---

100. Eugène Pellissier de Reynaud, *Annales algériennes*, new ed., 3 vols. (Paris, 1854), 3:268, 1:176–80.
101. *TEFA* (1837), 394.
102. Nouschi, *Enquête sur le niveau de vie*, 164–65, 175–76, 187.

the intentions of European purchasers. Whether made by civilians or administrators, wrote Baron Pichon, the colony's first civil intendant, such acquisitions "can have been made only with fraudulent, speculative intent and without any serious goal."[103]

In practical terms, speculation in land was believed to have two harmful consequences. First, it threatened already fragile relations with Algerians on whose cooperation the settler economy depended. "Shameful transactions" contributed to local people's suspicions of the French, discouraged them from selling their goods to the army or European civilians, and discredited commerce as a tool of rapprochement between colonizer and colonized.[104] Second, land speculators refused to cultivate their arable land yet also kept it out of the hands of "serious" colonists." "Adventurous speculators," the Algerian Commission reported in 1833, pounced on the colony "as if on easily exploited prey" and "neutralized all honest efforts" to fertilize the soil.[105] Land acquired by speculators lay fallow, as its new owners waited for its value to rise. When they did contract their land out to tenants or sharecroppers, they did so at inflated rates that excluded or bankrupted the small farmers that colonialists wished to encourage.[106] "Compared to the few individuals who truly cultivate for themselves the land they have legitimately acquired," a Lieutenant Adams asked in 1839, "how many idlers do we see speculating on the land as if on stock deals?"[107]

Adams was only one of many contemporaries to find the stock market an appropriate analogy for colonial land speculation. Where critics of café keepers, *cabaretiers*, and *débitants* invoked indigenous Algerians and the denizens of the Parisian *banlieue* to symbolize the dangers of alcohol and working-class sociability, land speculation was compared endlessly with the Paris Bourse.[108] Land speculators, a former Saint-Domingue colonist wrote to the minister of war in 1833, "have turned *the soil, the life-blood of the colony*, into a merchandise whose

103. [Louis-André] Pichon, *Alger sous la domination française; son état présent et son avenir* (Paris, 1833), 262, 298.
104. CAOM F80 10, "Note de Sidi Hamden, auteur du mémoire"; Charles Dupin, speech to the Chamber of Deputies, "La Question d'Alger," 29 April 1834, in *Mémoires de M. Dupin*, vol. 3, *Carrière politique, souvenirs parlementaires . . . (du 23 novembre 1832 au 26 mars 1839)* (Paris, 1860), 86.
105. "Rapport sur la Colonisation de l'Ex-Régence d'Alger, par M. de la Pinsonnière, député d'Indre-et-Loire, membre de la commission envoyé," in *Colonisation de l'Ex-Régence: Documens officiels déposés sur le bureau de la Chambre des députés* (Paris, 1834), 10.
106. *TEFA* (1837), 282.
107. CAOM F80 1586, lieutenant F. J. Adams to duc d'Orléans, "Quelques considérations sur l'état actuel des choses dans l'Algérie," 18 November 1839.
108. On the Bourse, see Victorian Thompson, *The Virtuous Marketplace: Women and Men, Money and Politics in Paris, 1830–1870* (Baltimore, 2000).

value is measured by the ups and downs of the Bourse."[109] The following year, Charles Dupin, president of the Chamber of Deputies, declared of Algerian speculators that "they have sold land just as they traffic in sugar, coffee, and spirits on the Paris Bourse!!"[110] The association of Algerian land speculation with the stock market had become so pervasive by the end of the 1830s that an 1840 New Year's caricature included "my land in Africa" in the bequest that the expiring year, depicted as a stereotypical bourgeois, would leave to its successor, along with "my [beet] sugar factories," stock for a "railroad [with trains going] 100 leagues in 2 minutes," and "my excellent letters of credit on Haïti, Spain, Greece, and the Republic of Argentina."[111] Algerian land, the artist implied, stood on a par with these other fantastical investments into which French speculators threw themselves in the 1830s and 1840s.

Like the urban metaphors used for petty merchants, the stock market analogy carried strong connotations of moral and social disorder. During the July Monarchy, the Paris Bourse became a locus of anxiety about new forms of industrial capitalism, and revived older concerns about the relationship between private and public interests. Founded in the eighteenth century to facilitate the sale of government loans and annuities, the Bourse was transformed in the 1830s, when the government began to sell stock to fund the building of the French railway system. With its growing financial importance, the stock market also gained greater potential to subvert critical national undertakings. In seeking to lower costs or negotiate contracts favorable to themselves, private investors might cut corners or alter plans, for example, thereby detracting from the projects' utility to the community. Gambling on the stock market, Victoria Thompson argues, thus came to be seen as "undermining a healthy balance between the public good and private interests."[112]

The stock market analogy indicates the extent to which land speculation seemed to threaten the creation of a new colonial regime in which private interests and the public good coincided. The African Commission's reporter, comte de la Pinsonnière, was representative of a widespread view that the "moral state of the colony" was seriously compromised by the invasion of speculators. "Algiers," he warned, "is becoming the theater of all kinds of fraudulent maneuvers which end by discrediting the French character in the eyes of the natives. We said that we are bringing these barbarous peoples *the benefits of civilization*, and yet from

109. CAOM F80 1161, Pavageau-Bretonnière to ministre de la Guerre (Soult), "Opinion d'un colon de St.-Domingue sur la Colonisation d'Alger," 2 May 1833 (emphasis in original).
110. Dupin, "Question d'Alger," 86.
111. BNEst Qb1 1839, *Testament de 1839, La Mode* (28 December 1839).
112. Thompson, *Virtuous Marketplace*, 149–50.

our hands escaped all the turpitudes of a worn-out social order."[113] Instead of building a virtuous New France, an Algeria of speculators simply reproduced those aspects of metropolitan society that colonization was meant to combat. "The Creation of Algeria is emminnently nationnal [sic]," wrote Alexandre Hersant-Desmares, from the Paris suburb of Montrouge, to the minister of war in the mid-1840s; "it cannot be left to speculation, which has no motive but private interest."[114]

Moral criticism of stock speculation did not entail a total rejection of the market as a tool for colonial development, however. Contemporary commentators on the Bourse distinguished between "good" and "bad" ways of profiting from the stock market. "The 'good' approach," Thompson writes, "which we might characterize as investment, was seen as that which produced wealth for the country as a whole; the 'bad' approach, making money by anticipating the rise and fall in the value of stocks and bonds, served only to enrich the individual playing the market."[115] Large Algerian landowners drew precisely this distinction between patriotic "speculations" and counterproductive forms of speculative investment. Men like himself, Ferdinand Barrot wrote to Prime Minister Guizot in 1847, "preferred agricultural speculations, always and everywhere difficult and uncertain, to the shorter-term and more brilliant speculations that urban construction, trade, industry, or legal usury offer capital."[116]

Under the July Monarchy's liberal economic regime, "good" investment was expected to play an important, even predominant role in public life, and this principle applied to the development of the Algerian colony as much as to the building of metropolitan railroads. The primary role of the state in this system was to ensure that private investment took a productive, rather than a speculative form. Thus, like colonial theorists who distinguished between "good" (productive) and "bad" (exploitative) forms of empire, officials in Paris and Algiers struggled to formulate a colonization policy that would encourage productive private investment in Algeria while forestalling unhealthy speculation. The former would constitute *véritable colonisation*, while the latter, contemporaries had no doubt, would simply revive the moral failings of Old Regime France and its slave colonies, while bringing to North Africa all the corruptions that plagued modern French society.

113. De la Pinsonnière, "Rapport sur la Colonisation," 10–12 (emphasis in original).
114. CAOM GGA L4 (d. 4/13), Alexandre Hersant-Desmares, "Affrique [sic] Française. Projet de Colonnie [sic] Général en Algérie, ayant pour base La Nationalité et Composée de divers Eléments," 5 January 1846.
115. Thompson, *Virtuous Marketplace*, 149.
116. CAOM F80 1791, letter of 28 August 1847.

Regulating Land Use

During the 1830s and 1840s, colonial officials took a series of measures to control speculation and to put fertile land into the hands of immigrants willing to cultivate it. First, they sought to regulate and, if necessary, to restrict land transactions to prevent speculators from acquiring property. Doing so, they hoped, would control prices and ensure that land remained available to colonists who would live and work on it. Similarly, when the state began to promote colonization by distributing confiscated Algerian lands to emigrants, administrators sought to ensure that concessions were granted only to those with "serious" intentions to settle and cultivate the land. Second, the colonial administration developed a framework for property rights that made titles contingent on land use and gave preference to small-scale landholding over large estates. The implementation of these policies, however, was dependent on officials' ability to distinguish productive from speculative investment and "good" from "bad" colonists. And making such distinctions ran counter to the prevailing notions of property ownership under the July Monarchy. At a time when property constituted the bedrock of citizenship, restricting property rights in a colony envisaged as an integral part of the polity posed a delicate problem. The desire to control speculation had to be balanced against the rights of individual property owners and officials' belief in the transformative powers of private capital.

Bans on some kinds of land transactions were the earliest and most direct means of preventing speculation. Since speculative activity was especially heated in areas newly occupied by French forces or where French occupation was anticipated, the first governors general banned property acquisition outside the immediate vicinity of Algiers. Decrees in 1832 and 1833 annulled all prior land transactions between Muslims and Christians in the province of Oran, in Bône and its environs, and in the towns of Arzew and Mostaganem. In 1836 and 1837, the commanders of the Constantine expeditions were instructed to institute and strictly enforce prohibitions on land sales to Europeans. Criticism of corruption within the colonial administration led to a March 1834 decree forbidding military or civilian officials to buy buildings or hold a stake in agricultural or industrial enterprises.[117] Metropolitan officials, however, soon found these controls to

---

117. "Arrêté qui maintient l'obligation de faire enregistrer tous les actes de cessions immobilières," 6 April 1832; "Arrêté qui interdit toute transmission de biens immobiliers entre Chrétiens et Musulmans, à Bône et dans la province de Constantine," 7 May 1832; "Arrêté qui autorise la vente des propriétés immobilières à l'extérieur de Bône," 8 May 1833; "Arrêté qui interdit les transmissions d'immeubles entre européens et indigènes à Arzew et Mostaganem," 3 September 1833; "Arrêté qui suspend toute transmission d'immeubles dans les provinces de Bône et de Constantine," 28 October 1836; "Arrêté qui interdit provisoirement toutes transmissions d'immeubles dans la

be both ineffective and an overly comprehensive check on the rights of private capital, which left no space for "legitimate" investment. In July of 1837, Paris saw fit to lift Governor General Valée's ban on transactions between Europeans and Algerians, and most areas of the colony were gradually opened to European buyers in the following decade.[118] An 1846 government circular explained, "as our conquest has been assured and as the European element has [expanded], the government felt the need to accord landed property the liberty that gives it life."[119] Bans were maintained in the *territoires mixtes*, areas of mixed European and Algerian habitation subjected to military administration, but in the *communes civiles* where European residents were administered by French law, new arrivals could now buy land freely.

At the same time, the French state sought to direct lands claimed for the public domain into productive hands by setting conditions on their rental, sale, and concession. Under the earliest rules governing the alienation of domain lands, the desire to limit speculators' access to real property was combined with the administration's wish to protect its own claim to the lands formerly owned by or managed for the dey and beys of Ottoman Algiers. As John Ruedy shows in his study of the Algerian public domain, French officials in Paris were primarily concerned in the 1830s and 1840s to identify and lay claim to the beylical lands that were believed to constitute the Algerian state's major source of wealth. In their search to minimize the costs of the occupation, they expected the rental and exploitation of these lands to finance the military conquest and administration of the new colony.[120]

To simultaneously protect and generate revenue from the public domain, a series of decrees in the early 1830s established that such property could only be rented or leased for a limited time, rather than sold outright. A maximum term of three years was established for rentals and leases in 1832.[121] Two years later,

---

province d'Alger, en dehors de certaines limites," 10–19 July 1837, in *RAGA*, 12, 21, 43, 46, 95, 106; *TEFA* (1837), 262–63.

118. *TEFA* (1837), 264; "Arrêté qui interdit provisoirement toutes transmissions d'immeubles dans la province d'Alger, en dehors de certaines limites," 10–19 July 1837; "Arrêté qui détermine les villes et territoires dans lesquels les transactions relatives aux biens immeubles sont et demeurent autorisées," 12–26 March 1844, in *RAGA*, 106, 275. Transactions were banned in Constantine until 1844, when the city was divided into European and indigenous quarters and Europeans were authorized to acquire real estate in the European section only. "Ordonnance qui règle le mode d'administration de la ville de Constantine, et régularise les prohibitions dont sont frappées les transactions immobilières dans cette ville depuis sa conquête," 9 June–11 July 1844, in *RAGA*, 283–85.

119. "Circulaire rappelant les dispositions générales de la législation sur les transactions immobilières," 5–17 December 1846, in *RAGA*, 467.

120. Ruedy, *Land Policy*, chap. 1.

121. "Arrêté qui interdit l'aliénation des immeubles du Domaine," 8 November 1830; "Arrêté qui réglemente les locations et les baux d'immeubles du Domaine," 4 June 1832, in *RAGA*, 4, 27–28.

this limit was raised to nine years for urban structures and ninety-nine years for empty urban lots or rural property, although any lease of more than nine years would require an act of the Algiers Administrative Council, which advised the governor general.[122] These decrees were designed to allow the colonial administration to begin filling its coffers while retaining the power to reclaim property from leaseholders or *concessionnaires* who failed to maintain, improve, or exploit their land. The decrees also laid the groundwork for the system of concessions, or grants, by which land would be transferred directly from the state to European settlers.

At first, the Administrative Council acted on a case-by-case basis in granting requests for long-term leases, but in September 1836, General Clauzel systematized the conditions under which concessions could be made from the domain to individual colonists.[123] The prescribed administrative formalities were modified in the 1840s, but the basic provisions of Clauzel's decree governed concessions throughout the rest of the July Monarchy. Under its terms, land was apportioned to settlers in accordance with their resources for exploiting it, and *concessionaires* were required to make certain improvements to their land and to cultivate it within a fixed period in order to gain full title. The territory to be conceded was subdivided into lots of four hectares, and each applicant would receive a number of lots proportional to his "means of action" in capital, labor, farm animals, and tools. In order to create smaller estates that would attract colonists with modest ambitions, rather than those seeking great fortunes, the decree set a maximum of three lots per *concessionaire*. Although this limit was eliminated in 1841, the state kept control over the size of grants in new colonial villages (*centres de population*) by requiring approval from the director of the interior, the governor general, and the minister of war for all new concessions.[124] The granting of smaller concessions was gradually turned over to local authorities in Algeria, but concessions of over twenty-five hectares continued to require approval from the highest levels of the colonial and metropolitan administration.[125]

---

122. "Arrêté concernant la location d'immeubles domaniaux, la propriété des emplacemens provenant de démolitions et les concessions," 2 April 1834, in *RAGA*, 49–51.

123. Ibid., 51; Decree of 27 September 1836, in CAOM F80 1162; CAOM F80 1162, Urtis, avocat consultant (Direction des affaires de l'Algérie), "Chronologie de la colonisation, 1830–1846."

124. "Arrêté concernant la concession des terres et la formation des centres de population," 18 April–7 May 1841, in *RAGA*, 159–60.

125. "Ordonnance qui détermine les formes suivant lesquelles les concessions pourront avoir lieu à l'avenir," 21 July–1 September 1845; "Ordonnance qui règle le mode d'administration des biens du Domaine de l'Etat," 9 November–15 December 1845; "Ordonnance qui détermine les conditions de délivrance des concessions de terres," 5 June–1 July 1847; "Ordonnance qui détermine les nouvelles conditions dans lesquelles les concessions pourront être faites en Algérie," 1–30 September 1847, all in *RAGA*, 359–60, 373–74, 515–17, 523.

The foundational decree of September 1836 required that each *concession-aire* build a house, enclose his land with a protective ditch or hedge, and clear and sow one-third of the arable land each year until the entire concession had been "cultivated," meaning that natural meadowland had been cleared and occupied no more than a quarter of the concession's total area. The *concessionaire* was obliged to plant fifty trees per hectare, to drain any wetlands, and to allow the public works department to extract sand and stone from uncultivated areas. If the grantee agreed to make additional expenditures on buildings and other improvements beyond these minimum requirements, the three-lot limit could be suspended. Only upon completion of these contractual requirements did the concession become definitive. After gaining full title, *concessionaires* were still forbidden to rent, resell, or mortgage their concessions, and title holders owed the domain an annuity of up to two francs per hectare, unless they paid it off in advance to gain free and clear ownership of the land. The goal of these conditions, Clauzel explained, was to discourage speculation without discouraging settlement. He wanted to promote colonization by "according a certain amount [of land] to those who have [the] capital and means of exploitation at the ready," rather than by making vast concessions to men without the means to cultivate effectively. The offer of land would attract farming families, and the terms under which it was granted would guarantee both their success and the interests of the new colony as a whole.[126]

Colonial officials were quickly disappointed by the results of the large concessions made under Clauzel's decree. At the end of 1837, in a report on the state of colonial agriculture, Civil Intendant Bresson condemned the "apathy" of large landowners, which he contrasted with praiseworthy efforts being made by smaller farmers to cultivate their lands. Around Bône, Bresson informed the minister of war, on fourteen large estates totaling 7,218 hectares, only 207 hectares (2.9 percent) were under cultivation. By contrast, twelve small proprietors who together controlled only 84 hectares had cultivated 52 of them (62 percent). In the environs of Algiers, Bresson observed a similar phenomenon. The Ferme modèle and the large farms of the Société algérienne de colonisation and the Polish refugee aristocrat, Prince de Mir, had produced little. In the Algiers plateau, by contrast, "small- and medium-sized properties dominate, and it is on these that vines are being planted, olive trees grafted, and . . . the most grain is being harvested and the best fodder furnished."[127] Bresson had initially thought that land companies

---

126. Clauzel to Maison, 12 September 1836, quoted in Julien Franc, *La colonisation de la Mitidja* (Paris, 1933), 163.
127. CAOM F80 1162, Bresson to Bernard, "Rapport sur l'agriculture," 6 January 1838.

and large proprietors with fallow holdings would redistribute these lands to small farmers, but found instead that they simply raised land prices beyond the reach of modest colonists. "Seeing the workers arrive, the monopolists raised their expectations rather than lowering them, and the former retreated in discouragement."[128] By 1838, War Minister Bernard had concluded that those who had acquired land in the preceding years could not be counted on to show such selfless "disinterest" as to make it available to large numbers of small colonists on acceptable terms. As Bernard declared in a set of critical instructions to the new governor general, Valée, private individuals should be free to contract as they saw fit, but where large landowners imposed "harsh" or "unacceptable" conditions on tenants or buyers of their land, the colonial administration needed to be ready to remedy the situation.[129]

By July of 1838, authorities in Paris and Algiers were ready to step in to assist small-scale settlement. Bernard therefore ordered Valée to inventory the available domain lands with the aim of identifying sites for villages in which land could be granted to *petits colons*. Since officials' shared aim was "to put arable lands into the hands of real cultivators very soon," the concessions of twelve hectares or less allowed by the September 1836 decree were deemed to be "among the most appropriate dispositions to encourage the recommendable emigrant and to assure the progress of colonization."[130] A member of the Chamber's Commission on Algerian Colonization, created in 1842 to oversee settlement policy, later explained that in limiting concessions to twelve to fifteen hectares, "we wanted inhabitants and not tenants; we did not want Parisians to be able to have tenants in Algeria."[131] Although the plans for new villages were soon halted by the resumption of hostilities with 'Abd al-Qadir, this first step into "official colonization" was an important shift away from the *laissez-faire* approach that had characterized colonization policy thus far, and it was prompted in large part by the failure of large *concessionnaires* to cultivate or settle their land.

In addition to making land available to colonists, Governor General Valée proposed a new land tax to force larger proprietors to cultivate. Since cultivation was a basic obligation of good landownership, he argued, the state ought not to offer positive inducements such as cash bonuses for production. Instead, failure

128. Bresson to Clauzel, 18 October 1836, quoted in Franc, *La colonisation*, 164.
129. CAOM F80 1793, Bernard to Valée, "Sur l'arrivée de nouveaux travailleurs, la culture des terres et la colonisation," 4 July 1838.
130. CAOM F80 1793, Bernard to Valée, "Sur le passage des ouvriers et cultivateurs et leur emploi aux travaux publics," 7 November 1838; *TEFA* (1838), 124, 137.
131. CAOM F80 1128, Félix Réal, Procès-verbaux des séances de la Commission de colonisation de l'Algérie, 24 April 1843.

to do so should be penalized by a property tax from which cultivated lands were exempted.[132] This proposition modified a provision in the September 1836 decree that made all concessions tax-exempt for five years and taxed only uncultivated land thereafter. Two years later, no tax had yet been instituted, and Valée's new proposal also remained a dead letter. The governor general's efforts nevertheless reflected his desire "to force the buyers of rural properties to cultivate the land they own":

> As long as speculators can maintain the hope that the growth of colonization will give their properties some considerable value without their being obliged to cultivate them or to use their capital to buy the equipment necessary for exploitation, they will not take the path of improvement that alone can give colonization a prosperous future. The costs that a property tax would impose on uncultivated lands will become for them an obligation to exploit, either by themselves or with *petits colons*, and the capital that today is tied up in speculations with no utility for the country will become an element of new prosperity.[133]

Despite its nonapplication, Valée's proposal to tax uncultivated lands marked the first suggestion that colonial land policy be shifted away from a regime that combated speculation by regulating the acquisition of property towards a legal framework that defined property rights by productivity. Rather than seeking to stem speculation at the point of transaction, key ordinances issued in 1844 and 1846 sought to force landholders to cultivate the land they had acquired. Liberal economic theory required that free trade in land be allowed wherever the military situation permitted, but to ensure that land be made productive, definitive legal title to property was made dependent on how it was used. Legitimate, legally protected property was redefined as that which was put to use (specifically agricultural use) by its owner. Land left fallow, on the other hand, was deemed "unoccupied" and became subject to appropriation by the state, which was then free to redistribute it to others.

In the 1830s, the administration's main priority with regard to property had been to identify and repossess beylical, *'arsh*, *hubus*, and *makhzan* lands to constitute the public domain of the new colonial state. This was in itself a massive and contentious undertaking, accompanied by considerable legal and bureaucratic

---

132. CAOM F80 1793, Bernard to Valée, "Sur l'arrivée de nouveaux travailleurs, la culture des terres et la colonisation," 4 July 1838.
133. Valée to Bernard, 18 May 1838, quoted in Franc, *La colonisation*, 186.

confusion in the surveying of these lands, serious misinterpretations of local land tenure laws, and protests against the dispossession (*séquestration*) of Algerian colonial subjects. And its effects were immediate and devastating for Algeria's rural people, who saw their holdings drastically reduced at the same time that the religious corporations that provided aid in times of need were deprived of the land from which they drew their revenues. French policymakers, however, showed little awareness of the humanitarian consequences of expropriation. Instead, their predominant concern was the property rights of Algerian landowners subjected to sequestration by the public domain. As an administrative mechanism gradually emerged to handle the questions surrounding the public domain in the late 1830s, attention turned to resolving the chaos that reigned in matters of individual property. Creating order from a documentary morass and finding a solid basis for colonial property law became the new priorities for authorities in Paris and in Algiers.

As John Ruedy points out, criticism of colonial expropriation came primarily from those who saw the colonial government's confiscation of Algerian lands as an unacceptable violation of personal property rights. "The fact that the July Monarchy passes as the government par excellence of the bourgeoisie, and stood for nothing if not for the sanctity and prerogatives of individual property, made of the Algerian sequestrations a paradox . . . difficult to explain."[134] French lawmakers, such as Alexis de Tocqueville, clearly understood this contradiction as an inevitable product of the colonial situation. While, in principle, Tocqueville firmly opposed government expropriation of private property, he came to believe that in Algeria it was the only way to make sufficient land available for European settlers and to end the disorder created by early speculators. Seizing land from both Algerian and European landholders was thus acceptable in this exceptional circumstance. Expropriating the land of Algerian tribes who fought for 'Abd al-Qadir could be justified under Muslim law, he argued, which allowed for the seizure of enemy lands. Even taking land from Algerian noncombatants posed less of a legal and philosophical problem for Tocqueville than taking it from Europeans, speculators or not, however, and only the "prodigious disorder of property" in Algeria made it necessary. The creation of "a secure landowner and an alienable property" required that the state determine "for once and for all" the ownership and boundaries of land, and then, "if the recognized owner does not cultivate his land within a term we indicate, this land will fall to the state," which would reimburse the original purchase price. "These are undoubtedly violent and irregular procedures," Tocqueville concluded, "but I defy anyone to come up with another

---

134. Ruedy, *Land Policy*, 37.

way to extricate ourselves from this problem."[135] Tocqueville's views in this regard largely coincided with those of his colleagues in the Commission on Algerian Colonization, which endorsed the use of expropriation to tie property rights to cultivation.

A series of decrees in the mid-1840s reaffirmed the right of the colonial state to seize land from private owners and laid out new criteria for their property rights. Although hotly contested by French and Algerian proprietors, the seizure of land was relatively easily reconciled with the existing French law. The capitulation of 5 July 1830 had transferred control of the property of Hussein Dey and his government to the French state, and the colonial administration claimed the right to sequester other "vacant" Algerian lands under Article 538 of the Civil Code, which held that "all parts of the French territory not determined to be private property are considered to be dependencies of the public domain."[136] A decade later, when colonial authorities began to clear space for the settlement of European immigrants, they argued that absent Algerians had abandoned their lands and, in addition, had done so to join France's enemies, giving the French a double claim to the vacant lands of enemy combatants.[137] In the following years, the government also seized land for colonial villages under its right to expropriate private property for public use (*utilité publique*).[138] This step also had its basis in metropolitan law, where both the Civil Code (Article 545) and the Charter (Article 9) allowed the state to "require the sacrifice of a property in the legally certified public interest."[139] In 1841, colonization was declared a duly recognized public good for which even legitimate landholders could be expropriated.[140] Article 5 of the 18 April 1841 decree on expropriations for colonization purposes did violate metropolitan law by allowing the colonization service to take immediate possession of expropriated property and to assess an indemnity at a later date, rather than paying prior to the transfer. Nonpayment of indemnities gave rise to

135. Alexis de Tocqueville, "Essay on Algeria," in *Writings on Empire and Slavery*, ed. and trans. Jennifer Pitts (Baltimore, 2001), 87–88.
136. *Code civil*, bk. 2, title 1, chap. 3, art. 538, [1804], http://www.legifrance.gouv.fr/WAspad/ UnArticleDeCode?code=CCIVILL0.rcv&art=538. The relevant Algerian decree is "Arrêté concernant la recherche des propriétés domaniales," 26 July 1834, in *RAGA*, 53.
137. E.g. "Arrêté qui met sous le séquestre les propriétés de la ville de Cherchell qui ne seraient pas réclamées au 1er octobre 1840," 20–29 September 1840, in *RAGA*, 144–45.
138. E.g. "Arrêté portant qu'il est formé dans le district de Kouba un village de 51 familles," 10 January–12 February 1842, in *RAGA*, 182–83.
139. *Code civil*, bk. 2, title 2, art. 545, [1804], http://www.legifrance.gouv.fr/WAspad/UnArticle DeCode?code=CCIVILL0.rcv&art=545; "Charte constitutionnelle du 14 août 1830," in *Les constitutions de la France depuis 1789*, ed. Jacques Godechot (Paris, 1970), 247.
140. "Arrêté sur l'expropriation pour cause d'utilité publique," 9–15 December 1841, in *RAGA*, 180.

a great deal of litigation in colonial courts, but since the basic principle of *utilité publique* conformed to existing French law, there was little legal wrangling over the decree itself. By 1852, some 18,414 hectares had been seized and turned over to the colonization service under the flag of *utilité publique*.[141]

The second part of the property solution imagined by French policymakers in the 1840s, the redefinition of the property rights of recognized landowners, was, as Tocqueville noted, legally exceptional and specific to the Algerian context. Whereas Article 8 of the Charter of 1830 declared that "all properties are inviolable, without any exception,"[142] colonial authorities pushed through two major pieces of legislation in 1844 and 1846 that differentiated between properties in Algeria. Building on the idea that the expansion of colonization constituted a public good that justified exceptional measures, these laws drew crucial distinctions between the rights of property owners who cultivated their land and the rights of those who did not. The 1844 and 1846 land laws played a critical role in loosening Algerians' hold on their own land, as historians have recognized, but they were also shaped by policymakers' ongoing concerns about the deleterious effects of European speculators on colonization efforts.

The first of the two laws, signed by Louis-Philippe on 1 October 1844, attempted to systematize the evolving complexities of colonial land policy. Drawn up by the minister of war in consultation with a special subcommittee of the parliamentary Commission on Colonization, the October ordinance sought to make "cultivation the sovereign law" governing property in Algeria.[143] Its first provisions reaffirmed the principles governing land transactions between Europeans and Algerians, the prohibitions on land acquisition by colonial officials, and the use of eminent domain to create or expand colonial villages, which had the effect of dramatically easing European acquisition of Algerian lands. The new law's most important legal innovation, however, was Title 5, concerning "Uncultivated Lands." According to Title 5, the minister of war was to draw boundaries around each town, village, and hamlet in which Europeans had settled and within which cultivation would become obligatory. European and indigenous proprietors with fallow lands in the designated areas would have three months to present their titles to the director of finances in Algiers, who oversaw the public domain. Any uncultivated land that went unclaimed would be declared vacant and absorbed

141. Ruedy, *Land Policy*, 81–85.
142. In Godechot, *Les constitutions*, 247.
143. CAOM F80 1129, Auguste Martineau des Chesnez, rapporteur, *Affaires de l'Algérie: Rapport au Ministre sur les travaux de la réunion intérieure formée par décision de M. le Maréchal duc de Dalmatie en date du 7 octobre 1842* (7 February 1843) (Paris, 1843), 6; "Ordonnance relative au droit de propriété en Algérie," 1–21 October 1844, in *RAGA*, 299–304.

into the domain, while anyone holding a title predating Hussein Dey's capitulation (5 July 1830) that had not been confirmed by the French authorities or was deemed otherwise insufficient would lose their property. Landholders within the cultivation zones who had undertaken cultivation, reforestation, drainage, or irrigation work would be considered free and clear owners of their lands, regardless of the terms of their concessions. Finally, a special tax of five francs per hectare, described by the subcommittee as a "fine imposed on bad colonists," would be imposed on uncultivated land inside the new boundaries. If the tax went unpaid for six months, the taxed land would be considered "given" to the domain. In lip service to the "inviolability" of private property, the land thus transferred to the domain would be "exchanged" for an equivalent holding elsewhere. Although the exchange could be put off at the convenience of either the colonist or the state, this substitute concession would also be subject to the cultivation requirements.[144]

In his instructions for implementing Title 5, War Minister Soult made clear its aims: "It is indispensable that the holders of lands situated in these selected territories put them under cultivation, so that the State not make its sacrifices [building roads, creating villages, settling colonists] for nothing and, as a consequence, to the detriment of the public good." The system of land exchanges was, he claimed, less radical than outright expropriation, for it would give a reprieve to those not yet ready to begin agricultural work and preserve their hopes for a future increase in their holdings' value, which a one-time cash indemnity did not. Soult argued further that such a landowner would not be injured by the exchange, since he could have developed "neither the value of affection, nor that real interest which attaches to things one has created and whose growth one has pursued" for land he had not worked with his own hands.[145] Implicit in this concluding statement was the conviction that the rights of speculators, whose interest in land lay solely in its commodity value, ran less deep than those of "true colonists" who invested their capital or labor in the improvement and cultivation of their property. The tenuousness of speculators' property claims was evident to the Commission on Algerian Colonization, which considered the very state of noncultivation to be in itself proof of speculative intent. The owners of vacant lands, the commission reported, really owned nothing more than a hope for future profits. "They played the lottery, they accepted the risks," of which expropriation was one. Compared to the overwhelming public interest in cultivation, speculators' dreams of "fairytale profits" constituted nothing more than

144. CAOM F80 1129, Martineau des Chesnez, *Rapport*, 74.
145. "Instructions sur l'exécution des dispositions ordonnées par l'ordonnance du Roi du 1er octobre 1844, titre V, à l'effet de faire cesser l'inculture des terres dans l'étendue des territoires compris dans les périmètres déterminés par les arrêtés ci-dessus," 2–20 February 1845, in *RAGA*, 326.

"accidental interests" unworthy of protection by the government's guarantees on private property.[146]

The second major land ordinance was issued by the king in July 1846 in order to "assure the settlement of Algeria and the fertilization of its soil by constituting rural property on henceforth unshakeable bases."[147] It addressed difficulties in the execution of the previous law but did not alter its guiding principles. The verification of land titles had proved almost impossible for the colonial courts to manage, so the new ordinance transferred this responsibility to an arbitration council and a cadastral surveying corps, both of which were deemed to have more time and expertise to devote to this essential activity. The conditions under which property could be declared vacant or unimproved and seized by the state were clarified, as well. The 1844 law had declared somewhat equivocally that cultivation might constitute "a title, the best perhaps, to possession of the soil." "Since the State has an interest in settlement and fertilization, it would be illogical to withdraw possession of land from someone using it in accordance with the public interest," whatever the status of his or her other claims. The new ordinance therefore spelled out the legal sources of the right of possession and declared that rights acquired through agricultural labor had to be given equal weight to those of parties claiming prior ownership. Article 20 of the 1846 ordinance specified the conditions under which land would be considered legally cultivated: for each twenty hectares of land granted, a *concessionaire* had five years to settle one European family in a house and farm buildings worth at least five thousand francs and to plant and maintain thirty trees. A colonist could claim definitive title to whatever portion of the land he occupied that met these conditions, regardless of his other legal claims to it.[148]

The 1846 law thus reaffirmed the principles behind the 1844 ordinance and further enshrined the idea that cultivation conveyed property rights, while failure to do so carried the risk of dispossession. The punitive aspects of both laws, however, remained almost entirely without effect. Here, as so often in early colonial policy, prescription and reality diverged quite dramatically. The government reclaimed very little property, and the tax on uncultivated lands was never enforced before it was taken off the books in 1851.[149] By 1850, only 19,497 hectares had been reclaimed under the two laws, although other decrees

146. CAOM F80 1129, Martineau des Chesnez, *Rapport*, 67, 72.
147. *TEFA* (1846–49), 253.
148. "Ordonnance sur la constitution de la propriété en Algérie," 21 July–8 August 1846, in *RAGA*, 428–34.
149. AN C899, "Réponse du ministre à la demande de la Commission d'Afrique, no. 14," [25 March 1847].

allowing the state to declare land vacant did yield some 33,000 hectares more.[150] The ordinances fell with greatest force on Algerians, who found themselves required to produce "unimpeachable" written proof of property rights that were rarely written down in forms acceptable to French authorities. These procedures facilitated the transfer of previously protected lands to Europeans, who gained access to some 168,000 hectares "forfeited" by Algerians who were unaware of or could not meet the new standards of proof.[151]

Ruedy attributes the paucity of these results to ineptitude and obstructionism on the part of the Algerian bureaucracy, which resisted attempts by Paris to impose its view on the colonial administration, but there was more to the problem than interoffice rivalries. The lack of political will in either Paris or Algiers to enforce a coherent, effective policy on land and property rights also reflected a long-standing ambivalence about the role of private capital in the colonial enterprise. As we have seen, critics insisted that to encourage large-scale private investment was to open the door to dangerous speculation and to sacrifice the broader goals of colonization for the benefit of a few big landowners. Supporters, however, maintained that wealthy capitalists were better positioned than small colonists or the government to make the kind of improvements necessary to a prospering colonial economy and that the economic development effected by private capital would outweigh the harm done by illegitimate speculation. In practical terms, these contrasting views manifested themselves in an ongoing policy debate over the relative merits of small and large colonial estates. Conflicting beliefs were held on this question by key players at all levels of the colonial policymaking hierarchy.

In formulating legislation to govern Algerian land policy, the Chamber of Deputies' Colonization Commission heard evidence from both sides and ultimately sought to steer a middle course between these two positions, thereby creating what might be called a colonial *juste milieu*, which would reflect the liberal values of the July Monarchy yet take into account the colonial situation. On one side of the debate, General Berthois testified that "only small proprietors can become attached to the soil. Possessing little, they hold on all the tighter to what they do own. . . . Great landowners, [however], will exploit their lands using tenant farmers who will leave at the first sign of war."[152] On the other side, the wealthy settler Baron Augustin de Vialar argued just as forcefully that capital was indis-

---

150. Ruedy, *Land Policy*, 95–97.
151. Grangaud, "Prouver," 37; Charles-André Julien, *Histoire de l'Algérie contemporaine*, vol. 1, *La conquête et les débuts de la colonisation (1827–1871)* (Paris, 1964), 240–41; Ruedy, *Land Policy*, chap. 7.
152. CAOM F80 1128, Procès-verbaux des séances de la Commission de colonisation de l'Algérie, 19 March 1842.

pensable for colonization: "only the landowner's money will suffice" to cover the expense of creating a new agricultural enterprise. Vialar protested that expropriating large landholders in order to concede their land to small colonists "shakes the rights of property, the principal basis of society."[153] He went on to accuse the Ministry of War of seeking to destroy "that ancient property right on which the existence of all societies rests," and claimed that 1844 and 1846 ordinances created a system of colonization by "spoliation and theft" whose cultivation standards even the wealthiest and most compliant landowner could not meet.[154] The commission's own members were largely unable to reconcile their own divided views on the question of large and small property. One subcommittee restricted itself to a general statement that "the first need of colonization in Africa is the existence of certain, guaranteed, and inviolable property rights," while another left the question of large and small property to local or higher authorities.[155]

The same disagreements emerged in discussion of three plans for systematic colonization that were tested by the government in the 1840s. Governor General Bugeaud, a conservative provincial landowner in his own right and a firm advocate of yeoman farming, proposed a scheme in which the government made small grants of land directly to army veterans. In civilian colonization, too, he advocated small colonists rather than large landowners. "I would much prefer," he claimed, "a hundred families each with 2,000 francs to a capitalist with 600,000 francs to whom I gave 1,000 hectares. In that space, I would make 100 proprietors attached to the soil forever, and the capitalist, if he did anything at all, would settle only a score of proletarian tenants or sharecroppers of the worst sort."[156] For his part, General de Lamoricière, the Saint-Simonian commander of Oran province, proposed a system of *grandes concessions* in which capitalists would be granted large tracts of land on which to settle tenant farmers. Finally, General Bedeau, commander of Constantine province, suggested a compromise that mixed small colonists with large capitalists.[157] The Chambers, split among

153. CAOM F80 1128, Procès-verbaux des séances de la Commission de colonisation de l'Algérie, 18 February 1842.
154. Augustin de Vialar, *Première lettre à M. le maréchal Bugeaud, duc d'Isly, gouverneur-général de l'Algérie* (Algiers, 1846), 10–11.
155. *Rapport fait au nom de la seconde sous-commission par M. Gustave de Beaumont, le 20 juin 1842: Organisation civile, administrative, municipale et judiciaire* (Paris, 1843), 17; *Rapport fait au nom de la troisième sous-commission par M. Lingay, le 3 juin 1842: Sécurité, salubrité, desséchements, villages et enceinte* (Paris, 1843), 43.
156. CAOM GGA 2EE 12, Bugeaud to général De Larue, 5 March 1846.
157. Bugeaud, *L'Algérie*; CAOM F80 1676, Direction des affaires de l'Algérie (Bureau de la colonisation et de l'agriculture), "Crédits extraordinaires à demander pour la Colonisation, en 1847," 7 November 1846; *Projets de colonisation pour les provinces d'Oran et de Constantine, présentés par MM. les lieutenants-généraux de Lamoricière et Bedeau* (Paris, 1847).

supporters of these systems, ultimately chose to fund experiments with all three in 1846.

This wavering on property and settlement regimes, so characteristic of colonial policy during the July Monarchy, was the result not only of French policymakers' reluctance to commit to a single, costly program but also of the parliamentarians' application of the July Monarchy's foundational philosophy to the colonial arena. The duc de Decazes, the president of the Colonization Commission, asked early in the commission's deliberations on land concessions if there was not some way to find a "juste milieu" between grants of ten hectares and six thousand.[158] This choice of wording is critical for understanding the halting development of Algerian settlement policy in the 1830s and 1840s. The subcommittee that played the key role in formulating the land ordinances of 1844 and 1846 explained its refusal to recommend either small landholding by the poor or large property ownership in precisely these terms: "The truth rarely lies in exclusive systems, in extreme opinions. It is in borrowing from each of the social elements its particular strength and in combining these united forces that we will obtain serious and prompt results."[159] Both the terms and the inefficacy of the land laws that resulted from attempts to settle the property question in Algeria stemmed from precisely this effort to draw together the various elements of society, to balance small proprietorship with the freedom of capital, and to reconcile the aims of *peuplement* and *fertilisation* with the rights of private property. This multifaceted balancing act aimed to create a *juste milieu* between the extremes of unbridled speculation and state control of colonization and to give rise to a colonial society that reproduced as closely as possible the ideals of the *juste milieu* in France itself.

Formulated as a way to bring "good" kinds of speculative investment to bear in the collective task of reviving the fertility of the Algerian soil, the colonial *juste milieu* largely accepted the argument of wealthy landowners that "the foundation of a colony is nothing less than a gigantic speculation undertaken by the nation," in which private capital had a necessary and noble role to play.[160] Whether the land was owned by many or few, however, the ultimate goal of colonization remained the introduction of a large, permanent European population dedicated to cultivating Algeria's rich soil. Conditioning land concessions and property rights upon cultivation had this underlying concern. In practice, however, it proved very difficult for administrators in Algiers or Paris to determine which investors would actually further this aim and which would not.

158. CAOM F80 1128, Procès-verbaux des séances de la Commission de colonisation de l'Algérie, 4 February 1842.
159. CAOM F80 1129, Martineau des Chesnez, *Rapport*, 122.
160. Cochut, "De la colonisation de l'Algérie.—Les essais et les systèmes," 537.

The problem of speculative involvement in colonization manifested itself in the case of individuals or companies that stepped forward to recruit colonial emigrants. Baron Pichon, the first civil intendant in Algiers, declared himself aghast at "the extent of the deception that had been perpetrated in Paris and in France on those unfortunates who have been brought here to settle" by interested parties.[161] Speculators' dishonesty had disastrous effects on the individuals concerned, Pichon noted, and the state bore the financial and political consequences of their lies. When emigrants misled and then abandoned by recruiters ended up on the public assistance rolls in the colony or returned to France destitute, the government found itself accused of failing to safeguard the well-being of its subjects. As a consequence, the Ministry of War tried to distance itself from speculators by supporting only those who clearly identified their efforts as private initiatives with "no commitment from the King's Government or from its agents in their public capacity." In the mid-1830s, the minister sponsored free passage on navy ships for emigrants recruited by private individuals in the Sarthe and in the French and German Rhineland, but refused to allow recruiters to use the French government's name to promote their activities.[162]

In the 1840s, when a more systematic rural colonization scheme was instituted, the Ministry of War took stronger measures to control recruitment by requiring all colonization agents to obtain ministerial approval before enrolling emigrants for Algeria. The difficulties of determining the trustworthiness of such individuals can be seen in the example of François Lacroutz, a banker-trader, who formulated a plan to settle Basque emigrants in Algeria in 1842. Working with two businessmen from the southwestern city of Bayonne and with Soult's encouragement, he recruited over fifty families to populate two new villages in the Sahel. After two years of planning, however, a last-minute inquiry into the backgrounds of Lacroutz and his partners revealed the plan to be unacceptably speculative in character. The prefect of the Basses-Pyrénées reported that the men were generally mistrusted in the region and that Lacroutz himself had originally gone to Algeria to escape business obligations in Pau. In addition, the prefect warned, their recruits were far from model colonists; some did not intend even to go to Algeria but planned to send servants to work their land. A project initially welcomed as "totally patriotic" had in fact "been conceived with the aim of private interest and not to come to the aid of colonization by bringing serious colonists." With its speculative intent unmasked, the project was

---

161. CAOM 6X 8, Pichon to Casimir Périer, 12 February 1832.
162. CAOM F80 1162, Maison to Clauzel, 18 September 1835, 23 October 1835, and 26 October 1835.

canceled by the Ministry of War.[163] Similar suspicions drove the administration to reject other offers to establish private recruitment agencies both in France and abroad in this period. The agents who obtained government sanction were those who recognized these attitudes and took care to insist that they were not selfish speculators, but sought to promote colonization.

Landowners and wealthy men seeking large concessions followed the same logic in presenting their actions as guided by the interests of the colony and the nation, although they framed these claims with an emotional defense of productive speculation. The wealthy legitimist aristocrat Jules Du Pré de Saint Maur, who amassed an estate of over two thousand hectares in Oran province during the July Monarchy and Second Empire, argued in requesting his first land concession in 1846 that "for the great landowner of France, . . . it is honorable to risk capital to render productive a land drenched in the blood of so many Frenchmen." "I have not come to seek a fortune," he continued, "I have come to risk part of my own."[164] Government officials could, as we have seen, be persuaded by such arguments, and most often granted land and contracts to found private villages to men like Du Pré de Saint Maur, even as their projects repeatedly failed.

That such enterprises were never discredited is evident from the involvement of prominent metropolitan figures in Algerian land investment schemes. One of the first private colonization companies, the Compagnie algérienne de colonisation, founded in 1834 with eight million francs of capital for what its prospectus called "the peaceable speculations of agriculture, commerce, and industry," counted among its primary investors Louis-Philippe's eldest son, the king's aide-de-camp, six deputies, two peers, the mayors of Rouen and of Paris's second arrondissement, a former prefect, and a number of other, noble luminaries.[165] An 1846 government report reveals the extent to which investment in Algerian estates remained the business of metropolitan elites. A list of 89 individuals requesting grants of over one hundred hectares in the preceding year was dominated by landowners (42), politicians (13), bankers and merchants (11), and men of law (8). A handful of liberal professionals and military men rounded out the list. The professional status and geographical origins of the applicants, most of whom reported legal residences in Paris, Lyon, and Marseille, suggest

163. CAOM GGA L1/6, préfet des Basses-Pyrénées to ministre de la Guerre, 29 December 1843; Guyot to Lacroutz, 16 November 1842 [copy]; Soult to Bugeaud, 26 January 1844.
164. Letter to Louis-Philippe, quoted in Roland Villot, *Jules Du Pré de Saint-Maur, colon oranien*, 2nd ed. (Oran, 1955), 40; Narcisse Faucon, "Du Pré de Saint Maur, Jules," in *Livre d'or de l'Algérie* . . . (Paris, 1889), 213–14.
165. CAOM F80 1162 and F80 1671, *Compagnie algérienne de colonisation, sous la raison A. Thayer, Soulié et Cie.: Prospectus* (Paris, 1834), 1, 9.

that most were wealthy urban investors who saw Algerian land as an opportunity for profit rather than as a place to settle themselves. It seems likely that, at best, the seven self-identified *agriculteurs* might have been prepared to relocate to Algeria to direct agricultural work personally, but the report does not record their intentions.[166]

Colonial administrators on both sides of the Mediterranean continued to favor large landowners throughout the July Monarchy, despite the frequently spectacular and not infrequently criminal collapses of their enterprises. In 1843, for example, Baron Vialar and his partner, Auguste Caussidou, received permission to settle twenty families on land they owned near Douéra. Interior Director Guyot questioned the merits of an enterprise where "'it is the administration that does all the work and provides all the funds'" for a private venture, but Vialar's standing as one of the most prominent members of the settler community convinced the government to build a village on their Hadj-Yakoub farm. The two men were given twenty thousand francs to provide shelter, tools, farm animals, and other assistance to the immigrants, who would then receive title to the land they cleared and cultivated. Colonial officials, however, soon realized that Vialar and Caussidou had no intention of turning the land over to the families they had recruited. Instead, the partners had established a kind of sharecropping arrangement that would provide them with European labor at below-market wages. Vialar and Caussidou's contract was canceled, and the episode ended with Caussidou embezzling part of the money the state had advanced for the migrant families.[167]

By the end of the July Monarchy, at least a dozen large grants of hundreds or thousands of hectares had been made to individuals or groups promising to settle French or European colonists on their farms. For the most part, these concessions failed to produce the desired results, from Clauzel's Ferme modèle (1831) to the Union agricole d'Afrique, which received 2,059 hectares to settle three hundred families along the Sig River in Oran province in 1846. One of the few successes was a settlement created by Trappist monks at Staouëli in 1843. A monastery of sixty monks and forty civilian employees prospered on a concession of 1,020 hectares in the Sahel until the death of the community's founder in the 1880s. Even the Trappists, however, succeeded only with massive state aid. In addition to sixty-two thousand francs allocated with the initial concession, the monks used the influence

166. CAOM F80 1166, "État des demandes en concession de terres formées pour des étendues de 100 hectares et au dessus," 10 January 1846.
167. Julien, *La conquête*, 245; CAOM F80 1162, Urtis, "Chronologie de la colonisation, 1830–1846."

of Queen Marie-Amélie and Catholic deputies to obtain free construction materials, horses, oxen, seeds, farm implements, and, later, further cash subsidies.[168] Although religious commitment may have contributed to their perseverance as Charles-André Julien suggests, other religious communities created in the same period failed miserably without similar infusions of government money. It seems likely that the Trappists' powerful friends played at least as important a role in the longevity of their settlement as did their piety.[169]

Contractual obligations required large *concessionaires* to invest their own capital to improve the land, build farm buildings, and settle certain numbers of European colonists, but as the example of Vialar and Caussidou demonstrates, these obligations often went ignored and unenforced. The state's primary legal recourse was to reclaim the land granted for such colonies, but officials usually did so only after *concessionnaires* had reneged on their commitments, having already pocketed significant amounts of money. Throughout the 1840s especially, the principles of economic liberalism continued to obtain at the top levels of the Algerian administration in Paris and to override generalized concerns about the dangers of speculation by colonial investors. The director of Algerian affairs declared in 1841 that it was "above all in agriculture that the maxim *laissez-faire* must be put into practice," and that the government should limit itself to protecting and guiding private investment.[170]

Attempts to counter land speculation were contested by defenders of the colonial *juste milieu* as an attack against the property rights on which the modern French polity was founded, but there were fewer qualms about regulating the movements and activities of more modest colonial emigrants. For whether land was owned by many or by few, realizing the Algerian fertility myth required *peuplement* as well as *fertilisation*. Shaping the flow of migration from France to Algeria was therefore the logical complement to efforts to regulate the distribution and use of land. Let us turn now to this final, critical aspect of French settlement colonization in Algeria: the formulation and implementation of emigration policy in France itself.

---

168. Bugeaud to Borel de Brétizel, 19 August 1843, in Bugeaud, *Par l'épée et par la charrue: Écrits et discours de Bugeaud*, ed. Paul Azan (Paris, 1948), 149.
169. Julien, *La conquête*, 243–44; "Arrêté qui concède à la société civile établie à Aiguebelles, 1,020 hectares de terres dans la plaine de Staouëli," 11–29 July 1843, in *RAGA*, 247–48.
170. CAOM GGA L4/1, directeur des Affaires de l'Algérie (Laurence), "Rapport au ministre: Colonisation du Territoire de Bône," 8 March 1841 (*laissez-faire* emphasized in original).

6

Settling Algeria

Labor, Emigration, and Citizenship

ALMOST IMMEDIATELY AFTER Algiers's capitulation in 1830, French officials, especially in large towns, began to dream of sending the poor and unemployed to Algiers. The Paris municipal council and the new prefect of police, Baron Jean-Jacques Baude, were the first to seize on this possibility in the winter of 1830–31, which was marked by a worsening economic and commercial slump, widespread working-class protests, and political unrest surrounding the trial of Charles X's ministers.[1] The crisis reached its height in early January 1831, when crowds of Parisian workers demanding jobs and bread overran the public workshops at Saint-Denis, overwhelming the local police *commissaire* and forcing the National Guard to step in to dispel the rioters. In July 1830, Baude had proposed in vain to Polignac that settling dissidents in North Africa might calm the country's troubles. When the Saint-Denis riots broke out in 1831, he and the Paris councilors turned their attention back to Algiers. Emigration, Baude argued once again, could provide a permanent prophylactic against such disturbances and even permit the abolition of the workshops, a source of constant disruption, altogether. "There is perhaps no way to escape this painful position other than enlarging the outlet for a restless and needy population [by] facili-

---

1. André Jardin and André-Jean Tudesq, *La France des notables*, vol. 1, *L'évolution générale, 1815–1848* (Paris, 1973), 130–31; H. A. C. Collingham with Robert S. Alexander, *The July Monarchy: A Political History of France, 1830–1848* (London, 1988), 36–39.

tating emigration to the coast of Africa," Baude proposed to Interior Minister Montalivet on January 4.[2]

Baude's plan to send twenty thousand unemployed men to Algiers was swiftly approved by King Louis-Philippe and the Conseil d'État, on condition that the city of Paris, which would reap the greatest benefit, also cover its costs.[3] Consultation with military authorities led to a modification in the initial proposal—rather than forming militarized settlements, as Baude suggested, the "Parisian volunteers" would enlist for five years in a new regiment of the Armée d'Afrique—but within a week, the revised plan, supported by the prefect of the Seine and funded by the Paris city council, was put into action.[4] By January 21, over 1,700 men had been dispatched to Marseille to embark for Algiers, and another 1,300 had registered to go by the end of April.[5] All told, some 4,500 Parisians were sent the nascent colony in the ensuing months.[6]

Baude's primary concern in organizing the Parisian volunteers was for the capital's stability and the power of military discipline and governmental lar-gesse to transform men of "hostile sentiments" into "faithful subjects of the July Throne."[7] "Disorderly Riot will no longer dare show his face upon our public squares," he maintained, if unemployed men could be lured to North Africa with promises of free land after a period of service.[8] Montalivet concurred, and a year later, the minister opened the regiment of Parisian volunteers to freed vaga-bonds and criminals nationwide.[9] Similar considerations led authorities across France to sponsor the emigration of beggars, criminals, and other troublemakers. A number of deputies and the prefect of the Calvados, for example, endorsed a plan to create villages for local convicts in Algeria.[10] Notables in Lyon created a

2. Jean-Jacques Baude, *L'Algérie*, vol. 2 (Paris, 1841), 271–73; AN F7 3885, Bulletin de Paris, 4 January 1831.
3. SHD 1M 1318, général Pelet, "Compte-rendu d'un projet de colonisation," and "Minute de la lettre écrite par Pelet au préfet de Police," both 19 January 1831.
4. SHD 1H 6, Berthezène to Soult, 8 February 1831, 9 February 1831; 1H 7, Soult to Clauzel, March 1831; Clauzel to Soult, dépêche télégraphique, 1 March 1831.
5. AN F7 3885, Bulletin de Paris, 21 January 1831; SHD 1H 7, préfect de Police (Vivien) to Soult, 30 April 1831.
6. Baude, *L'Algérie*, 2:273–74, 478–79; Baude, speech to the Chamber of Deputies, 30 April 1834, *AP* 89:615.
7. AN F7 3885, Bulletin de Paris, 2 November 1831.
8. AN F7 3885, Bulletin de Paris, 7 October 1831.
9. AD Var 3Z 171, [Sous-préfecture de Toulon], "Individus (vagabonds libérés) annoncés par M. le Ministre de l'Intérieur pour venir contracter des engagemens volontaires pour les corps formés à Alger," 19 June–8 October 1832.
10. CAOM F80 1161, préfet du Calvados to ministre de la Guerre, letter accompanying Gouré, *Considérations sur Alger*, November 1831.

society to lobby for Algeria's colonization in 1835, partly on the grounds that it would relieve discontent in industrial cities like their own.[11] Later, officials in the Corrèze supported a local man trying to found a settlement for poor inhabitants of the department.[12]

If metropolitan officials were enthusiastic about the idea that domestic ills could be cured by emigration to Algeria, officials of the new colonial state were not. Unrestricted emigration, they worried, would simply displace social and political problems from metropole to colony. In 1831, the commander of the Armée d'Afrique, General Berthezène, responded to Baude's emigration scheme with hostility:

> It would be a great and fatal error to think that tossing indigent families from the heart of the cities or the countryside onto the Algerian coast is enough to provide them with bread. They would find, to the contrary, fewer resources than in Europe, because they can find no work here. . . . *Consider then in what difficulty we would be if we were sent an excess of population, which we would have either to let die of hunger or to feed from the State's storehouses; already we are overburdened by a crowd of disreputable men* (gens sans aveu) *with no livelihood and of whom we cannot rid ourselves because they have no means of returning home.*[13]

It was vain to hope, Berthezène asserted, that unemployed workers could find jobs in Algiers.[14] Colonization might be possible in the future, if undertaken gradually and carefully controlled. At present, however, the ex-regency could not support the poor families arriving on its shores.

The conflict between Baude and Berthezène reveals the extent to which metropolitan views of colonization's potential benefits clashed with Algerian officials' fears that disorderly elements would contaminate colonial society and impede military operations. Exactly how many poverty-stricken emigrants there were in the first years of the French occupation, or how they got to Algeria, is difficult to gauge. Population statistics were not gathered in the early 1830s, although Berthezène estimated the European population at just over five hundred in March 1831 and nearly three thousand six months later.[15] Whatever their

---

11. Louis-François Trollier, *Mémoire sur la nécessité et sur les avantages de la colonisation d'Alger* (Lyon, 1835), 3–5.
12. CAOM GGA L3/43, préfet de la Corrèze to ministre de la Guerre (Saint-Yon), 10 April 1847.
13. SHD 1H 7, Berthezène to Soult, 21 March 1831 (emphasis added by minister in original).
14. SHD 1H 7, Berthezène to Soult, 2 April 1831.
15. SHD 1H 10, Berthezène to editor of *Le Constitutionnel*, 20 August 1831.

precise number, these individuals were seen by colonial officials as a source of financial and social difficulties to be mitigated as much as possible. In the case of Baude's Parisian volunteers, by 1834, Berthezène's successors had resorted to simply sending them back to France.[16]

The conviction that working-class emigrants would hurt the colony was driven by preexisting suspicions of poor urban workers and shaped the policies developed to regulate emigration to Algeria during the July Monarchy. Authorities in Paris and Algiers used controls on the issuance of passports and the influence of local officials in France to prevent "undesirable" individuals from reaching the colony. When subsidized passages were introduced as a means of encouraging "desirable" emigrants, eligibility criteria were designed to limit the access of the poor, unskilled, and unemployable to government assistance. The overriding concern to limit "undesirable" emigration to Algeria had to be balanced, however, against the practical needs of the growing colony, particularly for labor, and worked out through an administrative network that that stretched from new colonial settlements through Algiers and Paris into the smallest villages of rural France. Efforts to find an equilibrium between the countervailing priorities of these diverse state agents highlight the tensions that emerged between metropolitan and imperial reform movements, as well as between the different branches of the expanding French imperial state and emigrants themselves. Adding these conflicts to the better-known struggles between civilian and military authorities in North Africa, especially the colonization services and the Bureaux arabes, will help us better understand the Algerian colonial state as a trans-Mediterranean entity that sought to regulate the movements and behavior of European emigrants as much as those of indigenous Algerians.

From Exclusion to Assisted Emigration

The first regulations imposed on emigration to Algeria were prompted by Berthezène's complaints about Baude's Parisian volunteers and other poor migrants arriving unbidden in North Africa. Many of these newcomers were not French—the invasion of 1830 had unleashed a growing stream of spontaneous migration from around the Mediterranean basin, and migrants from southern Italy, Spain, Greece, Malta, and the Balearic Islands outnumbered French nationals until 1847. Although French diplomats did work with European states to stem the tide of unwanted migrants, controlling foreign immigration fell largely to po-

---

16. AD Var 3Z 171, colonel du 67e régiment de ligne, "État nominatif des militaires dudit régiment qui doivent s'embarquer pour rentrer en France . . . ," 7 March 1834.

lice officials in Algiers. As early as November 1830, colonial officials began to require all new arrivals to present passports and obtain residence permits upon landing in Algerian ports. Shortly thereafter, merchant captains were forbidden to take on or to discharge any passenger without a passport or other documentation from French authorities.[17] The logic of exclusion that governed these measures continued to shape policies towards foreign migrants, whose entry into French territory was subject to the discretion of the French state. Nineteenth-century laws requiring French citizens to obtain passports to travel within the national territory, however, gave the state power to regulate emigration from France to Algeria at both the sending and receiving ends of the migration path.[18] The balance between exclusion at the point of arrival and restriction at the point of departure fluctuated, but gradually shifted towards the latter over the course of the July Monarchy.

Prior to the French invasion, travel from France to Algeria was regulated according to the practices long used for foreign trading posts (échelles), which gave privileged metropolitan corporations authority over voyagers departing from France. In the case of Ottoman Algiers, this privilege was held by the Marseille Chamber of Commerce, whose rights were reaffirmed in July of 1830.[19] In May of 1831, however, Casimir Périer, then minister of the interior, president of the council of ministers, and an enthusiastic backer of colonial emigration as a means of social reform, transferred to the metropolitan prefects responsibility for issuing passports to enter Algiers.[20] In doing so, Casimir Périer asserted that Algeria should no longer be considered an échelle like those of the Levant, but instead should be treated as a French colony. Travel there would require the Interior Ministry documentation that permitted travel within metropolitan departments

---

17. "Arrêté concernant la police des passages en Algérie," 15 November 1830, and "Arrêté du général en chef," 25 April 1831, in RAGA, 4, 9. On European migration to Algeria, see Marc Donato, *L'émigration des Maltais en Algérie au XIXème siècle* (Montpellier, 1985); Jean-Maurice Di Costanzo, *Allemands et Suisses en Algérie, 1830–1918* (Calvisson, 2001); Gérard Crespo, *Les Italiens en Algérie, 1830–1960: Histoire et sociologie d'une émigration* (Nice, 1994); Jean-Jacques Jordi, *Espagnol en Oranie: Histoire d'une migration, 1830–1914* (Nice, 1996); Jennifer Sessions, "'L'Algérie devenue française': The Naturalization of Non-French Colonists in French Algeria, 1830–1849," *Proceedings of the Western Society for French History* 30 (2002), 165–77; Julia Clancy-Smith, "Exoticism, Erasures, and Absence: The Peopling of Algiers, 1830–1900," in *The Walls of Algiers: Narratives of the City through Text and Image*, ed. Zeynep Çelik, Julia Clancy-Smith, and Frances Terpak (Los Angeles, 2009), 19–61.

18. On passport laws, see Gérard Noiriel, "Surveiller les déplacements ou identifier les personnes? Contribution à l'histoire du passeport en France de la Première à la Troisième République," *Genèses* 30 (1998): 77–100.

19. Pierre Guiral, *Marseille et l'Algérie, 1830–1841* (Aix-en-Provence, 1957), 60–61.

20. AD Haut-Rhin 6M 354, ministre de l'Intérieur, "Passeports pour Alger," 18 May 1831.

and French overseas possessions, rather than the document issued by diplomatic authorities that allowed French citizens to exit the national territory.

Although they eased travel to Algiers for some wealthy individuals, the new regulations also sought to answer complaints from the Ministry of War about the influx of penniless emigrants into Algiers.[21] In the face of "increasing numbers of requests from travelers desiring to go there in hopes of procuring resources," the prefects were deemed best situated "to judge which are the persons who offer guarantees in terms of both conduct and means of existence and can go to this part of Africa without inconvenience to themselves or to the administration." To guide their judgments, the May circular distinguished four classes of people who might wish to travel to Algiers and indicated the official stance towards each group. First were established merchants with trading interests in North Africa, who could be accorded passports without inconvenience because they would return to France once their business was concluded. Second, the prefects could safely give passports to persons seeking to found agricultural enterprises, if they possessed the means and expertise to run a large estate successfully. In contrast to this second group, which constituted the earliest official incarnation of the *véritable colon*, the circular stipulated that the third and fourth classes of emigrants, indigents and needy workers, were not, under any circumstances, to receive passports:

Individuals who have no resources in France and have heard talk of the colonization of Algiers are asking to be sent there, most at the Government's expense. Neglect nothing in making clear to them that you cannot grant their requests in their own interest, that the territory of Algiers offers at this moment no estate where they could be taken on to work, and that they would soon be forced to return after exhausting the bit of money they had taken with them.[22]

These restrictions elicited protests from procolonization journalists, who saw any limits on travel to Algeria as neglect or even obstruction of aspiring colonists, and were thus followed a month later by a short notice in the *Moniteur universel* announcing that the Ministry of War would provide free passage to Algiers on government ships for "families and individuals from the working and agricultural classes who are capable of living from their own work and of taking to Africa some means of existence." Emigrants would have to pay their own way to the port of departure, however, and they would receive no allocation or subven-

21. CAOM F80 1670 (1), Casimir Périer to Soult, 11 July 1831.
22. AD Haut-Rhin 6M 354, ministre de l'Intérieur, "Passeports pour Alger," 18 May 1831.

tion from the state after reaching Algiers. Ostensibly a defense of the ministry's commitment to colonization, the notice was in fact intended to discourage "those who might believe they were improving their position by going to Africa."[23] The emphasis on prospective emigrants' need for self-sufficiency was aimed directly at the working-class and agricultural families who made up the third and fourth groups of emigrants in the May circular.

Behind these measures lay the desire to prevent a recurrence of the difficulties created by the Parisian volunteers, and this imperative continued to govern Algerian emigration rules until 1838. Passports were issued to those who could prove they had the resources to pay for the voyage and to live in Algeria at their own expense. Free passage on government ships was accorded to wealthy individuals scouting out property or formulating plans for large estates, while poorer colonists were treated with suspicion and refused passports. In theory any modest cultivators or workers in "useful professions" who could certify "their industry and their morality" could obtain free passage from Toulon to Algiers,[24] but access to this benefit depended on the applicant's holding a passport, which was granted only when public works authorities or wealthy settlers required labor.[25] Except when they were asked to recruit workers for specific purposes, local officials in France were enlisted to discourage workers and peasants contemplating emigration to Algeria. Subprefects and mayors were to make clear to "the unfortunate working class" that there was neither land nor employment to be had in Algiers, and that those who went there would be inevitably forced to return to France after exhausting their meager savings.[26] The metropolitan press reiterated warnings to prospective emigrants about the lack of travel funds or assistance for those who found themselves indigent once they arrived in Algiers.[27] Prefects, mayors, and police *commissaires* were called upon to provide citizens with "all the information necessary to understand the current situation of this country [with] the principal goal of warning the public against risky speculations that might be occasioned by this lack of clarification and to show how, in undertaking them, it might expose itself to disappointment."[28]

23. CAOM Afrique IV (5), "Extr. du *Moniteur universel* du mardi 21 juin 1831."
24. CAOM 1E 59², instructions of 19 February 1833, in "Résumé mensuel de la correspondance d'Afrique en mars 1834," 1 April 1834; AD Meurthe-et-Moselle 6M 290, "Extr. du *Moniteur* du jeudi 18 février 1836: No. 49, 'Alger: Passage gratuit de Toulon à Alger.'"
25. *TEFA* (1838), 121.
26. AM Marseille 13F 1, ministre de l'Intérieur to préfet des Bouches-du-Rhône, 22 February 1833, in maire de Marseille, "Avis: Ouvriers nécessaires à la colonie d'Alger," 20 April 1833; AD Yvelines 5M 71, préfet de la Haute-Saône, "Passeports pour Alger," *Recueil administratif de la Haute-Saône* 17 (1832), 156–57.
27. *Moniteur algérien*, 10 October 1835.
28. APP DB 364, préfet de Police to commissaires de police, 30 May 1831.

Authorities' efforts to filter out poor emigrants on the metropolitan end of the migration path were only partly successful, however. Casimir Périer's successors at the Ministry of the Interior found themselves forced to remind subordinates repeatedly about the passport regulations of May 1831, because local authorities eager to rid themselves of troublesome or burdensome individuals continued to provide passports to Algiers without seeking prefectoral approval.[29] As De la Pinsonnière, author of the African Commission's 1834 report on colonization, observed, certificates of morality, intended to guarantee the character of passport holders, could not be trusted because they were often falsified by mayors seeking to rid themselves of corrupt, useless, or dangerous people.[30] Algerian administrators tried to strengthen the 1831 circular by requiring that each new arrival immediately obtain a *carte de sûreté* (security card) from the local police, but to little avail.[31] The colony's indeterminate borders remained extremely porous, and both Europeans and Algerians moved with relative ease in and out of coastal towns.

In France, the government's cautionary notices appear to have been drowned out by rumors and popular misunderstandings of official emigration policy. At least some prospective migrants interpreted the new regulations as an invitation. For example, Lorrainer François Étienne Gin requested not only free passage but also an indemnity for travel to the port of embarkation and lodgings in Algeria, after "having learned from the newspapers that the Government was calling for workers . . . to be placed there under its protection."[32] Indeed, the repeated ministerial reminders to local authorities indicate the extent to which emigrants from France continued to expect aid. We can see such misunderstandings at work in the case of three brothers, Ferdinand, Frédéric, and Eugène Sarrobert, and their friend, Pierre Lambert, who left a small village in the Hautes-Alpes for North Africa in November 1835. As agricultural laborers, they were given free passage from Toulon, but on reaching Bône, they wrote immediately to the minister of war to ask for further assistance. They explained their belief that a ministerial decree guaranteed them food rations and claimed that they would be forced to return to France if they did not receive them. The minister responded that no such decree existed but nevertheless ordered the governor general to help the men, for whom jobs were eventually found with a French landowner.[33] Such impro-

29. AD Haut-Rhin 6M 354, ministre de l'Intérieur to préfets, 2 May 1832.
30. "Rapport sur la Colonisation de l'Ex-Régence d'Alger, par M. de la Pinsonnière, député d'Indre-et-Loire, membre de la commission envoyé," in *Colonisation de l'Ex-Régence: Documens officiels déposés sur le bureau de la Chambre des députés* (Paris, 1834), 28.
31. "Arrêté concernant la police des passeports," 27 June 1833, in *RAGA*, 44; *Moniteur algérien*, 27 June 1833.
32. AD Meuse 6M 96, François Étienne Gin to préfet de la Meuse, n.d. [summer 1831].
33. CAOM F80 1162, Sarrobert frères to ministre de la Guerre, 3 November 1835.

vised aid, which also included clothing, shelter in army tents, and food rations from military stores, was in fact frequently provided by the colonial administration in order to keep poor emigrants off the streets, since the sight of impoverished Europeans was considered dangerous to the conquerors' status in the eyes of Muslim Algerians. Although far from universal—many would-be colonists did find themselves reduced to misery and shipped back to the metropole—this kind of ad hoc assistance must have helped to perpetuate misunderstandings in France about the assistance available to emigrants in the colony.

The signature of the Treaty of Tafna with 'Abd al-Qadir in May 1837 and the fall of Constantine in October expanded the area under French occupation and paved the way for a significant expansion of colonization efforts the following year. In January 1838, War Minister Bernard declared to the Chambers that "our situation in Algeria finally allows us to set about creating a permanent establishment" and requested eighteen million francs to fund new infrastructure projects. In practical terms, these were primarily military installations: fortifications, barracks, hospitals, drainage, roads, and port facilities that would "ensure the army's material well-being and the care due to the wounded and ill in its ranks."[34] European settlement was also considered essential to the health and success of the army, however. Colonialists and military officials both believed that full territorial control called for more than treaties and force of arms; it required that "the country be settled and cultivated" by European colonists.[35] The new public works projects were therefore expected to serve the interests of civilian colonization, as well as those of the military occupation. Shoring up the army's capabilities and improving the transportation network would "provide for the defense and guard of the country, ensure protection, security, salubrity for its inhabitants [the settlers], [and] open easy and free communications for trade."[36]

The expansion of the *travaux publics* provided the impetus for the first significant program of government-subsidized emigration and settlement in French Algeria. As soon as the requested credits were approved, the minister of war set about recruiting workers and cultivators for the planned construction. Citing improvements in security and the new funding for public works, the ministers of war and of the interior announced to the prefects that "the moment [had] come to reduce the rigor of the precautionary measures still being observed with regard

34. "Exposé des motifs et projet de loi relatifs à l'ouverture d'un Crédit extraordinaire de 18,171,408 fr., au titre de l'exercice 1838, pour le service des possessions françaises dans le nord de l'Afrique," 24 February 1838, *PVD* (1838), 2:823.
35. CAOM F80 1793, Valée to Bernard, 25 May 1838, cited in Bernard to Valée, 4 July 1838.
36. "Exposé des motifs . . . ," 24 February 1838, *PVD* (1838), 2:831.

to the passage to Africa of workers without employment in France."[37] In a series
of dispatches through the summer and fall of 1838, an enthusiastic Bernard ordered Governor General Valée to prepare for the arrival of a large number of new
colonists who would, for the first time, be eligible for assisted passage to Algeria
and land grants in the colony. Valée was to inventory domain lands, survey sites
for new settlements, construct temporary shelters, and make plans to employ emigrant workers on newly expanded public works projects.[38] New instructions sent
to the prefects on 30 August 1838 extended the authority over Algerian passports
to all metropolitan officials ordinarily empowered to deliver passports for France
and its colonies, including subprefects and mayors. In addition, the Ministry of
War would now provide free passage on government ships to emigrants in professions judged to be of particular use to the colony, upon application to either
the minister or the under-quartermaster (*sous-intendant militaire*) in charge of
embarkation at Toulon. To publicize this new benefit, the Ministry of War made
announcements in the *Moniteur universel* as well as several Parisian newspapers,
and prefects in many departments inserted notices in local and regional journals.[39]

Although the financial criteria established in May 1831 were dropped under
the new system—even the indigent could now get passports—the August circular
nonetheless contained a number of provisions that reflected ongoing concerns
about working-class emigrants. Passport applicants would be required to provide
certificates of morality and professional capacity for themselves and any family members or domestic servants traveling with them. To protect the Algerian
administration from an influx of *misérables*, the prefects were instructed to cat-
egorically reject several groups of individuals considered physically, morally, or
professionally deficient: disabled people, individuals over seventy or under sixteen traveling alone, vagabonds, recidivists, and "all persons, married women
and children excepted, who exercise no profession or have no known trade that
can ensure their means of existence."[40] Free passage would be offered on demand but only to able-bodied workers exercising one of twenty-three specific

37. CAOM F80 1793, ministre de l'Intérieur to préfets, "Nouvelles instructions sur la délivrance des
passe-ports pour nos possessions d'Afrique," 30 August 1838.
38. CAOM F80 1793, Bernard to Valée, 4 July 1838; F80 1253, Bernard to Valée, 22 August 1838;
Bernard to Valée, 31 October 1838; Bernard to intendant civil (Bresson), 7 November 1838 (also in
F80 1162, F80 1793).
39. CAOM F80 1793, ministre de l'Intérieur to préfets, "Nouvelles instructions . . . ," 30 August
1838; *TEFA* (1838), 122–23.
40. CAOM F80 1793, ministre de l'Intérieur to préfets, "Nouvelles instructions . . . ," 30 August
1838.

trades or otherwise suited for the projected road, construction, and agricultural work. Local officials charged with certifying the status of assisted emigrants were reminded that the new system was intended, "in facilitating French or foreign emigration, to recruit the European population of Africa among workers whose capacity and morality give them a right to the government's benevolence."[41] The practical implications of this view were clearly understood by departmental authorities, like the prefect of the Côte-d'Or, who forwarded the circular to his subordinates with a note explaining that "the Government desires to recruit the European population of Africa and is disposed to encourage persons who intend to form industrial establishments in our colony. But it is indispensable that the emigrants possess capital or exercise professions that allow them to earn their livelihood."[42]

Finally, the August circular warned that the state's role under the new regulations was limited to providing access to passports and free passage across the Mediterranean. These measures were not to be construed as a departure from the noninterventionist colonization policy followed since 1830 or to be interpreted as a right to which French citizens might feel entitled. General Bernard's goal "in facilitating truly useful immigration," was to do so "under reassuring conditions, to recruit the European population of Africa from the laboring classes, not to commit the French administration beyond its current activity by keeping down the costs of its intervention, which in any other system would risk giving rise to unreasonable pretensions and unlimited [financial] sacrifices."[43] Bernard's language reflects the extent to which he and other officials viewed the Algerian emigration scheme as a form of public assistance, which was guided in this period by the principle of limited state intervention. Rémusat, then minister of the interior, neatly summarized this philosophy in an 1840 letter to the prefects explaining that private charity was preferable to government aid because "the poor man never gets the idea that he can claim it as a right."[44] Beyond transportation, provisional shelter, and temporary employment, no other assistance was offered to emigrants, especially if it entailed any sort of expense. Cash advances were strictly out of the question, as was money for travel from home villages to Toulon. As prefects and mayors were repeatedly reminded, any aid in reaching the port of embarkation was the responsibility of local officials who ordinarily paid *secours*

41. AM Nantes I2 C 14, doss. 10, maire de Nantes to commissaires de police, 28 November 1838.
42. AD Côte-d'Or SM 8453, préfet de la Côte-d'Or to sous-préfets and maires, 14 September 1838.
43. CAOM F80 1253, Bernard to Valée, 22 August 1838.
44. Charles de Rémusat, *Du paupérisme et de la charité légale: Lettre adressée à MM. les préfets du Royaume* (Paris, 1840), 57.

de route to indigent travelers, and would come out of departmental public assistance funds.[45]

Despite these ministerial efforts to limit the state's commitments, the liberalization of emigration policy renewed earlier conflicts between colonial and metropolitan authorities over poor and unsuitable working-class emigrants. By 1838, however, anxieties about emigrants' morality and poverty were counterbalanced by concerns about the colony's growing demand for European labor. At the end of the decade, the ministries of War and the Interior began to actively promote colonial emigration with two contradictory aims. First, they hoped to consolidate France's position in Algeria by increasing the size of the settler population, as statements from the War Ministry's Algerian bureaus made clear. Second, they wished to provide assistance to metropolitan workers affected by the recession and food crisis that struck France in 1837, raising bread prices by over 25 percent at the peak of the slump in 1839.[46] This view was often less explicit, but can be distinguished in the language of poor relief that was adopted in policy debates over the aid now being offered to emigrants.

Foremost among the disagreements raised between metropolitan and colonial officials by the 1838 assisted emigration scheme was a dispute about the capacity of the Algerian labor market to absorb a sudden increase in French migrants. When ordered by the minister to make room on colonial public works projects for new arrivals, Governor General Valée responded that he would do as instructed but that the administration's needs, especially for artisans, were limited, as were employment opportunities in the private sector. "It frequently happens," he wrote, "that workers who have come to Africa hoping to find work more easily than in France demand passage home after searching futilely for work for several days and exhausting the little money they had brought with them." Valée agreed to prepare for the new arrivals, while insisting on the need to proceed with caution. He would do all he could to speed up the immigration process, but only to the extent that the colony's budget allowed and as long as it did not revive the difficulties of 1831.[47]

The civil intendant, director of fortifications, and head engineer of the Ponts et Chaussées all raised similar concerns that urban workers' skills would not fit

45. AD Saône-et-Loire M1 639, préfet de la Saône-et-Loire, "Passe-ports pour l'Algérie," in *Recueil des actes administratifs de Saône-et-Loire* 42 (1838): 223–24; AD Bas-Rhin 6M 354, préfet du Bas-Rhin, "Police: Instructions relatives à la délivrance des passe-ports pour les possessions françaises en Afrique," 11 October 1838, in *Recueil des actes administratifs du Bas-Rhin*, 45 (1838): 189–91; préfet to ministre de l'Intérieur, 18 October 1838; directeur de la Police Général du Royaume (for ministre de l'Intérieur) to préfet du Bas-Rhin, 24 October 1838.
46. Collingham, *July Monarchy*, 360–61.
47. CAOM F80 1253, Valée to Bernard, 31 August 1838.

the labor needs of the *grands travaux* they oversaw. Army engineers did purely military work, often in excessively dangerous conditions, and thus had no use for civilian workers. Among the civilian projects, only the port and jetty in Algiers called for particular skills, and these were so specialized that few emigrants could be expected to possess them. The road construction and ditch digging that would account for the vast majority of the new public works projects required only brute manual labor that, the officials predicted, skilled artisans would resent. In any case, they argued, all the French workers in the colony were currently employed, so even hiring every new arrival was unlikely to speed up public projects as quickly as the government wished. Finally, an immigrant labor force would cost the administration much more than military or Algerian workers. Immigrants would have to be paid enough to sustain a higher standard of living than they had left behind in France, and skilled or specialized artisans would have be offered special rates. Yet, at the same time, the administration would have to limit wages in order to prevent the public works from drawing workers away from private enterprises.[48] Although they had a brighter view than Valée of immigrants' employment prospects, the directors nonetheless shared his skepticism towards the new, more liberal emigration policy. Their collective opposition translated into such sluggish implementation of the orders from Paris that Bernard eventually interpreted their slow progress as deliberate obstruction.[49]

Colonial administrators' general hostility to the new emigration plan contrasted sharply with the views of the settler elite, who had been lobbying since the early 1830s for a loosening of restrictions on European immigration. Through the press, through bodies such as the Algiers Chamber of Commerce, the Société des colons, and the Société coloniale d'Alger, and through individual delegates from the local European notability, the colonists had long pressured Paris about the elevated labor costs that hampered their efforts to build profitable agricultural or industrial enterprises.[50] Wages, especially for skilled workers, were significantly higher in Algeria than in France, and the colonists argued that until an increase in immigration brought wages down, French capitalists would hesitate

48. CAOM F80 1253, note on meeting between Valée, directeur des Fortifications, intendant civil (Bresson), and chef du service des Ponts et Chaussées, n.d. [summer/fall 1838].

49. CAOM F80 1162, Bernard to Valée, 21 November 1838.

50. E.g. CAOM F80 1253, [Chambre de commerce d'Alger] to ministre de la Guerre (Maison), 28 October 1835, copy; same to Clauzel, 28 October 1835; CAOM F80 1791, "Programme des Instructions données à MM. de Guiroye & Bon. de Vialar, délégués des Colons d'Alger par les Membres de la Commission spéciale de correspondance et de renseignement," 17 February 1836; J.P. Pagès (deputy, Arièges), "Alger," *L'Afrique française*, July 1837; "De l'émigration française," *L'Afrique*, 6 September 1844; "De la protection qu'il faut accorder à la Culture des céréales," *Revue d'Afrique*, 15 January 1846.

to invest in the new colony. In addition to lobbying, settler groups also acted to facilitate local employers' access to European workers. In 1835, the Société coloniale created a Workers' Placement Bureau to recruit workers in France and place them with wealthy colonists. The bureau was subsequently closed, but by 1839, the Société coloniale had obtained permission from the civil intendant to reopen it.[51] Landowners later pushed successfully for a system of workers' *livrets* (passbooks) in order to prevent laborers they recruited from being lured away by competitors. The passbook system was instituted in 1843 by a decree that forbade the hiring of any worker who had not been officially released from the service of his previous employer.[52]

Settler pressure was critical to the reform of emigration rules in 1838. The directors of the Algerian public works suggested that providing wealthy settlers the labor they needed was "what the Government had in mind above all . . . in facilitating passage to Africa for workers," and War Minister Bernard himself responded to Valée's protests with a reminder that "hands are lacking in Algeria" and that the expanded public works and a growing private sector would provide jobs for all the assisted emigrants.[53] Later ministerial instructions asked the governor to put greater energy into moving new arrivals out of the public works sites and into private employment.[54] The Algerian administration's attention to private sector labor needs continued through the 1840s, when "to facilitate the execution of public and private works and to lower the cost of labor, which is very high in all parts of the colony" became the official goals of state-assisted emigration policy.[55]

Within two months of the August 1838 circular's implementation, colonial officials in Algiers began to complain to Paris about the new immigrants. Some 650 permits for free passage had been issued by early November and another 3,300 by mid-April of the following year, although permit holders did not always use these authorizations immediately.[56] Algerian administrators did not consider

51. CAOM F80 1162, Rozey to directeur de l'Intérieur (Guyot), 16 April 1839; CAOM F80 1253, intendant civil (Bresson) to intendant militaire d'Alger, 9 March 1836.
52. Alexis de Tocqueville, "Notes on the Voyage to Algeria in 1841," entry for 23 May 1841, in *Writings on Empire and Slavery*, ed. and trans. Jennifer Pitts (Baltimore, 2001), 43; "Arrêté qui règle d'une manière plus complète les rapports des maîtres avec les ouvriers et domestiques à gages des deux sexes," 22 September–8 October 1843, in *RAGA*, 253.
53. CAOM F80 1253, note on meeting between Valée, directeur des Fortifications, intendant civil (Bresson), and chef du service des Ponts et Chaussées, n.d. [summer/fall 1838]; Bernard to Valée, 31 October 1838.
54. Bernard, dépêche of 26 September 1838, cited in *TEFA* (1838), 123.
55. CAOM F80 1253, Urtis, chef du 2e Bureau de la Direction des Affaires d'Algérie, "Note pour Monsieur le Chef du 3e Bureau," 8 November 1843.
56. CAOM F80 1162, Bernard to Valée, 7 November 1838; CAOM F80 1253, ministre de la Guerre (Despans-Cubières) to Valée, 17 April 1839. See also *TEFA* (1838), 126; (1845–46), 183.

the first migrants assisted under the new scheme to be suitable for the work available, however. They were mostly artisans in trades which, while allowed under the August circular, were "principally exercised in towns" and therefore of limited use in the colony.[57] Of the 551 workers who arrived in the colony between 1 October and 31 December 1838, there were only 200 manual laborers, 75 carpenters and joiners, 61 masons, and 11 blacksmiths. The rest belonged to an assortment of trades, including 11 furniture makers, 11 bakers, 3 tailors, and a butcher.[58] Furthermore, the *sous-intendant militaire* in Toulon was distributing embarkation permits to individuals who did not meet any of the criteria spelled out in the regulations.

The response from Paris to colonial authorities' complaints made clear that from the metropolitan perspective, the goal of the 1838 regulations was to increase the colonial population. Whereas Algerian officials focused their attention on restricting the labor supply to fit demand, authorities in Paris ordered the governor general and the civil intendant to bend demand to supply: "all the [public] workshops already founded or to be created are given a level of activity that corresponds, by the law of the labor supply, to the demands and needs of arriving workers." The types of projects specified for the extraordinary credits, especially road building and drainage work, were to be undertaken in all parts of the colony; arriving immigrants were to be given preference over foreigners and indigenous Algerians on public job sites, and the use of military labor was to be suspended; any expenses "that do not have as their goal the employment of labor" were to be reduced and halted altogether if necessary. The extraordinary credits made available for 1838 were to be entirely expended and any funds not needed for other services diverted to pay immigrant workers. The minister calculated that one thousand men could be employed daily in the months of November and December and that new credits in the 1839 budget would carry this policy into the following year. The goal of these instructions—rather extraordinary from a minister who claimed to be doing nothing deliberate to provoke emigration from France—was to guarantee emigrants a wage in exchange for their labor and thus to "settle in Africa a population attracted by hope that must not be chased away by discouragement or abandonment." The task of administrators in the colony would be "above all to employ every worker coming from France," to offer work even to those who did not seek it out, and to ignore only those who actively refused the work offered.[59]

57. CAOM F80 1162, Bernard to Valée, 7 November 1838.
58. CAOM F80 1253, commissaire central de police d'Alger, "État numérique des ouvriers, laboureurs et manœuvres venus en Afrique sur les Bâtiments de l'État depuis le 1er 8bre jusqu'au 7 Xbre 1838," 7 December 1838.
59. CAOM F80 1253, Bernard to intendant civil (Bresson), 7 November 1838 (also in F80 1793).

The logic underlying these measures was colonialist in its aims and typical of contemporary poor relief doctrine in its terms. Repeatedly, ministerial officials insisted that employment in the public workshops was a temporary benefit that would enable new arrivals to survive until they could find permanent employment elsewhere. The potential for indefinite reliance on public works raised the specter of state intervention in public welfare, with the attendant danger that poor colonists would become "lazy and demanding" of government support.[60] Wages on the *travaux publics* were therefore set below those offered by private employers, "so as to encourage the emigrant to seek definitive placement" in the private sector.[61] Thus, for example, smiths employed by the Ponts et Chaussées earned 3.50–4.00 francs per day instead of the 4.00–6.00 francs offered by private employers in Algiers, Oran, Bône, and Bougie. Only *manœuvres* (unskilled laborers) were paid a daily wage comparable to the prevailing rate of 1.00–1.75 francs in the private sector.[62] From the point of view of the Ministry of War, the expansion of the *travaux publics* served simultaneously the interests of the colony, the colonial administration, and workers affected by the economic slump in France. The goal was to create "a new, vigorous population in need of work in order to live from it," and "the labor required by these [public] works is the best of subventions and the most useful of encouragements [to this end] because it imposes on the State no sacrifice without compensation and benefits the worker whose existence it ensures."[63] This language was precisely that of metropolitan poor relief officials, who sought to restrict aid to the "deserving," that is to say the hardworking, morally upstanding poor, and believed in forms of public assistance that profited both state and subject through productive labor.

Although Parisian authorities agreed that colonists with some capital and savings were preferable to destitute emigrants, they also rebuked their colonial colleagues for complaining about the poverty of emigrant workers. Metropolitan officials reminded their counterparts in Algeria that it would be unreasonable to expect the relatively well off to emigrate to a nascent colony. In the risky early days of a new society, with labor running short, the administration would have to accept those who possessed "only robust health and the love of labor."[64] In this context, the conditions imposed on applicants for free passage to Algeria were those that defined the "good colonist." Youth, honesty, hardiness, laboriousness,

60. [Louis-André] Pichon, *Alger sous la domination française: Son état présent et son avenir* (Paris, 1833), 303.
61. *TEFA* (1838), 124–25.
62. Ibid., 125, 127.
63. CAOM F80 1162, Bernard to Valée, 7 November 1838.
64. CAOM F80 1162, Bernard to Valée, 7 November 1838.

and lack of the *esprit de retour* were more realistic traits to demand of emigrants, and "a population firmly decided to draw its living in Africa from labor" was a more realistic goal for emigration policy.[65]

The minister of war nonetheless refined the provisions of the 1838 circular to "better regulate the impulse already imparted to emigration" and to satisfy some of the Algerian administrators' concerns. His new instructions reiterated the limited assistance available to emigrants, who had continued to demand unauthorized benefits such as the transportation of their baggage to Toulon or support in Algiers, and the need to exclude families with large numbers of small children. Mayors were told to clearly warn all applicants that they would have to rely on their own labor alone in Algeria. To ensure that emigrant families were self-supporting and to protect the government from accusations of disregard for their well-being, any family one-third of whose members were under the age of fourteen or which included individuals over fifty became ineligible for assistance. Finally, to improve the fit between the pool of emigrants and the colony's labor needs, the prefects were told that the workers most likely to find jobs in the colony were those fit for road excavation or agricultural work. Of all the professions listed in the original circular, road navvies, manual laborers, and rural stone, wood, and iron workers who were also suited for agriculture, would be in the best position to find useful employment in the colony.[66]

Shortly after these instructions were issued, the professional qualifications for free passage to the colony were tightened to reflect this preference for primarily unskilled workers. The director of Algerian affairs wrote directly to metropolitan mayors in early November 1838 to inform them that the administration could provide work only for quarrymen, unskilled laborers, and road workers. Men in other trades would be given *permis de passage* only if they declared formally before the mayor of their home commune that they were willing to work on public road excavations, regardless of their primary profession.[67] Requests for free passage from artisans in more specialized trades, including smiths, farriers, joiners, and carpenters, who could or would not accept unskilled manual labor, were therefore turned down in the winter of 1838–39.[68] Even with these modifications, however, Algerian officials continued to insist that Paris did not appreciate the realities of the colonial economy or the true character of the new colonists. In

---

65. CAOM F80 1162, Bernard to Valée, 21 November 1838.
66. CAOM F80 1253, Bernard to Valée, 31 October 1838; CAOM F80 1793, ministre de la Guerre (Bernard) to préfets, "Règlement de l'exécution de la circulaire du 30 août 1838," 29 October 1838.
67. AD Corrèze 6M 400, directeur des Affaires d'Afrique to maires, 10 November 1838.
68. AD Haut-Rhin 6M 354, préfet du Haut-Rhin to sous-préfet de Belfort, 17 January 1839; same to sous-préfet d'Altkirch, 19 January 1839, and maire de Widensohlen 17 January 1839.

May of 1839, under ministerial pressure to speed up the placement of immigrant workers, the governor general responded that it was impossible to guarantee "the employment, subsistence, ranking, and placement of the many arrivals of all ages and sexes [who are] emigrating with very little and many with no financial means at all. Without even the desire to work, [they] bring only illusions that the sight of the African soil does not tend to dissipate." To think otherwise was "not to see things from their truest point of view."[69] The scheme had become such a disaster that the colonial state was forced to establish a system of free passages back to France for new arrivals who could not find work, fell ill, or otherwise failed to realize "the advantages they had imagined" in the colony. By the spring of 1839, every steamship leaving Algiers for Toulon was carrying numerous indigent emigrants who had become "a cause of difficulties or expense to the local administration."[70]

Recruiting a "Laborious and Useful" Population

A change in the French government at the end of March 1839 coincided with a formal request from Governor General Valée that the minister of war slow the pace of emigration from France.[71] A system now developed to regulate emigration in accordance with security conditions on the ground in North Africa and the state of the Algerian labor market as defined primarily by the needs of public works sites, but also those of private employers. The precise reasons for the improvement in relations between Paris and Algiers are unclear, but it is likely that the composition of the new government helped pave the way for better coordination. The new war minister, General Cubières, had ambitions on the governor-generalship and perhaps sought to cultivate support among colonial officials, but he was also relatively weak-willed and unable to impose his views on the strong-minded Valée.[72] The stabilization of the government under Marshal Soult in late 1840 and the appointment of Bugeaud, a firm advocate of colonization, as governor general early in 1841 gave Algiers a stronger voice in policymaking. Circumstances in Algeria likely contributed as well. The resumption of hostilities with 'Abd al-Qadir in November 1839 diverted army resources away from public

---

69. CAOM F80 1793, "Note de M. le Maréchal," attached to directeur de l'Intérieur (Guyot) to Valée, 22 May 1839 (copy); original in CAOM F80 1253.
70. CAOM F80 1253, Guyot to Valée, 22 May 1839.
71. CAOM F80 1253, Bernard to Valée, 31 October 1838; Cubières to Valée, 17 April 1839.
72. Charles-André Julien, *Histoire de l'Algérie contemporaine*, vol. 1, *La conquête et les débuts de la colonisation (1827–1871)* (Paris, 1964), 144, 198. Cubières was replaced by Lieutenant General Schneider in May 1839, then returned briefly in March 1840 before Soult took over the war portfolio in October 1840.

works, increasing the demand for civilian labor. Finally, as an early chronicler of emigration policy noted, the disastrous results of the August 1838 liberalization doubtless pushed administrators on both sides of the Mediterranean to regulate emigration more closely.[73]

The 1840s thus saw the emergence of a more smoothly functioning mechanism that opened and closed the emigration spigot on the demand of the Algerian authorities. Abuses by the *sous-intendant militaire* in Toulon had led Bernard to revoke this officer's right to accord permits for free passage in November 1838, and new instructions issued in May 1839 reasserted the minister's sole authority over emigration assistance.[74] Using this power, Paris cut back sharply the number of *permis d'embarquement*. After distributing 3,794 permits between October 1838 and March 1839, the ministry granted only 221 in April, May, and June of 1839, all to workers bound for ongoing road excavations. When military circumstances seemed to improve that summer and the Chambers voted significant supplementary funds for the *travaux publics*, the Parisian Bureau of Algerian Affairs asked Valée to indicate the number and professions of workers required before issuing more permits.[75] Although concerned that it would be difficult to restart the flow of emigration if free passages were completely suspended, the Second Bureau of the Directorate of Algerian Affairs nonetheless answered the 7,500 requests for passage received in 1839 in accordance with fluctuations in the demand for labor in Algiers.[76]

Under the new regulatory mechanism, civilian and military functionaries in Algeria tracked the local labor market and advised the Ministry of War of the colony's needs. The governor general reported the number and professions of workers required in the various parts of the colony to the minister of war, and the Second Bureau granted free passages and instructed the prefects to encourage or discourage emigration as appropriate. In the winter of 1839–40, for example, the minister asked the governor general whether the military engineering corps and civilian administration would need masons, carpenters, or other artisans for construction work then beginning in Constantine and Philippeville. Emigration had been scaled back for the season, but Valée's subordinates judged that masons and carpenters should be sent, citing the decreased availability of soldiers, the effects of illness, the number of unsuitable civilian workers, and competition from private sector employers. There were, however, sufficient numbers of joiners and

73. "De l'émigration française," *L'Afrique*, 6 September 1844.
74. CAOM F80 1793, Bernard to préfets, 5 November 1838; Cubières to préfets, "Nul individu ne peut passer gratuitement en Algérie sans autorisation du Ministre de la Guerre," 10 May 1839.
75. CAOM F80 1253, Schneider to Valée, 3 July 1839.
76. *TEFA* (1839), 12.

TABLE 5. "WORKERS WHOSE PASSAGE TO ALGERIA CAN BE AUTHORIZED AND THE PLACES TO WHICH THEY SHOULD BE DIRECTED," 1840

Locality	Professions														
	Manœuvres	Carpenters	Cartwrights	Caulkers	Sailmakers	Coopers	Pit sawyers	Blacksmiths	Metalworkers	Iron turners	Boiler-/Pumpmakers	Masons	Stonecutters	Pavers	Fountainmakers
Algiers	600	50	10	10	6	3	8	40	5	2	1	25	10		
Oran	100	3	2					4				10	5		
Bône	100	5	2				2						10	2	4
Philippeville	200	4	2					3				5	3		
Bougie	18		1					1				2		2	
Totals	1,018	62	17	10	6	3	10	48	5	2	1	42	28	4	4

Source: CAOM F80 1253, directeur de l'Intérieur (Guyot) to Valée, 29 August 1840.
Note in original: "Reduce manœuvres to 618 because of imminent arrival of 400 Spanish refugees."

ironworkers, as well as excess numbers of manœuvres in these towns, where indigenous Algerians and soldiers provided most of the manual labor. Count Guyot, director of the interior in Algiers, responded that the available workers in Algiers and Bône met the needs of private employers, but that the administration needed labor since soldiers were being redeployed into combat.[77] He attached to this report a chart specifying the workers needed and where they could be employed. Guyot's precision in evaluating the colony's labor needs can be seen from the table itself (table 5), which Valée forwarded to Paris along with a suggestion that Guyot had underestimated the number of masons needed. The Second Bureau then authorized passage for the workers enumerated in Guyot's table, as well as two hundred others.[78] Word went out to the prefects that recent improvements in the military situation and the resumption of construction work would permit the emigration of individuals exercising one "of the professions that currently offer the most opportunities in Algeria."[79]

77. CAOM F80 1253, Schneider to Valée, 25 December 1839; Valée to directeur de l'Intérieur (Guyot) and directeur des Fortifications, 11 January 1840; directeur des Fortifications to Valée, 17 January 1840; directeur de l'Intérieur to Valée, 29 August 1840.
78. CAOM F80 1253, Valée to Cubières, 12 September 1840; Cubières to Valée, 9 October 1840.
79. AD Haut-Rhin 6M 354, ministre de la Guerre (Soult) to préfets, "Nouvelles instructions sur les demandes de passage gratuit en Algérie," 19 November 1840.

In early 1841, the expansion of Algerian road construction prompted more active recruitment of navvies, *manœuvres*, and men in several other building trades. Special publicity measures were taken to ensure that news of the assistance available to these emigrants reached the French countryside and those groups particularly targeted by the circular. The ministry inserted notices in the *Moniteur universel* and other national newspapers; prefects were instructed to publish *avis* in local newspapers and in their departments' official bulletins, and mayors were asked to publicize the *avis* according to the "usual rules," by posting notices in public buildings and making announcements at public gatherings.[80] When the circular did not produce the desired results—the Second Bureau speculated that French workers were fully employed during the agricultural season or feared not finding profitable employment in Algiers—the call was renewed, with new exhortations to the prefects to post the announcement in every commune and to make clear to villagers that no able-bodied man would be turned away, as long as he did not have small children.[81]

The colony's labor needs increased again six months later, when work began on a protective ditch (the *obstacle continu*) that was to surround the area set aside for rural colonization in the Mitidja. This new project, the *Moniteur algérien* announced in September 1841, would offer employment to "all road navvies, stoneworkers, woodworkers, and ironworkers who present themselves." To the free passage and high wages already available to workers on public construction sites, the administration now added an indemnity of fifteen centimes per league for travel to Toulon, meals and a double wine ration once in Algeria (whose cost would be deducted from the worker's wages), free treatment in military hospitals for workplace accidents, and priority for land concessions the following year. For brick and tile makers from northern France, the colonial administration promised a piece rate more than double what they could expect at home. Workers in all professions who provided their own tools would also earn a higher wage.[82]

That the colony's labor needs were of primary concern here is evident from the clear preference for single male workers under the new assisted emigration scheme. Although the November 1840 circular did allow families to request free passage, they were eligible only if two-thirds of their members were of an age and physi-

80. CAOM F80 1793, ministre de la Guerre (Soult) to préfets, "Sur les demandes de passage gratuit et de concessions en Algérie," 28 February 1841. The list included road navvies, *manœuvres*, stonecutters, carpenters, masons, blacksmiths, carters, pit sawyers, and pavers.

81. AD Haut-Rhin 6M 354, ministre de la Guerre (Soult) to préfets, "Nouvelles dispositions à prendre pour activer le mouvement d'émigration en Algérie," 31 August 1841.

82. "3e avis aux terrassiers et aux ouvriers en pierre, en bois et en fer disposés à passer en Algérie," *Moniteur algérien*, 27 September 1841.

cal condition to work. Families with young children were not allowed to participate, and, in September 1841, the program was restricted to unaccompanied males.
Married men could obtain free passage for their wives and children only if they
met the criteria for obtaining concessions, suggesting that heads of households
were expected to move quickly out of the labor market and onto the land. Potential
emigrants were required to provide the same certifications of professional status,
health, and reputation demanded by earlier regulations, but it was clear that for colonial officials, "a truly laborious and useful population" now consisted of "young,
very healthy, and, especially, . . . single individuals."[83] The priority given to unmar-
ried young men was reiterated in the Second Bureau's correspondence with departmental officials and its responses to individuals seeking free passage to Algeria.[84]

Privileging emigration by single men was a matter of practical necessity rather
than of ideological commitment, however. The colonial administration's instrumental view of working-class laborers can be seen in the way that emigration policy was designed to follow the evolution of the colonial labor market. To ensure
a balance between the supply of and the demand for labor, the ministry of war
maintained a list of French and some foreign (mostly German) workers who had
applied for emigration assistance. When the colony needed men for a particular
task, the Second Bureau issued permits for free passage to the requisite number
of applicants in the indicated professions, in the order in which their dossiers
had been received.[85] For instance, when the measures taken in the fall of 1841
had brought enough workers to fully staff the *travaux publics*, the prefects were
informed that the ministry would cease according free passage to *ouvriers* and
that they should stop delivering certificates of health and morality to prospective
working-class emigrants.[86] "As a consequence of the large numbers of workers
who have emigrated into the colony," the director of Algerian affairs wrote repeatedly to provincial officials in 1842, "the local administration no longer needs
anything except road navvies at the moment."[87] Requests for *permis de passage*

83. AD Haut-Rhin 6M 354, ministre de la Guerre (Soult) to préfets, "Nouvelles instructions sur les
demandes de passage gratuit en Algérie," 19 November 1840.
84. E.g. AD Drôme 6Ma 3, directeur des Affaires de l'Algérie to préfet de la Drôme, 23 February
1842; AD Haut-Rhin 6M 354, "Avis: Émigrations pour l'Algérie," 28 February 1842, extract from
Recueil des actes de l'administration du Haut-Rhin (1842): 80.
85. *Guide du colon et de l'ouvrier en Algérie . . . Rédigé d'après les documents officiels du Ministère de
la guerre et du Ministère de l'intérieur, et les renseignements puisés près des autorités locales à Alger*
(Paris, 1843), 82–83.
86. AD Haut-Rhin 6M 354, ministre de la Guerre (Soult) to préfets, "Dispositions à prendre pour
arrêter le mouvement d'émigration d'ouvriers en Algérie," 27 May 1842.
87. E.g. AD Haute-Garonne 4M 57, Laurence to préfet de la Haute-Garonne, 22 January 1842; AM
Nantes I2 C 14, Martineau to maire de Nantes, 25 February 1842; AD Bas-Rhin 3M 685, Martineau
to préfet du Bas-Rhin, 24 March 1842.

from men in all other trades were rejected. When work once again became available in 1843, the ministers of war and of the interior asked the prefects to seek out just over 1,000 workers to emigrate, specifying the need for some 700 navvies and *manœuvres*, 150 masons, 100 stonecutters, 40 quarrymen, 80 carpenters, 20 cartwrights, and 10 smiths.[88] This emigration continued, reaching a rhythm of about two thousand individuals per month in the summer of 1843, before being trimmed to five or six hundred each month when work slowed during the winter.

The system of assisted emigration that developed in the 1840s reflected the triumph of a pragmatic, instrumental attitude towards the *colon-ouvrier*, but the ideological preference for rural families that underpinned contemporary colonization theory and official propaganda persisted. Even as the rules governing labor migration were being worked out, the War Ministry continued to lament the youth, mobility, and masculinity of Algeria's European population.[89] The economic realities of colonial development, however, made the nascent colony dependent on the working-class men so disdained in texts and images shaped by mythical visions of Algeria's agricultural fertility. Despite policymakers' moralizing views of impoverished workers, professional qualifications prevailed over financial resources in the selection of assisted emigrants. The Ministry of War acceded to warnings from Algiers that failing to sort migrants by profession risked "sending useless hands and mouths to the colony, which would cause more than one sort of difficulty" for the colonial administration.[90] At the same time, authorities on both sides of the Mediterranean came to recognize French workers as essential to expanding the infrastructure of colonial rule. The dependence of the colonial enterprise on working-class emigrants was formally acknowledged in 1845, when the Ministry of War agreed to reimburse communes and departments for the *secours de route* paid out to poor emigrants making their way across France to the ports of Marseille and Toulon.[91]

As the administration sought to meet the needs of growing public construction projects, it also took into account the extension of agricultural colonization and the diversification of the colonial economy. The construction of colonial villages and the institution of a large-scale system of land concessions in 1841 significantly increased the settler population and its demand for labor, and co-

---

88. AD Haut-Rhin 6M 354, ministre de l'Intérieur to préfets, "Mesures à prendre pour organiser une émigration continue d'ouvriers en Algérie," 19 April 1843.
89. *TEFA* (1839), 51.
90. AD Haut-Rhin 6M 354, ministre de l'Intérieur to préfets, "Algérie. Émigration d'ouvriers," 26 December 1843.
91. AD Corrèze 6M 400, ministre de la Guerre (Saint-Yon) to préfets, "Dispositions à prendre pour le remboursement aux communes, à partir du 1er janvier 1846, des avances faites pour secours de route à des cultivateurs et ouvriers autorisés à se rendre en Algérie," 30 December 1845.

lonial authorities took corresponding steps to make European workers available to new *concessionnaires*. In 1842, a municipal placement office was created in Algiers to act as an intermediary between emigrants and civilian employers, and funds were allocated in 1844 to establish additional *dépôts d'ouvriers* (also called *dépôts d'émigrants*) in Bône, Philippeville, Constantine, and Oran, where new arrivals could recuperate from their sea voyages, search for work, or wait to take possession of their land grants.[92] At the same time, the *Moniteur algérien* began publishing a weekly list of new arrivals for the benefit of colonists seeking to hire European workers.

The hundreds of emigrants arriving each month soon overwhelmed the *dépôts d'ouvriers*, but Europeans' wages remained high and agricultural labor, in particular, scarce.[93] Large colonial landowners were still unable to find tenants or farm hands. French prefects were thus instructed to encourage healthy, morally upstanding agricultural workers to emigrate.[94] As the prefect of the Ariège explained to his subordinates, "it is the duty of the administration to inform the populations about the advantages they can find in this French colony," where "hands are lacking and wages are very high." As a consequence, "the [relatively] low price of labor in the Ariège should encourage able-bodied men to seek out the resources that are so often lacking to them in their country." Agricultural laborers were "assured of finding work at a much higher rate than at home, [and] with care, they will reach the status of proprietor or landlord." Even young women of good morals would easily find advantageous positions as domestics, the prefect predicted, since laundresses, seamstresses, and domestic servants were in short supply and therefore paid as much in Algeria as in Paris.[95]

Assisted emigration policies reflected the bind in which the colonial administration found itself in the 1840s. Public construction work was a far cry from the agricultural settlement that was expected to transform urban workers into peasant proprietors. Yet officials in Paris and Algiers were confronted with a set of social and institutional realities over which they had little control. Urban workers seldom transitioned successfully from proletarian to farmer and, indeed,

92. CAOM GGA L5/18, ministre de la Guerre (Soult) to directeur de l'Intérieur, 10 June 1843 and 30 September 1844; *TEFA* (1846–49), 258; Louis Baudicour, *La colonisation de l'Algérie: Ses éléments* (Paris, 1856),152–53.
93. CAOM F80 1253, comptable du Dépôt des colons et ouvriers civils de Philippeville to sous-directeur de l'Intérieur et de la Colonisation, 2 December 1846 and 14 December 1846; CAOM GGA L5/18, "Note pour le Ministre au sujet d'un article inséré dans le *Courrier français*," 10 January 1845; F80 1253, directeur de l'Intérieur (Guyot) to Valée, 29 August 1840; *TEFA* (1845–46), 185.
94. CAOM Alger 5M 1, ministre de l'Intérieur to préfets, "Nécessité de seconder le départ pour l'Algérie des ouvriers cultivateurs," 15 February 1845.
95. AD Ariège 10M 15, préfet de l'Ariège, "Émigration en Algérie," 23 October 1845, in *Recueil des actes administratifs de la préfecture de l'Ariège*, 30th ser., no. 36 (1845), 254–56.

rarely seemed to want to do so. Moreover, colonial development projects actually demanded that they not be transformed into farmers. Efforts to control working-class emigration were undermined by local officials in France, as well, where prefects, subprefects, and mayors regularly misapplied the regulations on assisted emigration. A note from an unnamed Strasbourg police official requesting a certificate of morality for a certain Charles Mühlbach "in order to rid the city of this young man, who has already been arrested twice for begging," is revealing of the deliberation with which local agents often subverted these rules.[96] Complaints emanated continuously from Algiers about the unreliability of the certificates of morality and profession issued by metropolitan mayors.[97]

Authorities in Paris and Algiers did eventually come to see *colons-ouvriers* as a productive part of colonial society, "doubly useful, in that they provide the land with hands and defenders" at minimal cost to the public treasury.[98] Changes in rural colonization policy helped to make this shift in official attitudes possible, but also ensured that the *colon-ouvrier* was never fully integrated into the broader ideological foundations of settlement colonization. Construction and road workers were as necessary as the agricultural colonists themselves to rural colonization, which required not only the protective *obstacle continu* but also houses, roads, wells, and other infrastructure. Founding rural villages and distributing arable land to settler-farmers, however, were still considered "the principal elements of colonization,"[99] and the laborers and artisans who made them possible remained auxiliary to this primary objective.

Thus, despite the recognition in emigration policy of the need for manual and skilled labor, the "acceptable" and "unacceptable" categories of emigrants outlined in the passport regulations of the early 1830s continued to define the settler population in the eyes of French observers and officials. At the end of the July Monarchy, colonial authorities were still dividing colonists into three groups: *le colon-ouvrier, le colon-laboureur,* and *le colon sérieux.* The *colon-ouvrier,* an Algerian official wrote in 1846, "possesses and . . . brings to Africa only the need to create a better position for himself than the one he had when he left: [these are] chimerical dreams that soon dissipate." Like *colons-laboureurs,* such men were only "supposed colonists," whose penury inevitably forced them to wander the

96. AM Strasbourg 271 MW 67, note attached to gérant de la Maison de Refuge, certificat de bonne conduite for Charles Mühlbach, 23 November 1847.
97. E.g. CAOM F80 1253, général Lamoricière to Bugeaud, 29 January 1844; AD Haut-Rhin 6M 354, ministre de l'Intérieur to préfets, "Les emigrans en Algérie doivent attendre le permis d'embarquement, avant de vendre ce qu'ils possèdent et faire des préparatifs de départ," 8 December 1845.
98. *TEFA* (1838), 14–15.
99. CAOM 1162, Bernard to Valée, 21 November 1838.

colony "until misery forces them into hospital or until they are arrested on the roads as vagabonds." The *colon sérieux*, on the other hand, was characterized by his possession of "sufficient capital to provide for the costs of his installation" on the land. His position as a person of means distinguished him from the wage laborer or hired plowman, and made him a "good" colonist.[100] The ideals of rural landowning remained the goals of French colonization policy in Algeria, even if in practice colonial officials were forced to accept and even encourage emigration by ideologically undesirable workers.

From France to Algeria:
The Sociology of Assisted Emigration

I have thus far considered the question of assisted emigration primarily from the perspective of the French state and colonial policymakers. To understand the full import of the policies they elaborated, it is necessary to consider how French citizens answered the state's calls for emigration to Algeria. If the ideals of settlement colonization depended on the creation of a strong and steady stream of migration by desirable individuals, we must ask to what extent assisted emigration policies created such a stream. Who were the men and women who emigrated to Algeria? Why did they make this momentous decision? How did their understandings of colonial emigration and settlement compare with those of colonial theorists and policymakers?

The first concern of colonization advocates was the size of the settler population. As we have seen, those who envisioned a North African landscape emptied of its native inhabitants and filled with French farmers found the slow realization of this vision to be an ongoing source of anxiety. Their worries about Frenchmen's apparent reluctance to emigrate seem at first glance to be borne out by migration patterns in nineteenth-century France, which contributed little to the Great Migration out of industrializing Europe. Historians of French overseas migration have explained this "French exception" as a demographic phenomenon: a relatively low birthrate and low population density meant that population pressures weighed much less heavily in France than elsewhere in Europe. The populations of Great Britain and the German states, for instance, more than doubled during the nineteenth century, while the French population increased by a relatively modest 55 percent. As a result, the French stayed

---

100. CAOM Alger 5M 1, commissaire de police d'Alger to directeur de l'Intérieur (Guyot), 20 November 1846.

home, while other Europeans rushed off to the United States, South America, and Australia.[101] The scale of the French exception can be seen in the records of U.S. immigration officials, who counted 1.25 million Germans and 1.3 million Britons and Irish, but fewer than 200,000 French entering American ports between 1820 and 1855.[102] By this standard, Frenchmen's slow rate of emigration to Algeria is unsurprising. Except in the early 1840s, when the state was most actively recruiting colonial migrants, emigration from France to the North African colony ran largely parallel with French emigration to the United States in this period (fig. 52).[103]

Closer examination of Algeria in the conquest period, however, calls into question the basic assumptions behind demographic interpretations of French colonial emigration. In the first place, the settler population was not increasing as slowly as either contemporaries or historians believed, but rather grew at rates quite comparable with those of other "Neo-Europes" in the early nineteenth century.[104] For example, Australia, where colonization began with the arrival of the first British convict ships in 1788, had 400,000 Europeans by 1850, while Algeria's settlers numbered 483,501 sixty years after the Algiers expedition. Only 267,672 of the latter were French citizens as of 1891, but many of the rest would soon be naturalized under the Nationality Law of 1889.[105] Indeed, of all the European settler societies of the period, only the United States did not struggle to attract emigrants. What is more, the great divergence in European population growth rates took place in the *second* half of the century and is thus less helpful in explain-

101. Claude Fohlen, introduction to *L'émigration française. Études de cas: Algérie, Canada, États-Unis* (Paris, 1985), 11–12; Émile Temime, "La migration européenne en Algérie au 19e s.: Migration organisée ou tolérée?" *Revue de l'Occident musulman et de la Méditerranée* 43 (1987): 42; Dudley Baines, *Emigration from Europe, 1815–1930* (Cambridge, 1995), 16; Michael Heffernan, "French Colonial Migration," in *The Cambridge Survey of World Migration*, ed. Robin Cohen (Cambridge, 1995), 34. On population and migration more generally, see André Armengaud, "Le rôle de la démographie," in *Histoire économique et sociale de la France*, vol. 3, *L'avènement de l'ère industrielle (1789–années 1880)*, bk. 1 (Paris, 1976), 161–238. Population figures from André Armengaud, "Population in Europe, 1700–1914," trans. A.J. Pomerans, in *The Fontana Economic History of Europe*, vol. 3, *The Industrial Revolution, 1700–1914*, ed. Carol M. Cipolla (London, 1976), 30.

102. William J. Bromwell, *History of Immigration to the United States . . . from September 30, 1819, to December 31, 1855 . . .* (New York, 1856; repr., New York, 1969), 176–79.

103. The curves were likely even closer. Due to high turnover, loose border controls, and faulty record keeping, census figures undercount emigration to Algeria. European departures varied between 35 and 65 percent of arrivals in the 1840s, but this includes soldiers and temporary visitors, as well as Europeans of all nationalities.

104. The term "Neo-Europes" is Alfred Crosby's. *Ecological Imperialism: The Biological Expansion of Europe, 900–1900*, 2nd ed. (Cambridge, 2004).

105. Hugh Tinkler, "The British Colonies of Settlement," in Cohen, *Cambridge Survey*, 16; Victor Demontès, *Le peuple algérien: Essais de démographie algérienne* (Algiers, 1906), 39.

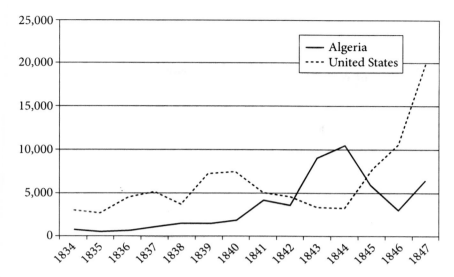

FIGURE 52. French emigration to Algeria and the United States, 1834–47.
Source: TEFA (1837–49); Bromwell, *History of Immigration*, 177.

ing the relatively low French emigration rates of the earlier decades. Population pressures in France peaked during the July Monarchy, when rural areas boomed and urbanization rates reached their high point for the century.[106] Before 1850, the French multiplied faster than their neighbors in the German states, for example, yet emigration from Germany far outpaced that from France as a percentage of total population.[107]

Nineteenth-century observers, who felt these patterns acutely, were more likely to explain the French reluctance to emigrate as a result of cultural factors than of demographic factors. Mid-century discussions of Algerian colonization saw repeated laments about France's "so-called ineptitude for colonizing," particularly in comparison with the prolifically expansive British.[108] The collapse of the

106. Armengaud, "Population," 32–33; Armengaud, "Le rôle de la démographie," 222; Louis Chevalier, *Laboring Classes and Dangerous Classes in Paris during the First Half of the Nineteenth Century* (1958), trans. Frank Jellinek (New York, 1973), 181–84; Patrice Bourdelais, "Le paysage humain," in *Histoire de la France*, ed. André Burguière and Jacques Revel (Paris, 1989), 230–32.
107. The French population grew from 26.9 to 36.5 million, while the German population grew from 24.5 to 31.7 million between 1800 and 1850. Armengaud, "Population," 29.
108. Baron de Volland, *Réfutation du rapport de la Commission du Budget, en ce qui concerne nos possessions en Afrique* (Paris, 1835), 21.

early modern French empire, especially the loss of Quebec and Saint-Domingue, offered proof that France did not share the colonial genius of its cross-Channel rival. "The Frenchman is not a colonizer," opined one avid colonialist with a wistful eye on the British settlements in Australia and New Zealand.[109] Along with deficiencies in patience, perseverance, and the spirit of adventure, administrative centralization and the nation's pervasive *esprit du clocher*, or love for the native soil, hampered French colonization efforts. "What prevents the French from having good colonies?" Alexis de Tocqueville asked in 1833. The fact that "the Frenchman loves the domestic hearth, . . . rejoices at the sight of his native parish, [and] cares about family joys like no other man in the world."[110] Unlike the model emigrant described by Jean-Baptiste Say, who argued that "to succeed in a distant settlement, a man must be young, because he must lose his old habits and acquire new ones, [and] must feel his character to be firm and persevering," the French character contained simultaneously too much attachment to home and "too much ardor, too much impatience . . . , too much mobility" for the slow, difficult business of overseas emigration and settlement.[111]

   The shared belief of historians and contemporary commentators in Frenchmen's reluctance to emigrate has overshadowed Algeria's place among the European settler colonies of the nineteenth century, as well as diverted attention from historical questions about those who surmounted their *esprit du clocher* to become the first agents of French settler colonialism in North Africa. Ironically, we know more about emigration to Algeria from other parts of Europe, including Spain, Italy, Germany, and Malta, than from France.[112] Extant sources do not permit analysis of the full stream of French migration to Algeria, but data collected by the Ministry of War and ministerial correspondence with local authorities in provincial France do allow for detailed examination of government-assisted emigration in the 1840s. Registers kept by the ministry's Directorate of Algerian Affairs paint a collective portrait of some 19,518 individuals who were

109. Noël-Jacques Lefebvre-Duruflé, "Avant-propos du traducteur," in Charles Rowcroft, *Le colon de Van Diémen ou aventures d'un émigrant: Contes des colonies . . .*, trans. Noël-Jacques Lefebvre-Duruflé, vol. 1 (Paris, 1847), xiii.
110. "Some Ideas about What Prevents the French from Having Good Colonies," in *Writings*, 1–2.
111. Jean-Baptiste Say, *Cours complet d'économie politique pratique . . .*, 2nd ed., ed. Horace Say, 2 vols. (Brussels, 1840), 1:401, 294, 402; Baron Mounier, "Rapport général sur l'occupation des divers points de la Régence, sur l'organisation du gouvernement et sur les dépenses de 1834 et 1835, adopté dans la séance du 7 mars 1834," in *Procès-verbaux et rapports de la Commission d'Afrique instituée par ordonnance du Roi du 12 décembre 1833* (Paris, 1834), 400–401.
112. Temime, "La migration," 32–33; works cited in note 17 above. Only Alsace and Lorraine have received close attention from historians of France. Fabienne Fischer, *Alsaciens et Lorrains en Algérie: Histoire d'une migration, 1830–1914* (Nice, 1999).

granted free passage to the colony between 1841 and 1845.[113] Many elected not to use their *permis de passage*, and there is no way to know how many of them actually left. Nor do the registers include the thousands of free emigrants who made their own way across the Mediterranean. But they nonetheless provide a unique overview of the geographical origins, professions, and family status of those who sought and obtained emigration assistance in the first years of French colonization. To understand their reasons for emigrating, we can turn to the files of provincial officials, including prefects, subprefects, mayors, and police commissioners, responsible for processing requests for free passage. Both of these sets of documents have important flaws, but together they shed invaluable light on the identities, understandings, and motivations of those who responded most directly to state recruitment efforts in the first years of official colonization.

Overall, the assisted migrants of the early 1840s embodied the contradictions that had provoked the trans-Mediterranean conflicts with which this chapter began. The vast majority were urban workers of precisely the sort that metropolitan social reformers hoped to transform into stable yeoman farmers, but this meant that very few belonged to the agricultural families desired by colonial officials. The mobility of assisted emigrants is visible in their geographic origins, which were heavily concentrated along France's eastern frontier and in the Paris basin, with secondary concentrations in the southwestern Basque country and the eastern Midi (map 2 and map 2 table).[114] These were the primary centers of mobility in nineteenth-century France, with strong traditions of regional migration, as well as the highest rates of emigration overseas.[115] These three areas continued to figure among those furnishing the largest number of emigrants in the 1850s, when the French state began to collect systematic data on out-migration.[116]

It seems unexceptional that emigration to Algeria was most appealing in these relatively peripatetic areas. Yet the 1840s present significant differences from the patterns observed later in the century that require further examination. Of the ten departments that furnished the most assisted migrants in the 1840s, only the

---

113. CAOM F80 *1998–2000, "Passages gratuits, autorisations, 1841–1845." The registers cover 1,934 permits issued October 19, 1841–March 25, 1842, and 8,035 from September 13, 1843 to July 11, 1845. I thank John Sessions, Noelle Yasso, and Sarita Patnaik, whose help in preparing this and other quantitative data made the analysis in this chapter possible.
114. A department of residence in France was recorded for 9,457 permits. In addition, 255 permits were sent to foreign destinations, mostly in the Rhineland German states; 6 went to Europeans resident in Algeria; and no residence was recorded for 228 permits.
115. Louis Chevalier, "L'émigration française au XIXe siècle," *Études d'histoire moderne et contemporaine* (1947): 147–48; Armengaud, "Le rôle de la démographie," 207.
116. Alfred Legoyt, *L'émigration européenne: Son importance, ses causes, ses effets . . .* (Paris, 1861), 61; Jules Duval, *Histoire de l'émigration européenne, asiatique et africaine au XIXe siècle: Ses causes, ses caractères, ses effets* (Paris, 1862), 105–6.

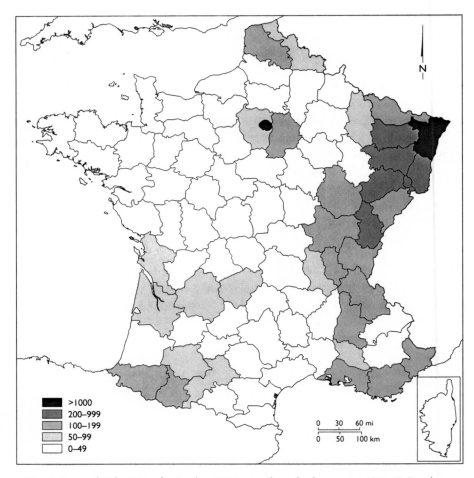

MAP 2. Geographical origins of assisted emigration to Algeria by department, 1841–45. Based on data in CAOM F80 *1998–2000.

Seine and the Haute-Saône remained leading sources of colonial emigrants in 1858. Otherwise, the centers of Algerian emigration shifted southwards, and the Spanish frontier region replaced Alsace as the largest source of emigrants. The Basque departments of the Basses- and Hautes-Pyrénées stood at the very bottom of the top-twenty list for the 1840s, but ten years later they, along with the Haute-Garonne, Tarn, Aude, and Pyrénées-Orientales, accounted for six of the ten principal departments for Algerian emigration. Equally striking is the rise of the Midi. The Bouches-du-Rhône, which received a modest 122 permits for free passage in the early 1840s, became the single largest source of emigrants in

GEOGRAPHICAL ORIGINS OF ASSISTED EMIGRANTS (LEADING DEPARTMENTS), 1841–45

Department	Permits issued	Number of emigrants
> 1000 permits		
Seine	2,459	3,326
Bas-Rhin	1,462	2,401
200–999 permits		
Haut-Rhin	820	2,350
Jura	371	957
Vosges	315	753
Haute-Saône	249	677
Meurthe	217	385
100–199 permits		
Isère	198	608
Doubs	172	433
Rhône	145	261
Saône-et-Loire	141	247
Var	128	375
Bouches-du-Rhône	122	202
Drôme	113	204
Seine-et-Oise	113	155
Moselle	110	294
Ain	109	208
Côte-d'Or	105	180
Basses-Pyrénées	103	241
Hautes- Pyrénées	102	140
Pas-de-Calais	100	146
50–99 permits		
Corrèze	94	243
Dordogne	94	161
Vaucluse	88	213
Seine-Inférieure	84	142
Loire	82	187
Haute-Garonne	72	120
Charente-Inférieure	71	166
Meuse	71	139
Gers	59	88
Nord	58	104
Gironde	50	74

Source: CAOM F80 *1998–2000.

the following decade, when the neighboring Vaucluse also entered the top ten. There was surely significant free migration from these departments, whose contribution is thus underrepresented in the assisted emigration data, but including unassisted emigrants cannot account for the whole of the increase. At the same time, the eastern regions of Alsace-Lorraine and the Franche-Comté nearly disappeared from the emigration stream. The Bas-Rhin and Haut-Rhin, which together accounted for nearly a quarter of all permit recipients in the 1840s, were no longer a noteworthy source of departures for Algeria in 1858, although they remained the chief point of origin for French out-migration overall in the 1850s. Only after Germany annexed Alsace-Lorraine following the Franco-Prussian War did the region again send significant numbers to the colony, which received twelve hundred refugee families seeking to retain their French nationality.[117]

The July Monarchy data show an extraordinary degree of geographical concentration that broadened significantly by the 1850s. Three departments—the Seine and the Bas- and Haut-Rhin—accounted for fully half of the permits for free passage issued in the 1840s, with the cities of Paris and Strasbourg alone accounting for a third. On the one hand, this overrepresentation reflects the overwhelmingly urban character of assisted emigrants, which can be seen in table 6. At a time when less than one-quarter of French citizens lived in communes of over 2,000 inhabitants, three-quarters of the free passages to Algeria went to residents of such urban communities, including 23 percent from metropolises of over 100,000. On the other hand, the predominance of city dwellers, and especially of Parisians and Strasbourgeois, supports the view that local traditions of mobility played a key role in colonial emigration. Both Paris and Strasbourg were growing rapidly at this time, largely through relatively long-distance migration. In Strasbourg, for instance, only 41 percent of residents had been born in the city in 1825, compared with 20 percent born outside of the surrounding towns and villages.[118] The capital was likewise a city of immigration in the second quarter of the century, when it saw 16,000 to 25,000 new arrivals from the provinces each year.[119] Passport records from these two cities help to confirm the linkage between prior migration and emigration to Algeria. In Strasbourg, two-thirds of those given free passports for Algerian destinations had been born elsewhere.[120] The percentage was even

117. See Fischer, *Alsaciens et Lorrains*, pt. 2.
118. Roland Schwab, *De la cellule rurale à la région: L'Alsace, 1825–1960. Essai de dynamique régionale* (Paris and Strasbourg, 1980), 51.
119. Chevalier, *Laboring Classes, Dangerous Classes*, 227.
120. AD Bas-Rhin 3M 682, "État des passeports d'indigents avec secours de route délivrés dans le Bas Rhin du 10 Juillet 1841 au 1 Janvier 1843." This register includes 371 passports and records a birthplace for all but 42.

TABLE 6. URBAN AND RURAL ORIGINS OF ASSISTED EMIGRANTS FROM FRANCE, 1841-45

Commune type (population)	Number of permits	Percentage
Rural		
Village (0-999)	1,465	15.5
Bourg (1,000-1,999)	788	8.3
Total	2,253	23.8
Urban		
Large bourg (2,000-4,999)	1,063	11.2
Town (5,000-9,999)	1,063	11.2
Small city (10,000-19,999)	694	7.3
City (20,000-49,999)	834	8.8
Large city (50,000-99,999)	1,281	13.5
Metropolis (over 100,000)	2,168	22.9
Total	7,103	75.1

Sources: CAOM F80 *1998-2000. Commune sizes from 1841 census, in Pierre Augustin Eusèbe Girault de Saint-Fargeau, Dictionnaire géographique, historique, industriel et commercial de toutes les communes de France..., 3 vols. (Paris, 1844-46).
Note: Percentages do not add up to 100 because commune size could not be determined for 101 of the 9,457 permits issued to French residents.

higher in Paris, where a register of certificates of morality issued to prospective Algerian colonists by the mairie of the second arrondissement shows that four-fifths had birthplaces outside of the capital.[121]

The prominence of Paris and Strasbourg also highlights the final important feature of the geography of assisted emigration: the significant overrepresentation of administrative centers. Together, departmental, arrondissement, and cantonal chefs-lieux accounted for a striking 69 percent of the permits issued to French residents.[122] The preponderance of departmental, arrondissement, and cantonal chefs-lieux suggests that industrialization was not the primary driver of emigration, as contemporary social reformers believed. The Nord, for instance,

121. AM Paris VD6 171, no. 1, "Recensement des colons algériens, 1834-1848." These three registers cover the years 1834-60. One is devoted to the colons of 1848 and has been analyzed by Yvette Katan in "Les Colons de 1848 en Algérie: Mythes et réalités," Revue d'histoire moderne et contemporaine 31 (April-June 1984): 177-202, and "Le 'voyage organisé' d'émigrants parisiens vers l'Algérie, 1848-1849," in L'émigration française, 17-47. Birthplaces are recorded for 1,010 of 1,768 individuals in the three registers.
122. Of the 9,457 permits issued to French residents, 6,523 went to administrative seats: 4,455 (47.1%) to departmental chefs-lieux, 865 (9.1%) to arrondissement chefs-lieux, and 1,218 (12.9%) to cantonal seats.

home to the manufacturing cities of Lille, Roubaix, and Tourcoing, received only 58 free passages in the 1840s. Lyon, the center of the French textile industry, was the most underrepresented of France's big cities, with only 121 permits issued to residents of the city and its *banlieue*. The primacy of administrative over industrial centers is apparent even within Alsace, where Strasbourg and Colmar, the two departmental capitals, received the vast majority of permits (1,138), while the booming textile and mining towns of Mulhouse and Sainte-Marie-aux-Mines were accorded only 225 and 87, respectively. Administrative capitals did tend to be poles of attraction for internal migrants and thus home to more mobile populations, but equally important, their predominance suggests that official recruitment efforts played a determinant role in emigration to Algeria. Prefects and subprefects were charged with publicizing the "advantages" offered to emigrants, and it was in administrative centers that placards, emigrant handbooks, and prefectoral circulars would have been most visible. By contrast, the frequent confusion or ignorance of rural mayors about emigration policies may help to explain the underrepresentation of rural people, who had less reliable access to accurate information about the assistance available.

If the people selected for emigration assistance were overwhelmingly urban people from administrative and service centers, the occupations recorded by ministry officials show that their social origins lay primarily in the working class. Many permit seekers exercised multiple occupations, and they often represented themselves strategically to officials, so this data must be treated with some caution. Their occupational distribution is nonetheless revealing. Tables 7 and 8 show that the assisted emigrants of the 1840s still worked primarily in trades "principally exercised in towns," as War Minister Bernard had noted in 1838.[123] Agricultural colonists, who had been awarded a place in official settlements, were relatively few, although many *concessionaires* did not apply for their land grants until after arriving in the colony. Agricultural laborers made up a significant proportion of the emigrants, but only 547 of the nearly 10,000 permits were issued to men categorized as *colons*, *colons-concessionaires*, or *concessionaires*. Skilled artisans and unskilled laborers, by contrast, made up a full third of the total number of assisted emigrants and received three-quarters of the permits.

In its broad outlines, the occupational structure of assisted emigration conformed quite closely to the priorities hammered out by Parisian and colonial officials, as they sought to meet the labor demands of European employers and the ever-expanding public works programs. Three-quarters of working-class emigrants were skilled artisans in the building and metal trades or unskilled laborers destined for the *travaux publics*, while the remainder were tradespeople who pro-

123. CAOM F80 1162, Bernard to Valée, 7 November 1838.

TABLE 7. OCCUPATIONAL DISTRIBUTION OF ASSISTED EMIGRANTS, 1841–45

	Number of emigrants	Percentage
Business and professional	127	1.4
Rentier	79	0.8
Sales and clerical	27	0.3
Small business	31	0.3
Skilled artisans	3,619	38.9
Service	292	3.1
Agriculture	1,939	20.8
Unskilled labor	3,464	37.2
Miscellaneous	124	1.3
Total	9,702	100.0

Source: CAOM F80 *1998–2000.
Note: Recipients' occupations are recorded for 8,726 of the 9,969 permits issued. Some permits included multiple
  individuals, and some individuals appear in more than one category.

TABLE 8. OCCUPATIONS OF WORKING-CLASS EMIGRANTS BY SECTOR, 1841–45

Sector	Number in sector	Percentage
Building trades	2,237	29.9
Metal work	675	9.0
Wood work	76	1.0
Leather trades	66	0.9
Textile production	111	1.5
Clothing trades	533	7.1
Luxury trades	47	0.6
Arts	10	0.1
Food	220	2.9
Transport	169	2.3
Road work (including unskilled manual labor)	3,328	44.5
Total	7,472	99.8

Source: CAOM F80 *1998–2000.
Note: Percentages do not add up to 100 due to rounding.

vided goods and services, from such necessities as bread and clothing to luxury
goods like candy and jewelry, to the army and the growing European population
in Algeria's coastal towns and cities. The number of unaccompanied women (452)
is somewhat surprising until we consider that most of them were traveling to join
male relatives already settled there. Otherwise, the sex ratios among assisted emi-

grants were largely consistent with those of Algeria's European population as a whole. Women made up only 14 percent of the assisted emigrants, although almost a quarter of the permits issued included the recipient's wife. As we would expect, single men received the large majority (68 percent) of free passages, although groups of male friends, neighbors, or relatives not infrequently sought to travel together. The predominance of single men was especially marked in the Seine and Bas-Rhin, where they made up over 80 percent of permit recipients, further reinforcing the importance of prior mobility among these emigrants.

The patterns that emerge from the ministerial registers are largely confirmed by the records of French provincial authorities, which offer a more detailed view of the mechanisms and reasoning that led thousands of men and women to consider leaving France for the North African colony in its first years. According to the prefects who responded to an 1844 Interior Ministry inquiry into the causes of emigration to Algeria, government assistance, including free passages, *secours de route*, land concessions, and official promises of high wages, was critical. In the Bas-Rhin, for instance, the prefect noted that Alsatians began to emigrate to Algeria when *secours de route* became available for travel to Toulon in 1838 and that departures reached a critical mass in 1841 with the liberalization and better publicizing of free passages.[124] "The facilities accorded to indigent workers to take passage for Africa are producing the best effects among the population of this town," the mayor of Wissembourg reported in 1838; "in ordering these measures, the Government has given a true blessing to areas in which the population is overflowing and where, as a consequence, means of existence are becoming daily harder to find."[125] Other mayors mentioned public announcements about available jobs, "the rumors spread" about higher salaries and the progress of colonization, and hopes for a small land grant as prompting departures.[126]

The attitude of local officials who mediated between citizens and the Ministry of War seems to have had a discernible impact on the response to emigration schemes. Officials in Paris and in Alsace, for instance, were consistently enthusiastic about emigration as an antidote to overpopulation and unemployment, and they actively sought out information about Algeria, publicized emigration assistance, and supported local people's requests for free passage. This attitude was exemplified by the justice of the peace in Marmoutier (Bas-Rhin), who urged his subprefect to intervene with the minister on behalf of Anselme Obermeyer, a

---

124. AD Bas-Rhin 6M 685, report for department of the Bas-Rhin, [1844].
125. AD Bas-Rhin 3M 695, maire de Wissembourg to sous-préfet de Wissembourg, 26 October 1838.
126. AD Haut-Rhin 6M 356, report for commune of Ribeauville, [1844]; AD Haut-Rhin 1Z 382, report for commune of Mulhausen, [1844]; AD Gard, 6M 747, maire de Nîmes, "Émigration pour l'Algérie, du 1er Janvier 1842 au 30 Juin 1844," 28 October 1844.

thirty-eight-year-old worker from the commune, where there was "an excess of Proletarians, whom it is very difficult to employ and to feed in our unfortunate country. It is urgent to create a future for them and above all to rid the country of them at any cost."[127] Officials elsewhere promoted emigration to solve local economic problems, too. At the other end of France, the mayor of Saleix (Arièges), a tiny village high in the Pyrenees near the Spanish border, orchestrated free passage for nine men from his commune, "because we almost need to weaken our population in our country even if only because of the forests," which were increasingly strained under the 1827 forestry code that severely restricted traditional use rights.[128] In the Haute-Garonne, emigration was not significant, but one subprefect suggested that economic pressures made his arrondissement ripe for departures, which could be encouraged by publicizing the assistance offered to colonists.[129] Economic pressures were not the only ones that led local authorities to promote emigration, however. The mayor of the town of Stenay, in the Meuse, for example, pressed the prefect to use his influence to obtain free passage for a seventeen-year-old printer's assistant, Léon Phée, in hopes that "Algeria will do some good for his young head and that he will return to us a good subject and a friend of work after spending a few years in a foreign country." Phée's parents supported their son's desire to go to North Africa, but "had already made too many sacrifices for the young featherbrain" to pay for his passage themselves.[130]

Local officials' decisive influence can be seen in the case of Charles Batut, one of the few residents of the Lot to be accorded free passage to Algeria. A thirty-two-year-old mason and stonecutter, Batut had moved away from his family's home village in the Dordogne as a young man. Returning to Martel in 1841, he found himself reduced to "the most complete [sic] indigence" when he could not find work. The mayor of the village reported that "seeing him in this miserable state, persons who cared about his fate and knew his remarkable capacities advised him to go to Algeria." Batut was apparently persuaded by this advice and applied to go to Algeria with his wife, Jeanne, and two young children in August of 1844. Shortly after receiving his permit, however, Batut informed the mayor that the family could not leave without additional assistance from the commune. Their economic situation, desperate enough to push them to emigration, did not provide them the resources to do so.[131] Somehow the family found the necessary

127. AD Bas-Rhin 3M 690, justice de paix de Marmoutier to sous-préfet de Saverne, 12 March 1849.
128. AD Ariège 10M 15, maire de Saleix to préfet de l'Ariège, 6 July 1845.
129. AD Haute-Garonne 4M 57, report for arrondissement of Saint-Gaudens, [1844].
130. AD Meuse 146M 3, directeur des Affaires d'Afrique to préfet de la Meuse, 28 February 1838; maire de Stenay to préfet de la Meuse, 22 March 1838.
131. AD Lot 6M 317, maire de Martel to sous-préfet de Gourdon, 1 October 1844.

funds, and they eventually settled near Algiers in the village of El Biar. Jeanne Batut died there two years later, but Charles Batut remarried and remained in the colony.[132]

The tale of Charles Batut also highlights the role of social networks in Algerian emigration, although the archives provide no detail about his relation to the concerned persons who encouraged him to emigrate. Prefectoral responses to the ministerial inquiry of 1844 are more specific about the development of local migration chains, in which individuals established in Algeria recruited family, friends, or neighbors to follow at a later date. Thus the mayor of Colmar reported that a few workers from a recently closed cotton mill had left for North Africa, where they had prospered and were now urging former colleagues to join them.[133] Other mayors and subprefects reported individuals solicited to emigrate by family members already settled in the colony. These kinds of networks could not only provide the initiative for emigration, but as in most cases of chain migration, they also helped following emigrants negotiate the bureaucratic requirements for obtaining free passage.

The few personal letters preserved in departmental archives are especially illuminating on this aspect of the Algerian migratory mechanism. A Madame Pérdix, for example, wrote from Algiers to her mother in Lyon with very explicit instructions for obtaining free passage to the colony: She was to begin at the *mairie*, where she would say that she did not have sufficient work to survive and request a certificate of indigence that would entitle her to *secours de route* for the voyage to Marseille. At the prefecture, she would request her *permis de passage* and explain that her daughter, a seamstress, would be able to support her in Algiers. Before departing, Pérdix asked that her mother retrieve her jewelry from the municipal pawnshop to bring with her to Africa.[134] Similar letters were sent by other emigrants to friends and relatives, containing much the same advice about how to present themselves to the officials responsible for issuing certificates of morality, passports, and permits for free passage, as well as requests for sundry items from France, ranging from tools to furniture, household linens, clothing, butter, even a good butcher's apprentice. A few letters offer a glimpse of the arguments emigrants used to convince their correspondents to join them in Algeria. Some cajoled with accounts of the beautiful climate and inexpensive food; others threatened recalcitrant relations with force.[135]

132. CAOM État-civil (Algérie), acte de mariage for Charles Batut and Prudence Clément, 26 January 1850, http://anom.archivesnationales.culture.gouv.fr/caomec2.
133. AD Haut-Rhin 6M 356, maire de Colmar to préfet du Haut-Rhin, 11 October 1844.
134. AD Rhône 6Mp 2/4, Madame Pérdix to her mother, 10 November 1850.
135. AD Rhône 6Mp 2/4, Grévet to Madame Grévet, 9 May 1850; AD Haute-Garonne, 6M 755, ministre de la Guerre (Saint-Yon), "Note sur la correspondance de la femme Berger-Andrien avec son mari," 28 September 1845–24 February 1846.

Regardless of emigrants' procedures, French officials saw the causes of emigration as self-evident and essentially economic. To the minister of the interior's query about the "material and moral causes" of emigration to Algeria, the prefects responded with one voice that most emigrants were poor and "have been convinced [to leave] solely by the hope of better fortune."[136] Departures for North Africa, one claimed, "must be attributed to the emigrants' state of financial difficulty, which has led them to go to Algeria in order to create for themselves more fortunate positions."[137] The prefects' reading of the situation contrasts quite sharply with that of historian Louis Chevalier, who argued that overseas migration in France had little to do with "living or simply living better. Most of the time it was a question of making one's fortune." There is remarkably little sign, however, in the surviving prefectoral responses of "the mirage of Eldorado" that Chevalier saw leading Frenchmen overseas.[138] Only a few mentioned emigrants' desire for rapid enrichment.[139] Most emphasized instead their hopes of overcoming poverty, unemployment, or family crises. Where emigration was heaviest, as in Alsace and Lorraine, respondents put the greatest emphasis on emigrants' misery. For the most part, however, the prefects shared the views of their colleague in the Ariège, who wrote, "it is neither the desire for change nor the attraction of novelty, much less the need to escape the sanction of society that has caused the little emigration we have seen in the department. The only motive for abandoning the country, so rare among the cultivators of our area, is nothing other than the desire to improve one's position by seeking a more useful occupation."[140]

The prefects' assessment of the economic motives driving Algerian emigration is borne out by the glimpses we can get of the experiences and understandings of emigrants themselves. Together, the archives of French officials in Algiers, Paris, and the provinces conserve a small, but invaluable corpus of several hundred letters composed by prospective emigrants or by mayors, priests, and public letter writers on their behalf. Although shaped by these various intermediaries and their authors' views of those who would rule on petitions for assistance, these documents nonetheless open a rare window onto the perspectives of a few of the thousands of assisted emigrants profiled above.

136. AD Lot 6M 317, sous-préfet de Figeac, "Relevé des émigrants en Algérie: Dressé par le sous-préfet de l'arrondissement de Figeac," 24 October 1844; AD Haute-Saône 550E dépôt 999, maire de Vesoul, "Causes générales et matérielles de l'émigration," [August–September 1844].
137. AD Corrèze 6M 408, "Enquête sur l'émigration en Algérie depuis 1842, tableau pour le Département de la Corrèze," [1844].
138. Chevalier, "L'émigration," 159.
139. E.g. AD Haut-Rhin 6M 356, report on commune of Wintzenheim; AD Gard 6M 747, sous-préfet de Vigan, report on arrondissement of Vigan, 18 October 1844.
140. AD Ariège 10M 18/1, "Émigration pour l'Algérie," [1844].

The primary themes of these emigrant letters can be seen in one written in 1845 by a Tarascon joiner to the prefect of the Ariège. With unsteady grammar, spelling, and handwriting, he explained:

> I am the father of a family, named Jean François Delaunay . . . who, for some time as work has been paralyzed in our country, have been finding myself barely able to live. Since we have no real hope of exercising our profession, having no other resources to live from, and knowing that our government is encouraging some French citizens to go to Algeria, I desire to be among that number, to exercise the trade of Cultivator, having from youth the knowledge and experience and good will to work.

"I beg you," Delaunay concluded, "have some care for a Father who until now has merited public esteem. Not wanting to sacrifice my family by going to live in an entirely unknown country, I lay myself at your mercy and your wisdom, and beg you further to give us your protection to settle us in a safe place so that we will not be sacrificed to the rage of the unsubdued" Algerians.[141] Delaunay's request stands out for its reference to the indigenous population, although there are hints that other prospective emigrants shared contemporary racist views of Algeria's supposedly ferocious native inhabitants. But his insistence on his status as a father, his professional skills, and his will to work, as well as his appeal to the generosity and wisdom of the prefect, were quite typical.

The letter writers are predominantly male and therefore speak, as Delaunay did, largely as men. Fatherhood figured with particular prominence in their letters, such as one from an 1848 petitioner who described himself "as an unfortunate father of a family" responsible for "the existence of ten people." Distasteful as he found the idea of expatriation, the man wrote, "because it was a matter of my family, because I owe bread to my Wife and Children, I will leave happily, since I will be fulfilling my duties as a Husband and a father."[142] Antoine Delpeuch, a cultivator from the rural Corrèze who requested free passage in 1842, did so in order "not to leave his wife, his children, and his mother in misery." Although he recognized that he did not meet the criteria for assistance, Delpeuch proposed that this honorable motive made him worthy of an exception to the rules.[143] When they did write, women also addressed themselves to authorities as mothers and daughters, much as younger men presented themselves as sons. Thus a Madame Chambon of Lyon, who wanted to join her husband in Algiers, appealed to the

141. AD Ariège 10M 18/1, Jean François Delaunay to préfet de l'Ariège, [1845].
142. AD Bas-Rhin 3M 690, Félix Birer to préfet du Bas-Rhin, 13 October 1848.
143. AD Corrèze 6M 406, Antoine Delpeuch to préfet de la Corrèze, 12 November 1842.

prefect "to take into consideration her position (*qualité*) as a good wife [and] a good mother" to four children suffering from the ongoing separation of the family.[144] An unemployed young railway worker in Strasbourg likewise presented his request for passage to "Affrique" as a matter of family welfare, "my father being unable to support me as well as his other children."[145]

In laying out for the prefect the hardships caused by unemployment, Delaunay also emphasized his professional knowledge, work ethic, and frustration at being unable to exercise his trade. Emphasizing the desire to work was at least partly a tactical appeal to a bourgeois officialdom whose conception of public assistance was predicated on distinctions between the deserving and the undeserving poor. But the ubiquity of such claims suggests that they also gave voice to a deeper conception of working-class honor defined by skilled labor and economic independence. For men, in particular, independence, work, and manliness went hand in hand. A collective letter from a rope maker, two plasterers, and a cotton-cloth maker proclaimed not only their shared status as "pères de famille" but also that they were each "able to work as a man" and "know their trades perfectly."[146] The Alsatian stonecutter Anselme Obermeyer similarly claimed assistance as a "skillful worker" and asked to be employed in Algeria "not as a simple *colon*, but in my specialty in skilled work and construction."[147]

Unemployed men argued for help in avoiding the emasculating state of idleness. Another Alsatian petitioner, although illiterate, used the services of a public letter writer to explain to the prefect of the Bas-Rhin that "I shudder to see my wife and my seven children, who want to live well, see me unable to provide for them even the basic necessities." Emigration, he believed, offered an honorable way out of this "embarrassing position."[148] A third emigrant from the same department stated simply, "in the country where I live, I can do nothing except vegetate."[149] Although less frequently, women sometimes also invoked their honor in soliciting emigration assistance. The example of Marie Catherine Masser, a domestic servant in Strasbourg who had lost her place, illustrates the particularities of working women's honor, which was endangered less by idleness than by its alternative: prostitution. This was implicit in Masser's letter, in which she described herself as a "poor girl . . . not knowing how to earn my living honorably"

144. AD Rhône, 6Mp 2/4, Madame Chambon to préfet du Rhône, [c. October 1850].
145. AD Bas-Rhin 3M 694, Thuilier fils to maire de Strasbourg, 21 February 1849.
146. AD Bas-Rhin 3M 685, S. Bouzé to préfet du Bas-Rhin on behalf of Charles Dinies, Bernard Leberlé, Henry Heller, and Christophe Heller, 3 February 1846.
147. AD Bas-Rhin 3M 690, Anselme Obermeyer to sous-préfet de Saverne, 28 February 1849.
148. AD Bas-Rhin 3M 690, Xavier Kres to préfet du Bas-Rhin, 19 February 1852.
149. AD Bas-Rhin 3M 689, Ambiehl to préfet du Bas-Rhin, 3 March 1845.

and begged for the prefect's "kind assistance and protection" in reaching Algiers, where she had friends or family to help her in her hour of distress.[150]

Whether framed by the ideals of the male breadwinner or virtuous working womanhood, the self-representations of prospective assisted migrants sketched out an alternative to the *véritable colon* enshrined in contemporary colonization theory and policy. Although some declared their aspirations to landownership, most, including those who identified themselves as farmers, viewed emigration primarily as a strategy for coping with economic or family crises. At the same time, the emphasis they placed on their professional skills and honor suggests that this economic strategy had a deeper significance in defining their place in a French society increasingly understood in imperial terms. Applicants for emigration assistance, particularly men, looked overseas to free themselves and their families from dependency and to reassert themselves as autonomous subjects at a time of rapid economic and political change.

The independence and self-sufficiency stressed by letter writers did very nearly mirror the qualities of the *véritable colon* enshrined in colonial policy, however, although they also suggest that the impetus for early French emigration to Algeria had relatively little to do with imperialist ideology. Rare were those who declared any patriotic affection for the colony before the February Revolution of 1848 made Algerian colonization a centerpiece of republican politics. During the July Monarchy, prospective emigrants laid claim to state assistance in more subtle terms that drew on their understandings of equality before the law and an implicit social contract that held government officials responsible for ensuring citizens' well-being. Despite policymakers' efforts to avoid creating a sense of entitlement among potential settlers, the language in which requests for free passage were couched makes clear that emigrants did presume that they had a legitimate claim to state aid as they sought to restore their lost or precarious status as male heads of households and autonomous economic actors.

Prospective emigrants grounded claims first in their understandings of the legal regulations governing assisted emigration and in their assumption that free passage to Algeria and other forms of assistance were being offered equally to all French citizens. Even though this was not in fact the case, as we have seen, officials found themselves confronted with requests from individuals confident that they would receive the free passages "that are being accorded to all indigents."[151] Petitioners cited the relevant circulars and decrees, or simply asserted, like Jean-François Delaunay, the joiner from the Ariège, that a travel indemnity and other benefits, including free transportation of household belongings, land concessions,

150. AD Bas-Rhin 696, Marie Catherine Masser to préfet du Bas-Rhin, 27 June 1842.
151. AD Haute-Garonne 6M 757, Jean Platard to préfet de la Haute-Garonne, 8 April 1847.

and financial support, were being accorded to "people of good will."¹⁵² Some of this misunderstanding arose from the circulation of rumors exaggerating the assistance offered to emigrants, but its persistence is indicative of the resonance these broader claims had with popular understandings of the government's obligations to its citizens. This underlying sense of equality and an incipient sense of a right to labor was, on its own, an inherent challenge not only to the conditions imposed on assisted colonial migration but also to the restrictions placed on citizenship by the censitary July Monarchy.

The second basis on which those seeking free passages to Algeria founded their demands also presumed government officials' obligation to aid those less fortunate, but located this obligation in a kind of updated *noblesse oblige* rather than a conception of rights. A letter addressed to the minister of the interior in 1839 by Louis Rougé, a twenty-five-year-old mason, exemplified this approach. A native of the Aude, Rougé had recently moved to Marseille, where local workers' hostility had made it impossible to find work: "Being young, I ask nothing more than to work, but work is found only with great difficulty, especially for an outsider. The goal of my request would be, Monsieur Minister, to beg you to transfer me at the Government's expense on a state ship to the part of Africa that needs workers the most. Since you seek only the occasion to relieve the unfortunate, I dare to hope, M. Minister, that my petition will have a happy outcome."¹⁵³ Such supplicating appeals to the kindness and generosity of government officials appeared to subscribe to the paternalistic attitudes of bourgeois social reformers and charity workers, who saw the working class as "more an object of solicitude than an active agent in social transformation."¹⁵⁴ That the propertyless should beg social and administrative elites for the salvation of their families and their dignity would appear to conform to the *juste milieu* principle of rule by men whose propertied "capacity" made them the natural stewards of the nation's well-being. Yet by confronting the constitutional monarchy's defining social principles directly, prospective Algerian emigrants also revealed the limitations of these principles. Like the popular Bonapartism that undermined the Orleanist image of the royal citizen-soldier, appeals for state aid that went unheeded laid bare the July Monarchy's failure to live up even to its own limited social commitments to its citizens.

152. AD Ariège 10M 18/1, Jean François Delaunay to préfet de l'Ariège, [1845]; AM Marseille, 13F 1, Paliro to maire de Marseille, 10 January 1839; AM Lyon 4 WP 059 2, Frédéric Brottin, Louis Eugène Robert, and Auguste Bernard to préfet du Rhône, 1 November 1847.
153. AM Marseille 13F 1, Louis Rougé to ministre de l'Intérieur, [c. August 1839].
154. William Sewell, *Work and Revolution in France: The Language of Labor from the Old Regime to 1848* (Cambridge, 1980), 235.

Requests for free passage challenged the monarchy to prove itself a generous protector of the sovereign people without resolving the tensions between metropolitan and colonial views of Algerian colonization, but such tensions did not prevent emigration and settlement from proceeding apace, either. On the eve of the February Revolution that drove Louis-Philippe from power, Algeria had become home to a combined European population of 109,400 souls. The 42,274 French citizens among them accounted for less than half this number, but colonial officials were optimistic about "the tendency of our nationals to surpass the foreigners."[155] By 1848, Algeria's future as a colony of European settlement had been sealed, and the assisted migrants discussed in this chapter made up a critical element of the nascent settler population. Under the Second Republic and its successors, their numbers would only grow, rooting French rule ever deeper in the North African soil.

155. *TEFA* (1843–44), 56.

Conclusion

Politics and Empire in Nineteenth-Century France

THE JULY MONARCHY ended as it had begun, with insurrection in the streets of Paris. As one observer later noted, the citizen-king "crowned by a revolution" in 1830 was "discrowned by a revolution" in February 1848.[1] On 22 February, while Louis-Philippe met with Horace Vernet to commission a portrait of the recently captured 'Abd al-Qadir, crowds of angry workers gathered under the windows of the Tuileries, singing the *Marseillaise* to protest the cancellation of a liberal reform banquet scheduled for that evening. When violent clashes broke out between the protesters and the forces of order, barricades went up in the capital's working-class quarters. Louis-Philippe mobilized the army to put down the insurrection and called in former Algerian governor general Bugeaud to command the military forces in the capital. Determined "to employ extreme measures to reestablish order," the general issued orders "as severe as many of those upon which *rhazzias* had been based in Algeria," directing his men to give no quarter and announcing that "blood will be spilled" to punish the "troublemakers" of the Parisian "canaille" (rabble).[2] Daunted by these promises of bloodshed, however, the king renounced his hard-line stance and instructed Bugeaud to stand down rather than risk civil war. Troops were ordered not to

1. Z., quoted in Nassau William Senior, *Journals Kept in France and Italy from 1848 to 1852, with a Sketch of the Revolution of 1848*, ed. Mary Charlotte Mair Simpson, 2nd ed., vol. 2 (London, 1871), 217.
2. Quoted in Jean-Pierre Bois, *Bugeaud* (Paris, 1997), 533; Antony Thrall Sullivan, *Thomas-Robert Bugeaud: France and Algeria, 1784–1849. Politics, Power, and the Good Society* (Hamden, 1983), 135.

fire on the rioters, and at midday on February 24, as a mob gathered once again outside the Tuileries, Louis-Philippe abdicated "this Crown that the national will called upon me to wear" eighteen years earlier.[3] The erstwhile King of the French then slipped, largely unheeded, out of the palace while radical deputies, cheered on by the crowd, proclaimed the Republic and instituted a Provisional Government at the Hôtel de Ville.

Algeria was as intimately entangled in the revolutionary politics of 1848 as it had been in 1830. In the chaos of the February Days, all eyes turned south, just as they had done eighteen years earlier, in hope or fear that the Armée d'Afrique would sail to the monarchy's rescue. But like General de Bourmont before him, the duc d'Aumale was persuaded to accept the will of the Parisian crowd. Declaring himself "subject to the national will," the prince called for public calm and remained at his post until the Provisional Government appointed General Eugène Cavaignac to replace him. Then, no longer "useful to the service of the country," he relinquished his command and sailed to England to join his family in exile. Down to the monarchy's final hours, Aumale clung to the ideal of the self-sacrificing royal citizen-soldier. In a farewell proclamation to Algeria's soldiers and settlers, the prince expressed sorrow that he would no longer fight alongside them "for the *patrie*" and insisted that even in exile, he would continue to pray for the colony's prosperity and "the glory of the France I would have liked to serve longer."[4] Popular disillusionment with such royal self-representations had helped to bring down the monarchy, but Algeria's importance in elaborating the Orleanist model of meritocratic kingship makes it fitting that its last public performance took place in Algiers.

I have argued in this book that the origins of French Algeria lay in the contested political culture of the postrevolutionary period. Rather than attributing imperial expansion to the triumph of a particular party or ideology, I have sought to demonstrate how conflicts over the sources of sovereignty and definitions of citizenship pushed France back onto the colonial stage after the imperial collapse of the eighteenth century. As we have seen, the struggle between Bourbon ultraroyalism, meritocratic Orleanism, and populist, egalitarian Bonapartism led the Restoration and the July Monarchy to undertake the invasion, conquest, and colonization of the former Ottoman regency of Algiers, even as these regimes' conduct in North Africa challenged their claims to sovereignty in France itself.

3. Act of abdication, quoted in H. A. C. Collingham with Robert S. Alexander, *The July Monarchy: A Political History of France, 1830–1848* (London, 1988), 412.
4. Proclamation to the Armée d'Afrique and inhabitants of Algiers, 3 March 1848, in Émile Carrey, ed., *Recueil complet des actes du gouvernement provisoire (février, mars, avril, mai 1848)* . . . (Paris, 1848), 118–19.

Despite their ideological differences, both Charles X and Louis-Philippe sought legitimacy in military conquest, which in turn created new imperatives for the settlement colonization proposed by reformers, economists, and officials anxious about the moral and political consequences of colonial slavery overseas and modernization at home. Like the prosecution of the war of conquest, the formulation of colonial land and emigration policies provoked conflict between metropolitan and colonial officials. Their disagreements over who should settle in Algeria and under what circumstances made colonization a halting, uneven process. But even when the terrible realities of colonial warfare and the disappointing results of early emigration unmasked the "chimerical" nature of the ideals of settler colonialism, lawmakers, administrators, and publicists clung to these ideals, making tactical adjustments in policy that did little to alter the ultimate goal of making Algeria a "new France" across the Mediterranean.

Reconsidering the origins of French Algeria from the perspective of political culture suggests that we need to rethink the history of nineteenth-century France as well. Algeria's central place in the political culture of the period highlights the imperial character of regimes usually viewed in exclusively domestic terms. I do not mean by this only that empire constituted a space where categories of belonging were worked out on the margins, for the colonial enterprise was intended to and did directly impact political, cultural, and social life at the heart of the metropole. The war of conquest was explicitly designed to sustain the ruling institution of the French state, the monarchy; those who formulated colonization policies anticipated that they would transform the economic, demographic, and moral structures of French society. Whether they wielded the sword or the plow, the agents of French colonization were expected to emerge from the process as new men, redeemed, revitalized, and revirilized by combat and contact with the land. Political and administrative assimilation of the society these men built would literally redraw the map of France, transforming its territorial, human, and political boundaries. Contemporaries, moreover, understood the Algerian conquest in terms of a larger imperial heritage that encompassed both the slave colonies of the French Atlantic world and the continental Empire of Napoleon Bonaparte. Although throughout this book I have insisted on Algeria's unique status within the French empire, it is equally important to recognize that it stood at the historical and ideological crossroads where the multiple empires of nineteenth-century France—Atlantic, Afro-Asian, and European—came together.

These interconnected ways of "thinking like an empire"[5] suggest an alternative narrative of nineteenth-century French history in which war weighs as heav-

---

5. Frederick Cooper, "States, Empires, and Political Imagination," in *Colonialism in Question: Theory, Knowledge, History* (Berkeley, 2005), 154.

ily as commercial expansion, emigration counts as much as urbanization, and Napoleon's legacy looms as large as that of Robespierre. If we carry forward such a perspective, the conquest of Algeria emerges as one of the century's major developments and the postrevolutionary decades become, as David Pinkney has suggested, the "decisive years" of the period.[6] The processes of conquest and colonization begun during the July Monarchy continued into the subsequent decades, when Algeria was fully integrated into the legitimizing rituals, citizenship debates, and social policies of the Second Republic, the Second Empire, and the Third Republic.

Colonial warfare and its politicized staging for French citizens presents perhaps the most striking continuity from the 1830s and 1840s into the second half of the century. The advent of the Second Republic brought dramatic reforms in the colonial arena, most important among them the abolition of colonial slavery by decree of the Provisional Government in April 1848.[7] But in Algeria, despite the Republic's repudiation of aggressive war, the French army pursued the conquest with a vengeance equal to and, in some ways, more extreme than that of the monarchy. The push south into the Sahara after the defeat of 'Abd al-Qadir and the surrender of Ahmad Bey in 1848 saw some of the most horrific violence of the conquest period, as the oasis towns of Zaatcha and Laghouat were besieged and sacked, and thousands of their residents butchered.[8] After the declaration of the Second Empire, the Armée d'Afrique marched into Kabylia, where the tribes had hitherto maintained their independence. The conquest of Algeria was finally deemed complete with the hard-fought submission of Greater Kabylia in 1857, but the generations of French military men trained in the Armée d'Afrique, along with thousands of North African auxiliary forces, were dispatched to new wars in Europe and Mexico, and to new colonial conquests in Sub-Saharan Africa and Asia.

The importance of the Armée d'Afrique in later nineteenth-century French imperial expansion is paralleled by its ongoing influence in domestic politics. Whereas Louis-Philippe called upon Bugeaud for the last, abortive defense of the monarchy, the Second Republic looked to his lieutenants in June of 1848, when radical Parisian workers revolted in defense of the "right to labor" proclaimed during the February Days. The Provisional Government appointed Cavaignac

6. David Pinkney, *The Decisive Years in France, 1840–1847* (Princeton, 1986).
7. "Décret relatif à l'abolition de l'esclavage dans les colonies et possessions françaises," 27 April 1848, in Carrey, *Recueil*, 317–19. See also Lawrence Jennings, *French Anti-Slavery: The Movement for the Abolition of Slavery in France, 1802–1848* (New York, 2000), 276–84.
8. Charles-André Julien, *Histoire de l'Algérie contemporaine*, vol. 1, *La conquête et les débuts de la colonisation (1827–1871)* (Paris, 1964), 383–85, 390–93; Benjamin Brower, *A Desert Named Peace: The Violence of France's Empire in the Algerian Sahara, 1844–1902* (New York, 2009), 81–89.

to put down the insurrection, first naming him minister of war and then giving him unrestricted executive powers to restore order. The repression of the June Days uprising, carried out by the *Africain* generals Lamoricière and Bedeau, was brutal, leaving Parisians with "a sentiment of retrospective terror that survived long after the danger"[9] and prompting accusations that the government had unleashed the tactics of colonial warfare against its own citizens. Although most famously expressed by Friedrich Engels, who described the use of artillery shells and incendiary rockets against the barricades as "a commendable display of Algerian barbarity,"[10] many others also saw a substantiation of earlier warnings that the violence of the Armée d'Afrique could be turned against the people at home.[11] One grisly souvenir of the June Days graphically embodies the ways that insurgents and their supporters equated the *Africains'* conquest of Algeria with their reconquest of Paris (fig. 53). A commemorative medal made of a flattened musket ball, engraved with the date, "June 22," and the phrase, "Example of a Ball from Overseas," clearly identified the bullets fired at Parisian workers with those aimed at indigenous Algerians. Moderate republicans and conservatives who endorsed harsh efforts to stem the tide of working-class radicalism also saw revolutionary violence as an extension of colonial conquest. Like Algerians, they argued, the Parisian rebels posed an existential threat to modern social and political order: "Family, institutions, liberty, fatherland, all were stricken to the heart, and, under the blows of these new barbarians, the civilization of the nineteenth century was threatened with destruction," the National Assembly declared in the aftermath of the June Days. Implicit in this analogy was the belief that defense of these foundational values demanded that the "new barbarians" of the metropole be treated with the same force as the "old barbarians" who resisted French conquest in North Africa.[12]

Building on this equation between domestic order and colonial domination, the Second Republic and its successors continued to foreground imperial conquest in their quest for legitimacy in the second half of the century. Like the conservative defenders of order during the June Days, they sought to justify their rule at home by associating the institutions of state power with the

---

9. Daniel Stern [Marie d'Argoult], *Histoire de la Révolution de 1848,* 2nd ed., vol. 2 (Paris, 1862), 478.

10. Friedrich Engels, "The June Revolution (The Course of the Paris Uprising)," *Neue Rheinische Zeitung,* 2 July 1848 (Marxists Internet Archive, n.d.), http://www.marxists.org/archive/marx/works/1848/07/01c.htm.

11. Jennifer Sessions, "'Unfortunate Necessities': Violence and Civilization in the Conquest of Algeria," in *France and Its Spaces of War: Experience, Memory, Image,* ed. Patricia Lorcin and Daniel Brewer (New York, 2009), 40.

12. Proclamation of the National Assembly, 28 June 1848, *CRANL,* 2:238.

FIGURE 53. "Example of a Musket Ball from Overseas," Paris, 1848. Courtesy University of Iowa Libraries, Special Collections, Mabbot Collection.

unquestioned legitimacy of colonial conquest abroad. Following the festivities that marked the Bourbons' Algiers expedition in 1830 and Algeria's starring role in Orleanist ceremonial, both Republic and Empire made imperial expansion—and especially the Armée d'Afrique—a pillar of their legitimizing rituals. In the historical spectacle planned to celebrate the first anniversary of the Second Republic, for example, it was an "Episode of Our War in Africa" that was to crown a series of scenes of "the emancipation of peoples and the French glories attached to them."[13] During the Second Empire, the August 15 festivals marking Napoleon I's invented name day entertained the crowds by reenacting recent French conquests in the Algerian Sahara, Indochina, and Sub-Saharan Africa. At the same time, military parades cast an army that now included both French and indigenous Algerian troops as a mainstay of the Imperial regime (fig. 54). And like the Orléans princes, Napoleon III went ostentatiously to war, proclaiming to the French people that "I will . . . put myself at the head of the Army" as it marched into Italy in 1859, for example, "to show the world that [our country] has not degenerated."[14] After 1871, when the desperate struggles of the Franco-Prussian War and the Paris Commune inscribed warfare at the heart of the Third Republic's citizenship practices, public schools, military

---

13. AN F21 720, "Rapport au ministre de l'Intérieur," n.d. [March 1849], and J. Charpentier to directeur des Beaux-Arts, 19 March 1849. The pageant was ultimately canceled for budgetary reasons. *Moniteur universel,* 4–6 May 1849.

14. AM Lyon 2Fi 1589, "Proclamation de l'Empereur au peuple français," 3 May 1859 (Lyon, 1859).

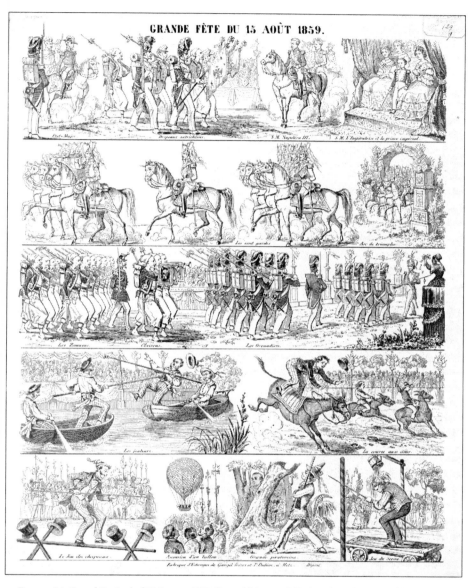

FIGURE 54. *Grand Festival of 15 August 1859*, Gangel frères et P. Didion (Metz), 1859. Bibliothèque nationale de France, Département des Estampes et de la photographie

rituals, and festivals were all mobilized to celebrate colonial armies' contributions to French imperialism, grandeur, and military strength.[15]

What Algeria signified within French political culture changed, but the ways in which the colony offered Frenchmen and their rulers both a stage and a vocabulary for politics persisted. As this book has shown, there was more to the relationship between culture and imperialism in nineteenth-century France than the expression of popular nationalist fervor, an attempt to shore up national grandeur, or a discursive funhouse mirror reflecting a distorted vision of an Occidental Self. The cultural origins of French Algeria certainly had a great deal to do with nationalism, grandeur, and French self-image, but these were not conceived solely or even always primarily in terms of the racialized binary between colonizer and colonized. Instead, images of Algeria and its conquest were embedded within broader domestic contests over citizenship, sovereignty, and empire. In their century-long struggle for legitimacy, the successive iterations of the French state and their respective opponents all looked to North Africa to express and enact competing understandings of political virtue and vice. In doing so, they established the foundations for the settler colonialism that brought Algeria into the French polity and integrated the colony into modern French life.

The linkages between military conquest and colonial settlement that created the political will behind state emigration and colonization initiatives endured after 1848, when a series of reforms aimed to assimilate Algeria fully into the French political and administrative order. Eighteen forty-eight was a critical turning point in this process, which decisively consolidated developments already underway. Colonial policymakers had begun to discuss territorial integration and the extension of French citizenship to all of Algeria's Europeans in the mid-1840s, and plans were in motion by 1847 to expand significantly the state's involvement in emigration and settlement.[16] As they did for the abolition of slavery, the February Days dramatically accelerated these processes. Republican lawmakers discussed several large-scale colonization schemes in the spring and summer of 1848, as the social anxieties that shaped the settler colonial movement moved to the center

15. Bertrand Taithe, *Citizenship and Wars: France in Turmoil, 1870–1871* (London and New York, 2001); 67–69; Rémi Dalisson, "Les 'Journées d'Afrique et des colonies' pendant la Grande Guerre: Un exemple d'instrumentalisation de l'image africaine (1914–1917)," *Trames* 9 (2001): 77–79; Jean-Pierre Bois, *Histoire des 14 juillet, 1789–1919* (Rennes, 1991), 180–82; Alain Morot, "Le soldat indigène de l'armée d'Afrique dans *Le Charivari* sous le Second Empire," in *La caricature entre République et censure. L'imagerie satirique en France de 1830 à 1880: Un discours de résistance?* ed. Raimbond Rütten, Ruth Jung, and Gerhard Schneider (Lyon, 1996), 314–24.
16. Jennifer Sessions, "'L'Algérie devenue française': The Naturalization of Non-French Colonists in French Algeria, 1830–1849," in *Proceedings of the Western Society for French History* 30 (2002): 171–73.

of French political life. When these tensions exploded in June, the Republic did not reopen the National Workshops whose closure had triggered the uprising. Instead, legislators sought to replace them by developing the first comprehensive plan for official colonization in Algeria. Approved by the National Assembly on 19 September 1848, the scheme aimed to send twenty thousand Frenchmen to settle in forty-two Algerian villages, where the state would provide them with land, houses, agricultural tools, seeds, animals, and three years of cash subsidies. Rather than guarantee them labor at home, the Republic would offer its unemployed citizens the means to create their own work on Algeria's fertile soil.[17] As a recruiting poster issued by the mayor of Lyon's Croix-Rousse neighborhood explained, the decree would "guarantee [workers without work] an existence based on property in the African colony."[18]

By almost any practical measure, the *colonies agricoles* of 1848 were an abysmal failure. Some fourteen thousand colonists were dispatched to Algeria between 1 October and 10 December 1848, and almost immediately, the trans-Mediterranean conflicts that had long dogged emigration policy resurfaced. Officials in Algiers complained about "the faulty choice of colonists, recruited almost entirely from the workshops of Paris and . . . altogether unsuited to working in the fields," while the *colons* themselves protested the conditions in the hastily built settlements. Hundreds of disillusioned emigrants quickly returned to France, having abandoned their villages or been expelled for infractions ranging from laziness to debauchery and political dissent. An outbreak of cholera in 1849 left over fifteen hundred dead, and thousands more fled infected communities.[19] Yet French lawmakers confronted with this near-catastrophe did not rescind the September decree and reclaim the credits for other projects. Instead, they revised the scheme to admit to the *colonies* only experienced farmers who possessed fifteen hundred francs in capital, and sent some five thousand new colonists who

17. On the colonies of 1848, see *TEFA* (1846–49), 238–39; Yvette Katan, "Les Colons de 1848 en Algérie: Mythes et réalités," *Revue d'histoire moderne et contemporaine* 31 (April–June 1984): 177–202, and "Le 'voyage organisé' d'émigrants parisiens vers l'Algérie, 1848–1849," in *L'émigration française. Études de cas: Algérie, Canada, États-Unis* (Paris, 1985), 17–47; Michael Heffernan, "The Parisian Poor and the Colonization of Algeria during the Second Republic," *French History* 3, no. 4 (1989): 377–403; Yvette Katan, "La Seconde République et l'Algérie: Une politique de peuplement?" in *1848: Actes du colloque international du cent cinquantenaire, tenu à l'Assemblée nationale à Paris, les 23–25 février 1998*, ed. Jean-Luc Mayaud (Paris, 2002), 389–412.
18. AM Lyon 6Fi 669, "Établissement de colonies agricoles en Algérie," 9 October 1848.
19. *TEFA* (1846–49), 238; letters of complaint in CAOM F80 1409, "Instructions relatives au retour en France des colons, 1849–1850"; CAOM F80 1792, Dutrône, "Rapport fait à la Commission des colonies agricoles de l'Algérie," 17 December 1849; Julien, *La conquête*, 367–73; Heffernan, "Parisian Poor," 392–93.

met these criteria to fill vacancies in the villages.[20] Although only a fraction of the original colonists remained, the population of the forty-two villages had returned to over ten thousand by the time the September decree expired on 31 December 1851.[21] Unassisted emigration continued throughout the Second Republic as well. Despite fluctuations due to disease and political unrest, Algeria's French population rose by nearly 25 percent, from 53,700 to 66,000, between the February Revolution and the end of 1851, and the European settler community as a whole increased in similar proportion from 104,000 to 131,000.[22]

The Second Empire, ushered in by Louis-Napoleon Bonaparte's coup d'état of 2 December 1851, is usually seen as a period of retrenchment in Algerian colonization. Guided by a Saint-Simonian belief in the complementarity of European and "Oriental" cultures, Napoleon III declared that "Algeria is not a colony, properly speaking, but an Arab kingdom." "I am as much the Emperor of the Arabs as the Emperor of the French," he continued, and as such his "native" subjects had as much right to his protection as the European settlers.[23] The areas open to European colonization and the government's role in emigration were therefore limited in the 1860s, and the Bureaux arabes were given broad powers to "protect" Algerians from the settlers and to "guide" them towards French civilization.[24]

Despite the Arabophile rhetoric of his "Arab kingdom" policy, the reign of Napoleon III saw a dramatic strengthening of settler colonialism in Algeria. Paradoxically, "policies instigated for the benefit of the indigenous population turned out in the end to be harmful to them," as Patricia Lorcin points out.[25] In particular, legislation intended to reinforce Algerian property rights actually made it easier for colonists to acquire land, and the amount of land in European hands increased more than sixfold from 115,000 hectares in 1850 to 765,000 hect-

---

20. AD Bas-Rhin 15M 63, ministre de l'Intérieur, circulars of 12 August 1850 and 31 July 1851; "Rapport fait par M. Passy, au nom de la commission du budget sur le projet de budget pour l'exercice 1852 (Dépenses)," 8 July 1851, CRANL, annexes to vol. 15, 233.
21. "Rapport fait par M. Thém. Lestidoubois, au nom de la commission chargée d'examiner le projet de loi tendant à ouvrir au ministre de la guerre un crédit de 300,000 fr. destiné à pourvoir à la continuation des colonies agricoles commencées en 1849, en Algérie, et au peuplement des centres," 10 June 1851, CRANL, annexes to vol. 14, 163–64; TEFA (1850–52), 260.
22. TEFA (1846–49), 92; (1850–52), 83.
23. Letter to gouverneur général Pélissier, 6 February 1863, in Œuvres de Napoléon III, vol. 5, Discours, proclamations, messages (Paris, 1869), 193.
24. Julien, La conquête, 376–77, 403–4; Patricia Lorcin, Imperial Identities: Stereotyping, Prejudice and Race in Colonial Algeria (1995; repr., London, 1999), 79–85; Osama Abi-Mershed, Apostles of Modernity: Saint-Simonians and the Civilizing Mission in Algeria (Stanford, 2010), 174–78.
25. Lorcin, Imperial Identities, 77.

ares in 1870.[26] At the same time, continued emigration and rising fertility nearly doubled the size of the settler population, giving rise in France to powerful new arguments for colonial emigration. Malthusianism gave way to fears of under-population after 1850, but economists and social reformers now began to argue, however counterintuitively, that settlement overseas would strengthen the French "race" and resuscitate the falling national birthrate.[27]

These changes came at deadly cost to Algeria's indigenous population. Algerian rural society crumbled under the massive land sequestrations that resulted from the Imperial reforms, leaving the tribes with few defenses against the disease and famine that followed in their wake. It is estimated that 20 to 25 percent of the 4.2 million Muslim Algerians died in the mid-1860s, as a direct result of the land transfers of the previous decade.[28] This terrible toll generated harsh criticism in some French humanitarian circles, and European settlement expanded less than it might have done because of these highly publicized attacks. But the growth in colonization was nonetheless tremendous, and the settler population became entrenched in French Algeria in these years. The census of 1872 counted 245,000 Europeans, including 130,000 French citizens, whose increase only accelerated under the Third Republic. By the eve of World War I, Algeria had 681,000 settlers, two-thirds of them French.[29] The proper relationship between France and its North African colony was still open to debate, but it had become a near-certainty in the minds of most Frenchmen that the relationship was permanent and was embodied in the hundreds of thousands of French citizens living on Algerian soil.

Equally important, that soil was now considered an integral part of the French national territory, organized into three departments where European civilians were governed by French law. Here too, it was the Second Republic that consolidated developments of the 1830s and 1840s into a solid armature for the full assimilation

26. Mahfoud Bennoune, *The Making of Contemporary Algeria, 1830–1987: Colonial Upheavals and Post-Independence Development* (Cambridge, 1988), 48–50.

27. Yves Charbit, "La population, la dépopulation et la colonisation en France," in *L'économie politique en France au XIXe siècle*, ed. Yves Breton and Michel Lutfalla (Paris, 1991), 452, 464; Margaret Cook Andersen, "A Colonial Fountain of Youth: Imperialism and France's Crisis of Depopulation, 1870–1940" (Ph.D. diss., University of Iowa, 2009).

28. André Nouschi, *Enquête sur le niveau de vie des populations rurales constantinoises de la conquête jusqu'en 1919: Essai d'histoire économique et sociale* (Paris, 1961), bk. 3; Bertrand Taithe, "Humanitarianism and Colonialism: Religious Responses to the Algerian Drought and Famine of 1866–1870," in *Natural Disasters, Cultural Responses: Case Studies toward a Global Environmental History*, ed. Christoph Mauch and Christian Pfister (Lanham, 2009), 137–65.

29. Kamel Kateb, *Européens, "indigènes" et juifs en Algérie (1830–1962): Représentations et réalités des populations* (Paris, 2001), 187. These figures do not include naturalized Algerian Jews, who numbered 34,574 in 1872 and 70,211 in 1911.

of Algeria to metropolitan France. Just days after Louis-Philippe's abdication, the Provisional Government proclaimed to the *colons* that "the Republic will defend Algeria like the soil of France itself" and "the progressive assimilation of Algerian institutions to those of the metropole . . . will be the object of the most serious deliberations of the National Assembly." French citizens in Algeria were accorded the right to elect representatives to the National Constituent Assembly, and the constitution produced by that body in November declared Algeria to be part of the national territory that would eventually be placed under direct legislative control and civilian rule by metropolitan law.[30] A series of measures in the fall of 1848 began to reassign jurisdiction over Algerian affairs to the appropriate metropolitan ministries and reorganized the colony's administrative structure according to the metropolitan system of departments, arrondissements, and communes.[31] Although the July Monarchy had itself begun to draft an assimilation law, the architects of the Second Republic's Algerian policy celebrated these measures as a realization of republican ideals. A monarchy might colonize in order to dominate and an aristocratic regime to usurp the profits of monopolistic trade, but

> a democracy sees in the colonists sons as dear as those who remained on the old national territory. It assimilates them to itself by institutions and laws; it demands from them the same obligations for the same rights. The colonists are a democracy [themselves], a means of diminishing the exuberant intensity of the population and balancing its well-being. . . . Under the fecundity of these principles, Algeria will soon be not a magnificent and profitable possession for France, but a rich part of France herself.[32]

As historians of French colonial law have appreciated—and contemporaries clearly recognized—the assimilation of 1848 was partial: political rights were extended only to natural-born or naturalized French men, while administrative assimilation covered only the European *colons*. Departmentalization differentiated *territoires civiles*, where European settlement was concentrated and civilian rule applied, from *territoires militaires*, populated by few Europeans, in which military administration of indigenous Algerians would continue. In some re-

30. "Proclamation du Gouvernement provisoire aux colons de l'Algérie," 2 March 1848, and "Instruction du Gouvernement provisoire pour l'exécution, en Algérie, du décret du 5 mars 1848, relatif aux élections générales," 12 March 1848, in Carrey, *Recueil,* 43, 118–27; François Luchaire, *Naissance d'une constitution: 1848* (Paris, 1998), 157–60, 238.

31. Julien, *La conquête,* 349–54; André Mallarmé, *L'organisation gouvernementale de l'Algérie* (Paris, 1900), 27–28.

32. CAOM F80 1792, Commission des colonies agricoles de l'Algérie, "Rapport sur les opérations de 1848," 24 January 1849.

spects, the regime of differential rights that had prevailed in France itself under the July Monarchy was now given new life in Algeria, with race and religion replacing property in defining the boundaries of French citizenship. These limits were gradually extended in the ensuing decades: the government of National Defense conferred French nationality on Algerian Jews in 1871, and non-French European settlers were naturalized en masse by the Third Republic's Nationality Law of 1889. But even after the colony's "Muslim indigenes" were recognized as French nationals by *sénatus-consulte* in 1865, they remained subjects whose "nationality was denatured [and] emptied of its rights." The *sénatus-consulte* offered them the possibility of "naturalization" as full citizens, but only if they renounced the personal status that allowed them to remain subject to Islamic law in civil affairs.[33] The exclusion of Algerians is revealing of the ways that empire challenged universalist French conceptions of nationality, but colonial citizenship law was equally significant as an affirmation of the settlers' incorporation into the French body politic. By extending citizenship to the *colons*, the Second Republic ratified and strengthened the idea that "Algeria must be nothing other than a continuation of France over the Mediterranean."[34] Its implementation was long and uneven, but this principle would not be seriously challenged again until the beginning of the Algerian War of Independence in 1954.

The intimate ties between settlement and assimilation, as well as their symbolic entanglement with the military conquest of the previous decades, was expressed with great clarity in the public rituals surrounding the colonization scheme of 1848. Republican officials organized elaborate departure ceremonies for each of the sixteen convoys of colonists that left Paris in the fall of 1848. Designed to maximize public awareness of the colonization scheme, these were events of mixed solemnity and joy that drew thousands of family, friends, and curiosity seekers to the banks of the Seine to bid farewell to the new *colons* (fig. 55). They were also, as speakers reminded the crowds, intended to consecrate the ties that had developed between France and Algeria since 1830. Newspapers, engravings, and *canards* brought the farewell ceremonies to thousands more and offer historians a detailed account of the speeches and rituals that composed them.

Running through all of the ceremonies was an affirmation of Algeria's status as part of the French *patrie* and of the departing colonists' uninterrupted mem-

33. Patrick Weil, *Qu'est-ce qu'un Français? Histoire de la nationalité française depuis la Révolution* (Paris, 2002), 225; Laure Blévis, "Les avatars de la citoyenneté en Algérie coloniale ou les paradoxes d'une catégorisation," *Droit et Société* 48 (2001): 557–80; Todd Shepard, *The Invention of Decolonization: The Algerian War and the Remaking of France* (Ithaca, 2006).
34. Colonists' petition of 1840, quoted in Mallarmé, *L'organisation*, 26.

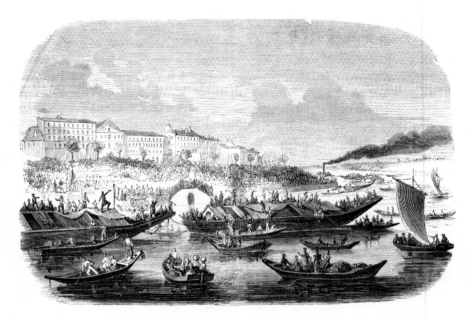

FIGURE 55. *Departure of the First Convoy of Algerian Colonists from Bercy, 8 October 1848*, in *L'Illustration*, 14 October 1848. Courtesy University of Iowa Libraries, Special Collections.

bership in the republican national community.[35] Each convoy received from the hands of the minister of war or another dignitary a tricolor flag blessed by the archbishop of Paris. Planted in the center of their new Algerian village, the banner would symbolize the providential and fraternal bond between the settlement and the Parisian homes the colonists were leaving behind. Speeches by parliamentary, ministerial, municipal, and clerical dignitaries reminded the *colons* of the benefits the Republic had bestowed on them, the prosperous future that awaited all who committed themselves to work Algeria's rich soil, and above all, the sacrifices that had made Algeria part of France. War Minister Lamoricière's speech to the first convoy, which left Paris on 1 October, captures perfectly the ways that the Republic mobilized the language of military sacrifice. The republican virtue of *fraternité*, Lamoricière declared, required that the new *colons* take up the standard previously carried by their brothers-in-arms in the Armée d'Afrique: "It is now up to you to guarantee to [the *patrie*] the possession of this conquest that cost her so much gold and blood. It is up to intelligent and civilizing labor to achieve what

35. My account is based on *Départ des colons pour l'Algérie* (Paris, 1848); "Histoire de la semaine," *L'Illustration*, 11 October 1848.

force began. Powder and the bayonet have done what they had to do in Algeria, and it is up to the hoe and the plow to finish their task." Conquest and colonization, which had been given mutually reinforcing meanings during the 1830s and 1840s, now merged into a single patriotic mission to restore the fertility of the Algerian land. On arrival in Africa, Lamoricière begged the emigrants, they should offer "a tear or a prayer for that poor child of the people, your brother, who has died for the *patrie* and sacrificed himself entirely so that you might one day, without even knowing his name, reap the fruits of his courage and devotion."

The colonists of 1848 would fulfill these emotional appeals only in part, and the settler community would wait until 1881 for total administrative *rattachement* and civilian rule—as well as full political exclusion of Muslim Algerians under the *code de l'indigénat*—but ceremonies and speeches like this one reflected the power that the patriotic logics of sacrifice and fertilization had gained by 1848. Together, they had driven the processes of conquest and colonization during the July Monarchy, despite significant opposition to their costs and consequences. The Second Republic now consolidated them into a formidable symbolic force that would sustain French policies of emigration and settlement through the rest of the century. "Native affairs" officers in the Bureaux arabes protested the destructive impact of colonization on the indigenous people, Algerians fought colonists' incursions on their land, and French humanitarians attacked the settlers' voracious appetite for land and power. Nevertheless the European population continued to grow with the active support of the French state.

Because settler colonialism is a structure rather than an event, as Patrick Wolfe argues,[36] these developments had a decisive impact on both Algerian colonial society and Algeria's relationship with France. By aiming to occupy land rather than exploit its inhabitants' labor and to create new societies rather than control existing ones, settler colonialism roots deeper into social, political, and physical landscapes than do colonies of extractive exploitation. Once established, its structural nature makes settler colonialism far more tenacious than other imperial forms and increases the likelihood that decolonization will require extraordinary violence.[37] French Algeria was a textbook case of this pattern. Despite their often humble origins, the *Français d'Algérie* came to enjoy tremendous economic privilege that was defended by their elected representatives and a pow-

---

36. Patrick Wolfe, *Settler Colonialism and the Transformation of Anthropology: The Politics and Poetics of an Ethnographic Event* (London, 1999).
37. Caroline Elkins, "Race, Citizenship, and Governance: Settler Tyranny and the End of Empire," in *Settler Colonialism in the Twentieth Century: Projects, Practices, Legacies,* ed. Caroline Elkins and Susan Pedersen (New York, 2005), 203; Ian Lustick, *Unsettled States, Disputed Lands: Britain and Ireland, France and Algeria, Israel and the West Bank–Gaza* (Ithaca, 1993); Shepard, *Invention,* pt. 3.

erful lobby in Paris, and their sense of familial affinity with the metropole was strengthened by the assimilationist fiction that Algeria was part of France itself. As a consequence, it took eight years of fighting for Algerian nationalists to uproot the settlers in the twentieth century, and the horrific violence of that struggle left scars that endure long after the Evian Accords recognized Algerian independence in 1962. The Algerian War gave birth to new regimes on both sides of the Mediterranean, and the trauma of that conflict now stands at the heart of political culture and historical debate in both postcolonial states. The founding myths of the independent Algerian Republic are grounded in the revolutionary struggle of the National Liberation Front, while the Fifth Republic has been marked by cultural schisms opened up by the French army's use of torture during the war, the repatriation of 1.1 million *colons*, and the immigration of thousands of Algerian Muslims accorded French citizenship in a last-ditch effort to stave off independence.[38] For these reasons alone, it is important to understand how Algeria came to be a colony of large-scale European settlement under French rule. But as I hope the preceding chapters have shown, the origins of French Algeria are equally critical to a full understanding of the history of France in the nineteenth century.

It has been argued that the "allure of empire" in nineteenth-century France lay in its power to distract public attention from the conflicts roiling the postrevolutionary polity. Imperialism "function[ed] as a surrogate, mask and displacement of Revolution," and constituted a unifying national mission that transcended the political divisions of the day.[39] Such an interpretation only partially captures the political dynamics of empire in these decades. The conquest and colonization of Algeria were intimately entwined with postrevolutionary politics, and the colonies did function to a certain extent as a screen onto which domestic anxieties were projected. But imperialism was far more than a simple displacement of political tensions. In the process of projection, imperialism and domestic politics became one. To the men who laid the foundations of the new French empire in Africa, imperial conquest and settlement enacted fundamental principles of sovereignty and citizenship, whether those principles were legitimist, Orleanist,

---

38. The literature on the Algerian War's legacy is rapidly growing. See, among others, James McDougall, *History and the Culture of Nationalism in Algeria* (Cambridge, 2006); Shepard, *Invention*; Jeannine Verdès-Leroux, *Les Français d'Algérie de 1830 à aujourd'hui: Une page d'histoire déchirée* (Paris, 2001); Patricia Lorcin, ed., *Algeria and France, 1800–2000: Identity, Memory, Nostalgia* (Syracuse, 2006); Andrea Smith, *Colonial Memory and Postcolonial Europe: Maltese Settlers in Algeria and France* (Bloomington, 2006); Benjamin Stora, *La guerre des mémoires: La France face à son passé colonial* (La Tour d'Aigues, 2007).
39. Todd Porterfield, *The Allure of Empire: Art in the Service of French Imperialism, 1798–1836* (Princeton, 1998), 5.

Bonapartist, or republican. The intimacy of this linkage made empire integral to French political life throughout the modern period.

Imperialism was not necessarily a unifying force, however. As domestic political culture changed, the meanings of imperial expansion shifted and gave rise to new conflicts on both sides of the Mediterranean. Legitimist Bourbons, "bourgeois" Orleanists, radical republicans, and authoritarian Bonapartists all endorsed and extended French colonial rule in Algeria, but they presented their actions through the very different lenses of divine kingship, royal meritocracy, republican fraternity, and Saint-Simonian paternalism, respectively. Members of the French public countered official stagings of the conquest with their own interpretations of the conquest as an embodiment of popular Bonapartism, which endowed military service and colonial settlement alike with the "values of 1789": individual male liberty, autonomy, and citizenship. To understand the origins of French colonization in Algeria, then, and especially the genesis of its unique status as a colony of European settlement and an integral part of the national territory, we must look not to a transcendent imperial ideology, but to the intimate and dynamic interactions between empire and a political culture that increasingly encompassed both metropole and colony.

Selected Bibliography of
Primary Sources

ARCHIVAL AND VISUAL SOURCES

Archives Condé, Chantilly

Ms 1349–52. Frédéric Nepveu, reports on Louis-Philippe's visits to Versailles, 1833–47
Bibliothèque 50. Henri Philippoteaux, *Album: le Duc d'Aumale en Algérie* (1840)

Archives de la Préfecture de Police, Paris

D^B 77. Passeports
D^B 364. Émigration

Archives départementales de l'Ain, Bourg-en-Bresse

4M 31. Police administrative: Troubles particuliers, 1832–56
4M 224. Police: Passeports, 1800–1890
Belley 2I 2, 5. Archives communales de Belley: Passeports, An VIII–1909

Archives départementales des Alpes-de-Haute-Provence, Digne-les-Bains

6M 26. Émigration: Demandes de concessions en Algérie, 1843–1908

Archives départementales de l'Ardèche, Privas

10M 222. Émigration en Algérie

Archives départementales de l'Ariège, Foix

10M 15, 17, 18/1. Colonisation de l'Algérie: Instructions et circulaires, états nominatifs, demandes de concessions, correspondance, 1832–89

Archives départementales de l'Aude, Carcassonne

1MD 407. Affaires militaires: Troubles associés au 17e léger en garnison à Limoux, 1834
1MD 410. Administration générale: Événements locaux, monarchie de juillet (E–L)
4E 069/I68. Archives municipales de Carcassonne: Programmes et affiches des fêtes publiques, 1807–47

Archives départementales du Bas-Rhin, Strasbourg

3M 20. Police: Contrôle de l'esprit public (expédition de l'Algérie)
3M 672, 678, 680–706. Police: Passeports, secours de route, émigration et colonisation, passages gratuits et concessions de terre, 1822–70
15M 24. Esprit public, seconde restauration
15M 63. Colonisation de l'Algérie, 1839–1865
15M 199. Répression du vagabondage et de la mendicité; saltimbanques, colportage, An XI–1868

Archives départementales des Bouches-du-Rhône, Marseille

1M 546, 553. Cabinet du préfet: Affaires politiques, correspondance générale, 1819–46
1M 582. Fêtes et cérémonies officielles, 1830–43
1M 585. Voyages officiels et privés, 1831–47
1M 1093. Colonisation de l'Algérie: Correspondance et réglementation, 1848–52
6M 527–28. Colonisation et concessions de terre en Algérie, 1838–57

Archives départementales de la Charente-Maritime, La Rochelle

8M 3/1. Émigration pour l'Algérie, 1831–1924

Archives départementales de la Corrèze, Tulle

6M 400–408. Colonisation en Algérie: Instructions, correspondance, secours de route, passages gratuits, enquête statistique, 1830–1923

Archives départementales de la Côte-d'Or, Dijon

1M 256. Événements politiques, Restauration: Prise d'Alger, 1830
1M 453. Fêtes publiques: *Te Deum* pour la prise d'Alger, 1830
1M 500. Voyages officiels: Personnalités françaises, Monarchie de Juillet

1M 567. Hommages particuliers où intéressant pas le seul département

20M 470–71. Colonisation et émigration: Secours aux colons et voyageurs, 1847–81

E dépôt 404/32. Commune de Ménétreux-le-Pitois: Police, misc.

E dépôt 432/31. Commune de Montigny-sur-Vigneanne: Population

M13 XI/1. Colonisation de l'Algérie, agriculture

SM 8452–53. Colonisation et émigration: Agences d'émigration, 1831–1926

Archives départementales des Côtes-d'Armor, Saint-Brieuc

6M 809. Colonisation agricole de l'Algérie, 1839–77

Archives départementales de la Dordogne, Périgueux

6M 429–30. Population: Émigration en Algérie, à l'étranger ou aux colonies, 1845–96

1T 277. Colportage: Instructions et affaires générales, 1815–1914

1T 280*. Presse, déclarations d'imprimeurs, dépôt légal, 1836–41

2Z 140. Sous-préfecture de Nontron: Affaires politiques et confidentielles, 1830–47

Archives départementales du Doubs, Besançon

M 1176. Haute police [fêtes publiques, affaires politiques]

M 1234–35. Passeports

4T 120, 128. Théâtres: 17e–9e arrondissement théâtral, Montbéliard, An IX–1868

Archives départementales de la Drôme, Valence

6M 542–50. Colonisation de l'Algérie, 1831–1914

6 Ma 3. Algérie et colonies: Émigrations, An V–1891

12T 6/1A. Colportage, 1806–53

Archives départementales du Gard, Nîmes

4M 674, 705, 711. Police: Passeports, secours de route, 1844–50

6M 393, 397, 406. Colonisation de l'Algérie: Instructions, correspondance, concessions, passages gratuits, 1848–84

6M 747. États numériques des français émigrés en Algérie, 1842–44

Archives départementales de la Gironde, Bordeaux

8J 65. Conquête de l'Algérie, XIXe siècle

Archives départementales du Haut-Rhin, Colmar

1 M 81. Réactions de l'opinion publique à la conquête de l'Algérie, 1830

4M 117–18, 125, 137. Police: Passeports, instructions, correspondance, demandes, 1801–59
6M 349. Émigration: Instructions, correspondance, 1834–70
6M 354–68. Émigration vers l'Algérie, 1830–69
6M 376. Émigration vers d'autres destinations, 1801–64
1Z 380, 382. Sous-préfecture d'Altkirch: Population, émigration, 1808–70

Archives départementales de la Haute-Garonne, Toulouse

4M 57. Police: Événements politiques, colonisation de l'Algérie, 1830–45
6M 754–57, 762. Population: Colonisation de l'Algérie, concessions de terres 1845–1912

Archives départementales de la Haute-Marne, Chaumont

85M 7. Émigration en Algérie, 1831–64

Archives départementales de la Haute-Saône, Vesoul

550E dépôt 999. Algérie, enquête statistique, 1844

Archives départementales de la Haute-Vienne, Limoges

6M 284. Émigration en Algérie, 1847–1901

Archives départementales des Hautes-Pyrénées, Tarbes

4M 282, 284. Police: Passeports, An VIII–1874
6M 175, 179. Population: Émigration, agences, 1810–1929
E dépôt Vic-Bigorre/I47. Archives communales de Vic-en-Bigorre: Police, passage gratuit en Algérie, 1841–86

Archives départementales du Jura, Montmorot

6M 1061–62. Passeports et émigration, 1844–51

Archives départementales de la Loire, Saint-Étienne

1M 575. Voyages officiels, 1830–45
6M 759, 762–65. Colonisation: Circulaires et instructions, passages gratuits, concessions de terres, 1841–1938
T 1883–85, 1904. Théâtres, 1833–53

Archives départementales de la Loire-Atlantique, Nantes

1M 1783–84. Émigration pour la colonisation de l'Algérie, 1831–99

Archives départementales du Loiret, Orléans

O suppl. 509 1M 3. Archives communales de Malesherbes: Édifices communaux, statue du capitaine Lelièvre
O suppl. 509 5M 5–7. Archives communales de Malesherbes: Bâtiments militaires et commémoratifs, défense de Mazagran

Archives départementales du Lot, Cahors

6M 317. États des émigrés en Algérie, 1844

Archives départementales de la Meurthe-et-Moselle, Nancy

1M 659. Fêtes publiques, Restauration
4M 234. Passeports, An VIII–1859
6M 290. Colonisation: Généralités, Algérie, 1830–97
2Z 87. Sous-préfecture de Lunéville: Émigration en Algérie, 1838–1911

Archives départementales de la Meuse, Bar-le-Duc

6M 95–96. Population: Colonisation et émigration, 1831–1921
146M 1, 3. Police: Passeports à l'intérieur, An XII–1871
2Z 228. Sous-préfecture de Commercy: Départs pour l'Algérie et la Nouvelle Calédonie, 1850–1912
E dépôt 460 I2. Archives communales de Bar: Passages gratuits en Algérie, 1841–48

Archives départementales de la Moselle, Saint-Julien-lès-Metz

88M 1/2. Émigrants: Affaires diverses, états, 1837–39
95M 1/2. Émigrants: Rapatriement des émigrants sans ressources, 1810–70
106M 1–2. Passeports: Instructions, correspondance, An VIII–1870
110M. Remise de passeports et de secours de route aux indigents, 1808–70
1T 95. Dépôt légal: Images déposées, 1848
1T 103*. Librairie et imprimerie: Registre des déclarations et des dépôts, 1840–57

Archives départementales des Pyrénées-Orientales, Perpignan

6M 371. Colonisation et déportation en Algérie, XIXe siècle–1940

Archives départementales du Rhône, Lyon

1M 164. Fêtes publiques, 1837–48
4M 397. Demandes de passeports, 1830–54
4M 406. Police des étrangers, émigration en Algérie

6Mp 2/1. Colonisation: Affaires diverses, généralités
6Mp 2/4–5. Colonisation de l'Algérie: Passages gratuits, dossiers individuels, 1846–59

Archives départementales de Saône-et-Loire, Mâcon

M1 639. Colonisation en Algérie, 1831–76

Archives départementales de la Seine-Maritime, Rouen

6M 849–50, 854. Émigration: Généralités, rapports, statistiques, agences, recrutement, transports, 1825–1906
6M 858–64. Colonisation de l'Algérie: Dossiers individuels et collectifs

Archives départementales du Var, Draguignan

6M 18/4. Cérémonies publiques, 1831–48
7M 5/1–2. Passeports, 1814–82
11M 3/1–5. Colonisation de l'Algérie, 1835–1909
3Z 171. Sous-préfecture de Toulon: Affaires militaires, recrutement, expédition d'Alger

Archives départementales de la Vaucluse, Avignon

1M 877. Fêtes publiques: Cérémonies, Restauration
6M 324–25. Population: Colonisation et émigration, 1834–99

Archives départementales des Vosges, Épinal

15M 51. Émigration, 1839–84
26R 1–3. Algérie: Renseignements statistiques, demandes de passages gratuits, 1838–57

Archives départementales des Yvelines, Versailles

4M 2/24. Colonisation de l'Algérie, 1830–49
5M 71. Passeports, 1802–61

Archives municipales de Lyon, Lyon

3WP 216 1. Commune de la Croix-Rousse: Émigration vers l'Algérie, 1850–51
4WP 59 2. Commune de La Guillotière: Passage de colons en Afrique, 1844–51
4WP 90 4. Commune de La Guillotière: Secours aux colons, 1837–44
469 WP 6. Monuments: Statue du sergent Blandan, 1842–85
784 WP 1. Colonisation de l'Algérie, 1848–49
Fi. Série iconographique: Affiches

Archives municipales de Marseille, Marseille

1D 61. Délibérations du Conseil municipal, April 1835
13F 1. Population: Colonisation de l'Algérie, 1828–39
1I 672–73. Fêtes publiques, 1844–56

Archives municipales de Nantes, Nantes

I2 C 14, dossier 10. Police: Passeports et permis de passage gratuit pour l'Algérie, 1831–60

Archives municipales de Paris, Paris

V.D6 171. Mairie du 2e arrondissement (ancien): Colons pour l'Algérie, 1832–60

Archives municipales de Strasbourg, Strasbourg

271MW 67. Police: Émigrés en Algérie, 1836–47

Archives des Musées nationaux, Paris

P30 3, 9. Fonds Delaroche-Vernet: Correspondance et voyages d'Horace Vernet, 1824–58
V0–4. Musée de Versailles: Histoire, correspondance, catalogues, acquisitions, 1792–1970

Archives nationales de France, Paris

82AP 5, 20. Papiers Bro de Comères: Campagnes d'Algérie, correspondance
222AP 3. Fonds La Bonninière de Beaumont: Commission de l'Algérie
223AP 17. Fonds Berryer: Territoires d'outre-mer
238AP 2. Papiers Trézel: Trézel en Algérie, 1831–37
270AP 1^, doss. 2. Papiers Chanzy: Voyage de Paris à Alger, 1839–40
281AP 1–2. Papiers Édouard Charton
300AP III 40–41, 43, 45, 48, 51, 85, 102, 114, 119, 168–70, 172. Fonds de la Maison de France (branche d'Orléans). Affaires du roi Louis-Philippe: Correspondance familiale, correspondance politique, papiers militaires
300AP IV 172, 174, 192, 198–99, 210. Fonds de la Maison de France (branche d'Orléans). Fonds Nemours: Correspondance, voyages, affaires militaires
C 898–99. Chambre des députés: Commission d'Afrique, Budget 1847
C 2100–226. Chambre des députés: Pétitions, 1830–48
C 2425–31*. Chambre des députés: Enregistrement des pétitions, 1830–48
F7 3884–93. Police générale: Bulletins de Paris, 1830–47
F7 6760. Police générale: Voyages des membres de la famille royale, 1827–30

F7 6767–72. Police générale: Esprit public, situation politique des départements, 1815–30

F13 1022. Bâtiments civils: Fêtes de juillet, 1836–39.

F21 717–19. Beaux-Arts: Fêtes publiques et nationales, 1799–1847

O4 1723–24, 1789, 1916, 1972. Maison du Roi: Voyages des princes, 1837–41

Bibliothèque nationale de France, Département des Estampes et de la photographie, Paris

Collection De Vinck

Collection Hennin

Li 59. Images d'Épinal de l'Imprimerie de Pellerin, 1810–57

Nz-42 (2)-Boîte fol. Benjamin Roubaud, *Souvenirs d'Afrique* (Paris: Gihaut frères, 1842)

Of 2 a. Commandant Leblanc [and possibly Baccuët]. Album d'Afrique, dessins, 1837

Pd. Fêtes et cérémonies publiques

Qb 1. Histoire de France

SNR 1. Genet (A.). Alexandre Genet

Tf. Caricatures politiques

Centre des archives d'outre-mer, Aix-en-Provence

Séries géographiques

Afrique IV/5. Algérie, 1783–1872; colonisation, 1830–72

Archives ministérielles

F80 9–10. Commission d'Afrique, 1833–34

F80 1128–30. Commission de Colonisation de l'Algérie, 1842–49

F80 1131. Projets de colonisation, 1838–60

F80 1161–67. Colonisation (mémoires, projets, rapports), 1830–49

F80 1177. Émigration en général, 1843–47

F80 1179. Subventions aux colons, 1844–57

F80 1237. Passages, affaires générales, 1837–57

F80 1253. Dépôts d'ouvriers, 1835–58

F80 1303, 1306, 1313, 1372, 1390–91, 1399–1400. Colonies agricoles, 1848–53

F80 1332–39. Colons, 1841–48

F80 1409. Ouvriers d'art, retours en France, 1848–55

F80 1584. Souscriptions diverses: Statue du duc d'Orléans, 1842

F80 1586–99. Commission scientifique de l'Algérie, 1835–65

F80 1670 (1)–1676. Colonisation (notes, plans, rapports), 1830–50

F80 1733. Publications conçernant l'Algérie, 1833–1908

F80 1791–93. Colonisation (projets, rapports, mémoires), 1835–93; immigration et créations de centres, 1838–69

F80 1804. Émigration étrangère, 1847–48

F80 1998–2000*. Passages, demandes d'autorisation, 1841–47

Gouvernement-Général de l'Algérie

1E. Cabinet du Gouverneur-Général: Correspondance politique, 1830–47
2E. Fonds Bugeaud: Correspondance politique, 1836–49
2EE. Fonds Bugeaud: Registres de correspondance, 1841–47
L 1–16, 32, 37, 61, 65. Colonisation, 1832–54
6L 13–43. Projets de colonisation
32L 44. Colonisation: Principes, instructions, programmes, 1830–1914
6X 8. Papiers Pelet
18X 18, 23, 53, 56, 65, 68, 84, 89. Collection Merle: Clauzel, Dauzats, Lelièvre, Louis-Philippe, Morris, Aumale, Thiers, Vernet

Département d'Alger

5M 1. Colonisation, instructions, circulaires ministériels, 1841–76

État-civil de l'Algérie

Digitized registers, http://anom.archivesnationales.culture.gouv.fr/caomec2

Archives privées

83 APC 1. Fonds Musée de la France d'Outre-Mer: Collection d'autographies

Séries Iconographiques

7Fi 4–5. Images d'Épinal
7Fi 17. Auguste Raffet, *Marche sur Constantine, octobre 1847* (Paris: Gihaut, 1838)
8Fi 6. *25 Lithographies de Canquoin, Toulon, d'après croquis de Letuaire et Courdouan* (c. 1856)
8Fi 7. Guyon, *D'Alger aux Ziban* (lithograph album, 1850)
8Fi 11. *Souvenirs de l'Algérie: Vues et costumes. Vues prises au Daguerréotype par Bettinger et lithographiées par Mrs. Champin et H. Walter* (Paris: Wild, [c. 1845–47])
8Fi 12. R. Jungmann, *Costumes, mœurs et usages des Algériens: Ouvrage orné de 40 lithographies* (Strasbourg, 1837)
8Fi 20. Album de croquis et dessins par un capitaine du 41ème de Ligne, 1839
8Fi 425. Gobaut, album d'aquarelles, Campagnes de Mascara, 1835
8Fi 426. Gobaut, album d'aquarelles, Campagnes du duc d'Orléans, 1835, 1846
8Fi 458. Gobaut, album d'aquarelles, Campagnes du duc de Nemours en Algérie, 1840
21X 1C. Ben[jamin] Schauenberg, *Aquarelle de Birmandreis,* 1833

Getty Research Institute, Special Collections, Los Angeles

850807. Louis-Philippe, King of the French, letters and memoranda, 1817–28
860593. Musées royaux de France, letters received, 1819–71
860751. Horace Vernet, letters, 1812–55
870473. Henri d'Orléans, duc d'Aumale, letters, ca. 1841–71

Fac Simile des tableaux exposés au Salon de 1839, sous les nos. 2050, 2051 et 2052, par M. Horace Vernet, et représentant le Siège de Constantine (Paris: Vinchon, Impr. des musées royaux, 1839)

Musée ou magasin comique de Philipon: contenant 800 dessins par Cham de N . . . , Eustache, Fontallard (Charles), Forest, Gavarni, Grandville, Jacque, Provost-Dumarchais, Ch. Vernier; Testes par MM. Cham de N. . . . , L. Huard, Des O. . . . . , E. Martus et Ch. Philipon (Paris: Aubert, [1842–43])

Musée de la Civilisation de l'Europe et de la Méditerranée, Paris and Marseille

Collections of *imagerie populaire*

Musée nationale de Versailles, Versailles

Works from the African galleries
MV. Documentation files for works from the African galleries

Service historique de la Défense, Vincennes

E5 172. Ministère de la Guerre, correspondance générale: Voyages des princes en Algérie
1H 1–105. Expéditions d'Outre-Mer, Algérie: Correspondance, 1830–45
1H 225–28. Expéditions d'Outre-Mer, Algérie: Mémoires diverses, 1830–39
1H 391. Expéditions d'Outre-Mer, Algérie: Colonisation
1M 1317–19. Dépôt de la Guerre: Mémoires et reconnaissances, Algérie, 1796–1864
1M 2068, 2070, 2074. Papiers Pelet: Correspondance, discours, travaux, 1831–45
1M 2371. Musée de Versailles, aquarelles Bagetti
3M 66, 125–26, 138, 139, 141, 181, 231–33. Dépôt de la Guerre: Correspondance, notes et rapports au ministre de la Guerre, 1829–53
3M 881. Dépôt de la Guerre: Mémoires, Algérie, 1732–45

Dossiers du personnel

6Yd 49. Maréchal de Saint-Arnaud
7Yd 1096. Baron Pelet
3Yf 70408. Alexandre Genet
5Yg 62. Félix Mornand
6Yg 25. George Julien Fellmann

Collections iconographiques

Gb 33. Ferdinand de Trélo, Vues d'Alger (1831–32)
SH/D 77–95, 77bis–95bis. Dessins d'Alexandre Genet, aquarelles par Jung (c. 1830–37)
SH/D 96–121. Duboc, Vues d'Oran (1831–32)
SH/D 122–97. Album, Vues du Capitaine Genet

PRINTED GOVERNMENT DOCUMENTS

Archives parlementaires de 1787 à 1860: Recueil complet des débats législatifs & politiques des Chambres françaises. Seconde série: 1800–1860. Edited by J. Madival and E. Laurent. 127 vols. Paris: Paul Dupont, 1862–1913.

Bulletin des lois du Royaume de France. Paris: Impr. royale, 1830–48.

Carrey, Émile ed. *Recueil complet des actes du gouvernement provisoire (février, mars, avril, mai 1848). . . .* Paris: Auguste Durand, 1848.

Code civil. République française, http://www.legifrance.gouv.fr/affichCode.do?cidTexte=LEGITEXT000006070721.

Colonisation de l'Ex-Régence d'Alger. Documens officiels déposés sur le bureau de la Chambre des députés: 1° Rapport sur la colonisation; 2° Extraits des rapports sur l'occupation militaire, les travaux publics, l'organisation judiciaire, les douanes, les domaines, les impôts, la marine, l'administration; 3° Rapport de la Grande Commission d'Afrique; 4° Discours de M. de la Pinsonnière, prononcé à la Chambre des députés le 29 avril 1834. Avec une carte de l'État d'Alger. Paris: Delaunay, 1834.

Commission de colonisation de l'Algérie. *Rapport fait au nom de la première sous-commission par M. Macarel, sur le domaine en Algérie. Le 21 juin 1842.* Paris: Impr. royale, 1843.

——. *Rapport fait au nom de la seconde sous-commission par M. Gustave de Beaumont, le 20 juin 1842: Organisation civile, administrative, municipale et judiciaire.* Paris: Impr. royale, 1843.

——. *Rapport fait au nom de la troisième sous-commission par M. Lingay, le 3 juin 1842: Sécurité, salubrité, desséchements, villages et enceinte.* Paris: Impr. royale, 1843.

——. *Rapport fait au nom de la quatrième sous-commission par M. Magnier de Maisonneuve, le 15 février 1843: Régime commercial, impôts directs et indirects, organisation des services financiers.* Paris: Impr. royale, 1843.

Commission de colonisation de la Guyane Française. *Extrait du procès-verbal de la séance du 4 mars 1842: Explications présentées par M. Jules Lechevalier.* Paris: Impr. de C. Bajat, 1842.

Compte-rendu des séances de l'Assemblée nationale: Exposés des motifs et projets de lois présentés par le gouvernement; rapports de MM. les représentants. 10 vols. Paris: Impr. de l'Assemblée nationale and Panckoucke, 1848–49.

Compte-rendu des séances de l'Assemblée nationale législative: Exposés des motifs et projets de lois présentés par le gouvernement; rapports de MM. les représentants. 17 vols. Paris: Panckoucke, 1849–51.

Documents statistiques relatifs aux Possessions Françaises dans le Nord de l'Afrique (Exécution de l'article 5 de la loi du 23 mai 1834). [Paris, 1836].

Godechot, Jacques, ed. *Les constitutions de la France depuis 1789.* Paris: Garnier-Flammarion, 1970.

Martineau des Chesnez, Auguste. *Affaires de l'Algérie: Rapport au Ministre sur les travaux de la réunion intérieure formée par décision de M. le Maréchal duc de Dalmatie en date du octobre 1843.* Paris: Impr. royale, 1843.

Peyerimhoff, Henri de. *Enquête sur les résultats de la colonisation officielle de 1871 à 1895: Rapport à Monsieur Jonnart, gouverneur général de l'Algérie.* Algiers: Impr. de Torrent, 1906.

Procès-verbaux des séances de la Chambre des députés. Paris: Impr. A. Henry, 1831–48.

Procès-verbaux et rapports de la Commission d'Afrique instituée par ordonnance du Roi du 12 décembre 1833. Paris: Impr. royale, 1834.

Programme des instructions pour la Commission spéciale à envoyer en Afrique, 22 juin 1833. Paris: A. Henry, April 1834.

Recueil des actes du gouvernement de l'Algérie, 1830–1854. Algiers: Impr. du Gouvernement, 1856.

Tableau de la situation des établissements français dans l'Algérie. 19 vols. Paris: Impr. royale, 1838–68.

OTHER PUBLISHED PRIMARY SOURCES

À l'Armée d'Afrique! Une Victoire, ou la prise d'Alger. Paris: Selligue, 1830.

À l'Assemblée nationale: Pétition et projet de colonisation en Algérie par associations temporaires, présentes au nom de 20,000 familles. Août 1848. Paris: A. Appert, 1848.

Abinal, [Joseph-Auguste]. *Relation de l'attaque et de la défense de Mostaganem et de Mazagran au mois de février 1840.* Paris: G. Laguionie et J. Dumaine, 1843.

Achard. *Algérie: Projet de colonisation présenté par M. Achard, membre du Conseil général du département du Bas-Rhin.* Paris: Impr. royale, May 1842.

Album de vues et paysages: Petit voyage pittoresque et en zig-zag de Paris aux Îles Marquises. Paris: Magasin des familles, 1850.

Album du Salon 1844: Collection des principaux ouvrages exposés au Louvre reproduits par les artistes eux-mêmes ou sous leur direction. Paris: Challamel, 1844.

Alby, Ernest. *La captivité du Trompette Escoffier.* 2 vols. Paris: Roux, 1848.

——. *Histoire des prisonniers français en Afrique depuis la conquête.* 2 vols. Paris: Dessart, 1847.

Amaury, A. *Colonisation de l'Algérie: Observations, pour appendice et à l'appui d'un plan d'établissement en Algérie de colonies agricoles, proposé comme un d'entre les moyens les plus efficaces de parvenir à une diminution sensible de la mendicité et même du paupérisme en France, suivies du plan, établi sur une plus grande échelle.* Paris: P.-F. Beaulé, 1842.

——. *De l'Algérie et du paupérisme en France.* Algiers: Bastide, 1847.

——. *Établissement de colonies agricoles en Algérie, proposé comme moyen des plus puissants pour arriver à l'extinction de la mendicité en France.* Algiers: n.p., 1844.

——. *Projet d'établissement de colonies agricoles à fonder en Algérie, proposé comme un des plus puissants moyens d'extinction de la mendicité et même du paupérisme en France.* Paris: Pollet, 1842.

Annuaire de l'état d'Alger, publié par la Commission de la Société Coloniale. Marseille: Feissat aîné; Paris: Firmin Didot Frères, 1832.

Aperçu historique, statistique et topographique sur l'État d'Alger, à l'usage de l'armée expéditionnaire d'Afrique avec plans, vues et costumes; rédigé au Dépôt Général de la Guerre. 2nd ed. Paris: Ch. Picquet, 1830.

Arbaud, François-Antoine. *Recueil des circulaires, mandemens, etc. de Mgr. Arbaud, évêque de Gap: Précédé d'un aperçu sur les traditions religieuses de cette église et d'une notice sur chacun des évêques qui l'ont gouvernée jusqu'à ce jour.* Edited by abbé Aucel. Gap: J. Allier et Fils, 1838.

Assailly, Charles d', et al. *Pétition aux Chambres: Esclavage en Algérie.* Paris: Duverger, [1846].

Aumale, duc d' (Henri d'Orléans). *Correspondance du duc d'Aumale et de Cuvillier-Fleury.* Edited by Henri Limbourg. 4 vols. Paris: Plon-Nourrit, 1910–14.

Avert, Eugène. *Épître royaliste à un officier de l'Expédition d'Alger, par Eugène Avert. Lue à la Société Royale des Bonnes-Lettres, dans sa séance du 5 avril 1830.* Paris: Félix Lequin, 1830

B., C. *L'Algérie ou la civilisation conquérante: Poème dédié à l'Armée et à la Marine françaises.* [Paris]: La Crampe et Fertiaux, Janvier 1848.

B. . . . , H. . . . de la. *De l'Algérie et de la colonisation.* Paris: Crochard, 1834.

Baillet, A. *Réflexions sur l'Algérie et les moyens de contribuer à sa colonisation: À l'aide des cultivateurs choisis dans le département de la Seine-Inférieure, et sur les modifications à introduire dans diverses ordonnances qui régissent cette colonie.* Rouen: A. Surville, 1848.

Barante, Prosper Brugière de. *Souvenirs du baron de Barante de l'Académie française, 1762–1866.* Edited by Claude de Barante. 6 vols. Paris: Calmann Lévy, 1890–97.

Barat, S.-B.-F. *La prise d'Alger: Ode.* [Paris]: Carpentier-Méricourt, [1830].

Barbier, Jean. *Itinéraire historique et descriptif de l'Algérie, avec un vocabulaire français-arabe des mots les plus usités et un résumé historique des guerres d'Afrique.* Paris: Hachette, 1855.

Barchou de Penhoën, Auguste Théodore Hilaire. *Mémoires d'un officier d'état major.* Paris: Charpentier, 1835; repr., Geneva: Slatkine, 1977.

Barclay, Francis. *Les castagnettes africaines: Poésies lyriques inédites. Romances, chansonnettes, nocturnes, chants populaires, ballades, gaudrioles, chansons barcarolles.* Oran: A. Perrier, 1850.

Barthélemy, [Auguste]. *La Colonne de Mazagran, par Barthélemy.* Paris: Béthune et Plon, 1840.

———. *Constantine: Chant de guerre dédié à l'armée d'Afrique, par Barthélemy.* Paris: Dezauche, 1857.

Barthélemy, [Auguste], and Joseph Méry. *La Bacriade, ou la guerre d'Alger: Poëme héroi-comique en cinq chants.* Paris: A. Tastu, 1827.

Baude, Jean-Jacques. *L'Algérie.* 2 vols. Paris: Arthus Bertrand, 1841.

Baudelaire, Charles. *Curiosités esthétiques.* Paris: Michel Lévy, 1868.

Baudicour, Louis. *La colonisation de l'Algérie: Ses éléments.* Paris: Lecoffre et Cie., 1856.

Belaïs, Abraham. *Ode hébraïque, traduite en français, suivi du psaume de David no. XVIII, en l'honneur de S. M. Louis-Philippe, de LL. AA. RR. les ducs de Nemours et Joinville, et de l'armée française, à l'occasion de la prise de Constantine.* Paris: Wittersheim, 1837.

Belfort-Devaux, Pierre-Louis. *La Guerre d'Alger: Chanson composée par M. Belfort.* Ajaccio: M. Marchi, [1830].

Belmas, Louis. *Prières ordonnés par Mgr. l'Évêque de Cambrai pour le succès de l'expédition d'Alger.* Roubaix: Beghin, 1830.

———. *Prières pour le succès de l'Expédition d'Alger, ordonnés par Mgr. l'Évêque de Cambrai.* Roubaix: Beghin, 1830.

Berard, Victor. *Indicateur général de l'Algérie renfermant la description géographique, statistique et historique de chacune des localités des trois provinces: Suivi d'un recueil d'arrêtés et d'actes administratifs et d'un annuaire pour 1848 contenant les noms des fonctionnaires civils et militaires; ainsi que les noms, professions et demeures des principaux commerçans et notables habitans de l'Algérie.* Algiers: Bastide, 1848.

Berbrugger, Adrien. *L'Algérie historique, pittoresque et monumentale, ou Recueil de vues, costumes et portraits faits d'après nature dans les Provinces d'Alger, Bône, Constantine et Oran par Bour, Ol. Bro, A. Genet, E. Flandin, Philippoteaux, Raffet, &c. avec texte descriptif par Mr. Berbrugger, conservateur au Musée et de la Bibliothèque d'Alger. Dédié au Roi. Lithographies par Bour, Genet, Bayot, Courtin, Collignon.* 2 vols. Paris: Delahaye, 1843.

Bertholon, J. and C. Lhote. *Horace Vernet à Versailles, au Luxembourg et au Louvre: Critique et biographie.* Paris: Cournol, 1863.

Bertier, Ferdinand de. *Souvenirs d'un ultraroyaliste (1815–1832).* Edited by Guillaume de Bertier de Sauvigny. Paris: Tallandier, 1993.

Bertrand, G. J. J. *Stances héroïques sur la prise d'Alger.* Paris: n.p., 1830.

Bertrand, Henri Gratien. *Sur la détresse des colonies françaises et de l'île Martinique en particulier; et de la nécessité de diminuer le taxe exorbitante établie sur le sucre exotique.* Paris: F. Didot frères, 1838.

Beulé, Charles Ernest. *Éloge de M. Horace Vernet par M. Beulé, secrétaire perpétuel de l'Académie des Beaux-Arts, prononcé dans la séance publique du 3 octobre 1863.* Paris: Didier, 1863.

Bigot de Morogues, Pierre-Marie-Sébastien. *De la misère des ouvriers et de la marche à suivre pour y remédier.* Paris: Huzard, 1832.

———. *Du paupérisme, de la mendicité, et des moyens d'en prévenir les funestes effets.* Paris: Dondey-Dupré, 1834.

———. *Projet de colonies agricoles libres, fondées par maisons dispersées dans les campagnes et y formant de petites propriétés, présenté au Conseil général du département du Loiret, par M. le Baron de Morogues, l'un de ses membres, à la session du 25 janvier 1833.* N.p.: A. Jacob, [1833].

———. *Trois opuscules sur les moyens de prévenir les misères des ouvriers.* Paris: Alex. Jacob, [n.d.].

Blanc, Louis. *History of Ten Years, 1830–1840.* 2 vols. London: Chapman and Hall, 1845.

Blanqui, Adolphe. *Algérie: Rapport sur la situation économique de nos possessions dans le nord de l'Afrique, lu à l'Académie des sciences morales et politiques, dans les séances des 16, 23 et 30 novembre, 7 et 15 décembre 1839.* Paris: Coquebert, 1840.

——. *Rapport sur l'état économique et moral de la Corse en 1838, lu dans les séances de 18 et 27 octobre, 10 et 17 novembre, 8 et 22 décembre 1838.* Paris: Didot, frères, 1840.

Boigne, Louise-Eléonore-Charlotte-Adélaide d'Osmond, comtesse de. *Memoirs of the Comtesse de Boigne, 1820–1830.* Edited by Charles Nicoullaud. New York: Charles Scribner's Sons, 1908.

Boissy, Adrien. *Réflexions d'un Français, au sujet de l'expédition d'Alger.* Paris: n.p., 1830.

Bolognini. *Scènes entre M. de Polignac, Charles X et le Dey d'Alger (les premiers jours d'août 1830).* Paris: Chassaignon, 1830.

Le bombardement de Mogador, et le drapeau français pour toujours victorieux en Algérie. Paris: Jules-Juteau, [1844].

Bonnebeault. *Ode: Clémence de S. A. R. Mgr. le duc de Nemours à la prise de Constantine.* Paris: Baudouin, 1839.

Bouniol, Bathild. *Gringalet au Salon, espèce de critique.* Paris: n.p., 1843

Bousquet, Dr. *Hussein, ou le dernier Dey d'Alger: Ode à S. A. R. Mgr. le Dauphin.* Marseille: M. Olive, 1830.

Boutet, Louis, ed. *Mazagran, ou 123 contre 12.000: Chansonnier nouveau pour 1840, choisi et chanté par Boutet (Louis).* Paris: Stahl, 1840.

Bromwell, William J. *History of Immigration to the United States, exhibiting the number, sex, age, occupation, and country of birth of passengers arriving in the United States by sea from foreign countries from September 30, 1819, to December 31, 1855.* New York: Redfield, 1856. Reprint, New York: Augustus Keller, 1969.

Brunet, Charles. *Table des pièces de théâtre décrites dans le catalogue de la Bibliothèque de M. de Soleinne.* 1914; The CESAR Project, 2002. http://www.cesar.org.uk/cesar2/books/soleinne.

Brunet, Jean. *La question algérienne.* Paris: Dumaine, 1847.

Bugeaud, Thomas-Robert. *L'Algérie: des moyens de conserver et d'utiliser notre conquête.* Paris: Dentu, 1842.

——. *Lettres inédites du Maréchal Bugeaud, duc d'Isly (1808–1849).* Edited by Captain Tattet. Paris: Émile-Paul Frères, 1922.

——. *Par l'épée et par la charrue: écrits et discours de Bugeaud.* Edited by Paul Azan. Paris: Presses Univérsitaires de France, 1948.

Bulwer, Henry Lytton. *France, Social, Literary, Political.* 2 vols. New York: Harper and Brothers, 1834.

Buret, Eugène. *De la misère des classes laborieuses en Angleterre et en France: De la nature de la misère, de son existence, de ses effets, de ses causes, et de l'insuffisance des remèdes qu'on lui a opposés jusqu'ici; avec l'indication des moyens propres à en affranchir les sociétés.* 2 vols. Paris: Paulin, 1840.

——. *Question d'Afrique: De la double conquête de l'Algérie par la guerre et la colonisa-tion, suivi d'un examen critique du gouvernement, de l'administration et de la situa-tion coloniale.* Paris: Ledoyen, 1842.

Burette, Théodore. *Musée Historique de Versailles, avec un texte historique.* 3 vols. Paris: Furne et Cie., 1844.

C., Charles. *Lettre du Dey d'Alger au Comte de Bourmont, général en chef de l'expédition d'Alger.* Paris: Jacques Ledoyen, 1830.

C., M. H. *Lettres sur l'Algérie.* Clermont-Ferrand: Auguste Veysset, 1844.

Capefigue, Baptiste. *Histoire de la Restauration et des causes qui ont amené la chute de la branche aînée des Bourbons, par un homme d'État.* 10 vols. Paris: Duféy, 1831–33.

Captivité du Trompette Escoffier et de ses Camarades chez Abd-el-Kader. Paris: Chassaignon, 1843.

Caramouche, [P.-F. Adolphe], and [Ch.-Désiré] Dupeuty. *Les Grisettes en Afrique, ou le Harem, pièce en deux actes et trois tableaux, mêlée de vaudevilles.* In *La Mosaïque, recueil de pièces nouvelles,* no. 30. Paris: Beck, 1842.

Castellane, Esprit-Victor-Élisabeth-Boniface, maréchal de. *Campagnes d'Afrique, 1835–1848. Lettres adressées au Maréchal de Castellane par les Maréchaux Bugeaud, Clauzel, Valée, Canrobert, Forey, Bousquet et les généraux Changarnier, de Lamorcière, Le Flo, de Négrier, de Wimpffen, Cler, etc. etc.* Paris: Plon, 1898.

——. *Journal du Maréchal de Castellane, 1804–1862.* 5 vols. Paris: Plon, 1895–97.

Caze, F. *Notice sur Alger.* Paris: Félix Locquin, 1831.

Cham. [Amédée-Charles-Henri Noé]. *Mœurs algériennes, chinoiseries turques: Nouvel album de Cham (de N.).* Paris: Audibert, [1837].

Chancel, Ausone de. *Première Algérienne.* Paris: Crapelet, 1845.

La chanson au XIXe siècle: Recueil de chansons populaires et contemporaines, de nos chan-sonniers les plus renommés. 2 vols. Paris: Durand, 1846.

Chapuys-Montlaville, Benoît-Marie-Louis-Alceste, Baron de. *Mazagran: Journées des 3, 4, 5 et 6 février 1840. Récit par M. Chapuys-Montlaville.* 2nd ed. Paris: Pagnerre, 1840.

Charles X et le Dey. Rouen: Bloquel, 1830.

Charton, Edouard. *Projets de Sociétés.* Paris: Crapelet, n.d.

Chateaubriand, François-René de. *Mémoires d'outre-tombe.* In *Œuvres complètes de F.-R. de Chateaubriand.* Paris: Acamédia, 1997. http://gallica.bnf.fr/ark:/12148/bpt6k1013503.

Chatelain, Le Chevalier. *Mémoire sur les moyens à employer pour punir Alger, et détruire la piraterie des puissances barbaresques; précédé d'un précis historique sur le caractère, les mœurs et la manière de combattre des musulmans habitant la côte d'Afrique, et d'un coup-d'œil sur les expéditions françaises tentées contre eux à diverses époques.* Paris: Anselin, 1828.

Chevalier, L. *La colonisation d'Alger, ou le géant de l'Atlas: Ode par M. L. Chevalier.* Versailles: Montalant-Bougleux, 1835.

Chevalier, Michel. *Lettres sur l'Amérique du Nord*. 4th ed. 2 vols. Brussels: Wouters et Cie., 1844.

Ch.-M***, ed. *L'Algérie, landscape africain: Promenades pittoresques et chroniques algériennes. Orné de six belles vues de l'Afrique française*. Paris: Louis Janet, [1840].

Christian, P. [Christian Pitois]. *L'Afrique française, l'empire de Maroc et les déserts de Sahara: Conquêtes, victoires et découvertes des Français, depuis la prise d'Alger jusqu'à nos jours. Vignettes par Henri Philippoteaux, Tony Johannot, Eugène Bellangé . . .* Paris: A. Barbier, 1846.

———. *L'Algérie de la jeunesse*. Librairie à illustrations pour la jeunesse. Paris: Alph. Desesserts, [1847].

Cogniard, Théodore, and Hippolyte Cogniard. *La cocarde tricolore, épisode de la guerre d'Alger: Vaudeville en trois actes. Représenté pour la première fois, à Paris, sur le théâtre des Folies Dramatiques, le 19 mars 1831*. 4th ed. Paris: Jules Didot, [1834].

A Collection of Twenty-Four Caricatures Which Have Appeared in Paris Since the Late Revolution; with an introduction, and explanatory remarks annexed to each text. Paris: Fain; London: Charles Tilt, 1831.

Colomel, Alex[andre]. *Du parti qu'on pourrait tirer d'une expédition d'Alger; ou de la possibilité de fonder dans le bassin de la Méditerranée un nouveau système colonial et maritime, à l'épreuve de la puissance anglaise*. Paris: Everat, 1830.

Comédon, Noël. *La Bataille d'Isly: Poème dédié à Monsieur le maréchal Bugeaud, duc d'Isly*. Paris: Stahl, 1845.

Constant, Benjamin. *De l'esprit de la conquête et de l'usurpation dans leurs rapports avec la civilisation européenne*. 1814; repr., Paris: Imprimerie nationale Éditions, 1992.

Constantine est à nous! Chanson dédiée à l'armée d'Afrique. Arras: Gouillot-Legrand, 1841.

Corbet, Th. *Mascara: Les Français en Afrique. Poème en huit Chants, suivi d'un aperçu sur le Koran*. Lyon: Pélagaud, 1837.

Coudrot. *Chant sur la prise d'Alger*. Troyes: Bouquot, [1830].

Coup-d'œil sur les colonies, et en particulier sur celle d'Alger. Paris: David, 1833.

Cuvillier-Fleury, Alfred-Auguste. *Journal et correspondance intimes de Cuvillier-Fleury*. Edited by Ernest Bertin. 2 vols. Paris: Plon, 1900–1903.

La dame de comptoir, ou le colon extravagant: Comédie en un acte. Algiers: J.-B. Philippe; Toulon: L. Laurent, 1835.

Dejob, Charles. "La Défense de Mazagran dans la littérature et les arts du dessin." In *Revue d'Histoire Littéraire de la France* 19 (1912): 318–40.

Demontès, Victor. *Le peuple algérien: Essais de démographie algérienne*. Algiers: Impr. algérienne, 1906.

Denfert-Rochereau, [Pierre-Marie-Philippe-Aristide]. *Lettres d'un officier républicain (1842–1871)*. Edited by William Serman. Vincennes: Service historique de l'Armée de Terre, 1990.

Départ des colons pour l'Algérie. Paris: Chassaignon, 1848.

Desjobert, Amédée. *L'Algérie en 1838*. Paris: P. Dufart, 1838.

———. *L'Algérie en 1844*. Paris: Guillaumin, 1844.

———. *L'Algérie en 1846*. Paris: Guillaumin, 1846.

———. *Discours prononcé par M. Desjobert, représentant du peuple, Seine-Inférieure, dans la discussion du projet de loi tendant à régler le régime commercial en Algérie, et note sur les effets de cette loi*. Paris: Panckoucke, 1850.

Dialogue entre Charles X et le dey d'Alger. Paris: E. Brière, 1830.

Dictionnaire de l'Académie française. 6th ed. Paris, 1832–35. Reprint, The ARTFL Project, http://artfl-project.uchicago.edu/node/17

Dopigez, M. (Abbé). *Souvenirs de l'Algérie et de la France méridionale*. Douai: V. Adam, 1840.

Du Barail, François-Charles. *Mes souvenirs*. 12th ed. 3 vols. Paris: Plon, Nourrit et Cie., 1897–98.

Dubois, Charles. *Journal d'un colon d'Algérie*. Strasbourg: Édouard Huder, 1864.

Le duc d'Aumale à Mâcon. Chalon-sur-Saône: J. Duchesne, 1841.

Le duc d'Aumale et le 17e régiment d'infanterie légère. Paris, 1841.

Duchesne, E.-A. *De la prostitution dans la ville d'Alger depuis la conquête*. Paris: Ballière and Garnier frères,1853.

Duclos, Louis. *L'Empereur, suivi de Mazagran, poème*. Paris: Worms, 1843.

Ducrocq, H.-Isaïe (Abbé). *Poème sur la bataille d'Isly*. Brissy: Impr. de Mgr. l'évêque d'Arras, 1845.

Dufour, Fanny. *Mazagran, par Mme. Fanny Dufour*. Paris: A. Aubrée, 1840.

Dumas, Alexandre. *Mes mémoires*. 10 vols. Paris: Lévy frères, 1863–84.

Dupias, Alexandre. *Expédition d'Alger: Poème, par Alexandre Dupias, chant premier, interrompu par le canon des Invalides*. Paris: Levavasseur, 1830.

Dupin, Charles. *Mémoires de M. Dupin*. Vol. 3, *Carrière politique, souvenirs parlementaires: M. Dupin président de la Chambre des députés pendant huit sessions (du 23 novembre 1832 au 26 mars 1839)*. Paris: Plon, 1860.

Durande, Amédée. *Joseph, Carle et Horace Vernet: Correspondance et biographies*. Paris: Hetzel, 1863.

Duteil, V. H. *Nécessité de la colonisation d'Alger et des émigrations*. Paris: Louis Janet, 1832.

Dutot, S. *De l'expatriation, considérée sous ses rapports économiques, politiques et moraux, suivi d'un mémoire de M. le Prince de Talleyrand de Périgord*. Paris: Arthus Bertrand, 1840.

Duval, Jules. *Histoire de l'émigration européenne, asiatique et africaine au XIXe siècle: Ses causes, ses caractères, ses effets*. Paris: Guillaumin, 1862.

———. "Tableaux de la situation des Établissements français dans l'Algérie." In *Bulletin de la Société de Géographie*, 5th ser., 2 (1865): 49–170.

Duvivier, Antony. *Mazagran! . . . Récit poétique des journées des 3, 4, 5 et 6 février, par Antony Duvivier*. Troyes: Anner-André, 1841.

Duvivier, Franciade Fleurus. *Algérie: Quatorze observations sur le dernier mémoire du Général Bugeaud*. Paris: H.-L. Delloye, 1842.

Enfantin, Prosper. *Colonisation de l'Algérie*. Paris: P. Bertrand, 1843.

Engels, Friedrich. "The June Revolution (The Course of the Paris Uprising)." In *Neue Rheinische Zeitung*, 2 July 1848; Marxists Internet Archive, n.d. http://www.marxists.org/archive/marx/works/1848/07/01c.htm.

Erivanne, Charles. *Constantine: ode à l'armée, aux jeunes princes.* Paris: Delaunay, 1837.

Estry, Stephen d'. *Histoire d'Alger, de son territoire et de ses habitants, de ses pirateries, de son commerce et de ses guerres, de ses mœurs et usages, depuis les temps les plus reculés jusqu'à nos jours.* 2nd ed. Bibliothèque de la Jeunesse Chrétienne. Tours: Ad. Mame et Cie., [1843].

Étienne, [Charles-Guillaume], and P.-Charles Nanteuil. *Le Dey d'Alger, ou la visite au pensionnat, comédie en un acte en prose, par MM. Étienne et Nanteuil, mise en vaudeville, représentée, pour la première fois, à Paris, sur le Théâtre du Gymnase Dramatique, le 30 septembre 1831.* Paris: E. Duverger, 1831.

L'expédition d'Alger. Toulon: Duplessis Ollivault, [1830].

Explication des ouvrages de peinture, sculpture, gravure, lithographie et architecture des artistes vivans, exposés au musée Royal. Paris: Vinchon, 1831–51.

Fabar, Paul-Dieudonné. *L'Algérie et l'opinion.* Paris: J. Corréard, 1847.

Fac Simile des tableaux exposés au Salon de 1839, sous les nos. 2050, 2051 et 2052, par M. Horace Vernet, et représentant le Siège de Constantine. Paris: Vinchon, 1839.

Faucon, Narcisse. *Livre d'or de l'Algérie: Histoire politique, militaire, administrative, événements et faits principaux, biographie des hommes ayant marqué dans l'armée, les sciences, les lettres, etc., de 1830 à 1889.* Paris: Challamel et Cie., 1889.

Faure, Henry. *Histoire de Moulins (Xe siècle–1830).* 2 vols. Moulins: Crépin-Leblond, 1900.

"Le fils du héros." In untitled brochure. Arras: Gouillot-Legrand, 1841.

Forbin-Janson, Charles-Auguste-Marie-Joseph. *Mandement de Monseigneur l'Évêque de Nancy et de Toul qui ordonne des prières publiques pour le succès de l'expédition d'Alger, et pour attirer les bénédictions de Dieu sur l'élection générale des députés du royaume.* Nancy: Haener, 1830.

——. *Mandement de Monseigneur l'évêque de Nancy et de Toul qui ordonne qu'un Te Deum solonnel sera chanté dans toutes les églises de son Diocèse, en actions de grâces de la* PRISE D'ALGER. [Nancy, 1830].

Forbonnais, François Veronde. "Colonie." In *Encyclopédie ou dictionnaire raisonné des sciences, des arts et des métiers, par une société de gens de letters.* Vol. 3. Paris: Briasson, David, Le Breton, Durand [1853]; repr., Stuttgart: Friedrich Frommann Verlag, 1988.

Fournier, Marc, François Fertiault, Bourget, Festeau, Hég. Moreau, Eugène Briffaut, etc. *Paris chantant: Romances, chansons et chansonnettes contemporaines.* Paris: Lavigne, 1845.

Les Français peints par eux-mêmes: Encyclopédie morale du dix-neuvième siècle. 10 vols. Paris: L. Curmer, 1840–42.

Franque, A., ed. *Lois de l'Algérie, année 1844: Recueil plus complet que l'édition officielle, comprenant les ordonnances royales, arrêtés ministériels et arrêtés du Gouverneur-Général et du Directeur de l'Intérieur.* Paris: Dubos frères et Marest, [1844].

Gabourd, Amédée. *Histoire contemporaine comprenant les principaux événements qui se sont accomplis depuis la Révolution de 1830 jusqu'à nos jours et résumant . . . le mouvement social, artistique et littéraire.* 12 vols. Paris, Firmin-Didot, 1863–74.

Galerie historique de l'Algérie: Les Princes en Afrique. 3 vols. Paris: Delahaye, 1845–46.

Garnier, J.-M. *Histoire de l'imagerie populaire et des cartes à jouer à Chartres, suivie de recherches sur le commerce du colportage des complaintes, canards et chansons dans les rues.* Chartres: Garnier, 1869.

Garnier-Pagès, Louis-Antoine, ed. *Dictionnaire politique: Encyclopédie du langage et de la science politiques.* Paris: Pagnerre, 1842.

Gautier, Théophile. *Histoire de l'art dramatique en France depuis vingt-cinq ans.* 6 vols. Paris and Brussels: Hetzel, 1858–59.

——. *Voyage en Algérie.* Edited by Denise Brahimi. 1856; repr., Paris: La Boîte à Documents, 1989.

Gavard, Charles. *Galeries historiques de Versailles, gravées sur acier par les meilleurs artistes français et étrangers, avec un texte explicatif par M. Jules Janin.* Paris: Bureau central des Galeries historiques de Versailles, 1837.

——. *Galeries historiques du palais de Versailles.* 9 vols. Paris: Impr. nationale, 1837–48.

——. *Supplément aux Galeries historiques de Versailles.* 6 vols. Paris: n.p., 1843–46.

Gomot, F. *Annuaire de l'Algérie.* Paris: Victor Magen; Algiers: L.-B. Philippe, 1842.

——. *Annuaire de l'Algérie pour 1843.* Paris: Victor Magen; Algiers: L-B. Philippe, 1843.

——. *Annuaire de l'Algérie.* Paris: Victor Magen; Algiers: L.-B. Philippe, 1844.

Gondrecourt, Aristide de. *Médine.* 2 vols. Paris: Alexandre Cadot, 1845.

Grandmaison, Geoffroy de. *La Congrégation (1801–1830).* Paris: Plon, 1889.

Le Grand Terrorifer d'Afrique. Cherbourg: Boulanger, [1830].

Guernon-Ranville, Martial de. *Journal d'un ministre: Œuvre posthume du Cte de Guernon-Ranville, ancien membre de l'Académie des Sciences, Arts et Belles-Lettres de Caen.* Edited by Julien Travers. Caen: F. Le Blanc-Hardel, 1874.

Guide des Français à Alger. Marseille: Achard, 1830.

Guide du colon et de l'ouvrier en Algérie, indiquant: 1° les sûretés, les garanties et les ressources assurées aux colons; 2° les conditions et formalités à remplir en France pour obtenir des concessions de terrain en Algérie; 3° les conditions et formalités à remplir par les colons en Algérie; 4° les avantages offerts aux ouvriers en Algérie. Rédigé d'après les documents officiels du Ministère de la guerre et du Ministère de l'intérieur, et les renseignements puisés près des autorités locales à Alger. Paris: Guiraudet et Jouaust, 1843.

Guilmot, [André-Nicolas-Joseph]. *Explication philosophique du Musée de Versailles, ou paradoxes sur la politique et sur le pouvoir royal.* Paris: A. Guyot, 1840.

Guizot, François. *Memoirs to Illustrate the History of My Time.* Vol. 7, *France under Louis-Phillipe from 1841 to 1847.* 1865; repr., London: Bentley; New York: AMS Press, n.d.

Guyot, Comte. *Algérie, Direction de l'Intérieur: Plan de colonisation pour la province d'Alger. Alger, le 12 mars 1842.* Algiers: n.p., n.d.

Hamdan Khodja. *Aperçu historique et statistique sur la Régence d'Alger, intitulé en Arabe le Miroir.* Paris: Goetschy fils, 1833.

Hatin, Eugène. *Histoire politique et littéraire de la presse en France: Avec une introduction historique sur les origines du journal et la bibliographie générale des journaux depuis leur origine.* 8 vols. Paris, 1859–61; repr., Geneva: Slatkine, 1967.

Haussez, Charles Lemercier de Longpré, baron d'. *Mémoires du baron d'Haussez, dernier ministre de la marine sous la Restauration.* Edited by duchesse d'Almazan. 3 vols. Paris: Calmann-Lévy, 1896–97.

Hautpoul, Alphonse d'. *Mémoires du général marquis Alphonse d'Hautpoul, pair de France, 1789–1865.* Paris: Perrin, 1906.

Henrichs, P. *Guide du colon et de l'ouvrier en Algérie, indiquant: 1° les sûretés, garanties et ressources offertes aux colons, 2° Les conditions et formalités à remplir en France pour obtenir des concessions de terres en Algérie, 3° Les conditions et formalités à remplir par les colons concessionnaires en Algérie; 4° Les avantages offerts et les conditions imposées aux ouvriers qui veulent se rendre en Algérie.* Paris: Garnier frères; Algiers: Philippe, 1843.

Les héros de Mazagran: Relation de la sublime défense de 123 Français contre 12,000 Arabes. Lyon: Boursy fils, 1840.

Hussein-Dey, Ex-Dey d'Alger, à Charles X, ex-Roi de France. Lyon: André Idt, 1830.

Indicateur du palais et du musée de Versailles: Description complète des salles de Constantine, des Croisades, galeries et appartements, précédée d'une notice historique sur le palais. Paris: Imp. de Baudouin, 1845.

Jacob, Henri. *Le songe d'Abd-el-Kader, ou Isly, Mogador et Tanger, poëme en 6 chants, suivi d'une ballade.* Ingouville: Gaffney, 1844.

Jal, A. *Panorama d'Alger, peint par M. Charles Langlos, chef de bataillon au corps royal d'état major, officier de la Légion d'Honneur, auteur du panorama de Navarin. Rue des Marais-Saint-Martin, no. 40, près la rue Lancri.* Paris: Selligue, 1833.

——. "Une visite au dey d'Alger." *Revue de Paris* 30 (1831): 36–52; repr., Geneva: Slatkine, 1972.

Jarry, Alexandre. *Constantine: Poème dédié à Mgr. le duc de Nemours.* Paris: Ebrard, 1837.

Joinville, Prince de (François d'Orléans). "Lettre du prince de Joinville au duc de Nemours." In *Revue rétrospective, ou Archives secrètes du dernier gouvernement. Recueil non périodique,* no. 31. Paris: Paul, 1848.

——. *Vieux souvenirs de Mgr. le Prince de Joinville 1818–1848.* Edited by Daniel Meyer. Paris: Mercure de France, 1986.

Jouhaud, Auguste. *Mazagran, ou 123 contre 12000, fait militaire en 3 tableaux, par M. Auguste Jouhaud, . . . musique de M. Lautz.* Paris: L. Vert, 1840.

Jouy, Étienne de, and Antoine Jay. *Salon d'Horace Vernet: Analyse historique et pittoresque des quarante-cinq tableaux exposés chez lui en 1822.* Paris: Ponthieu, 1822.

Kock, Paul de, and Valory [Charles Mourier]. *Le Débardeur ou Le Gros-Caillou et Alger: Vaudeville en deux actes.* Paris: E. Duverger, 1839.

Krako, Emile. *Vies et aventures surprenantes de M. Mayeux et de sa nombreuse famille: Ses relations avec les personnages les plus haut placés, son Voyage en ALGÉRIE et dans le MAROC, ses Visites à ABD-EL-KADER et à l'Empereur; Sa rencontre avec le JUIF ERRANT dont M. EUGENE SUE a raconté des choses si extraordinaires, son retour à Paris; sa présence à Fontainebleau le jour de l'attentat de l'infâme Lecomte.* Paris and Meulan: A. Hiard, 1846.

Laborde, Alexandre de. *Au Roi et aux Chambres, sur les véritables causes de la rupture avec Alger et sur l'expédition qui se prépare.* Paris: Gaultier-Laguionie, 1830.

Laborie, Ferdinand, and Charles Desnoyers [sic]. *Mazagran: Bulletin de l'armée d'Afrique en 3 actes, par MM. F. Laborie et Ch. Desnoyers* [sic]. Antwerp: H. Ratincx, n.d.

Ladimir, Jules. *Mazagran: Ode au Capitaine Lelièvre et à ses soldats. Précédée d'une notice historique.* Paris: Baudoin, 1840.

Lafaye, Léon. *Question d'Afrique, au mois de décembre 1843.* Paris: Libr. de Paul Dupont, 1843.

Laffillé, [Charles]. *La prise d'Alger: Poème, par Ch. Laffillé auteur de la Bataille de Bouvines, etc., etc.* Paris: Delaunay et Gossein, 1834.

Laisné, D. *La double victoire, ou les Barbares vaincus à Paris et à Alger: Hommage au Roi des Français, S.M. Louis-Philippe Ier.* Versailles: C.-G. Vitry, 1830.

Laisné, Pierre-Marie. *La Constantine, ou le Drapeau tricolore et Constantine, chant national . . . par P. Laisné.* Paris: Maulde et Renou, 1838.

Laloue, Ferdinand, and Charles Desnoyer. *Mazagran: Bulletin de l'armée d'Afrique, en trois actes, par MM. Ferdinand-Laloue et Ch. Desnoyer, décors de MM. Philastre et Cambon, représenté, pour la première fois, à Paris, sur le théâtre national du Cirque-Olympique, le 14 avril 1840.* Paris: Mifliez, 1840.

La Martinière, Émile. *Les amours dans le désert, ou les aventures d'un officier de l'armée française en Afrique.* Paris: Renault, 1846.

La Merlière, Eugène [Hugues-Marie-Humbert Bocon] de, and Joachim Duflot. *Sous Constantine: À-propos-vaudeville en un acte, mêlé de couplets, par MM. E. Delmerlière et Duflot. Représenté pour la première fois à Lyon, sur le théâtre du Gymnase, le 8 novembre 1837, sous la direction de M. Ch. Provence.* Lyon: Bertaud, 1837.

——. *Mazagran, ou 123, À-propos militaire en trois parties, par MM. Eugène de Lamerlière et J. Duflot.* Lyon: P. Nourtier, 1840; Paris: chez les Marchands de nouveautés, 1840.

Lamoricière, Christophe Louis Léon Juchault de, and Marie Alphonse Bedeau. *Projets de colonisation pour les provinces d'Oran et de Constantine, présentés par MM. les lieutenants-généraux de Lamoricière et Bedeau.* Paris: Impr. royale, 1847.

Landmann, J. M. (Abbé). *Exposé sur la colonisation de l'Algérie adressé à MM. les pairs de France, lors de la discussion des crédits supplémentaires 1846.* Paris: Schneider et Langrand, 1846.

——. *Les fermes du Petit Atlas, ou colonisation agricole, religieuse et militaire du nord de l'Afrique.* Paris: Périsse frères, 1841.

——. *Mémoires au Roi sur la colonisation de l'Algérie.* Paris: Lecoffre, 1845.

Larousse, Pierre, ed. *Grand dictionnaire universel du XIXe siècle.* 17 vols. Paris: Administration du grand Dictionnaire universel, 1866–77.

Laugier de Tassy. *Histoire du royaume d'Alger avec l'état présent de son gouvernement, de ses forces de terre et de mer, de ses revenus, police, justice, politique et commerce.* Edited by Noël Laveau and André Nouschi. 1724; repr., Paris: Éditions Loysel, 1992.

Launay, Robert. "Mazagran (février 1840), d'après des documents inédits." *Le Correspondant* 81 (10 February 1909): 550–64.

Leblanc, Capitaine. *Des levés à vue et du dessin d'après nature, par M. Leblanc, capitaine au corps royal du génie militaire.* Librairie encyclopédique de Roret. Amiens: Machart, 1838.

Leblanc, P.-E.-Z. *Première et dernière campagne d'Afrique de Jean Leblanc, dit Narcisse: Drame historique en quatre couplets, dédié à Joseph Habillon et au 19me Régiment d'Infanterie Légère, par P.-E.-Z. Leblanc, père.* Paris: Carré, 1846.

Lecomte, Louis-Henry. *Napoléon et l'Empire racontés par le théâtre, 1797–1899.* Paris: Jules Raux, 1900.

Ledoux, P. *Le départ pour Alger: Couplets à l'occasion de l'expédition d'Afrique.* Paris: E. Duverger, May 1830.

Le Duc, Louis-Charles. *Epître sur l'expédition d'Alger, dédiée à l'armée Française, suivie d'une anecdote militaire.* Saint-Esprit: Cluzeau, 1830.

Legoyt, Alfred. *L'émigration européenne: Son importance, ses causes, ses effets, avec un appendice sur l'émigration africaine, hindoue et chinoise.* Paris: Guillaumin, 1861.

Lelièvre, Félix, *De l'émigration en Amérique, depuis 1815 jusqu'en 1843: Ouvrage utile aux Commerçants des ports de mer et aux personnes qui s'expatrient.* Nantes: Hérault, 1843.

Lépine, N.-G. *La prise d'Alger: Hommage à la jeune armée.* Paris: Timothy Dehay, 1830.

Leroux, Pierre, and Jean Reynaud, eds. *Encyclopédie nouvelle: Encyclopédie pittoresque à deux sous.* Paris: Bourgogne et Martinet, 1834.

Leroy-Beaulieu, Paul. *De la colonisation chez les peuples modernes.* 2nd ed. Paris: Guillaumin, 1882.

Leynadier, [Camille], and [Bertrand] Clausel. *Histoire de l'Algérie française, précédée d'une introduction sur les dominations Carthaginoise, Romaine, Arabe et Turque, suivie d'un précis historique sur l'empire du Maroc.* 2 vols. Paris: H. Morel, 1846.

Lieutaud. *Société angévine pour le placement des colons en Algérie: Projet de colonisation présenté par M. Lieutaud, notaire à Alger.* Angers: Cosnier et Lachèse, 1847.

Lille, A.-L. de. *Ode sur la guerre d'Alger, juin 1830.* Paris: Guiraudet, [n.d.].

Limbourg, Henri. *Le duc d'Aumale et sa deuxième campagne d'Afrique (février à septembre 1841).* Paris: Plon-Nourrit, 1915.

——. *Le duc d'Aumale et sa troisième campagne d'Afrique: La Smalah (novembre 1842 à juin 1843).* Paris: Plon-Nourrit, 1915.

Lombard, J. B. *Rataplan, ou le petit tambour, vaudeville en un acte, représenté pour la première fois le 4 novembre 1827, modifié depuis la guerre d'Afrique.* Metz: Typog. S. Lamort, March 1845.

Malessart, A. G. *Le colon: Esquisses algériennes.* Paris: Recoules, 1845.

Malthus, Thomas. *Essai sur le principe de population, ou exposé des effets passés et présens de l'action de cette cause sur le bonheur du genre humain, suivi de quelques recherches relatives à l'espérance de guérir ou d'adoucir les maux qu'elle entraîne, par T. R. Malthus.* Translated by Pierre Prévost. 3 vols. Paris and Geneva: J. J. Paschoud, 1809.

Manuel de l'agriculteur du Midi de la France et de l'Algérie, ou la petite maison rustique méridionale. Avignon: Pierre Chaillot jeune, 1839.

Marcillac, Auguste. *Chant français: Couplets composés par M. Auguste Marcillac à l'occasion de la prise d'Alger.* Épinal: Pellerin, n.d.

Martin, L. *À l'armée d'Afrique: Mogador et l'Isly, poésie par L. Martin.* Paris and Grenoble: Prudhomme et Blanchet, 1844.

Martin, Victor and L.-E. Foley. *Histoire statistique de la colonisation algérienne au point de vue du peuplement et de l'hygiène.* Algiers: Impr. du Gouvernement, 1851.

Marx, Karl. "The Modern Theory of Colonization." In *Capital,* vol. 1, pt. 3, chap. 33. 1867; Marxists Internet Archive, 1999. http://www.marxists.org/archive/marx/works/1867-c1/ch33.htm.

Masson, A. *Dithyrambe sur la prise d'Alger.* Nantes: Mellinet-Malassis, 1830.

Matharel, Vor. de. *Vues des provinces d'Alger, de Constantine et d'Oran: Lithographiées par C. Mottet d'après des Dessins de Vor. de Matharel.* Paris; Gihaut, [1841].

Matterer, Amable. *Journal de la prise d'Alger par le Capitaine de Frégate Matterer, 1830.* Edited by Pierre Jullien. 1830; repr., Paris: Éd. de Paris, 1960.

Mendès da Costa, Raoul. *Le Dey d'Alger chez Monsieur Polignac: Scène dramatique.* Paris: Meneret, 1830.

Merivale, Herman. *Lectures on Colonization and Colonies, delivered before the University of Oxford in 1839, 1840, & 1841 and reprinted in 1861.* London: Longman, Green, Longman, and Roberts, 1861; repr., Oxford: Oxford University Press, 1928.

Merle, Jean-Toussaint. *Anecdotes historiques pour servir à l'histoire de la conquête d'Alger en 1830.* Paris: G.-A. Dentu, 1831.

Milliroux, Félix. *Émigration à la Guyane Anglaise.* Paris: Pagnerre, 1842.

Mir, Théophile de. *Discours prononcé par Théophile Prince Swiatopolk Piast de Mir Mirski, sur l'installation du Comité organisateur de la Compagnie chrétienne pour la colonisation et la civilisation de l'Afrique.* Marseille: Marius Olive, [1839].

Moll, Louis. *Colonisation et agriculture de l'Algérie.* 2 vols. Paris: Libr. agricole de la Maison Rustique, 1845.

Monbrion. *Ode sur l'expédition d'Alger, dédiée à Son Altesse Royale Monsieur le Dauphin, Grand-Amiral de France.* Paris: Moreau, April 1830.

Montagnac, Lucien de. *Lettres d'un soldat: Algérie, 1837–1845.* Edited by Elizé de Montagnac. Vernon: Éditions Christian Destremau, 1998.

Montbel, Guillaume-Isadore de. *1787–1831: Souvenirs du comte de Montbel, ministre de Charles X.* Edited by Guy de Montbel. Paris: Plon-Nourrit et Cie., 1913.

Montesquieu, Charles-Louis de Secondat. *De l'esprit des lois.* 1748; repr., Paris: Gallimard, 1995.

Morel. *Chanson nouvelle sur la guerre nouvelle d'Lager* [sic]. Lons-le-Saulnier: Fréd. Gauthier, [1830].

Morel, Noël. *Mazagran: Épisode lu au Théâtre du Panthéon, par Noël Morel.* Paris: Terzuolo, 1840.

Morgues, H. de. *Algérienne, ou chant de victoire en l'honneur de la prise d'Alger, par M. H. de Morgues.* Saint-Flour: Viallefont, 1830.

Mornand, Félix. *Le 1er mars en Algérie: Extraits de* L'Illustration *des 28 février et 7 mars 1851.* Paris: Plon frères, 1851.

——. *La vie arabe*. Paris: Michel Lévy frères, 1856.

Müller, Élisabeth. *Plaisir et savoir: Huit jours au Musée de Versailles, entretiens familiers sur les faits les plus mémorables de l'histoire de France*. Paris: Amédée Bédelet, 1846.

Muraton, Ad. *Mazagran: Ode dédiée aux chasseurs de la 1re compagnie du 3e bataillon de la 2e légion, par leur camarade A. Muraton*. Paris: Delanchy, 1840.

Muret, Théodore. *L'histoire par le théâtre, 1789–1851*. 3 vols. Paris: Amyot, 1865.

[Musset, Victor-Donatien de]. *1828: Nouveaux mémoires secrets pour servir à l'histoire de notre temps*. Paris: Casimir, 1829.

Napoleon III. *Œuvres de Napoléon III*. Vol. 5. *Discours, proclamations, messages*. Paris: Plon and Amyot, 1869.

Néoprytanée Central, société du progrès: Pièces dites par les auteurs dans les séances publiques de la Société, et surtout à sa grande solennité littéraire et musicale du Dimanche, 31 mai 1840. Paris: n.p., 1840.

Nettement, Alfred de. *Histoire de la conquête d'Alger écrite sur des documents inédits et authentiques*. Paris: Jacques Lecoffre et Cie., 1856.

——. *Histoire de la Restauration*. 8 vols. Paris: Jacques Lecoffre et Cie., 1860–72.

Nisard, Charles. *Histoire des livres populaires, ou de la littérature du colportage depuis le XVe siècle jusqu'à l'établissement de la Commission d'examen des livres du colportage (30 novembre 1852)*. 2nd ed. 2 vols. Paris: Amyot, 1864.

Nodier, Charles. *Journal de l'expédition des Portes de Fer*. Paris: Impr. royale, 1844.

Notes sur l'Algérie, par un ancien officier de l'Armée d'Afrique, en retraite. Niort: Robin et Cie., 1841.

Notice sur l'expédition qui s'est terminée par la prise de la Smalah d'Abd-el-Kader, le 16 mai 1843. Paris: Impr. des musées royaux, 1843.

La nouvelle gloire française: Récits des combats et hauts faits militaires de l'Armée d'Afrique, depuis la prise d'Alger jusqu'à la défense de Mazagran; contenant un précis historique et chronologique complet de l'Algérie ancienne et moderne, des détails curieux et authentiques sur l'aspect du pays et les mœurs de ses habitants, extraits des rapports adressés au gouvernement. Paris: L. Bouchard-Huzard, 1840.

Ode sur la conquête d'Alger, par l'auteur du Parnasse moderne. Paris: L. F. Hivert, [1830].

Orléans, duc d' (Ferdinand-Philippe d'Orléans). *Campagnes de l'armée d'Afrique, 1835–1839*. Paris: Michel Lévy frères, 1870.

——. *Lettres, 1825–1842*. Edited by Philippe d'Orléans, comte de Paris, and Robert d'Orléans, duc de Chartres. Paris: Calmann Lévy, 1889.

Pagès, A. *Mazagran, 4, 5 et 6 février 1840: Chant héroïque, par A. Pagés du Tarn*. Albi: Papailhiau, 1840.

Panorama d'Alger, peint par M. Charles Langlois, chef de bataillon au corps royal d'état major, officier de la Légion d'Honneur, auteur du panorama de Navarin. Rue des Marais-Saint-Martin, No. 40, près la rue Lancri. Paris: Selligue, 1833.

Parent-Duchâtelet, A.-J.-B. *De la prostitution dans la ville de Paris, considérée sous le rapport de l'hygiène publique, de la morale et de l'administration*. 3rd ed. Edited by A. Trebuchet and Poirat-Duval. 2 vols. Paris: J.-B. Ballière et fils, 1857.

Pascal, Adrien. *Histoire de l'armée et de tous les régiments depuis les premiers temps de la monarchie française jusqu'à nos jours: Art stratégique, organisation, costumes, victoires, conquêtes et faits glorieux de nos armées par une Société d'écrivains militaires.* Paris: A. Barbier, 1847.

Pasquier, Étienne-Denis. *Mémoires du chancelier Pasquier: Histoire de mon temps.* Edited by duc d'Audiffret-Pasquier. 6 vols. Paris: Plon, Nourrit et Cie., 1895.

Pelet, Jean-Jacques-Germain. *Note sur la situation de l'Algérie à la fin de janvier 1838. Demandée par le général Bernard, et remise le 3 février 1838. Avec une carte de la Province d'Alger.* Paris: Bourgogne et Martinet, 1839.

Pellissier de Reynaud, Henri-Jean-François-Edmond. *Annales algériennes.* 3 vols. Paris: Anselin et Gaultier-Laguionie, 1836–39.

——. *Annales algériennes: Nouvelle édition, revue, corrigée et continuée jusqu'à la chute d'Abd-el-Kader.* 2nd ed. 3 vols. Paris: J. Dumaine, 1854.

Péricaud, Louis. *Le Théâtre des Funambules, ses mimes, ses acteurs, et ses pantomimes depuis sa fondation, jusqu'à sa démolition.* Paris: Léon Sapin, 1897.

Pernier, J. *Alger conquis: Poème héroï-national précédé du chant patriotique de la Cocarde tricolore, dédié et présenté à S.M. Louis-Philippe, roi des Français.* Paris: Dentu, 1830.

Perrot, A[ristide]-M[ichel]. *La conquête d'Alger, ou relation de la campagne d'Afrique, comprenant les motifs de la guerre, les détails des préparatifs de l'expédition et des événemens qui ont précédé le débarquement, la composition de l'armée de terre et de l'armée navale, les noms des officiers supérieurs, et un précis des opérations militaires; d'après les documens officiels et particuliers, recueillis et mis en ordre par A.M. Perrot.* Paris: Langlois fils, 1830.

Philarmos [Marie de La Fresnaye]. *Ode sur l'expédition d'Alger par les Français, tirée de la formule générale de l'incantation trilogique d'Apollon.* Paris: Marchand du Breuil, n.d.

Pichon, Louis-André. *Alger sous la domination française: Son état présent et son avenir.* Paris: T. Barrois, 1833.

Pignel, Armand. *Conducteur ou Guide du voyageur et du colon de Paris à Alger et dans l'Algérie, avec carte itinéraire.* Paris: E.-J. Bailly, Sept 1836.

Plaidoyer de Me. Jean Bonhomme, en faveur du pouvoir absolu, dédié aux très-honorables Milord Polignac, Ibrahim-Labourdonnaye et Judas-Bourmont. Paris: Selligue, 1829.

Poirel. *De la colonisation militaire, agricole et pénale d'Alger.* Nancy: Impr. du Dard, February 1837.

Poisle-Desgranges. *Récit succinct d'une exploration sur le littoral d'Algérie, suivi de l'immortelle défense de Mazagran.* Paris: Violet, 1841.

Polignac, Jules de. *Considérations politiques sur l'époque actuelle, adressées à l'auteur anonyme de l'ouvrage intitulé* Histoire de la Restauration par un homme d'État. Brussels: Antoine Peeters; Leipzig: Allgemeine Niederländische Buchhandlung, 1832.

Polignac et ses confrères jugés par le Dey d'Alger: Grande dispute entre un jésuite et le Dey. Paris: Poussin 1830.

Pons, Antoine de. *Mandement de Monseigneur l'évêque de Moulins, qui prescrit des prières publiques pour le succès de nos armes en Afrique, et pour l'élection générale des députés du royaume.* Moulins: P.-A. Desrosiers, [1830].

Poujol, A. *Guerre d'Alger: Essai de poëme politique et morale en deux chants. Suivi de pièces fugitives. Plus de piraterie.* Montpellier: X. Jullien, 1830.

Prébois, François de. *Algérie: Conditions essentielles du progrès en Algérie.* Paris: Delaunay, 1840.

Prévost-Paradol, Anatole. *La France nouvelle.* 2nd ed. Paris: Michel Lévy frères, 1868.

Procès et acquittement du National, poursuivi pour avoir défendu l'égalité, les droits de l'armée, la loi contre le privilège et le régime des ordonnances; contenant l'article incriminé, les débats, le réquisitoire; la plaidoirie et la réplique de Me Michel (de Bourges), député de Niort. Paris: Pagnerre, 1838.

Procès-verbal de l'arrivée et du séjour à Marseille de S.A.R. Mgr le Duc d'Orléans. Marseille: Hoirs Feissat aîné et Demonchy, 1839.

Puységur. Ode, "En France." *Annales de la Société Académique de Nantes et du Département de la Loire-Inférieure* 12 (1841): 87–90.

Quélen, Hyacinthe-Louis de. *Mandement de Monseigneur l'archevêque de Paris, qui ordonne que le Te Deum solonnel sera chanté dans toutes les Églises de son Diocèse, en actions de grâces de la PRISE D'ALGER* [Paris, 1830].

[Quétin, E.] *Guide du voyageur en Algérie: Itinéraire du savant, de l'artiste, de l'homme du monde et du colon.* 2nd ed. Paris: L. Maison; Algiers: Dubox frères et Marest; Poitiers: Imp. de F.-A. Saurin, 1846.

Raineville, de. *Colonies agricoles, considérées comme moyens de venir au secours des indigens.* Amiens: Duval et Herment, [1841].

Raynal, Guillaume-Thomas. *Histoire philosophique et politique des établissements et du commerce des Européens dans les Deux Indes.* 10 vols. Geneva: Pellet, 1780.

Rédarez Saint-Remy, Jules-Henry. *Ode sur la prise de Constantine (ancienne Cirte).* [Paris]: Mevrel, [1837].

Remusat, Charles de. *Du paupérisme et de la charité légale: Lettre addressée à MM. les préfets du royaume.* Paris: Jules Renouard, 1840.

Reynaud, Jean. *Correspondance familière.* Paris: Motteroz, 1886.

Rispal, A. "Belmas (Louis)." In *Nouvelle biographie générale depuis les temps les plus reculés jusqu'à nos jours,* edited by [Jean-Chrétien-Ferdinand] Hoefer. Vol. 5, *Beaumarchais-Biccius,* 155–56. Paris: Firmin Didot, 1855.

Robert, Jules. *Album du Salon de 1840: Collection des principaux ouvrages. Avec une préface par le Baron Taylor.* Paris: Challamel, 1840.

R[ognat], A[drien]. *Hermès, ou le génie colonisateur: Essai politique contenant les principes fondamentaux en matière de colonisation.* Paris: Dupont et Laguionie, 1832.

Rossi, Pellegrino. *Mélanges d'économie politique, d'histoire et de philosophie publiés par ses fils.* 2 vols. Paris: Guillaumin, 1857.

Roubaud, Benjamin. *Album d'Afrique: Costumes français et indigènes, scènes de mœurs, sujets militaires au bivouac et en campagne. Dessinés d'après nature et lithogr. par Benjamin Roubaud.* Paris: Gihaut Frères, 1846.

Rousset, Camille. *L'Algérie de 1830 à 1840: Les commencements d'une conquête.* 2 vols. Paris: Plon, 1887.

Rowcroft, Charles. *Le colon de Van Diémen ou aventures d'un émigrant: Contes des colonies.* Translated by Noël Lefebvre-Duruflé. 3 vols. 5th ed. Paris: J. Renouard, 1847.

The Royal Menagerie: A Collection of the Best Caricatures Which Have Appeared in Paris since the Late Revolution. Paris: Fain; London: Charles Tilt, 1831.

Ruggieri, Claude. *Précis historique sur les fêtes, les spectacles et les réjouissances publiques.* Paris, 1830.

Ruscio, Alain, ed. *Que la France était belle au temps des colonies . . . : Anthologie de chansons coloniales et exotiques françaises.* Paris: Maisonneuve et Larose, 2001.

Sabourin de Nanton. *Épinal et l'imagerie dans les Vosges.* Strasbourg: Heitz, 1868.

Sagot. *Pétition à Messieurs les membres de la Chambre des députés de France, par Sagot, de Nantilly, ancien payeur à l'Armée d'Afrique, colon en Algérie.* Versailles: Klefer, 1844.

Saint-Arnaud, Arnaud-Jacques Le Roy de. *Lettres du maréchal de Saint-Arnaud (1832–1854).* Edited by Adolphe Leroy de Saint-Arnaud. 2 vols. Paris: M. Lévy frères, 1855.

Saint-Hypolite, [Achille-Hippolyte Blanc]. *De l'Algérie: Système du duc de Rovigo en 1832. Moyens d'affermir nos possessions en 1840.* Paris: Bourgogne et Martinet, 1840.

Saint-Marcel, J.-B. de. *L'indispensable au Palais-Musée de Versailles.* Versailles and Paris: n.p., 1839.

Salneuve, J.-F. *Cours de topographie et de géodésie fait à l'École d'Application du Corps royal d'État-Major.* Paris: Gaultier-Laguionie, 1841.

Salvaire, Félix. *Les deux expéditions de Constantine: Poème dédié à S.A.R. Mgr. le Duc de Nemours.* Algiers: Impr. Civile et Militaire, Jan 1838.

[Saudonard, Adolphe]. *De la colonisation en Afrique: Par un paysan du Danube.* Paris: Dumaine, 1843.

Say, Jean-Baptiste. *Cours complet d'économie politique pratique.* 2nd ed. Brussels: Hauman et Cie., 1840.

——. *De l'Angleterre et des Anglais.* Paris: Arthus Bertrand; London: Berthoud and Wheatley, 1815.

——. *Traité d'économie politique, ou simple exposition de la manière dont se forment, se distribuent et se consomment les richesses.* 6th ed. Edited by Horace Say. Paris: Guillaumin, 1841.

Schœlcher, Victor. *Esclavage et colonisation.* Edited by Émile Tersen. Paris: Presses universitaires de France, 1948; repr., Paris: Presses universitaires de France, 2007.

Senior, Nassau William. *Journals Kept in France and Italy from 1848 to 1852, with a Sketch of the Revolution of 1848.* Edited by Mary Charlotte Mair Simpson. 2nd ed. 2 vols. London: H. S. King, 1871.

Shaler, William. *Sketches of Algiers, Political, Historical and Civil.* Boston, n.p. 1826.

Shaw, Thomas. *Voyage dans la régence d'Alger, ou Description géographique, physique, philologique, etc., de cet état.* Translated and edited by J. MacCarthy. 2 vols. Paris: Marlin, 1830.

Simart, Isidor. *Isly et Mogador: Chant du peuple* [Paris]: Lange Lévy et Cie., [1844].

Sismondi, J[ean]-C[harles]-L[éonard] de. *De l'expédition contre Alger*. Paris: Plessan, 1830.

———. *Études sur l'économie politique*. 2 vols. Paris: Truettel et Würtz, 1838.

———. *Les colonies des anciens comparées avec celles des modernes, sous le rapport de leur influence sur le bonheur du genre humain*. Geneva: Lador et Raboz, 1837.

Smith, Adam. *An Inquiry into the Nature and Causes of the Wealth of Nations* (3rd ed., 1784). In *Glasgow Edition of the Works and Correspondence of Adam Smith*. Edited by R. H. Campbell and A. S. Skinner. Oxford: Clarendon Press, 1976.

Solms, E. de, and E. de Bassano. *Pétition à l'Assemblée Nationale: Projet de colonisation de l'Algérie*. Paris: Proux et Cie., 1848.

Solvet, Ch[arles]. *Voyage à la Rassauta: Lettre à M. A . . . député*. Marseille: Marius Olive, 1838.

Soult, Nicolas-Jean de Dieu. *Correspondance politique et familière avec Louis-Philippe et la famille royale*. Edited by Louis and Antoinette de Saint-Pierre. Paris: Plon, 1959.

Stern, Daniel [Marie d'Argoult]. *Histoire de la Révolution de 1848*. 2nd ed. 2 vols. Paris: Charpentier, 1862.

Suchet, Jacques [Abbé]. *Constantine et l'Algérie: Extrait des lettres de M. Suchet, missionaire en Algérie*. Tours: Mame, 1839.

———. *Lettres édifiantes et curieuses sur l'Algérie, par M. l'Abbé Suchet, vicaire générale d'Alger*. Tours: Mame, 1840.

Sur la guerre actuelle avec la Régence d'Alger, en réponse à un écrit de M. le comte de Laborde, député de la Seine. Paris: Fain, May 1830.

T ***. *Stances sur la prise d'Alger, dédiées à Mlle. Delphine Gay; précédées d'une Epître à la Muse de la Seine, et suivies d'une Imitation en vers de deux Odes d'Horace*. Lyon: Fontaine, 1830.

Talleyrand-Périgord, Charles-Maurice de. *Le Prince de Talleyrand et la maison d'Orléans: Lettres du Roi Louis-Philippe, de Madame Adélaïde et du Prince de Talleyrand*. Edited by Marie Le Harivel de Gonneville, comtesse de Mirabeau. Paris: Calmann Lévy, 1890.

Ténint, Wilhelm. *Album du Salon de 1841: Collection des principaux ouvrages exposés au Louvre, reproduits par les peintres eux-mêmes, ou sous leur direction*. 2nd year. Paris: Challamel, 1841.

Thoré, Théophile. *Salons de T. Thoré, 1844, 1845, 1846, 1847, 1848, avec une préface par W. Bürger*. Edited by W. Bürger. Paris: Lacroix, Verboeckhove, et Cie., 1868.

Tocqueville, Alexis de. *Writings on Empire and Slavery*. Edited and translated by Jennifer Pitts. Baltimore and London: Johns Hopkins University Press, 2001.

Touchard, Théodore. *Histoire pittoresque et militaire des Français, racontée par un Caporal à son Escouade*. 2 vols. Paris: Schneider et Langrand, 1840.

Toussenel, Alphonse. *Les juifs, rois de l'époque: Histoire de la féodalité financière*. Paris: École sociétaire, 1845.

Trédos, René. *Mazagran, ou le Serment des braves: Poème dédié aux 123 et à l'armée française, par M. René Trédos*. Marennes: J.-S. Raissac, 1840.

[Trévern, Jean-François-Marie Le Pappe de]. *Mandement de Monseigneur l'évêque de Strasbourg, qui ordonne des prières publiques pour demander le succès de l'expédition contre Alger*. Strasbourg: L. Fr. Le Roux, 1830.

Tripier, François. *Sur le désastre de Constantine, chant.* [Paris]: Fain, [1837].

Trollier, Louis-François. *Mémoire sur la nécessité et sur les avantages de la colonisation d'Alger.* Lyon: J. M. Barret, 1835.

Urtis. *Opinion émise par M. Urtis, propriétaire à Alger, devant la Commission de Colonisation de l'Algérie à la séance du 12 mars 1842.* Paris: Paul Dupont et Cie., [1842].

V***, L. de. [Thomas-Robert Bugeaud]. *La guerre d'Afrique: Lettre d'un lieutenant de l'Armée d'Afrique, à son oncle, vieux soldat de la Révolution et de l'Empire.* Paris: Cosse et G. Laguionie, 1838.

[Vallongue, P.] *Instruction sur le service des ingénieurs-géographes du Dépôt général de la guerre.* Paris: Impr. de la République, Thermidor An XI [1803].

Vaulabelle, Achille de. *Histoire des deux Restaurations jusqu'à l'avènement de Louis-Philippe (de janvier 1813 à octobre 1830).* 5th ed. 8 vols. Paris: Perrotin, 1860.

Veyrat, [Xavier], and [Ange-Jean-Robert Eustache] Angel. *L'oncle d'Afrique: Vaudeville en un acte, par MM. Veyrat et Angel, représenté pour la première fois, sur le théâtre de la Porte-Saint-Antoine, le 25 mai 1837.* Paris: Morain, 1837.

Vialar, Antoine-Étienne-Augustin de (Baron). *Alger: Appendice au rapport de M. Passy, par M. le Bon Vialar.* Paris: L.-E. Herhan, 1835.

———. *Première lettre à M. le maréchal Bugeaud, duc d'Isly, gouverneur-général de l'Algérie.* Algiers: A. Bourget, 1846.

———. *Simples faits exposés à la réunion algérienne du 14 avril 1835.* Paris: Firmin-Didot frères, 1835.

Vingtrinier, Aimé. *Mazagran: Poème, par Antonin Vidal.* Paris: Schwartz et Gagnot, 1841.

Volland. *Réfutation du rapport de la Commission du Budget, en ce qui concerne nos possessions en Afrique. Par M. le baron Volland, intendant militaire, délégué des colons d'Alger.* Paris: L.-E. Herhan, 1835.

Wains-des-Fontaines, Th[éodore]. "Mazagran: Fragment d'un poème couronné par l'Association-Lionnaise, le 18 juin 1840." *Affiches, annonces judiciaires, avis divers du Mans, et du département de la Sarthe,* 28 August 1840.

Wakefield, Edward Gibbon. *The Collected Works of Edward Gibbon Wakefield.* Edited by M. F. Lloyd Prichard. Auckland: Collins, 1969.

"The War in Algeria." *Chambers's Repository of Instructive and Amusing Tracts.* Vol. 3, no. 18. Philadelphia: Lippincott, Grambo; London and Edinburgh: William and Robert Chambers, 1854.

W[iesener], L. *Galeries historiques de Versailles: Description de la Salle de Constantine.* Versailles: Montalant-Bougleux, 1842.

Wyld, W[illiam], and Émile-Aubert Lessore. *Voyage pittoresque dans la Régence d'Alger, exécuté en 1833, et lithographié par E. Lessore & W. Wyld.* Paris: Charles Motte, 1835.

Index

CPSIA information can be obtained
at www.ICGtesting.com
Printed in the USA
LVOW12s2024251016

510222LV00003B/241/P